Rick Steves'

PRAGUE
& THE CZECH REPUBLIC

Rick Steves & Jan (Honza) Vihan

PRAGUE

1. Archbishop's Palace
2. Basilica & Convent of St. George
3. Bethlehem Chapel
4. Black Light Theaters (3)
5. Castle Square
6. Ceremonial Hall
7. Changing of the Guard
8. Charles Bridge
9. Charles University
10. Church of St. Mary the Victorious
11. Church of St. Nicholas (in Little Quarter)
12. Church of St. Nicholas (in Old Town)
13. To Dancing House
14. Dvořák Museum
15. Estates Theater
16. Golden Lane
17. Havelská Market
18. Jewish Quarter
19. Kampa Island
20. Karlova Street
21. Klaus Synagogue
22. Klementinum
23. Lennon Wall
24. Lobkowicz Palace
25. To Loreta Church
26. Lucerna Gallery
27. Maisel Synagogue
28. Monument to Victims of Communism Who Survived
29. Mucha Museum
30. Municipal House
31. Museum of Communism
32. Museum of Czech Cubism (in Black Madonna House)
33. Museum of Medieval Art at St. Agnes Convent
34. Na Příkopě Street
35. National Gallery in Sternberg Palace
36. National Museum
37. National Theater
38. Nerudova Street
39. Old Jewish Cemetery
40. Old Royal Palace
41. Old Town Hall, Astronomical Clock, Tower & Chapel
42. Old Town Square & Jan Hus Memorial
43. Old-New Synagogue
44. Petřín Tower & Mus. of Jára Cimrman
45. Pinkas Synagogue
46. Powder Tower
47. Prague Castle
48. Royal Gardens
49. Royal Summer Palace
50. Schwarzenberg Palace
51. Spanish Synagogue
52. St. Martin in the Wall
53. St. Vitus Cathedral
54. St. Wenceslas Statue
55. To Strahov Monastery & Library
56. Toy & Barbie Mus.
57. Týn Church
58. Ungelt Courtyard & House at the Golden Ring Gallery
59. Vrtba Garden
60. Wallenstein Palace Garden
61. Wenceslas Square

METRONOME

Letenské Park

To Holešovice Train Sation

NÁBŘEŽÍ EDVARDA BENEŠE

ČECHŮV MOST

ŠTEFÁNIKŮV MOST

NÁBŘEŽÍ LUDVÍKA SVOBODY

TĚŠNOVSKÝ TUNEL

TĚŠNOV

BARIKÁDNÍKŮ

ŠTARKOVA

HOLBOVA

SAMCOVA

MLYNÁŘSKÁ

PETRSKÁ

TESNÁ

DVOŘÁKOVO NÁBŘEŽÍ

KLÁŠTER SV. ANEŽKY ČESKÉ

33

ŘÁSNOVKA

LANNOVA

BARVÍŘSKÁ

BISKUPSKÁ

DUŠNÍ

KOŽNÁ

U MILOSRDNÝCH

ŘÁSNOVA

ZA HAŠTALEM

KLIMENTSKÁ

JEWISH QUARTER

BÍLKOVA

HAŠTALSKÁ

HRADEBNÍ

REVOLUČNÍ

SOUKENICKÁ

ZLATNICKÁ

PAŘÍŽSKÁ

BŘEHOVÁ

VĚZEŇSKÁ

DLOUHÁ

TRUHLÁŘSKÁ

HAVLÍČKOVA

NA POŘÍČÍ

To Florenc Bus Station

BŘEŽÍ

39

6

JDIŠTĚ

18

VALENTINSKÁ

21

43

45

ROKÁ

ŠIROKÁ

51

KOSTEČNÁ

V KOLKOVNĚ

MASNÁ

MASNÁ

ŠTUPARTSKÁ

RYBNÁ

BENEDIKTSKÁ

NA FLORENCI

KOTVA DEPT. STORE

KAPROVA

27

MAISELOVA

DUŠNÍ

12

4

DLOUHÁ

TÝNSKÁ

JAKUBSKÁ

RYBNÁ

TEMPLOVA

OBECNÍ DŮM

V CELNICI

MASARYK STATION

Staroměstská

LESLAVINOVA

TÝNSKÁ

57

58

ŠTUPARTSKÁ

KRÁLODVORSKÁ

30

Náměstí Republiky

HYBERNSKÁ

LATNĚRSKÁ

ČERNÁ

42

STAROMĚSTSKÉ NÁM.

CELETNÁ

32

CELETNÁ

46

U PRAŠNÉ BRÁNY

SENOVÁŽNÁ

DLÁŽDĚNÁ

BOLZANOVA

22

KLEMENTINUM

LINHARTSKÁ

41

ŽELEZNÁ

KAROLINUM

9

PRAŠNÁ BRÁNA

NEKÁZANKA

JERUZALEMSKÁ

Vrchuckého Park

OLD TOWN

KARLOVA

20

KARLOVA

U RADNICE

MARIÁNSKÉ

STAVOVSKÉ DIVADLO

15

NA PŘÍKOPĚ

34

PANSKÁ

WILSONOVA

4

ŘETĚZOVÁ

JILSKÁ

HAVELSKÁ

17

31

NÁM. MŮSTEK

Hlavní Nádraží

Hlavní Nádraží (MAIN TRAIN STATION)

OVOCNÝ

3

BETHLEHEM CHAPEL

MICHALSKÁ

KOŽNÁ

RYTÍŘSKÁ

M

Můstek

OVOCNÝ

29

U PŮJČOVNY

RŮŽOVÁ

PERLOVÁ

TŘÍMSKÁ

NVIKTSKÁ

52

NÁRODNÍ TŘÍDA

28. ŘÍJNA

P. MARIE SNĚŽNÁ

JINDŘIŠSKÁ

POLITICKÝCH VĚZŇŮ

ŠPANĚLSKÁ

TESCO DEPT. STORE

Franciscan Garden

M

Můstek

OPLETALOVA

ŠTÁTNÍ OPERA PRAHA

POLSKÁ

MANESOVA

NOVÁ SCÉNA

Národní Třída

VLADISLAVOVA

JUNGMANNOVA

PALACKÉHO

VODIČKOVA

VÁCLAVSKÉ NÁMĚSTÍ

26

61

WASHINGTONOVA

MEZIBRÁNSKÁ

VINOHRADSKÁ

STROVNÍ

V JIRCHÁŘÍCH

KŘEMENCOVA

LAZARSKÁ

NAVRÁTILOVA

ŠKOLSKÁ

NEW TOWN

KUBELÍKOVA

BALBÍNOVA

ITALSKÁ

BARTOLOMĚJSKÁ

KAROLÍNY

PŠTROSSOVA

VORŠILSKÁ

MIKULANDSKÁ

REZNICKÁ

VE SMEČKÁCH

ŠTĚPÁNSKÁ

KRAKOVSKÁ

54

M

Muzeum

NÁRODNÍ MUZEUM

36

RÍMSKÁ

MYSLÍKOVA

OZBORŮ

NOVOMĚSTSKÁ RADNICE

ŽITNÁ

LEGEROVA

BĚLEHRADSKÁ

ANGLICKÁ

To Vinohrady

Náměstí Míru

M

KARLOVO

Karlovo Náměstí

SPÁLENÁ

ŠTĚPÁNSKÁ

HÁLKOVA

— To **13**
RESSLOVA

T

JEČNÁ

DITTRICHOVA

ROJANOVA

Karlovo Náměstí

M

LIPOVÁ

KATEŘINSKÁ

NA BOJIŠTI

KE KARLOVU

DVOŘÁK MUSEUM

14

NA MORÁNI

U NEMOCNICE

VINIČNÁ

BENÁTSKÁ

VYŠEHRADSKÁ

KLÁŠTER NA SLOVANECH

Botanická Zahrada

To Vyšehrad

To Nuselský Bridge & E-50 To Brno

LEGEND

Pedestrian-Friendly Area

T Tram #22 Stop

M **M** Major Metro Stops

Landmark or Point of Interest

i Tourist Information Offices

Viewpoint

0 m   400 m

0 mi   400 yds

Rick Steves'

PRAGUE
& THE CZECH REPUBLIC

Rick Steves & Jan (Honza) Vihan

AVALON
TRAVEL

CONTENTS

Top Destinations in the Czech Republic

DAY TRIPS:
KUTNÁ HORA,
TEREZÍN &
CASTLES

WALLACHIA

PRAGUE

OLOMOUC

TŘEBOŇ, TELČ
& TŘEBÍČ

MORAVSKÝ
KRUMLOV

ČESKÝ
KRUMLOV

SLAVONICE

MIKULOV
WINE REGION

INTRODUCTION

Wedged between Germany and Austria, the Czech Republic is one of the most comfortable and easy-to-explore countries of the former Warsaw Pact. After the fall of communism in 1989, the Czech capital, Prague, quickly became one of Europe's most popular destinations. Come see what all the fuss is about...but don't overlook the rest of the country. Even in a quick visit, you can enjoy a fine introduction to the entire Czech Republic.

This book focuses on Prague, but also includes my favorite small-town and back-to-nature destinations in the countryside. If you want to experience the best two weeks that the Czech Republic has to offer, this book has all the information you'll need.

Experiencing Czech culture, people, and natural wonders economically and hassle-free has been my goal throughout three decades of traveling, tour guiding, and writing. With this guidebook, I pass on to you the lessons I've learned.

This book is selective, including only the top destinations and sights. For example, the Czech Republic has dozens of charming medieval towns, but I take you to only the most pleasant: Třeboň and Slavonice.

The best is, of course, only my opinion. But after spending a third of my adult life exploring and researching Europe, I've developed a sixth sense for what travelers enjoy.

About This Book

Rick Steves' Prague & the Czech Republic is a personal tour guide in your pocket. Better yet, it's actually two tour guides in your pocket: The co-author and researcher of this guidebook is Honza Vihan, a Prague native who leads Prague and Eastern Europe tours for my company, Rick Steves' Europe Through the Back Door. Together, Honza and I keep this book up-to-date and accurate. For simplicity we've shed our respective egos to become "I" in this book—though at times, you'll know from the intimacy of some of the comments that Honza is sharing his own, uniquely Czech perspective.

This book is updated regularly, but things change. For the latest, visit www.ricksteves.com/update, and for reports and experiences—good and bad—from fellow travelers, check www.ricksteves.com/feedback.

The first half of this book focuses on Prague, following this format:

Orientation to Prague includes helpful hints and easy-to-read maps, along with specifics on planning your time (with thoughts on how best to use your limited time), public transportation, local tour options, and tourist information (abbreviated **TI** in this book).

The **Old Town, New Town, Little Quarter,** and **Castle Quarter** chapters provide a succinct overview of Prague's most important sights, rated:

▲▲▲—Don't miss;

▲▲—Try hard to see;

▲—Worthwhile if you can make it;

No rating—Worth knowing about.

Sleeping in Prague describes my favorite hotels, from good-value deals to cushy splurges.

Eating in Prague serves up a range of options, from inexpensive take-out joints to fancy restaurants.

Shopping in Prague gives you tips for shopping painlessly and enjoyably, without letting it overwhelm your vacation or ruin your budget.

Entertainment in Prague is your guide to fun, including a wide array of concerts and nightclubs—as well as other Czech entertainment options, from the unique Black Light Theater to hockey and soccer matches.

Prague Connections lays the groundwork for your smooth arrival and departure, covering connections by train, bus, and plane.

The second half of the book, **Beyond Prague,** is devoted to the rest of the Czech Republic. It includes day trips from Prague, as well as farther-flung destinations elsewhere in the country. Each one is covered as a mini-vacation of its own.

At the end of the book, you'll find these sections:

Czech History explains the complicated, tumultuous, and ultimately uplifting background of this country.

The **appendix** is a traveler's tool kit, with telephone tips, useful phone numbers, transportation basics (on trains, buses, car rentals, driving, and flying), recommended books and films, a festival list, climate chart, handy packing checklist, a hotel reservation form, and Czech survival phrases.

Map Legend

⟱	View Point	✈	Airport	)━(	Tunnel
↑	Entry Arrow	Ⓣ	Taxi Stand	————	Pedestrian Zone
⊕	Tourist Info	▉	Tram Stop	- - - - -	Railway
WC	Restroom	Ⓑ	Bus Stop	··············	Ferry/Boat Route
▉	Castle	▯	Parking	⊢━⊢━⊣	Tram
⬆	Church	)(	Mtn. Pass	▥▥▥▥▥	Stairs
▪	Statue/Point of Interest		Park	· · · · ·	Walk/Tour Route
				- - - - - -	Trail

Use this legend to help you navigate the maps in this book.

Browse through this book and choose your favorite sights. Then have a great trip! Traveling like a temporary local and taking advantage of the information here, you'll enjoy the absolute most of every mile, minute, and dollar. I'm happy you'll be visiting places I know and love, and meeting some of my favorite Czech people.

Planning

This section will help you get started on planning your trip—with advice on trip costs, when to go, and what you should know before you take off.

Travel Smart

Your trip to the Czech Republic is like a complex play—easier to follow and really appreciate on a second viewing. While no one does the same trip twice to gain that advantage, reading this book in its entirety before your trip accomplishes much the same thing.

Design an itinerary that enables you to visit the various sights at the best possible times. Make note of festivals, colorful market days, and when sights are closed.

If you have only a few days for Prague, remember that the impressive sights of the Jewish Quarter are closed every Saturday, and other museums (particularly in the Old Town) are closed on Monday. Monday can be a problem day outside of Prague, as many Czech museums are closed. Saturday morning feels like any bustling weekday, but many shops close at lunchtime and don't reopen until Monday morning. Sundays have the same pros and cons as they do for travelers in the US—sights are generally open but may have limited hours, shops and banks are closed, city traffic is light, and public-transportation options are fewer.

Be sure to mix intense and relaxed periods in your itinerary. Every trip—and every traveler—needs at least a few slack days

INTRODUCTION

The Czech Republic at a Glance

▲▲▲**Prague** The Czech capital and one of Europe's most romantic cities, boasting a remarkably well-preserved Old Town with top-notch architecture from every era; a sprawling hilltop castle; a thriving New Town packed with slinky Art Nouveau facades; a historic and well-presented Jewish Quarter; fascinating and inspiring tales from a rocky recent history; countless lively pubs serving some of the world's best beer; and enough museums, churches, gardens, and other attractions to entertain any visitor.

▲▲**Day Trips from Prague** A wide range of easy side-trips, including Kutná Hora, a workaday Czech town with an offbeat bone church, fine cathedral, and silver mining museum; Terezín, a sobering concentration camp memorial to the victims of the Nazis; Konopiště Castle, the opulent but lived-in former residence of the Archduke Franz Ferdinand; dramatically situated Karlštejn Castle; and the genuinely Gothic hunting palace of Křivoklát Castle.

▲▲**Český Krumlov** Charming, picturesque, and popular mid-sized town huddled under a colorful castle and hugging a river bend in the Bohemian hills, made to order for canoeing, hiking, and people-watching.

▲**Třeboň, Telč, and Třebíč** Three different southern Bohemian towns, each with a claim to fame: Třeboň, surrounded by artifi-

(for picnics, laundry, people-watching, and so on). Pace yourself. Assume you will return.

Reread this book as you travel, and visit local TIs. Upon arrival in a new town, lay the groundwork for a smooth departure; write down (or print out from an online source) the schedule for the train or bus you'll take when you depart.

While traveling, take advantage of the Internet and phones to make your trip run smoothly. By going online at Internet cafés or your hotel and using the phone (buy a phone card or carry a mobile phone), you can get tourist information, learn the latest on sights (special events, tour schedules, etc.), book tickets and tours, make reservations, reconfirm hotels, research transportation connections, and keep in touch with loved ones.

Connect with the culture. Set up your own quest to find the most characteristically Czech pub you can. (Anything with an English menu doesn't count.) Once inside, get recommendations from the locals on the best type of beer, and make it your goal to get the most interesting story you possibly can out of them.

cial lakes; Telč, with a spectacular main square; and Třebíč, with echoes of Jewish history.

Slavonice Tiny town hugging the Austrian border, ideal for hiking into a pastoral countryside dotted with evocative, never-used WWII fortifications.

▲**Moravský Krumlov** Drab city notable only for housing Art Nouveau painter Alfons Mucha's stunning masterpiece, *Slav Epic*.

▲▲**Olomouc** Moravian cultural capital and thriving university city, with a grand square (crowned by Europe's biggest plague column), churches, museums, stinky cheese, vibrant everyday life, and an opportunity to side-trip to the country's top Rococo château in nearby Kroměříž.

▲**Wallachia** Time-passed, mountainous corner of Moravia, with a fine open-air folk museum at Rožnov pod Radhoštěm and a mountaintop retreat at Pustevny.

Mikulov Wine Region The Czech Republic's top wine-growing area, with the home-base village of Pavlov (wine cellars and fun water activities), the historical town of Mikulov (synagogue museum), and the impressive castles-and-gardens complex of Lednice and Valtice.

Enjoy the hospitality of the Czech people. Slow down and be open to unexpected experiences. Ask questions—most locals are eager to point you in their idea of the right direction. Keep a notepad in your pocket for organizing your thoughts. Wear your money belt, and learn the local currency and how to estimate prices in dollars. Those who expect to travel smart, do.

Trip Costs

There are two price tiers in the Czech Republic: Prague and everywhere else. Outside of Prague, you'll be amazed at the low prices for accommodations, food, transportation, and sightseeing. In Prague, you'll find prices closer to the Western European range. Prague hotels are particularly expensive, often surpassing Western prices. But even in Prague, things that natives pay for—such as transportation and food (in local-style, rather than in tourist-oriented, restaurants)—are very affordable. Despite the expense of Prague, if you avoid overpriced restaurants on the main tourist drag, and if you use my listings to stay only at

Major Holidays and Weekends

Popular places are even busier on weekends...and can be inundated on three-day weekends. Plan ahead and reserve your Prague accommodations and transportation well in advance during these times: any weekend, the months of May, June, and September, and major holidays such as Easter and New Year's. Christmas, on the other hand, is rather slow at most hotels and sights. Also check the list of festivals and holidays in the appendix.

the best-value hotels, a trip to the Czech Republic can still be substantially less expensive than a trip to Western European destinations.

Five components make up your trip cost: airfare, surface transportation, room and board, sightseeing and entertainment, and shopping and miscellany.

Airfare: A basic round-trip US-to-Prague flight costs $700–1,300, depending on where you fly from and when (cheaper in winter). If your travels take you beyond the Czech Republic, consider saving time and money in Europe by flying "open jaw" (into one city and out of another; for example, into Prague and out of Vienna).

Surface Transportation: Point-to-point train and bus tickets within the Czech Republic are inexpensive—a second-class train ticket from Prague to the farthest reaches of the country won't run you more than about $40. Renting a car is convenient for exploring the Czech countryside, but doing so is much more expensive than public transportation (figure about $770 per week, including gas and insurance). Leasing is worth considering for trips of two and a half weeks or more. Car rental and leases are cheapest when arranged from the US (see page 292). And those with more money than time could consider hiring a car with a private driver (a full-day, round-trip excursion from Prague to Český Krumlov runs about $220; see page 161).

Room and Board: Plan on spending an average of $130 a day per person for room and board in Prague. A $130-a-day budget per person allows an average of $10 for lunch, $20 for dinner, and $100 for lodging (based on two people splitting the cost of a $200 double room that includes breakfast). That's doable. Outside of Prague, hotel rates plummet to $70 or less for a decent double, and food prices also drop—making $50 a day per person a reasonable budget in the Czech countryside. Even in Prague, students and tightwads can eat and sleep for $40 a day ($25 per hostel bed, $15 for meals and snacks).

Sightseeing and Entertainment: Sightseeing is inexpensive here. Most sights generally cost about $4–8. A few biggies cost much more (such as Prague Castle—up to $20, or the Jewish Quarter—$28), but that's rare. Figure $25–30 for concerts, Black Light Theater performances, and other splurge experiences. You can hire a private guide for as little as $120 for four hours. An overall average of $25 a day works for most travelers. Don't skimp here. After all, this category is the driving force behind your trip— you came to sightsee, enjoy, and experience the Czech Republic.

Shopping and Miscellany: Figure a little over $1 per stamped postcard, coffee, beer, or ice-cream cone. Shopping can vary in cost from nearly nothing to a small fortune. Good budget travelers find that this category has little to do with assembling a trip full of lifelong and wonderful memories.

When to Go

The "tourist season" runs roughly from Easter through October. July and August have their advantages, with the best weather, very long days (daylight until after 21:00), fewer tourists in Prague than in the peak months of May, June, and September, and busy festivals held in small towns around the country. In spring and fall (May, June, Sept, and early Oct), the weather is milder, and the colors and scents are powerful.

Winter travelers find the concert season in full swing, with remarkably fewer tourists—but outside of Prague, many sights are either closed or open on a limited schedule. In December, you'll find Christmas markets on main squares around the country, fragrant with the scent of hot wine with cloves. After a quiet Christmas season, Prague explodes with fun on New Year's Eve, joined by thousands of Germans and other Europeans. In January and early February, when few tourists come, chances are you will wake up to a Prague silenced by the wistful glimmer of snow, which quickly melts in the Old Town but stays on the ground at Prague Castle and on top of Petřín Hill. Seeing the Charles Bridge blanketed by fresh snow makes the hours spent out in the cold worthwhile. Frequent pub stops, with lots of plum brandy and hot wine, are essential at this time of year—and they bring you closer to local life. Winter can linger, but Prague usually turns green with spring around mid-April. Use the climate chart in the appendix as your Prague weather guide.

Know Before You Go

Your trip is more likely to go smoothly if you plan ahead. Check this list of things to arrange while you're still at home.

You need a **passport**—but no visa or shots—to travel in the Czech Republic. You may be denied entry into certain European

The Czech Republic's Best Two-Week Trip by Car

Day	Plan	Sleep in
1	Arrive in Prague	Prague
2	Prague	Prague
3	Prague	Prague
4	Day-trip to Terezín Concentration Camp	Prague
5	To Český Krumlov	Český Krumlov
6	Český Krumlov	Český Krumlov
7	To Telč via Třeboň	Telč
8	Telč and Slavonice	Telč
9	To Pavlov via Třebíč and Moravský Krumlov	Pavlov
10	Mikulov Wine Region and Lednice	Pavlov
11	To Olomouc	Olomouc
12	Olomouc	Olomouc
13	Return to Prague	Prague
14	Prague	Prague

countries if your passport is due to expire within three to six months of your ticketed date of return. Get it renewed if you'll be cutting it close. It can take up to six weeks to get or renew a passport (for more on passports, see www.travel.state.gov). Pack a photocopy of your passport in your luggage in case the original is lost or stolen.

In 2008, the Czech Republic officially joined the open-borders Schengen Agreement, eliminating checks at **border crossings** when traveling to and from neighboring countries. You'll simply zip through the border without stopping. But when you

The Czech Republic's Best 12-Day Trip by Bus and Train

Day	Plan	Sleep in
1	Arrive in Prague	Prague
2	Prague	Prague
3	Prague	Prague
4	Day-trip to Terezín Concentration Camp	Prague
5	To Český Krumlov	Český Krumlov
6	Český Krumlov	Český Krumlov
7	To Telč via Třeboň	Telč
8	Telč and Slavonice	Telč
9	To Olomouc via Třebíč	Olomouc
10	Olomouc	Olomouc
11	Return to Prague	Prague
12	Prague	Prague

With more time in the Czech Republic, consider a pair of other destinations that are a little more difficult, but still possible, to reach by public transportation: Hikers enjoy Wallachia, which fits easily into the above schedule after Olomouc (make your home base in Trojanovice). Wine-lovers head for the Mikulov Wine Region, easiest to visit between Telč and Olomouc (make your home base in Pavlov).

Beyond the Czech borders, consider adding Budapest, Hungary, and Kraków, Poland—each an easy, direct night-train trip away from Prague (or an even quicker connection from Olomouc). For more on these destinations beyond the Czech Republic, see the current editions of *Rick Steves' Budapest* and *Rick Steves' Eastern Europe*.

change countries, you still change money, phone cards, and postage stamps.

Book your **rooms** well in advance, especially if you'll be traveling during peak season (May, June, and September) or any major holidays (see "Major Holidays and Weekends" sidebar).

Call your **debit- and credit-card companies** to let them know the countries you'll be visiting so that they won't deny your international charges. Confirm your daily withdrawal limit; consider asking to have it raised so you can take out more cash at each ATM stop. Ask about international transaction fees.

If you want to see Alfons Mucha's *Slav Epic,* confirm its location (it may still be in the town of Moravský Krumlov, or it may have been moved to Prague; see page 233 for details).

If you're interested in **travel insurance,** do your homework

INTRODUCTION

before you buy. Compare the cost of the insurance to the likelihood of your using it and your potential loss if something goes wrong. For details on the many kinds of travel insurance, see www.ricksteves.com/plan/tips/insurance.htm.

If you'll be **renting a car** in the Czech Republic, bring your US driver's license (to drive, you'll also need an International Driving Permit—see appendix). Confirm pick-up hours; many car-rental offices close Saturday afternoon and all day Sunday.

Because airline **carry-on restrictions** are always changing, visit the Transportation Security Administration's website (www.tsa.gov/travelers) for an up-to-date list of what you can bring on the plane with you...and what you have to check. Remember to arrive with plenty of time to get through security.

Sightseeing Priorities

Depending on the length of your trip, and taking geographic proximity into account, the following are my recommended priorities:

3 days:	Prague
4–5 days, add:	Your choice of nearby day trips (Kutná Hora, Terezín Concentration Camp, and the three castles: Konopiště, Karlštejn, or Křivoklát)
5 days, add:	Český Krumlov (and skip day trips)
7 days, add:	Olomouc
8–9 days, add:	Třeboň, Telč, and Třebíč
More:	Your choice among Moravský Krumlov, Šumava, Wallachia, Slavonice, or the Mikulov Wine Region with Lednice/Valtice

This list assumes you're primarily interested in the Czech Republic. But note that Prague also splices neatly into a wider-ranging trip that can include such nearby destinations as Vienna (4–6 hrs by train), Budapest (7–8.5 hrs), Kraków (7.5–9.5 hrs), Munich (6.25 hrs), and Berlin (4.5–5 hrs).

Practicalities

Emergency Telephone Numbers: Dial 112 for medical or other emergencies and 158 for police.

Time: In Europe—and in this book—you'll use the 24-hour clock. It's the same through 12:00 noon, then keep going—13:00, 14:00, and so on. For anything after 12, subtract 12 and add p.m. (14:00 is 2:00 p.m.)

The Czech Republic is generally six/nine hours ahead of the East/West Coasts of the US. The exceptions are the beginning and end of Daylight Saving Time: Europe "springs forward" the last Sunday in March (two weeks after most of North America), and "falls back" the last Sunday in October (one week before North

Where Do I Find Information On...?

Credit Card Theft	See page 13.
Packing Light	See the packing list on page 305.
Phoning	See "Telephones" on page 283.
Language	See page 282.
Making Hotel Reservations	See page 20.
Tipping	See page 14.
Tourist Information Offices	See page 281.
Updates to This Book	See www.ricksteves.com/update

America). For a handy online time converter, try www.timeand date.com/worldclock.

Watt's Up? Europe's electrical system is different from North America's in two ways: the shape of the plug (two round prongs) and the voltage of the current (220 volts instead of 110 volts). For your North American plug to work in Europe, you'll need an adapter, sold inexpensively at travel stores in the US. As for the voltage, most newer electronics or travel appliances (such as hair dryers, laptops, and battery chargers) automatically convert the voltage—if you see a range of voltages printed on the item or its plug (such as "110–220"), it'll work in Europe. Otherwise, you can buy a converter separately in the US (about $20).

Discounts: While discounts are generally not listed in this book, youths (under 18) and students (with International Student Identity Cards) often get discounts—but only by asking. To get a teacher or student ID card, visit www.statravel.com or www.isic .org. Senior discounts are technically available only to Czech citizens (age 65 and over), but sometimes are granted to travelers who ask.

News: Americans keep in touch in Europe with the *International Herald Tribune* (published almost daily through-out Europe). Every Tuesday, the European editions of *Time* and *Newsweek* hit the stands with articles of particular interest to travelers in Europe. Sports addicts can get their fix from *USA Today*. Good websites include www.prague.com, www.iht.com, http://news.bbc.co.uk, and www.europeantimes.com. For the local perspective, I pick up a copy of the English-language *Prague Post* (which also has a convenient events calendar). Many hotels have CNN or BBC television channels available.

Money

This section offers advice on getting cash, using credit and debit cards, dealing with lost or stolen cards, and tipping.

Exchange Rate

Though the Czech Republic joined the European Union in 2004, it'll be a while before they officially begin using the euro. For now, the Czech Republic continues to use its traditional currency, the Czech crown (*koruna,* abbreviated Kč).

18 Czech crowns (Kč) = about $1.

Although the Czech Republic hasn't officially adopted the euro, many hotels, restaurants, and shops accept euro bills (but not coins or large bills). You may even see hotel rooms or souvenirs priced in euros (€). In this case, remember that €1 = 25 Kč = about $1.40. If you're using euros, expect bad rates and your change in the local currency. If you're just passing through the country, your euros will probably get you by—and they can actually be helpful in an emergency. But if you're staying awhile, get the local currency. (To get the latest rates and print a cheat sheet, see www.oanda.com.)

Cash from ATMs

Throughout Europe, cash machines (ATMs) are the standard way for travelers to get local currency. Bring plastic—credit and/or debit cards. It's smart to bring two cards, in case one gets demagnetized or eaten by a temperamental machine. As an emergency backup, bring several hundred dollars in hard cash (in $20 bills rather than hard-to-exchange $100 bills). Don't use traveler's checks—they're a waste of time (long waits at slow banks) and a waste of money in fees.

To use an ATM (called a *Bankomat* in the Czech Republic) to withdraw money from your account, you'll need a debit card—ideally with a Visa or MasterCard logo for maximum usability—plus a PIN (Personal Identification Number). Know your PIN code in numbers; there are only numbers—no letters—on European keypads.

Before you go, verify with your bank that your cards will work overseas, and alert them that you'll be making withdrawals in Europe; otherwise, the bank may not approve transactions if it perceives unusual spending patterns. (Your credit-card company may do the same thing—let them know about your travel plans, too.) Also ask about international fees; see "Credit and Debit Cards," next.

When using a cash machine, try to take out large sums of money to reduce your per-transaction bank fees. If the machine refuses your request, try again and select a smaller amount (some cash machines limit the amount you can withdraw—don't take it personally). If that doesn't work, try a different machine.

To keep your cash safe, use a money belt—a pouch with a strap that you buckle around your waist like a belt, and wear under your clothes. Thieves target tourists. A money belt provides peace of mind, allowing you to carry lots of cash safely. Don't waste time every few days tracking down a cash machine—withdraw a week's worth of money, stuff it in your money belt, and travel!

Credit and Debit Cards

For purchases, Visa and MasterCard are more commonly accepted than American Express. Just like at home, credit or debit cards work easily at larger hotels and shops, but smaller businesses prefer payment in local currency (in small bills—break large bills at a bank or larger store). Although larger restaurants take credit cards, it makes sense to pay in cash—particularly in Prague, where it's unwise to entrust your credit card to a potentially unscrupulous waiter (see the Eating in Prague chapter). If receipts show your credit-card number, don't toss these thoughtlessly.

Fees: Most credit and debit cards—whether used for purchases or ATM withdrawals—often charge additional, tacked-on "international transaction" fees of up to 3 percent plus $5 per transaction. Note that if you use a credit card for ATM transactions, it's technically a "cash advance" rather than a "withdrawal"—and subject to an additional cash-advance fee.

To avoid unpleasant surprises, call your bank or credit-card company before your trip to ask about these fees. Ask your bank if it has agreements with any Czech banks for lower withdrawal fees. If the fees are too high, consider getting a card just for your trip: Capital One (www.capitalone.com) and most credit unions have low-to-no international transaction fees.

If merchants offer to convert your purchase price into dollars (called dynamic currency conversion, or "DCC"), refuse this "service." You'll pay even more in fees for the expensive convenience of seeing your charge in dollars.

Damage Control for Lost Cards

If you lose your credit, debit, or ATM card, you can stop people from using it by reporting the loss immediately to the respective global customer-assistance centers. Call these 24-hour US numbers collect: Visa (410/581-9994), MasterCard (636/722-7111), and American Express (623/492-8427).

At a minimum, you'll need to know the name of the financial institution that issued you the card, along with the type of card (classic, platinum, or whatever). Providing the following information will allow for a quicker cancellation of your missing card: full card number, whether you are the primary or secondary cardholder, the cardholder's name exactly as printed on the card, billing address, home phone number, circumstances of the loss or theft, and identification verification (your birth date, your mother's maiden name, or your Social Security number—memorize this, don't carry a copy). If you are the secondary cardholder, you'll also need to provide the primary cardholder's identification-verification details. You can generally receive a temporary card within two or three business days in Europe.

If you promptly report your card lost or stolen, you typically won't be responsible for any unauthorized transactions on your account, although many banks charge a liability fee of $50.

Tipping

Tipping in the Czech Republic isn't as automatic and generous as it is in the US, but for special service, tips are appreciated, if not expected. As in the US, the proper amount depends on your resources, tipping philosophy, and the circumstances, but some general guidelines apply.

Restaurants: Tipping is an issue only at restaurants that have table service. If you order your food at a counter, don't tip.

At Czech restaurants that have a waitstaff, service is included, although it's common to round up the bill after a good meal (usually 5–10 percent; e.g., for a 370-Kč meal, pay 400 Kč). If you warm up the waiter with a few Czech words, such as "please" (*prosím;* PROH-zeem) and "thank you" (*děkuji;* DYACK-khuyi), you'll get better service and won't be expected to tip more than a local. But if you greet your waiter in English, he'll want a 15 percent tip. Believe me: The slightest attempt at speaking Czech (see phrases on page 307) will turn you from a targeted tourist into a special guest, even in the most touristy restaurants.

Taxis: To tip the cabbie, round up about five percent. If the cabbie hauls your bags and zips you to the airport to help you catch your flight, you might want to toss in a little more. But if you feel like you're being driven in circles or otherwise ripped off, skip the tip. Again, if you use some Czech words, your cabbie will be less likely to try to scam you.

Special Services: It's thoughtful to tip someone who shows you a special sight and who is paid in no other way. Tour guides at public sights sometimes hold out their hands for tips after they give their spiels; if I've already paid for the tour, I don't tip extra unless they've really impressed me (about 20–30 Kč). At hotels, porters expect about 30 Kč for carrying bags (another reason to pack light). Leaving the maid about 30 Kč per overnight at the end of your stay is a nice touch. In general, if someone in the service industry does a super job for you, a tip (of up to about 50 Kč) is appropriate...but not required.

When in doubt, ask: If you're not sure whether (or how much) to tip for a service, ask your hotelier or the tourist information office; they'll fill you in on how it's done on their turf.

VAT Refunds for Shoppers

Wrapped into the purchase price of your souvenirs is a Value-Added Tax (VAT) of about 19 percent. If you make a purchase of more than 2,000 Kč (about $110) at a store that participates in the VAT-refund scheme, you're entitled to get most of that tax back.

Getting your refund is usually straightforward and, if you buy a substantial amount of souvenirs, well worth the hassle. If you're lucky, the merchant will subtract the tax when you make your purchase. (This is more likely to occur if the store ships the goods to your home.) Otherwise, you'll need to:

Get the paperwork. Have the merchant completely fill out the necessary refund document, called a "cheque" (not to be confused with a "Czech"). You'll have to present your passport at the store.

Get your stamp at the border or airport. Process your cheque(s) at your last stop in the EU (e.g., at the airport) with the customs agent who deals with VAT refunds. It's best to keep your purchases in your carry-on for viewing, but if they're too large or dangerous (such as knives) to carry on, track down the proper customs agent to inspect them before you check your bag. You're not supposed to use your purchased goods before you leave. If you show up at customs wearing your new chic Czech outfit, officials might look the other way—or deny you a refund.

Collect your refund. You'll need to return your stamped document to the retailer or its representative. Many merchants work with a service, such as Global Refund (www.globalrefund.com) or Premier Tax Free (www.premiertaxfree.com), which have offices at major airports, ports, or border crossings. These services, which extract a four percent fee, can refund your money immediately in your currency of choice or credit your card (within two billing cycles). If the retailer handles VAT refunds directly, it's up to you to contact the merchant for your refund. You can mail the documents from home, or quicker, from your point of departure (using a stamped, addressed envelope you've prepared or one that's been provided by the merchant). You'll then have to wait—it could take months.

Customs for American Shoppers

You are allowed to take home $800 worth of items per person duty-free, once every 30 days. The next $1,000 is taxed at a flat 3 percent. After that, you pay the individual item's duty rate. You can also bring in duty-free a liter of alcohol (slightly more than a standard-size bottle of wine; you must be at least 21), 200 cigarettes, and up to 100 non-Cuban cigars. You may take home vacuum-packed cheeses; dried herbs, spices, or mushrooms; and canned fruits or vegetables, including jams and vegetable spreads. Baked goods, candy, chocolate, oil, vinegar, mustard, and honey are OK. Fresh fruits or vegetables are not. Meats, even if canned, are generally not allowed. Remember that you'll need to carefully pack any bottles of *slivovice* and other liquid-containing items in your checked luggage, due to the three-ounce limit on liquids in carry-on baggage. To check customs rules and duty rates before you go, visit www.cbp.gov, and click on "Travel," then "Know Before You Go."

Sightseeing

Sightseeing can be hard work. Use these tips to make your visits to the Czech Republic's finest sights meaningful, fun, efficient, and painless.

Plan Ahead

Set up an itinerary that allows you to fit in all your must-see sights. For a one-stop look at opening hours in Prague, see "Prague at a Glance" on page 48. Most sights keep stable hours in the summer months, but hours tend to fluctuate in the winter. If you have your heart set on visiting particular sights, it's always smart to confirm the latest hours by checking their websites or asking at the local TI.

When possible, visit major sights first thing (when your energy is best) and save other activities for the afternoon. Hit the highlights first, then go back to other things if you have the stamina and time.

Study up. To get the most out of the self-guided walks and sight descriptions in this book, read them before your visit.

At Sights

Here's what you can typically expect:

At churches—which often offer interesting art (usually free) and a welcome seat—a modest dress code (no bare shoulders or shorts) is encouraged.

Galleries in Prague and castles outside the city require you to check daypacks and coats. They'll be kept safely. If you have something you can't bear to part with, stash it in a pocket or purse. To avoid checking a small backpack, carry it under your arm like a purse as you enter. From a guard's point of view, a backpack is generally a problem, while a purse is not.

Photography is sometimes banned at major sights or permitted only for a fee. Look for signs or ask. If cameras are allowed, video cameras are too. Flashes, which can damage oil paintings and distract others in the room, are sometimes forbidden. Even without a flash, a handheld camera will take a decent picture (or buy postcards or posters at the museum bookstore).

Some sights rent audioguides, which generally offer excellent recorded descriptions in English ($4–12). If you bring along your own pair of headphones and a Y-jack, you can sometimes share one audioguide with your travel partner and save money.

Guided tours at sights range from free to about $20. Though tours range widely in quality, many of the sights are quite dull until a local guide brings them to life. Monolingual Americans are in luck in Prague, where most tours are conducted in English. At sights outside of Prague, you will typically need to join a Czech tour and ask for an English handout—the guides rarely go beyond the information printed on the sheet. Tours are most likely to occur during peak season; however, there is often a guide on duty ready to whip into teaching mode—but only when engaged by a curious tourist.

Many sights also show educational videos about the attraction. These are generally well worth your time. I make it standard operating procedure to ask when I arrive at a sight if there is a video in English.

Expect changes—artwork can be on tour, on loan, out sick, or shifted at the whim of the curator. To adapt, pick up any available free floor plans as you enter. Ask the museum staff if you can't find a particular piece.

Major sights often have an on-site café or cafeteria (usually a good place to rest and have a snack or light meal). The WCs at some sights are free and clean.

Many places sell postcards that highlight their attractions. Before you leave, scan the postcards and thumb through the biggest guidebook (or skim its index) to be sure you haven't overlooked something that you'd like to see.

Most sights stop admitting people 30–60 minutes before closing time, and some rooms shut down early (often 45 minutes before the actual closing time). Guards usher people out, so don't save the best for last.

Every sight or museum offers more than what is covered in this book. Use the information in this book as an introduction—not the final word.

Sleeping

I favor accommodations (and restaurants) handy to your sightseeing activities. Rather than list hotels scattered throughout a city, I choose two or three favorite neighborhoods and recommend the best accommodation values in each, from $20 bunk beds to fancy-for-my-book $250 doubles.

I look for places that are friendly; clean; a good value; located in a central, safe, quiet neighborhood; English-speaking; and not mentioned in other guidebooks. I'm more impressed by a handy location and a fun-loving philosophy than hair dryers and shoe-shine machines.

I also like local character and simple facilities that don't cater to American "needs." Obviously, a place meeting every criterion is rare, and all of my recommendations fall short of perfection—sometimes miserably. But I've listed the best values for each price category, given the above criteria. I've also thrown in a few hostels, pensions, and other cheap options for budget travelers.

During these times of economic uncertainty, many hotels will likely be discounting deeply to snare what customers they can. Try to avoid paying their published "rack rate." If you email several places and ask for their best prices, you'll find that some are eager to discount. This can save you big bucks with prices potentially far below those listed in this guidebook.

Pay your bill the evening before you leave to avoid the time-wasting crowd at the reception desk in the morning, especially if you need to rush off to catch your train. And, as always, I appreciate feedback on your experiences.

Types of Accommodations

Hotels

Hotel prices in Prague are at Western European levels, but once you get out of the city, you'll pay half as much for a similar room. Plan on spending $150–250 per hotel double in Prague and $50–100 in smaller towns. A triple is much cheaper than a double and a single. Traveling alone can be expensive: A single room is often only 20 percent cheaper than a double. The price is usually posted in the room. Breakfast is generally included (sometimes continental, but often buffet).

The prices listed in this book are generally valid for peak season, but may go up during major holidays and festivals (see page 301). Prices can soften off-season, for stays of two nights or longer, or for payment in cash (rather than by credit card). Always mention that you found the place through this book—many of the hotels listed offer special deals to my readers.

Before accepting a room, confirm your understanding of the complete price. The only tip my recommended hotels would like is a friendly, easygoing guest.

For environmental reasons, towels are often replaced in hotels only when you leave them on the floor. In cheaper places, they aren't replaced at all, so hang them up to dry and reuse.

Sleep Code

(18 Kč = about $1)

To help you sort easily through the listings, I've divided the rooms into three categories based on the price for a standard double room with bath:

$$$ **Higher Priced**
$$ **Moderately Priced**
$ **Lower Priced**

To give maximum information in a minimum of space, I use the following code to describe the accommodations. Prices listed are per room, not per person. When a price range is given for a type of room (such as "Db-1,800–2,000 Kč"), it means the price fluctuates with the season, room size, or length of stay.

S = Single room (or price for one person in a double).

D = Double or twin. Double beds are usually big enough for nonromantic couples.

T = Triple (often a double bed with a single).

Q = Quad (usually two double beds).

b = Private bathroom with toilet and shower or tub.

s = Private shower or tub only (the toilet is down the hall).

According to this code, a couple staying at a "Db-2,700 Kč" hotel in Prague would pay a total of 2,700 Czech crowns (about $150) for a double room with a private bathroom. Unless otherwise noted, English is spoken, breakfast is included, and credit cards are accepted.

If I mention "Internet access" in a listing, there's a public terminal in the lobby for guests to use. If I list "Wi-Fi," you can generally access it in your room (usually for free), but only if you have your own laptop.

Private Rooms

A cheap option in the Czech Republic is a room in a private home (called "pension," sometimes advertised with the German phrase *Zimmer frei*, "room free," meaning vacancy). These places are inexpensive, at least as comfortable as a cheap hotel, and a good way to get some local insight. The boss changes the sheets, so people staying several nights are most desirable—and stays of less than three nights are often charged up to 30 percent more.

Hostels

For $20–25 a night, you can stay at a youth hostel. Travelers of any age are welcome, as long as they don't mind either dorm-style accommodations or a simple private room with the bathroom down the hall—and lots of traveling friends. Hostels are also a tremendous source of local and budget travel information. Cheap meals are sometimes available, and kitchen facilities are usually provided for do-it-yourselfers. Expect crowds in the summer, snoring, and lots of youth groups giggling and making rude noises while you try to sleep. Family rooms and doubles are often available on request; unlike in Western Europe, many hostels in the Czech Republic are in university dorms where two- or three-person rooms are the norm.

Hosteling is ideal for those traveling single: Prices are per bed, not per room, and you'll have an instant circle of friends. More and more hostels are getting their business acts together, taking credit-card reservations over the phone and leaving sign-in forms on the door for each available room.

Phoning

To make international calls to the Czech Republic to line up hotel reservations, you'll need to know its country code (420). To call the Czech Republic from the US or Canada, dial 011-420-local number. For detailed instructions on telephoning, see page 283 in the appendix.

Making Reservations

Given the quality of the places I've found for this book, I'd recommend that you reserve your rooms in advance, either directly with the hotel or through one of Prague's room-booking services (see page 117). Book several weeks ahead, or as soon as you've pinned down your travel dates. Note that some holidays jam things up and merit your making reservations far in advance (see "Major Holidays and Weekends" sidebar). Just like at home, holidays that fall on a Monday, Thursday, or Friday can turn the weekend into a long holiday, so book the entire weekend well in advance.

Requesting a Reservation: To make a reservation, contact hotels directly by email, phone, or fax. Email is the clearest and most economical way to make a reservation. Or you can go straight to the hotel website; many have secure online reservation forms and can instantly inform you of availability and any special deals. But be sure you use the hotel's official site and not a booking agency's site for my recommended hotels—otherwise you may pay higher rates than you should. If phoning from the US, be mindful of time zones (see page 10). Most recommended hoteliers are accustomed to guests who speak only English, though you might find a few near the Austrian border who communicate only in Czech and German.

The hotelier wants to know these key pieces of information (also included in the sample request form on page 306):

- number and type of rooms
- number of nights
- date of arrival
- date of departure
- any special needs (e.g., bathroom in the room or down the hall, twin beds vs. double bed, air-conditioning, quiet, view, ground floor, etc.)

When you request a room, use the European style for writing dates: day/month/year. Hoteliers need to know your arrival and departure dates. For example, for a two-night stay in July, I would request: "2 nights, arrive 16/07/10, depart 18/07/10." (Consider in advance how long you'll stay; don't just assume you can tack on extra days once you arrive.)

If you don't get a reply to your email or fax, it usually means the hotel is already fully booked (but you can try sending the message again, or call to follow up).

Confirming a Reservation: If the hotel's response includes its room availability and rates, it's not a confirmation. You must tell them that you want that room at the given rate. Many hoteliers will request your credit-card number for a one-night deposit to hold the room. While you can email your credit-card information (I do), it's safer to share that personal info via phone call, fax, two successive emails, or secure online reservation form (if the hotel has one on its website).

Canceling a Reservation: If you must cancel your reservation, it's courteous to do so with as much advance notice as possible—at least three days. Simply make a quick phone call or send an email. Family-run hotels and pensions lose money if they turn away customers while holding a room for someone who doesn't show up. Understandably, many hotels bill no-shows for one night.

Hotels in larger cities such as Prague sometimes have strict cancellation policies. For example, you might lose a deposit if you cancel within two weeks of your reserved stay, or you might be billed for the entire visit if you leave early. Ask about cancellation policies before you book.

If canceling via email, request confirmation that your cancellation was received to avoid being accidentally billed.

Reconfirm Your Reservation: Always call to reconfirm your room reservation a day or two in advance from the road. Smaller hotels and pensions appreciate knowing your time of arrival. If you'll be arriving after 17:00, be sure to let your hotelier know. On the small chance that a hotel loses track of your reservation, bring along a hard copy of your emailed or faxed confirmation. Don't have the TI reconfirm rooms for you; they'll take a commission.

Reserving Rooms as You Travel: If you enjoy having a flexible itinerary, you can make reservations as you travel, calling hotels

INTRODUCTION

a few days to a week before your visit. If you prefer the flexibility of traveling without any reservations at all, you'll have greater success snaring rooms if you arrive at your destination early in the day. When you anticipate crowds (weekends are worst), call hotels at about 9:00 on the day you plan to arrive, when the hotel clerk knows who'll be checking out and just which rooms will be available. If you encounter a language barrier, ask the fluent receptionist at your current hotel to call for you.

Eating

You'll find that the local cafés, cuisine, beer, and wine are highlights of your Czech adventure. This is affordable sightseeing for your palate.

When restaurant-hunting, choose a spot filled with locals, not the place with the big neon signs boasting "We Speak English and Accept Credit Cards." Incredible deals abound in the Czech Republic, where locals routinely eat well for $5. Venturing even a block or two off the main drag leads to authentic, higher-quality food for less than half the price of the tourist-oriented places. Most restaurants tack a menu onto their door for browsers and have an English menu inside. Most Czech restaurants are open Sunday through Thursday 11:00–22:00, and Friday and Saturday 11:00–24:00. Only a rude waiter will rush you. Good service is relaxed (slow to an American). You can stay in a pub as long as you want—no one will bring you the *účet* (bill) until you ask for it: *"Pane vrchní, zaplatím!"* (PAH-neh VURCH-nee zah-plah-TEEM; "Mr. Waiter, now I pay!"). The service charge is included in the bill, but it's customary to tip 5–10 percent (explained earlier, under "Tipping"). In Prague, it's smart to pay cash for your meals rather than let your credit card leave your sight; for more on scams in Prague, see page 38.

When you're in the mood for something halfway between a restaurant and a picnic, look for take-out food stands, bakeries (with sandwiches and small pizzas to go), delis with stools or a table, department-store cafeterias, salad bars, or simple little eateries for fast and easy sit-down restaurant food.

Czech Food

Czech cuisine is heavy, hearty, and tasty. Expect lots of meat, potatoes, and cabbage. Still, there's more variety than you might expect. Ethnic restaurants provide a welcome break from Slavic

Czech Dumplings

Czech dumplings *(knedlíky)* resemble steamed white bread. They come in plain or potato *(bramborové)* varieties; are meant to be drowned in gravy (dumplings never accompany sauceless dishes); and are eaten with a knife and fork. Sweet dumplings, listed in the dessert section on a menu, are a tempting option during summer, when they are loaded with fresh strawberries, blueberries, apricots, or plums, and garnished with custard and melted butter. Beware, though, that many restaurants like to cheat by filling the sticky dough with a smattering of jam or fruit preserve; before ordering, ask the waiter for details, or discreetly inspect that plate at your neighbor's table. Dumplings with frozen fruit lose some of the flavor, but are still good to try.

fare. Seek out vegetarian, Italian, or Chinese—these are especially good in bigger towns such as Prague, Olomouc, Český Krumlov, and Kutná Hora.

A Czech restaurant is a social place where people come to relax. Tables are not private. You can ask to join someone, and you will most likely make some new friends. After a sip of beer, ask for the *jídelní lístek* (menu).

Soups: *Polévka* (soup) is the most essential part of a meal. The saying goes: "The soup fills you up, the dish plugs it up." Some of the thick soups for a cold day are *zelná* or *zelňačka* (cabbage), *čočková* (lentil), *fazolová* (bean), and *dršťková* (tripe—delicious if fresh, chewy as gum if not). The lighter soups are *hovězí* or *slepičí vývar s nudlemi* (beef or chicken broth with noodles), *pórková* (leek), and *květáková* (cauliflower).

Bread: *Pečivo* (bread) is either delivered with the soup, or you need to ask for it; it's always charged separately depending on how many *rohlíky* (rolls) or slices of *chleba* (yeast bread) you eat.

Main Dishes: These can either be *hotová jídla* (quick, ready-to-serve standard dishes, in some places available only during lunch hours, 11:30–14:30) or the more specialized *jídla na objednávku* or *minuy* (plates prepared when you order). Even the supposedly quick *hotová jídla* will take longer than the fast food you're used to back home.

Hotová jídla come with set garnishes. The standard menu across the country includes *smažený řízek s bramborem* (fried pork fillet with potatoes), *svíčková na smetaně s knedlíkem* (beef tenderloin in cream sauce with dumplings), *vepřová s knedlíkem a se zelím* (pork with dumplings and cabbage), *pečená kachna s knedlíkem a se zelím* (roasted duck with dumplings and cabbage), *maďarský guláš s knedlíkem* (the Czech version of Hungarian goulash), and *pečené kuře s bramborem* (roasted chicken with potatoes).

In this landlocked country, fish options are typically limited to *kapr* (carp) and *pstruh* (trout), prepared in a variety of ways and served with potatoes or fries—although recently, Czech perch and Norwegian salmon have cropped up on many local menus. Vegetarians can go for the delicious *smažený sýr s bramborem* (fried cheese with potatoes) or default to *čočka s vejci* (lentils with fried egg). If you are spending the night out with friends, have a beer and feast on the huge *vepřové koleno s hořčicí a křenem* (pork knuckle with mustard and horseradish sauce) with *chleba* (yeast bread).

The range of the *jídla na objednávku* (meals prepared to order) depends on the chef. You choose your starches and garnishes, which are charged separately.

Salad: *Šopský salát*, like a Greek salad, is usually the best salad option (a mix of tomatoes, cucumbers, peppers, onion, and feta cheese with vinegar and olive oil). The waiter will bring it with the main dish, unless you specify that you want it before.

Dessert: For *moučník* (dessert), there are *palačinka* (crêpes served with fruit or jam), *lívance* (small pancakes with jam and curd), *zmrzlinový pohár* (ice-cream sundae), or fruit-filled dumplings. Many restaurants will offer different sorts of *koláče* (pastries) and *štrůdl* (apple strudel), but it's much better to get these directly from a bakery.

Beverages: No Czech meal is complete without a cup of strong *turecká káva* (Turkish coffee—finely ground coffee that only partly dissolves, leaving "mud" on the bottom, drunk without milk). Although espressos and instant coffees have made headway in the past few years, some Czechs regard them as a threat to tradition.

A good alternative to a beer is *minerálka* (mineral water). These healthy waters have a high mineral content. They're naturally carbonated because they come from the springs in the many Czech spas (Mattoni, the most common brand, is from Carlsbad). If you want still water, ask for *voda bez bublinek* (water without bubbles). Tap water is generally not served. Water comes bottled and generally costs more than beer.

Bohemia is beer country, with Europe's best and cheapest brew (for all the details, see the sidebar on page 129). Locals also like the herb liquor *becherovka*. Moravians prefer wine and *slivovice* (SLEE-voh-veet-seh)—a plum brandy so highly valued that it's the de facto currency of the Carpathian Mountains (often used for bartering with farmers and other mountain folk). *Medovina* ("honey wine") is mead.

In bars and restaurants, you can go wild with memorable liqueurs, most of which cost about a dollar a

How Was Your Trip?

Were your travels fun, smooth, and meaningful? If you'd like to share your tips, concerns, and discoveries, please fill out the survey at www.ricksteves.com/feedback. I value your feedback. Thanks in advance—it helps a lot.

shot. Experiment. *Fernet,* a bitter drink made from many herbs, is the leading Czech aperitif. Absinthe, made from wormwood and herbs, is a watered-down version of the hallucinogenic drink that's illegal in much of Europe. It's famous as the muse of many artists (including Henri de Toulouse-Lautrec in Paris more than a century ago). *Becherovka,* made of 13 herbs and 38 percent alcohol, was used to settle upset aristocratic tummies and as an aphrodisiac. This velvety drink remains popular today. *Becherovka* and tonic mixed together is nicknamed *beton* ("concrete"). If you drink three, you'll find out why.

Traveling as a Temporary Local

We travel all the way to Europe to enjoy differences—to become temporary locals. You'll experience frustrations. Certain truths that we find "God-given" or "self-evident," such as cold beer, ice in drinks, bottomless cups of coffee, hot showers, and bigger being better, are suddenly not so true. One of the benefits of travel is the eye-opening realization that there are logical, civil, and even better alternatives.

Americans are enjoying a surge in popularity in Europe these days. But if there is a negative aspect to the image Europeans have of Americans, it's that we are big, loud, aggressive, impolite, rich, superficially friendly, and a bit naive.

My Czech friends (and Europeans in general) place a high value on speaking quietly in restaurants and on trains. Listen while on the bus or in a restaurant—the place can be packed, but the decibel level is low. Try to adjust your volume accordingly to show respect for their culture.

While Europeans look bemusedly at some of our Yankee excesses—and worriedly at others—they nearly always afford us individual travelers all the warmth we deserve. Judging from all the happy feedback I receive from travelers who have used this book, it's safe to assume you'll enjoy a great, affordable vacation—with the finesse of an independent, experienced traveler.

Thanks, and happy travels!

Back Door Travel Philosophy
From *Rick Steves' Europe Through the Back Door*

Travel is intensified living—maximum thrills per minute and one of the last great sources of legal adventure. Travel is freedom. It's recess, and we need it.

Experiencing the real Europe requires catching it by surprise, going casual..."Through the Back Door."

Affording travel is a matter of priorities. (Make do with the old car.) You can eat and sleep—simply, safely, and enjoyably—anywhere in Europe for $120 a day plus transportation costs. In many ways, spending more money only builds a thicker wall between you and what you traveled so far to see. Europe is a cultural carnival, and time after time, you'll find that its best acts are free and the best seats are the cheap ones.

A tight budget forces you to travel close to the ground, meeting and communicating with the people. Never sacrifice sleep, nutrition, safety, or cleanliness to save money. Simply enjoy the local-style alternatives to expensive hotels and restaurants.

Connecting with people carbonates your experience. Extroverts have more fun. If your trip is low on magic moments, kick yourself and make things happen. If you don't enjoy a place, maybe you don't know enough about it. Seek the truth. Recognize tourist traps. Give a culture the benefit of your open mind. See things as different, but not better or worse. Any culture has plenty to share.

Of course, travel, like the world, is a series of hills and valleys. Be fanatically positive and militantly optimistic. If something's not to your liking, change your liking.

Travel can make you a happier American, as well as a citizen of the world. Our Earth is home to six and a half billion equally precious people. It's humbling to travel and find that other people don't have the "American Dream"—they have their own dreams. Europeans like us, but with all due respect, they wouldn't trade passports.

Thoughtful travel engages us with the world. In tough economic times, it reminds us what is truly important. By broadening perspectives, travel teaches new ways to measure quality of life.

Globetrotting destroys ethnocentricity, helping us understand and appreciate other cultures. Rather than fear the diversity on this planet, celebrate it. Among your most prized souvenirs will be the strands of different cultures you choose to knit into your own character. The world is a cultural yarn shop, and Back Door travelers are weaving the ultimate tapestry. Join in!

CZECH REPUBLIC

Česká Republika

The Czech Republic is geographically small. On a quick visit, you can enjoy a fine introduction while still packing in plenty of surprises.

Despite their difficult 20th-century experience, the Czechs have managed to preserve their history. In Czech towns and villages, you'll find a simple joy of life—a holdover from the days of the Renaissance. The deep spirituality of the Baroque era still shapes the national character. The magic of Prague, the beauty of Český Krumlov, and the lyrical quality of the countryside relieve the heaviness caused by the turmoil that passed through here. Get beyond Prague and explore the country's medieval towns. These rugged woods and hilltop castles will make you feel as if you're walking through the garden of your childhood dreams.

Of the Czech Republic's three main regions—Bohemia, Moravia, and small Silesia—the best-known is Bohemia. It has nothing to do with beatnik bohemians, but with the Celtic tribe of Bohemia that inhabited the land before the coming of the Slavs. A longtime home of the Czechs, Bohemia is circled by a naturally fortifying ring of mountains and cut down the middle by the Vltava River, with Prague as its capital. The winegrowing region of Moravia (to the east) is more Slavic and colorful, and more about the land.

Tourists often conjure up images of Bohemia when they think of the Czech Republic. But the country consists of more than rollicking beer halls and gently rolling landscapes. It's also about dreamy wine cellars and fertile Moravian plains, with the rugged Carpathian Mountains on the horizon. Politically and geologically, Bohemia and Moravia are two distinct regions. The soils and climates in which the hops and wine grapes grow are very different...

Czech Republic Almanac

Birth of Two Nations: The nation of Czechoslovakia—formed after World War I and dominated by the USSR after World War II—split on January 1, 1993, into two separate nations: the Czech Republic (Česká Republika) and Slovakia.

Population: 10.3 million people. About 90 percent are ethnic Czechs, who speak Czech. Unlike some of their neighbors (including the very Catholic Poles and Slovaks), Czechs are inclined to be agnostic: One in four is Roman Catholic, but the majority (60 percent) list their religion as unaffiliated.

Latitude and Longitude: 50°N and 15°E (similar latitude to Vancouver, British Columbia).

Area: 31,000 square miles (similar to South Carolina or Maine).

Geography: The Czech Republic comprises three regions—Bohemia (Čechy), Moravia (Morava), and a small slice of Silesia (Slezsko). The climate is generally cool and partly cloudy.

Biggest Cities: Prague (the capital, 1.2 million), Brno (380,000), Ostrava (336,000), and Plzeň (165,000).

Economy: The gross domestic product equals about $220 billion (similar to that of Indiana). The GDP per capita is approximately $26,000 (about half that of the average American). Some major moneymakers for the country are machine parts, cars and trucks (VW subsidiary Škoda has become a highly respected automaker), and beer (including Pilsner Urquell and the original Budweiser—called "Czechvar" in the US). The recent economic crisis caused a major decline in machine parts, cars, and trucks—but not in beer consumption, which dropped minimally (the vast

and so are the two regions' mentalities. The boisterousness of the Czech polka contrasts with the melancholy of the Moravian ballad; the political viewpoint of the Prague power broker is at odds with the spirituality of the Moravian bard.

Only a tiny bit of Silesia—around the town of Opava—is part of the Czech Republic today; the rest of the region is in Poland and Germany. (The Habsburgs lost traditionally Czech Silesia to Prussia in the 1740s, and 200 years later, Germany in turn ceded most of it to Poland.) People in Silesia speak a wide variety of dialects that mix Czech, German, and Polish. Perhaps due to their diverse genes and cultural heritage, women from Silesia are famous for being intelligent and beautiful.

Since 1989, the year that the Czechs won their independence from Soviet control, people have been working harder—but the average monthly wage is still only about $1,500. Roads have been patched up, facades have gotten facelifts, and supermarkets have been pushed out by hypermarkets.

majority of Czech beer is consumed domestically). More than a third of trade is with next-door-neighbor Germany; therefore, Germany's economic indicators one year will generally predict the Czech Republic's indicators the next year. Privatization of formerly government-run industries goes on. Next on the selling list are the airlines and the energy company.

Currency: 18 Czech crowns (*koruna*, Kč) = about $1.

Government: From 1948 to 1989, Czechoslovakia was a communist state under Soviet control. Today, the Czech Republic is a member of the European Union (since 2004) and a vibrant democracy, with 68 percent of its eligible population voting in the 2006 election. Its parliament is made up of 200 representatives elected every four years and 81 senators elected for six years. No single political party dominates. The two big parties—the conservative Civic Democrats and the left-of-center Social Democrats—each won just a third of the vote in the 2006 election. The other three parties—the Communists, Christian Democrats, and the Greens—hold enough sway that the leader of the winning party typically heads a coalition government. The president (currently Václav Klaus, a conservative) is selected every five years by the legislators.

Flag: The Czech flag is red (bottom), white (top), and blue (a triangle along the hoist side).

The Average Czech: The average Czech has 1.2 kids (slowly rising after the sharp decline that followed the end of communism), will live 76 years, and has one television in the house.

Freedom Versus Babies

In communist times, it was routine to be married and start a family by age 22. Once a Czech finished training school and (for men) the compulsory two-year military service, there was little else to aspire to. Everyone was assigned essentially the same mediocre job ("They pretended to pay us, we pretended to work"), with little hope of career progress—unless you were willing to cut ties with your friends by entering the Communist Party or working for the secret police. Children (and summer homes) were the only way for people to project their dreams. Parenting was subsidized. In the countryside, young families were guaranteed housing, and in cities, flats were allocated according to long waiting lists that gave priority to married couples with children.

But after the fall of communism in 1989, many more options became available to young people who, as children or teenagers, had not even dreamed of such possibilities. Young Czechs embraced the new freedoms: Everyone wanted to travel—to the

West to study law, or to the East to meditate in a cave. And everyone wanted to work—for big bucks at a multinational investment bank, or for pennies at a nonprofit organization in Afghanistan. Marriage was no longer the expected "next step." And shacking up was no longer a problem; you needed money, rather than a marriage certificate, to get a place to live. More and more young adults waited until after 30 to get married, and those already married reconsidered their choices in the light of new circumstances. Fewer Czechs had children, and many got divorced.

By 2004, the falling birthrate and shrinking size of the Czech nation was a regular topic in newspaper columns. To stimulate production, the socialist government began paying new parents a baby bonus—one month's wages—in addition to the standard three years of paid maternity leave already promised to one parent.

Ironically—as if to prove that Czechs will never listen to what the government tells them to do—as soon as the newly elected conservatives revoked the monthly wage pay-out in 2006, everyone between the ages of 25 and 35 suddenly decided to have children. The biggest baby boom in a generation is still on: Maternity wards are overflowing, signs regulating stroller traffic are being introduced into public parks, and politicians are blaming each other for imprudently closing down many state-run nurseries.

Yet, even though they're faced with a bright and baby-filled future, some Czechs maintain a healthy dose of pessimism and seem reluctant to dive headlong into the Western rat race. Life still goes a little slower here, and people find pleasure in simple things.

Ninety percent of the tourists who visit the Czech Republic see only Prague. But if you venture outside the capital, you'll enjoy traditional towns and villages, great prices, a friendly and gentle countryside dotted by nettles and wild poppies, and almost no Western tourists. Since the time of the Habsburgs, fruit trees have lined the country roads for everyone to share. Take your pick.

PRAGUE

ORIENTATION TO PRAGUE

It's amazing what two decades of freedom can do. Prague has always been historic. Now it's fun, too. No other place in Europe has become so popular so quickly. And for good reason: Prague—the only Central European capital to escape the bombs of the last century's wars—is one of Europe's best-preserved cities. It's filled with sumptuous Art Nouveau facades, offers tons of cheap Mozart and Vivaldi concerts, and brews the best beer in Europe. Beyond its architecture and traditional culture, it's an explosion of pent-up entrepreneurial energy jumping for joy after 40 years of communist rule. Its low prices can cause you to jump for joy, too. Travel in Prague is like travel in Western Europe...20 years ago and (except for hotels) for half the price.

Planning Your Time

A week in Prague is plenty of time to get a solid feel for the city and enjoy excursions to Český Krumlov and Kutná Hora. If you're in a rush, you need a minimum of two full days (with three nights, or two nights and a night train) for a good introduction to the city. From Munich, Berlin, and Vienna, Prague is a four- to six-hour train ride by day (you also have the option of a longer night train from Munich). From Budapest, Warsaw, or Kraków, you can take a handy overnight train.

With two days in Prague, I'd spend one morning seeing the castle and another morning in the Jewish Quarter. Use your afternoons for loitering around the Old Town, Charles Bridge, and the Little Quarter, and split your nights between beer halls and live music. Keep in mind that Jewish Quarter sights close on Saturday. Some museums, mainly in the Old Town, are closed on Monday.

Prague Overview

Prague unnerves many travelers—it's behind the former Iron Curtain, and you've heard stories of rip-offs and sky-high hotel

prices (both are real problems, but avoidable if you're smart). Despite your fears, Prague is charming, safe, and ready to show you a good time. The language barrier is tiny. It seems like every well-educated young person speaks English.

Locals call their town "Praha" (PRAH-hah). It's big, with 1.2 million people, but during a quick visit, you'll focus on its relatively compact old center. As you wander, take advantage of brown street signs directing you to tourist landmarks. Self-deprecating Czechs note that while the signs are designed to help tourists (locals never use them), they're only printed in Czech. Still—thanks to the little icons—the signs can help smart visitors who are sightseeing on foot.

The Vltava River divides the west side (Castle Quarter and Little Quarter) from the east side (New Town, Old Town, Jewish Quarter, Main Train Station, and most of the recommended hotels).

Prague addresses come with references to a general zone: Praha 1 is in the old center on either side of the river; Praha 2 is in the New Town, southeast of Wenceslas Square; Praha 3 and higher indicate a location farther from the center. Virtually everything I list is in Praha 1.

Tourist Information

TIs are at several key locations: **Old Town Square** (in the Old Town Hall, just to the left of the Astronomical Clock; Easter–Oct Mon–Fri 9:00–19:00, Sat–Sun 9:00–18:00; Nov–Easter Mon–Fri 9:00–18:00, Sat–Sun 9:00–17:00; tel. 224-482-018) and the castle side of **Charles Bridge** (Easter–Oct daily 10:00–18:00, closed Nov–Easter). For general tourist information in English, dial 12444 (Mon–Fri 8:00–19:00) or check the TIs' useful website: www.prague-info.cz.

The TIs offer maps, phone cards, a useful transit guide, information on guided walks and bus tours, and bookings for private guides, concerts, hotel rooms, and rooms in private homes.

Monthly event guides—all of them packed with ads—include the *Prague Guide* (29 Kč), *Prague This Month* (free), and *Heart of Europe* (free, summer only). The English-language weekly *Prague*

Post newspaper is handy for entertainment listings and current events (60 Kč at newsstands).

Arrival in Prague

For a comprehensive rundown on Prague's train stations, bus connections, airport, and hiring your own local driver, see the Prague Connections chapter.

No matter how you arrive, your first priority is buying a city map, with trams and Metro lines marked and tiny sketches of the sights drawn in for ease in navigating (30–70 Kč, many different brands; sold at kiosks, exchange windows, and tobacco stands). It's a mistake to try doing Prague without a good map—you'll refer to it constantly. The *Kartografie Praha* city map, which shows all the tram lines and major landmarks, includes a castle diagram and a street index. It comes in two versions: 1:15,000 covers the

ORIENTATION

city center, and 1:25,000 includes the whole city. The city center map is easier to navigate, and is sufficient unless you're sleeping in the suburbs.

Helpful Hints

Medical Help: A 24-hour **pharmacy** is at Palackého 5 (a block from Wenceslas Square, tel. 224-946-982). For standard assistance, there are two state hospitals in the center: the **General Hospital** (open daily 24 hours, moderate wait time, right above Karlovo Náměstí at U Nemocnice 2, Praha 2, use entry G, tel. 224-962-564) and the **Na Františku Hospital** (on the embankment next to Hotel InterContinental, Na Františku 1, go to the main entrance, for English assistance call Mr. Hacker between 8:00–14:00, tel. 222-801-278 or tel. 222-801-371—serious problems only). The reception staff may not speak English, but doctors do.

For above-standard assistance in English (including dental service), consider the top-quality **Hospital Na Homolce** (less than 1,000 Kč for an appointment, from 8:00 to 16:00

Prague's Four Towns

Until about 1800, Prague was actually four distinct towns with four town squares, all separated by fortified walls. Each town had a unique character, which came from the personality of the people who initially settled it. Today, much of Prague's charm survives in the distinct spirit of each of its towns.

Castle Quarter (Hradčany): Since the ninth century, when the first castle was built on the promontory overlooking a ford across the Vltava River, Castle Hill has been occupied by the ruling class. When Christianity arrived in the Czech lands, this hilltop—oriented along an east–west axis—proved a perfect spot for a church and, later, the cathedral (which, according to custom, had to be built with the altar pointing east). Finally, the nobles built their representative palaces in proximity to the castle to compete with the Church for influence on the king. Even today, you feel like clip-clopping through this neighborhood in a fancy carriage. The Castle Quarter—which hosts the offices of the president and the foreign minister—has high art and grand buildings, little commerce, and few pubs.

Little Quarter (Malá Strana): This Baroque town of fine palaces and gardens rose from the ashes of a merchant settlement that burned down in the 1540s. The Czech and European nobility who settled here took pride in the grand design of their gardens. In the 1990s, after decades of decay, the gardens were carefully restored. While some are open only to the successors of the former nobility—including the Czech Parliament and the American, German, and Polish Embassies—many are open to visitors.

Old Town (Staré Město): The Charles Bridge connects the Little Quarter with the Old Town. A boomtown since the 10th century, this area has long been the busy commercial quarter—filled with merchants, guilds, and supporters of Jan Hus (who wanted a Czech-style Catholicism). Trace the walls of this town in the modern road plan (the Powder Tower is a remnant of a wall system that completed a fortified ring, the other half of which was formed by the river). The marshy area closest to the bend—least inhabitable and therefore allotted to the Jewish community—became the ghetto (today's Josefov, or Jewish Quarter).

New Town (Nové Město): The New Town rings the Old Town—cutting a swath from riverbank to riverbank—and is forti-

call 252-922-146, for after-hours emergencies call 257-211-111; bus #167 from Anděl Metro station, Roentgenova 2, Praha 5). The **Canadian Medical Care Center** is a small, private clinic with an English-speaking Czech staff at Veleslavínská 1 in Praha 6 (3,000 Kč for an appointment, 4,500 Kč for a house call, halfway between the city and the airport, tel. 235-360-133, after-hours emergency tel. 724-300-301).

If a **massage** is all you need to cure your aches and pains,

Prague Overview

To Holešovice
Train Station

To
←Airport

CASTLE QUARTER
(Hradčany)

JEWISH
QUARTER

LITTLE
QUARTER
(Malá Strana)

River

Old Town
Square

PRAGUE
CASTLE

CHARLES
BRIDGE

OLD TOWN
(Staré Město)

MAIN TRAIN
STATION

Petřín
Hill

Wenceslas
Square

NEW TOWN
(Nové Město)

Vltava

VINOHRADY

SMÍCHOV

VYŠEHRAD

Not to scale

ORIENTATION

fied with Prague's outer wall. In the 14th century, the king created this town, tripling the size of what would become Prague. Wenceslas Square was once the horse market of this busy working-class district. Even today, the New Town is separated from the Old Town by a "moat" (the literal meaning of the street called Na Příkopě). As you cross bustling Na Příkopě, you leave the glass and souvenir shops behind, and you enter a town of malls and fancy shops that cater to locals and visitors alike.

The Royal Way: Cutting through the four towns—from St. Vitus Cathedral down to the Charles Bridge, and then from the bridge to the Powder Tower—is the Royal Way (Královská Cesta), the ancient path of coronation processions. Today, this city spine is marred by tacky trinket shops and jammed by tour groups. Use it for orientation only—try to avoid it if you want to see the real Prague.

walk into one of the numerous Thai massage parlors around the Old Town. For a more professional fix, contact **Patrick Kočica,** an experienced Hoshino therapist (750 Kč/hr, mobile 722-070-703, www.hoshino.cz, patrick.kocica@hoshino.cz).

Internet Access: Internet cafés are well-advertised and scattered through the Old and New Towns. Consider **Bohemia Bagel** near the Jewish Quarter (see page 135). **Káva Káva Káva Coffee,** on the boundary between the Old and New Towns, is

Rip-Offs in Prague

Prague's new freedom comes with new scams. There's no particular risk of violent crime, but green, rich tourists do get taken by con artists. Simply be on guard, particularly when traveling on trains (thieves thrive on overnight trains), changing money (tellers with bad arithmetic and inexplicable pauses while counting back your change), dealing with taxis (see "Getting Around Prague—By Taxi" on page 42), paying in restaurants (see the Eating in Prague chapter), and wandering through seedy neighborhoods.

Anytime you pay for something, make a careful note of how much it costs, how much you're handing over, and how much you expect back. Count your change. Someone selling you a phone card marked 190 Kč might first tell you it's 790 Kč, hoping to pocket the difference. If you call his bluff, he'll pretend that it never happened.

Plainclothes policemen "looking for counterfeit money" are con artists. Don't show them any cash or your wallet. If you're threatened with an inexplicable fine by a "policeman," conductor, or other official, you can walk away, scare him away by saying you'll need a receipt (which real officials are legally required to provide), or ask a passerby if the fine is legit. On the other hand, do not ignore the plainclothes inspectors on the Metro and trams who show you their badges.

Pickpockets can be little children or adults dressed as professionals—or even as tourists. They target Western visitors. Many thieves drape jackets over their arms to disguise busy fin-

in the Platýz courtyard off Národní 37.

Bookstore: For some good bookstores in Prague, see the Shopping in Prague chapter.

Laundry: A full-service laundry near most of the recommended hotels is at Karolíny Světlé 11 (200 Kč/8-pound load, wash and dry in 3 hours, Mon–Fri 7:30–19:00, closed Sat–Sun, 200 yards from Charles Bridge on Old Town side, mobile 721-030-446); another is at Rybná 27 (290 Kč/8-pound load, same-day pick-up, Mon–Fri 8:00–18:00, Mon and Wed from 7:00, closed Sat–Sun, tel. 224-812-641). Or surf the Internet while your undies tumble-dry at the self-service launderette at Korunní 14 (160 Kč/load wash and dry, Internet access-2 Kč/min, daily 8:00–20:00, near Náměstí Míru Metro stop, Praha 2).

Local Help: Magic Praha is a tiny travel service run by Lída Jánská. A Jill-of-all-trades, she can help with accommodations and transfers throughout the Czech Republic, as well as private tours and side-trips to historic towns (mobile 604-207-

gers. Thieves work the crowded and touristy places in teams. They use mobile phones to coordinate their bumps and grinds. Be careful if anyone creates a commotion at the door of a Metro or tram car (especially around the Národní Třída and Vodičkova tram stops, or on the made-for-tourists tram #22)—it's a smoke-screen for theft.

Car theft is also a big problem in Prague (many Western European car-rental companies don't allow their rentals to cross the Czech border). Never leave anything valuable in your car—not even in broad daylight on a busy street.

The sex clubs on Skořepka and Melantrichova streets, just south and north of Havelská Market, routinely rip off naive tourists and can be danger-ous. They're filled mostly with young Russian women and German and Asian men. Lately this district has become the rage for British "stag" parties, for guys who are happy to fly for cheap to get to cheap beer and cheap thrills.

This all sounds intimidating. But Prague is safe. It has its share of petty thieves and con artists, but very little violent crime. Don't be scared—just be alert.

ORIENTATION

225, www.magicpraha.cz, magicpraha@magicpraha.cz). Lída also speaks Spanish and Portuguese.

Bike Rental: Prague has recently improved its network of bike paths, making bicycles a feasible option for exploring the center of the town and beyond (see www.prahounakole.cz/mapa for an updated map). Two bike-rental shops located near the Old Town Square are **Praha Bike** (daily 9:00–22:00, Dlouhá 24, mobile 732-388-880, www.prahabike.cz) and **City Bike** (daily 9:00–19:00, Králodvorská 5, mobile 776-180-284, www.citybike-prague.com). They rent bikes for about 400 Kč for four hours or 500 Kč per day (with a 1,500-Kč deposit) and also organize guided bike tours.

Car Rental: All of the biggies have offices in Prague (check each company's website, or ask at the TI). For a locally operated alternative, consider **Alimex Thrifty** (toll-free tel. 800-150-170, www.alimex.eu). The cheaper models are a great value (584 Kč/day with basic insurance and limited mileage, plus 238 Kč/day for full theft and damage insurance; additional fees: 500-Kč tax for airport pickup, 357 Kč for delivery to your hotel; discounts if you book online, smart to reserve up to a week ahead in peak season). Note that the "super offer" cars have giant ads pasted on the side. Alimex has branches at the airport (daily 8:00–21:00, tel. 220-114-860) and near Holešovice Station (Mon–Fri 8:00–18:00, Sat 8:00–14:00, Sun 10:00–16:00, tel. 233-350-001).

Best Views: Enjoy the "Golden City of a Hundred Spires" during the early evening, when the light is warm and the colors are rich. Good viewpoints include the terrace at the Strahov Monastery (above the castle), the top of St. Vitus Cathedral (at the castle), the top of either tower on Charles Bridge, the Old Town Square clock tower (has an elevator), the Restaurant u Prince Terrace overlooking the Old Town Square (also with an elevator—see page 136), and the steps of the National Museum overlooking Wenceslas Square.

Getting Around Prague

You can walk nearly everywhere. But after you figure out the public transportation system, the Metro is slick, the trams fun, and the taxis quick and easy. For details, pick up the handy transit guide at the TI. City maps show the Metro, tram, and bus lines.

By Metro, Tram, and Bus

Excellent, affordable public transit is perhaps the best legacy of the communist era (locals ride all month for 550 Kč). The three-line Metro system is handy and simple, but doesn't always get you right to the tourist sights (landmarks such as the Old Town Square and Prague Castle are several blocks from the nearest Metro stops). Trams rumble by every 5–10 minutes and take you just about anywhere.

Tickets: The Metro, trams, and buses all use the same tickets:

- 20-minute basic ticket with limited transfer options (*základní s omezenou přestupností*)—18 Kč. With this ticket, no transfers are allowed on trams and buses, but on the Metro you can go up to five stops with one transfer (not valid for night trams or night buses).
- 1.25-hour transfer ticket with unlimited transfers (*základní přestupní*)—26 Kč.
- 24-hour pass (*jízdenka na 24 hodin*)—100 Kč.
- 3-day pass (*jízdenka na 3 dny*)—330 Kč.
- 5-day pass (*jízdenka na 5 dní*)—500 Kč.

Buy tickets from your hotel, at newsstand kiosks, or from automated machines (select ticket price, then insert coins). For convenience, buy all the tickets that you think you'll need—but estimate conservatively. Remember, Prague is a great walking town, so unless you're commuting from a hotel far outside the center, you'll likely find that individual tickets work best. Be sure to validate your ticket as you board the tram or bus, or in the Metro station, by sticking it in the machine (which stamps a time on it; watch locals and imitate). Inspectors routinely ambush ticketless riders (including tourists) and fine them 700 Kč on the spot.

Tips: Navigate by signs that list the end stations. When you come to your stop, push the yellow button if the doors don't automatically open. Although it seems that all Metro doors lead to the neighborhood of Výstup, that's simply the Czech word for

ORIENTATION

"exit." When a tram pulls up to a stop, two different names are announced: the name of the stop you're currently at, followed by the name of the stop that's coming up next. Confused tourists, thinking they've heard their stop, are notorious for rushing off the tram one stop too soon.

Schedules and Frequency: Trams run every 5–10 minutes in the daytime (a schedule is posted at each stop). The Metro closes at midnight, and the nighttime tram routes (identified with white numbers on blue backgrounds at tram stops) run all night at 30-minute intervals. There's more information and a complete route planner at www.dpp.cz/en.

Handy Tram: Tram #22 is practically made for sightseeing, connecting the New Town with the Castle Quarter (see my "Self-

Guided Tram Tour," later, and find the line marked on the color map at beginning of this book). The tram uses some of the same stops as the Metro (making it easy to get to—or travel on from—the tram route). Of the many stops this tram makes, the most convenient are two in the New Town (Národní Třída Metro stop, between the bottom of Wenceslas Square and the river; and Národní Divadlo, at the National Theater), two in the Little Quarter (Malostranské Náměstí and Malostranská Metro stop), and three above Prague Castle (Královský Letohrádek,

Pražský Hrad, and Pohořelec; for details, see "Getting to Prague Castle—By Tram" on page 98).

By Taxi

Prague's taxis—notorious for hyperactive meters—are being tamed. New legislation is in place to curb crooked cabbies, and police will always take your side in an argument. Still, many cabbies are crooks who consider it a good day's work to take one sucker for a ride. You'll make things difficult for a dishonest cabbie by

Prague Landmarks

English	Czech	Pronounced
Main Train Station	*Hlavní Nádraží*	hlav-NEE NAH-drah-zhee
Old Town	*Staré Město*	STAH-reh MYEHS-toh
Old Town Square	*Staroměstské Náměstí*	STAR-roh-myehst-skeh NAH-myehs-tee
New Town	*Nové Město*	NOH-vay myehs-toh
Little Quarter	*Malá Strana*	MAH-lah strah-nah
Jewish Quarter	*Josefov*	YOO-zehf-fohf
Castle Quarter	*Hradčany*	HRAD-chah-nee
Charles Bridge	*Karlův Most*	KAR-loov most
Wenceslas Square	*Václavské Náměstí*	VAHT-slahf-skeh NAH-myehs-tee
Vltava River	*Vltava*	VUL-tah-vah

ORIENTATION

challenging an unfair fare.

While most hotel receptionists and guidebooks advise that you avoid taxis, I find Prague to be a great taxi town and use them routinely. With the local rate, they're cheap (read the rates on the door: drop charge starts at 36 Kč; per-kilometer charge—29 Kč; and waiting time per minute—5 Kč). The key is to be sure the cabbie turns on the meter at the #1 tariff (look for the word *sazba*, meaning "tariff," on the meter). Avoid cabs waiting at tourist attractions and train stations. To improve your odds of getting a fair meter rate—which starts only when you take off—call for a cab (or have your hotel or restaurant call one for you). AAA Taxi (tel. 14-014) and City Taxi (tel. 257-257-257) are the most likely to have English-speaking staff and honest cabbies. I also find that hailing a passing taxi usually gets me a decent price, although at a slightly higher rate than when reserving by phone. If a cabbie surprises you at the end with an astronomical fare, simply pay 300 Kč, which should cover you for a long ride anywhere in the center. Then go into your hotel. On the miniscule chance that he follows you, the receptionist will back you up.

Tours in Prague

Walking Tours

Many small companies offer walking tours of the Old Town, the castle, and more. For the latest, pick up the walking tour fliers at the TI. Since guiding is a routine side-job for local university students, you'll generally get hardworking young guides at good prices. While I'd rather go with my own private guide (described next), public walking tours are cheaper (about 450 Kč for a 4-hour tour), cover themes you might not otherwise consider, connect you with other English-speaking travelers, and allow for spontaneity. The quality depends on the guide rather than the company. Your best bet is to show up at the Astronomical Clock a couple of minutes before 8:00, 10:00, or 11:00, then chat with a few of the umbrella-holding guides there. Choose the one you click with. Guides also have fliers advertising additional walks.

▲▲Private Guides

In Prague, hiring a local guide is particularly smart—they're twice as helpful for half the price compared with guides in Western Europe. Because prices are usually per hour (not per person), small groups can hire an inexpensive guide for several days. Guides meet you wherever you like and tailor the tour to your interests. Visit their websites in advance for details on various walks, airport transfers, countryside excursions, and other services offered, and then make arrangements by email.

Šárka Kačabová, who uses her teaching background to help you comprehend Czech culture, has hand-picked a team of personable and knowledgeable guides for her company, **Personal Prague Guide** (600 Kč/hr for 2–3 people, 800 Kč/hr for 4–8 people, mobile 777-225-205, www.prague-guide.info, saraguide@volny.cz). **Katka Svobodová,** a hardworking anthropologist-historian-guide who knows her stuff, runs **Praguewalker,** which offers enthusiastic and friendly guides (600 Kč/hr for 1–4 people, 800 Kč/hr for 5–8 people, mobile 603-181-300, www.praguewalker.com, katerina @praguewalker.com).

Jana Hronková has a natural style—a welcome change from the more strict professionalism of some of the busier guides (mobile 732-185-180, www.experience-prague.info, janahronkova@hot mail.com). My readers also recommend **Renata Blažková,** who has a special interest in the history of Prague's Jewish Quarter (tel. 222-716-870, mobile 602-353-186, blazer@volny.cz); **Martin Bělohradský,** whose main area of expertise lies in fine arts and architecture (martinb@uochb.cas.cz, mobile 723-414-565); and **Václav Štorek,** who specializes in history (vaclavstorek@post.cz). These guides typically charge about 2,000–2,500 Kč for a half-day tour.

Athos Travel's licensed guides can lead you on a general sightseeing tour or fit the walk to your interests: music, Art Nouveau, architecture, and more (600 Kč/hr for 1–5 people, 700 Kč/hr for 5 or more people, arrange tour at least 24 hours in advance, tel. 277-004-677, www.a-prague.com/tours, info@a-prague.com).

The **TI** also has plenty of private guides (rates for a 3-hour

Daily Reminder

Monday: The major sights—such as Prague Castle and the Jewish Quarter—are open, but a number of the lesser sights are closed, including the Bethlehem Chapel (in winter), Museum of Czech Cubism, House at the Golden Ring, Loreta Church, Sternberg Palace, Convent of St. George, and Museum of Medieval Art.

If you're day-tripping today, Terezín and Kutná Hora's Sedlec Bone Church are open. The three castles—Konopiště, Karlštejn, and Křivoklát—are closed.

In Prague's Old Town, classical musicians have a jam session at 17:00 at St. Martin in the Wall, and the cover is free at Roxy's music club, where concerts start at 20:00.

Tuesday–Friday: All sights are open.

Saturday: The Jewish Quarter sights are closed. In nearby Terezín, the Crematorium and Columbarium are closed.

Sunday: St. Vitus Cathedral at Prague Castle is closed Sunday morning for Mass. Some stores have shorter hours or are closed.

Crowd-Beating Tips: Visit Prague Castle either first thing in the morning (be at St. Vitus Cathedral at 9:00—except Sun morning, when it's closed for Mass) or before it closes (17:00 in summer, 16:00 in winter). Hiring your own local guide for a historic walk is relatively cheap and allows you to choose a time (evening or early morning) and route to avoid crowds.

Summer Activities: Outdoor movies on Střelecký Island are shown at about 21:00 from mid-July through early September (see page 87). And a paddle down the river is always fun in warm weather.

Evening Activities: Prague Castle's grounds stay open until 23:00, and the shop-lined Golden Lane is free and empty after 18:00 (17:00 in winter). Concerts in the National Theater, Municipal House, and Rudolfinum feature superb artists at bargain prices (see the Entertainment in Prague chapter).

tour: 1,200 Kč/1 person, 1,400 Kč/2 people, 1,600 Kč/3 people, 2,000 Kč/4 people; desk at Old Town Square TI, arrange and pay in person at least 2 hours in advance, tel. 236-002-562, guides @pis.cz). For a listing of more private guides, see www.guide -prague.cz.

Jewish-Themed Tours: Sylvie Wittmann, a native Czech Jew, has developed a diverse array of guides (some better than others) who aspire to bring Jewish traditions back to life in Prague. Consider her three-hour walking tour of the Jewish Quarter (880 Kč includes entry to the Jewish Museum and the Old-New Synagogue, May–Oct Sun–Fri at 10:30 and 14:00, Nov–Dec and mid-March–April Sun–Fri at 10:30 only, no tours Sat and Jan–mid-March) or her six-hour trip to Terezín Concentration Camp (1,150 Kč includes transportation and all entries, departs May–Oct daily at 10:00; mid-March–April and Nov–Dec no Mon, Wed, or Fri tours; Jan–mid-March by appointment only). All tours require prior reservation and meet in front of Hotel InterContinental at the end of Pařížská street (tel. & fax 222-252-472, mobile 603-168-427, www.wittmann-tours.com).

Outside Prague: To get beyond sights listed in most guide-books, call **Tom and Marie Zahn** from **P.A.T.H. Finders International.** Tom is an American who married into the Czech Republic (Marie), and together they organize and lead family-friendly day excursions (in Prague or throughout the country). Their tours are creative and affordable, and they teach travelers how to find off-the-beaten-track destinations on their own. Their specialty is Personal Ancestral Tours & History (P.A.T.H.), and with sufficient notice, they can help Czech descendants find their ancestral homes, perhaps even a long-lost relative. Tom and Marie can also help you with other parts of your Eastern European travel by hooking you up with associates in other countries, especially Germany, Hungary, Poland, Romania, Slovakia, and Ukraine (US tel. 360-450-5959, Czech tel. 257-940-113, www.pathfinders.cz, info@pathfinders.cz).

Reverend Jan Dus is another option. This enthusiastic pastor lived in the US for several years and now serves a small congre-gation about 100 miles east of Prague. Jan likes to help travelers connect with locals in little towns, particularly in northeastern Bohemia and Moravia. He has an outstanding track record in pro-viding genealogical services (toll-free US tel. 800-807-1562, www .revjan.com, rev.jan.services@gmail.com).

Bus Tours

Although I generally recommend cheap big-bus orientation tours for an efficient, once-over-lightly look at great cities, Prague just isn't built for bus tours. In fact, most bus tours of the city are walk-ing tours that use buses for pick-ups and transfers. The sightseeing core (Castle Quarter, Charles Bridge, and the Old Town) is not accessible by bus. So if you insist on a bus, you're playing basketball with a catcher's mitt.

Bus tours make more sense for day trips out of Prague. Several companies have kiosks on Na Příkopě, where you can comparison-shop. **Premiant City Tours** offers 20 different tours, includ-ing Terezín Concentration Camp, Karlštejn Castle, and Český Krumlov (1,750 Kč, 10 hrs), and a river cruise. The tours feature live guides and depart from near the bottom of Wenceslas Square at Na Příkopě 23. Get tickets at an AVE travel agency, your hotel, on the bus, or at Na Příkopě 23 (tel. 224-946-922, mobile 606-600-123, www.premiant.cz). Tour salespeople are notorious for telling you anything to sell a ticket. Some tours, especially those heading into the countryside, can be in as many as four different languages. Hiring a private guide, many of whom can drive you around in their car, can be a much better value (described earlier, under "Private Guides").

More Tours

Tram Tours—Prague's tram #22 is an easy way to get familiar with the city at very little cost (see "Self-Guided Tram Tour," next). Handy tram stops for this tour are located near the Národní Třída and Malostranská Metro stops.

Cruises—Prague isn't ideal for a boat tour because you might spend half the time waiting to go through the locks. Still, the hour-long Vltava River cruises, which leave from near the castle end of Charles Bridge about hourly, are scenic and relaxing, though not informative (150–200 Kč).

▲**Rowboat or Paddleboat Cruises**—Renting a rowboat or paddleboat on the island by the National Theater is a better way to enjoy the river. You'll float at your own pace among the swans and watch local lovers cruise by in their own boats (40 Kč/hr for rowboats, 60 Kč/hr for paddleboats, bring photo ID for deposit).

Self-Guided Tram Tour

▲▲Welcome to Prague: Tram #22

Tram #22 makes a good Prague orientation joyride. It runs roughly every 5–10 minutes, and you can hop on and off as you like (26-Kč transfer ticket valid for 1.25 hrs—described earlier, under "Getting Around Prague"). There are more seats and less traffic early, mid-day, and late. Be warned: Thieves like this route as much as the tourists.

Catch the tram in the New Town and ride it over the river, through the Little Quarter, and up to the castle (stop: Pohořelec). You'll see how easy it is to use the trams, get the lay of the land, and zip effortlessly up to the castle (saving lots of sweat or a 200-Kč taxi ride).

Start at the **Národní Třída** stop (facing the Metro stop of the same name, catch the tram closest to the Metro, on the same side of the street as the Tesco department store). The tram will turn

Prague at a Glance

Activities

▲▲Self-Guided Tram Tour Quick, scenic, and handy overview of the city and its excellent transit system. See page 47.

▲▲Tourist Concerts Good yet affordable concerts in sumptuous venues. **Hours:** Daily between about 13:00 and 21:00. See page 149.

▲▲Private Guides A worthwhile two- to three-hour tour of this complex city by a hired, hardworking young guide. See page 44.

▲Rowboat or Paddleboat Cruises An hour's paddle on the river on a hot, sunny day: peaceful, scenic, memorable...and good exercise. See page 47.

In the Old Town

▲▲▲Old Town Square Magical main square of Old World Prague, with dozens of colorful facades, the dramatic Jan Hus Memorial, looming Týn Church, and fanciful Astronomical Clock. **Hours:** Týn Church generally open to sightseers Tue–Sat 10:00–13:00 & 15:00–17:00; clock strikes on the hour daily 8:00–21:00, until 20:00 in winter; clock tower open Tue–Sun 9:00–17:30, Mon 11:00–17:30. See page 52.

▲▲▲Charles Bridge An atmospheric, statue-lined bridge that connects the Old Town to the Little Quarter and Prague Castle. **Hours:** Always open and crossable, though certain sections may be closed for renovation. See page 65.

▲▲▲Jewish Quarter The best Jewish sight in Europe, featuring various synagogues and an evocative cemetery. **Hours:** April–Oct Sun–Fri 9:00–18:00, Nov–March Sun–Fri 9:00–16:30, always closed Sat. See page 69.

▲▲Museum of Medieval Art The best Gothic art in the land, at St. Agnes Convent. **Hours:** Tue–Sun 10:00–18:00, closed Mon. See page 60.

▲Havelská Market Colorful open-air market that sells crafts and produce. **Hours:** Daily 9:00–18:00. See page 61.

▲Klementinum National Library's lavish Baroque Hall and Observatory Tower (with views), open by 45-minute tour only. **Hours:** Mon–Fri 14:00–19:00, Sat–Sun 10:00–19:00, shorter hours off-season. See page 63.

In the New Town

▲▲**Wenceslas Square** Lively boulevard at the heart of modern Prague. **Hours:** Always open. See page 75.

▲▲**Mucha Museum** Easy-to-appreciate collection of Art Nouveau works by Czech artist Alfons Mucha. **Hours:** Daily 10:00–18:00. See page 81.

▲▲**Municipal House** Pure Art Nouveau architecture, including Prague's largest concert hall and several eateries. **Hours:** Daily 10:00–18:00. See page 82.

▲▲**Museum of Communism** The rise and fall of the regime, from start to Velvet finish. **Hours:** Daily 9:00–21:00. See page 84.

In the Little Quarter

Church of St. Nicholas Jesuit centerpiece of Little Quarter Square, with ultimate High Baroque decor and a climbable bell tower. **Hours:** Church—daily 9:00–17:00; tower—April–Oct daily 10:00–18:00, closed Nov–March. See page 90.

Petřín Hill Little Quarter hill with public art, a funicular, a replica of the Eiffel Tower, and the quirky museum of a nonexistent Czech hero. **Hours:** Funicular—daily 8:00–22:00; tower and museum—daily 10:00–22:00. See page 97.

In the Castle Quarter

▲▲▲**St. Vitus Cathedral** The Czech Republic's most important church, featuring a climbable tower and a striking stained-glass window by Art Nouveau artist Alfons Mucha. **Hours:** Daily April–Oct 9:00–17:00, Nov–March 9:00–16:00, closed Sunday mornings year-round for Mass. See page 110.

▲▲**Prague Castle** Traditional seat of Czech rulers, with St. Vitus Cathedral (see above), Old Royal Palace, Basilica of St. George, shop-lined Golden Lane, and lots of crowds. **Hours:** Castle sights—daily April-Oct 9:00–17:00, Nov–March 9:00–16:00; castle grounds—daily 5:00–23:00. See page 107.

▲**Strahov Monastery and Library** Baroque center of learning, with ornate reading rooms and old-fashioned science exhibits. **Hours:** Daily 9:00–11:45 & 13:00–17:00. See page 100.

Toy and Barbie Museum Several centuries of toys, starring an army of Barbies. **Hours:** Daily 9:30–17:30. See page 116.

ORIENTATION

and rattle along National Street (Národní Třída).

At the next stop, **Národní Divadlo,** you'll see Café Slavia facing the National Theater, just before the tram crosses the river. Survey the boat-rental scene (island with rental wharfs) and the romantic beach island, and enjoy a great castle view. The Dancing House, while hard to see, is 400 yards upstream.

The next stop, **Újezd,** faces a park. See the Monument to Victims of Communism Who Survived—with devoured spirits on the steps (uphill at the corner, described on page 97). A funicular leads to the Eiffel-like Petřín Tower.

The tram then heads north from the **Hellichova** stop, paralleling Kampa Island on the river side (to the right). On the inland side, the tram passes St. Mary the Victorious Church, popular with pilgrims for its Infant Jesus of Prague. Entering the Little Quarter, the tram goes slightly uphill to the American Embassy (flying the Stars and Stripes).

The tram stops next at **Malostranské Náměstí,** on the Little Quarter's main square, dominated by the Church of Saint Nicholas. From here you can hike up Nerudova street to Prague Castle. Charles Bridge is just 100 yards away—catch a peek-a-boo view through the gate.

Fifteen yards beyond the **Malostranská** Metro stop (also a tram stop) is the entry to the Wallenstein Palace Garden. Past the park, with its memorial to World War II freedom fighters, a bridge leads across the Vltava River to Josefov, the Jewish Quarter. The tram now enters the longest stretch between stations—perfect for ticket-checkers to reveal themselves and catch anyone traveling without a valid ticket.

Immediately across the street from the **Královský Letohrádek** stop is the Royal Summer Palace, the Royal Gardens leading fragrantly to Prague Castle, and a public WC. On the tram side of the street is one of the few preserved gates of Prague's Baroque fortification system.

If you're in a hurry to hit the castle sights, jump out at the **Pražský Hrad** stop for the most direct route to the castle entrance. If you've got more time, stay on board for my favorite approach from Pohořelec, coming up soon.

The next stop is **Brusnice,** from which you can explore the Nový Svět (New World) neighborhood, a time capsule of cobblestone streets and tiny houses with no shops or tourists (to reach this area from the stop, walk across the small park with a statue, then down the steps).

The tram now winds through a greenbelt built along the top of the city wall (only remnants survive). The next stop, **Pohořelec,** is my preferred approach to the castle and the closest stop to the Strahov Monastery. Hop out here, and it's all downhill. Or catch a tram going the opposite direction to do this trip in reverse.

Extending the Route: You could start this tour earlier at the Náměstí Míru stop (four stops before Národní Třída), next to several recommended places to eat and sleep. And you could get off later at the Břevnovský Klášter stop (five stops after Pohořelec), at the peaceful Břevnov Monastery, next to two recommended hotels (see page 124).

THE OLD TOWN

Staré Město

From Prague's dramatic centerpiece, the Old Town Square, sightseeing options fan out in all directions. Get oriented on the square before venturing onward. You can learn about Jewish heritage in the Jewish Quarter (Josefov), a few blocks from the Old Town Square. Closer to the square, you'll find the quaint and historic Ungelt courtyard and Celetná street, which leads to the Museum of Czech Cubism and the landmark Estates Theater. If you're intrigued by Jan Hus, the preacher and martyr, look for his pulpit in the chapel on Bethlehem Square. Nearby, Karlova street funnels all the tourists to the famous Charles Bridge. All of the sights described here are within a five-minute walk of the magnificent Old Town Square.

▲▲▲Old Town Square (Staroměstské Náměstí)

The focal point for most visits, Prague's Old Town Square is one of the city's top sights. This has been a market square since the 11th century. It became the nucleus of the Old Town (Staré Město) in the 13th century, when its Town Hall was built. Today, the old-time market stalls have been replaced by outdoor cafés and touristy horse buggies. But under this shallow surface, the square hides a magic power to evoke the history that has passed through here. The square's centerpiece is a memorial to Jan Hus.

Prague's Old Town

1. Church of St. Nicholas
2. Ungelt Courtyard & House at the Golden Ring
3. Church of St. James
4. St. Agnes Convent & Museum of Medieval Art
5. Museum of Czech Cubism
6. Estates Theater
7. Havelská Market
8. Bethlehem Chapel
9. Family Museum of Postcards
10. Charles University
11. Klementinum (National Library)
12. Old Town Hall & Astronomical Clock
13. Czech Railways Ticket Office

THE OLD TOWN

Jan Hus and Martin Luther

The word *catholic* means "universal." The Roman Catholic Church—in many ways the administrative ghost of the Roman Empire—is the only organization to survive from ancient times. For more than a thousand years, it enforced its notion that the Vatican was the sole interpreter of God's word on earth, and the only legitimate way to be a Christian was as a Roman Catholic.

Jan Hus (c. 1369–1415) lived and preached a century before Martin Luther. Both were college professors, as well as priests. Both drew huge public crowds as they preached in their university chapels. Both condemned Church corruption and promoted a local religious autonomy. Both helped establish their national languages. (Hus gave the Czech alphabet its unique accent marks so that the letters could fit the sounds.) And both got in big trouble.

While Hus was burned, Luther survived. Thanks to the new printing press, invented by Gutenberg, Luther was able to spread his message cheaply and effectively. Since Luther was high-profile and German, killing him would have caused major political complications. While Hus may have loosened Rome's grip on Christianity, Luther orchestrated the Reformation that finally broke it. Today, both are honored as national heroes as well as religious reformers.

Jan Hus Memorial

This monument, erected in 1915 (500 years after the Czech reformer's martyrdom by fire), symbolizes the long struggle for Czech freedom. Walk around the memorial. Jan Hus stands tall between two groups of people: victorious Hussite patriots, and Protestants defeated by the Habsburgs in 1620. One of the patriots holds a chalice (cup)—in the medieval Church, only priests could drink the wine at Communion. Since the Hussites fought for their right to take both the wine and the bread, the cup is their symbol. Hus looks proudly at the Týn Church (described later), which became the headquarters and leading church of his followers. A golden chalice once filled the now-empty niche under the gold bas-relief of the Virgin Mary on the church's facade. After the Habsburg (and, therefore, Catholic) victory over the Czechs in 1620, the Hussite chalice was melted down and made into the image of Mary that shines from that spot high over the square today.

Old Town Square

THE OLD TOWN

Behind the statue of Jan Hus, the bronze statue of a mother with her children represents the ultimate rebirth of the Czech nation. Because of his bold stance for independence in the way common people worship God, Hus was excommunicated and burned in Germany, a century before the age of Martin Luther.

Old Town Square Orientation Spin-Tour

Whirl clockwise to get a look at Prague's diverse architectural styles: Gothic, Renaissance, Baroque, Rococo, and Art Nouveau. Start with the green domes of the Baroque **Church of St. Nicholas.** Originally Catholic, now Hussite, this church is a popular venue for concerts. (There's another green-domed Church of St. Nicholas—also popular for concerts—by the same architect, across the Charles Bridge in the Little Quarter.) The Jewish Quarter (Josefov) is a few blocks behind the church, down the uniquely tree-lined Pařížská—"Paris street." (For more on the Jewish Quarter, see page 69.) Pařížská, an eclectic cancan of mostly Art Nouveau facades, leads to a bluff that once sported a 100-foot-tall stone statue of Stalin. Demolished in 1962 after Khrushchev exposed Stalin's crimes, it was replaced in 1991 by a giant ticking **metronome**—partly to commemorate Prague's centennial exhibition (the 1891 exhibition is remembered by the Little Quarter's

Eiffel-esque Petřín Tower), and partly to send the message that for every power, there's a time to go.

Spin to the right, past the Hus Memorial and the fine yellow Art Nouveau building. The large Rococo palace on the right (with a public WC in the courtyard) is part of the **National Gallery** and will exhibit Asian art—particularly Chinese and Japanese works—when it opens in May 2010 (Tue–Sun 10:00–18:00, closed Mon).

To the right, you can't miss the towering Gothic **Týn Church** (pronounced "teen"), with its fanciful spires flanking the gold bas-relief of Mary. For 200 years after Hus' death, this was Prague's leading Hussite church (described later in more detail). A narrow lane leading to the church's entrance passes the **Via Musica,** the most convenient ticket office in town. Behind the Týn Church is a gor-geously restored medieval courtyard called **Ungelt.** The row of pastel houses in front of Týn Church has a mixture of Gothic, Renaissance, and Baroque facades. To the right of these buildings, shop-lined **Celetná street** leads to a square called Ovocný Trh (with the Estates Theater and Museum of Czech Cubism—see page 60) and, beyond

that, to the Municipal House and Powder Tower in the New Town (see pages 82–83).

Continue spinning right, taking in more gloriously colorful architecture, until you reach the pointed 250-foot-tall spire mark-ing the 14th-century **Old Town Hall** (which has the only elevator-

accessible tower in town—described later, under Astronomical Clock listing). The chunk of pink building attached to the tower of the Neo-Gothic City Hall is the town's "memorial" to sore losers. The building once stretched all the way to the Church of St. Nicholas. Then, in the last days of World War II (May 1945), German tanks knocked off this landmark—to the joy of many Prague citizens who considered it an ugly, over-sized 19th-century stain on the medieval square. Across the square from the Old Town Hall (opposite the Astronomical Clock), touristy **Melantrichova street** leads directly to the New Town's Wenceslas Square (see page 75), passing the craft-packed Havelská Market (see page 61) along the way.

Twenty-Seven Crosses

Embedded in the pavement at the base of the Old Town Hall tower (near the snack stand), you'll see white inlaid crosses marking the spot where 27 Protestant nobles, merchants, and intellectuals were beheaded in 1621 after rebelling against the Catholic Habsburgs. The execution ended Czech independence for 300 years and is still one of the grimmest chapters in the country's history.

▲▲Astronomical Clock

Join the gang for the striking of the hour on the Town Hall clock (daily 8:00–21:00, until 20:00 in winter). As you wait, see if you can figure out how the clock works.

With revolving discs, celestial symbols, and sweeping hands, this clock keeps several versions of time. Two outer rings show the hour: Bohemian time (gold Gothic numbers on black background, counts from sunset—find the zero, between 23 and 1...supposedly the time of tonight's sunset) and modern time (24 Roman numerals, XII at the top being noon, XII at the bottom being midnight). Five hundred years ago, everything revolved around the earth (the fixed middle background—with Prague marking the center, of course).

To indicate the times of sunrise and sunset, arcing lines and moving spheres combine with the big hand (a sweeping golden sun) and the little hand (a moon that spins to show various stages). Look for the orbits of the sun and moon as they rise through day (the blue zone) and night (the black zone).

If this seems complex to us, it must have been a marvel 500 years ago. Because the clock was heavily damaged during World War II, much of what you see today is a reconstruction. The circle below (added in the 19th century) shows the signs of the zodiac, scenes from the seasons of a rural peasant's life, and a ring of saints' names—one for each day of the year, with a marker showing today's special saint (at top).

Four statues flanking the clock represent the 15th-century outlook on time and prejudices. A Turk with a mandolin symbolizes hedonism, a Jewish moneylender is greed, and the figure staring into a mirror stands for vanity. All these worldly goals are vain in the face of Death, whose hourglass reminds us that our time is unavoidably running out.

At the top of the hour (don't blink—the show is pretty quick): First, Death tips his hourglass and pulls the cord, ringing the bell;

then the windows open and the 12 apostles parade by, acknowledging the gang of onlookers; then the rooster crows; and then the hour is rung. The hour is often off because of daylight savings time (completely senseless to 15th-century clockmakers). At the top of the next hour, stand under the tower—protected by a line

of banner-wielding concert salespeople in powdered wigs—and watch the tourists.

Clock Tour and Tower Climb: The main TI, to the left of the Astronomical Clock, contains an information desk and sells tickets for these two options: zipping up the Old Town Hall tower by elevator (60 Kč, Tue–Sun 9:00–17:30, Mon 11:00–17:30, good views); or taking a 45-minute tour of the Old Town Hall, which includes a Gothic chapel and a close-up look at the inner guts of the Astronomical Clock (plus its statues of the 12 apostles; 50 Kč, 2/hr).

▲Týn Church

Though this church has a long history, it's most notable for its 200-year stint as the leading church of the Hussite movement (generally open to sightseers Tue–Sat 10:00–13:00 & 15:00–17:00). It was Catholic before the Hussites, and was returned to Catholicism after the Hussites were defeated. As if to insult Hus and his doctrine of simplicity, the church's once elegant and pure Gothic columns are now encrusted with noisy Baroque altars. While Gothic, the church interior is uncharacteristically bright because of its clear Baroque windowpanes and whitewash. Read the church's story (posted in English, rear-left side) for a Catholic spin on the church's events—told with barely a mention of Hus. The fine 16th-century, carved John the Baptist altar (right aisle) is worth a look. As you enjoy this church, try to ignore its unwelcoming signs—other than the Catholic-slanted history, the only English words you'll see here are commands that tell you what not to do.

Outside, on the side of the church facing Celetná street, find a statue of the Virgin Mary resting on a temporary column against the wall. The Catholics are still waiting for a chance to reinstall Mary in the middle of the Old Town Square, where she stood for about 250 years until being torn down in 1918 by a mob of anti-Habsburg (and therefore anti-Catholic) demonstrators.

Behind Týn Church

▲Ungelt Courtyard (Týnský Dvůr)—Ever since the Old Town was established, the Ungelt courtyard—located directly behind the Týn Church—has served as a hostel for foreign merchants, much like a Turkish caravanserai. Here the merchants (usually German) would store their goods and pay taxes before setting up stalls on the Old Town Square. Notice that, for the purpose of guaranteeing the safety of goods and merchants, there are only two entrances into the complex. After decades of disuse, the courtyard had fallen into such disrepair by the 1980s that authorities considered demolishing it. Marvelously restored a few years ago, the Ungelt courtyard is now the most pleasant area in the Old Town for dining outdoors (such as at the recommended Indian Jewel), sorting through wooden crafts, and paging through English books (at Anagram Bookshop, described in the Shopping in Prague chapter). Although Prague has undoubtedly lost some of its dreamy character to the booming tourist industry, places such as Ungelt stand as testimony to the miracles that money can work. Had the communists stayed in power for a few more years, Ungelt would have been a black hole by now. Ungelt also reminds us that Prague, for most of its history, has been a cosmopolitan center quite alien to the rest of the country.

House at the Golden Ring (Dům u Zlatého Prstenu)—This medieval townhouse displays a delightful collection of 20th-century Czech art. Its exterior has rectangular sgraffiti etchings (designs scratched out of one layer, revealing a different-colored layer beneath). Since 1900, Czech artists have been refining the subtle differences between dream, myth, and ideal. The English descriptions of each room psychoanalyze this demanding art and recall the fact that Prague in the 1930s and 1960s was at the forefront of the European avant-garde. Notice the absence of Socialist Realism: The artists exhibited here chose deeply personal means of expression over regime-sponsored proclamations of universal optimism (90 Kč, Tue–Sun 10:00–18:00, closed Mon, just left of the entry into Ungelt courtyard as you approach it from the Old Town Square, Týnská 6, tel. 224-827-0224, www.citygalleryprague.cz). The house's courtyard is home to a lively-with-students café.

Church of St. James (Kostel Sv. Jakuba)—Perhaps the most beautiful church in the Old Town, the Church of St. James is just behind the Ungelt courtyard. The Minorite Order has occupied this church and the adjacent monastery almost as long as merchants have occupied Ungelt. A medieval city was a complex phenomenon: Side-by-side, there existed commerce, brothels, and a life of contemplation. (I guess it's not that much different from today.) Artistically, St. James (along with the Church of the Ascension of St. Mary at Strahov Monastery—see page 100) is a stunning example of how simple Gothic spaces could be transformed into sumptuous feasts of Baroque decoration. The blue light in the altar highlights one of Prague's most venerated treasures—the

THE OLD TOWN

bejeweled Madonna Pietatis. Above the *pietà*, as if held aloft by hummingbird-like angels, is a painting of the martyrdom of St. James (free, daily 9:30–12:00 & 14:00–16:00).

As you leave, find the black shriveled-up arm with clenched fingers (15 feet above and to the left of the door). According to legend, a thief attempted to rob the Madonna Pietatis from the altar, but his hand was frozen the moment he touched the statue. The monks had to cut off the arm in order for it to let go. The desiccated arm now hangs here as a warning—and the entire delightful story is posted nearby in English.

North of the Old Town Square, near the River

▲▲**Museum of Medieval Art**—The St. Agnes Convent houses the Museum of Medieval Art in Bohemia and Central Europe (1200–1550). The 14th century was Prague's Golden Age, and the religious art displayed in this Gothic space is a testament to the rich cultural life of the period. Each exquisite piece is well-lit and thoughtfully described in English. Follow the arrows on a chronological sweep through Gothic art history. The various Madonnas and saints were gathered here from churches all over Central Europe (100 Kč, Tue–Sun 10:00–18:00, closed Mon, two blocks northeast of the Spanish Synagogue, along the river at Anežská 12).

Princess Agnes founded this Clarist convent in the 13th century as the first hospital in Prague. Agnes was canonized by Pope John Paul II (who loved to promote the Slavic faithful) in 1989. Since local celebrations of her sainthood on November 26 coincided with the Velvet Revolution (the peaceful overthrow of the Communist government in 1989), Agnes has since been regarded as the patron of the renascent Czech democracy (you'll see her on the rare 50-Kč bill).

On Celetná Street, Toward the New Town

Celetná, a pedestrian-only street, is a convenient and relatively untouristy way to get from the Old Town Square to the New Town (specifically the Municipal House and Powder Tower, described on pages 82–83). Along the way, at the square called Ovocný Trh, you'll find these sights.

Museum of Czech Cubism—Cubism was a potent force in Prague in the early 20th century. The fascinating Museum of Czech Cubism in the Black Madonna House (Dům u Černé Matky Boží) offers the complete Cubist experience: Cubist architecture (stand back and see how masterfully it makes its statement while mixing with its neighbors...then get up close and study the details), a great café (one flight up), a ground-floor shop, and, of course, a museum. Take the elevator to the top floor and work your way down. On three floors you'll see paintings, furniture, graphics, and architectural drafts by Czech Cubists. This building is an example of what has long been considered the greatest virtue of Prague's architects: the ability to adapt their grandiose plans to the existing cityscape (100 Kč, Tue–Sun 10:00–18:00, closed Mon, corner of Celetná and Ovocný Trh at

Ovocný Trh 19, tel. 224-301-003, www.ngprague.cz). If you're not interested in touring the museum, consider a drink in the similarly decorated upstairs Grand Café Orient (described in the Eating in Prague chapter).

Estates Theater (Stavovské Divadlo)—Built by a nobleman in the 1770s, this Classicist building—gently opening its greenish walls onto Ovocný Trh—was the prime opera venue in Prague at a time when an Austrian prodigy was changing the course of music. Wolfgang Amadeus Mozart premiered *Don Giovanni* in this building—he directed many of his works here. Prague's theatergoers would whistle arias from Mozart's works on the streets the morning after they premiered. Today, the Estates Theater (part of the National Theater group) continues to produce *The Marriage of Figaro, Don Giovanni,* and occasionally *The Magic Flute.* For a more intimate encounter with Mozart, go to Villa Bertramka (see sidebar on page 148).

On Melantrichova Street

Skinny, tourist-clogged Melantrichova street leads directly from the Old Town Square's Astronomical Clock to the bottom of Wenceslas Square. But even along this most crowded of streets, a genuine bit of Prague remains...

▲**Havelská Market**—This open-air market, offering crafts and

produce, was set up in the 13th century for the German trading community. Though heavy on souvenirs these days, the market still keeps hungry locals and vagabonds fed cheaply. It's ideal for a healthy snack—merchants are happy to sell a single vegetable or piece of fruit—and you'll find a washing fountain and plenty of inviting benches midway down the street. The market is also a fun place to browse for crafts.

Czechs and Indians

The German writer Karl May (who did not visit America until 1908, very late in his life) used the time he spent in prison for fraud to write stories about the fictional noble Apache chief Winnetou and his German friend, Old Shatterhand—and ever since, the Czechs have been obsessed with Native Americans. Most kids spend summers in camps (as Boy Scouts and Girl Scouts), where they learn about the Native Americans' respect for nature, survival skills in the wilderness, courage, and the idealized noble spirit. A tune celebrating the Native Americans' victory at Little Big Horn is one of the most popular sagas sung at campfires around the country. When famous cancer survivor Lance Armstrong visited Prague's oncology ward in July 2004—just days after his unprecedented sixth consecutive victory in the rigorous Tour de France—child cancer patients rewarded their idol with the Native American name "Fast Wind." Prague's Náprstek Museum of Asian, African, and American Cultures actually displays attire worn by Lakota Chief Sitting Bull (Betlémské Náměstí 1).

THE OLD TOWN

It's a homegrown, homemade kind of place; you'll often be dealing with the actual artist or farmer (market open daily 9:00–18:00, produce best on weekdays; more souvenirs, puppets, and toys on weekends). The many cafés and little eateries circling the market offer a relaxing vantage point from which to view the action.

Bethlehem Square (Betlémské Náměstí)

This sight sits on the charming, relatively quiet Bethlehem Square (Betlémské Náměstí), a pleasantly untouristy chunk of Old Town real estate.

Bethlehem Chapel (Betlémské Kaple)—Emperor Charles IV founded the first university in Central Europe, and this was the university's chapel. In about the year 1400, priest and professor Jan Hus preached from the pulpit here (see sidebar on page 54). While meant primarily for students and faculty, Hus' Masses were open to the public. Standing-room-only crowds of more than 3,000 were the norm when he preached. Hus proposed that the congregation should be more involved in worship (i.e., actually drink the wine at Communion) and have better access to the word of God through services and scriptures written in the people's language, not in Latin. The stimulating, controversial ideas debated at the university spread throughout the city and, after Hus' death at the stake, sparked the bloodiest civil war in Czech history.

Each subsequent age has interpreted Hus to its liking: For the Protestants, Hus was the founder of the first Protestant church (though he was actually an ardent Catholic); for the revolutionaries, this critic of the Church's power was a proponent of social equality; for the nationalists, this Czech preacher was the defender of the language; and for the communists, Hus was the first ideologue to preach the gospel of socialism.

Today's chapel is a 1950s reconstruction of the original. Try the unbelievably bad acoustics inside—they demonstrate the sloppy restoration work sponsored by the communists (tiny upstairs exhibit and big chapel with English info sheets available; entry-40 Kč; April–Oct daily 10:00–18:30; Nov–March Tue–Sun 10:00–17:30, closed Mon and during frequent university functions; Betlémské Náměstí, tel. 224-248-595).

The recommended **Klub Architektů** restaurant, across from the entry, has a cave-like atmosphere inside, straw-chair seating outside, and good food both in and out.

The tiny **Family Museum of Postcards** is around the corner on Liliová street, which connects Bethlehem Square with Karlova. After learning how the Austrian Empire invented the postcard, you can buy your own early–20th-century specimen (entry-40 Kč, Tue–Sun 11:00–19:00, closed Mon, tel. 222-222-519).

From Old Town Square to the Charles Bridge

Karlova Street—Karlova street winds through medieval Prague from the Old Town Square to the Charles Bridge (it zigzags...just follow the crowds). This is a commercial gauntlet, and it's here that the touristy feeding frenzy of Prague is at its ugliest. Street signs keep you on track, and *Karlův most* signs point to the bridge. Obviously, you'll find few good values on this drag. Two favorite places providing a quick break from the crowds are just a few steps off Karlova on Husova street: **Cream and Dream Ice Cream** (Husova 12) and the recommended **U Zlatého Tygra**, a colorful pub that serves great, cheap beer in a classic and untouristy setting (Husova 17).

▲**Klementinum**—The Czech Republic's massive National Library borders touristy Karlova street. The contrast could not be starker: Step out of the most souvenir-packed stretch of Eastern Europe, and enter into the meditative silence of Eastern Europe's biggest library. Jesuits built the Klementinum in the 1600s to house a new college; they had been invited to Prague by the Catholic Habsburgs to offset the influence of the predominantly Protestant Charles University nearby. The building was transformed into a library in the early 1700s, when the Jesuits took firm control of the university. Their books, together with the collections of several noble families (written in all possible languages...except Czech), form the nucleus of the National and University Library, which is now six million volumes strong.

Prague's Charles University

Back in the 1300s, Charles University students studied the arts first, and only then proceeded to one of the other three faculties (medicine, law, and theology), of which theology was the most prestigious. Classes were taught in Latin, and the student body was cosmopolitan—Czechs made up only a fourth of all students.

During the chaotic period of Hussite reforms in the early 1400s, the university's policies were changed to give more power to the Czechs. In protest, many foreign students and professors left Prague and founded the first German university in Leipzig. Celebrated by Czech nationalists as a victory over foreigners, the new policies reduced Charles University from a European center of learning to a provincial institution.

In the 1600s, the predominantly Protestant university was handed over to the Jesuits. But in the 1780s, Habsburg Emperor Josef II abolished the Jesuit order, opened the university to non-Catholics, and changed the language of instruction from Latin to German. Czechs did not win the freedom to study in their own language until 1882, when the university split into two separate schools (the German school ceased to exist in 1945).

Today, the Old Town continues to live a double life as both a commercial center and a university campus. Though lined with souvenir stalls outside, many buildings hold classrooms that have been animated by lecturers for centuries. Some of the Old Town's most hidden courtyards have provided Czech scholars with their two most essential needs: good beer, and space for an inspiring conversation.

Charles University, always a center of Czech political thinking, has incited trouble and uprisings. Jan Hus initiated the reform of the Church here; the revolutions of 1618 and 1848 were sparked by university minds; and in the modern era, students rose up against totalitarian regimes in 1939, 1948, and 1968. The Germans closed down all Czech universities for the duration of

(Note that the Klementinum's Chapel of Mirrors is a popular venue for evening concerts.)

Library Tour and Tower Climb: While much of the Klementinum building is simply a vast library, its magnificent original Baroque Hall and Observatory Tower are open to the public by tour only (45 min, in English). You'll belly up to a banister at the end of the ornate library with its many centuries-old books, fancy ceilings with Jesuit leaders and saints overseeing the pursuit of knowledge, and Josef II—the enlightened Habsburg emperor—looking on from the far end. Then you'll climb the Observatory Tower, learning how early astronomers charted the skies over Prague. The tour finishes with a grand Prague view

World War II. Later, the communists fired professors unwilling to follow the party line and replaced them with applicants chosen on the basis of class background rather than ability. The Velvet Revolution, which swept communists out of power in November 1989, started as a student demonstration.

Although many professors returned to their classrooms after 1989, the education system itself has yet to escape the legacy of the authoritarian regimes. From an early age, students are taught to memorize rather than to think independently; knowledge is measured by facts rather than by the ability to use them; and even at the university level, few students dare to challenge the professor's view.

Charles University still attracts the best Czech and Slovak students. University education is, as in most of Europe, free in the Czech Republic, and student housing is heavily subsidized. You would expect that free admission would make education more accessible to students from poorer backgrounds, but this is not always true. Without enough money in the education system, the state doesn't have the means to build more schools. The demand exceeds the supply, so only a third of the people who apply to high school ("gymnasium") are accepted, and only half of university applicants are admitted. Students from better-educated backgrounds tend to do better in a system that begins selecting students from the age of 10.

Teachers are poorly paid (even a tenured university professor barely gets by), and libraries are underfunded. Consequently, even students have campaigned for the introduction of moderate fees that would improve access to education and allow professors to spend less time on side jobs and more time on lecture preparation and research. The final verdict on school fees lies with the politicians, who often pay more attention to public opinion than to students and teachers.

from the top (220 Kč, departs on the hour Mon–Fri 14:00–19:00, Sat–Sun 10:00–19:00, shorter hours off-season, tel. 221-663-165, mobile 603-231-241, www.klementinum.com; strolling down Karlova, turn at the intersection with Liliová through an archway into the Klementinum's courtyard).

▲▲▲Charles Bridge (Karlův Most)

Among Prague's defining landmarks, this much-loved bridge offers one of the most pleasant and entertaining 500-plus-yard strolls in Europe. Enjoy the bridge at different times of day. The bridge is most memorable early—before the crowds—and late, during that photographers' "magic hour" when the sun is low in the sky.

At the Old Town end of the bridge, in a little square, is a statue of the bridge's namesake, **Charles IV** (Karlo Quatro—the

guy on the 100-Kč bill), the Holy Roman Emperor who ruled his vast empire from Prague in the 14th century. This statue was erected in 1848 to celebrate Prague's university's 500th birthday. Charles is holding a contract establishing the university, the first in Northern Europe. The women around the pedestal symbolize the school's four subjects: the arts, medicine, law, and theology. (From the corner by the busy street, many think the emperor's silhouette makes it appear as if he's peeing on the tourists. Which reminds me, public WCs are in the passageway opposite the statue.)

Bridges had been built on this spot before, as the remnant tower from Judith Bridge testifies (see the smaller of the two bridge towers at the far end). All were washed away by floods. After a major flood in 1342, Emperor Charles IV decided to commission an entirely new structure rather than repair the old one. Until the 19th century, this was Prague's only bridge that crossed the river.

The Charles Bridge has long fueled a local love of legends— including one tied to numbers. According to medieval record, the bridge's foundation was laid in 1357. In the late 1800s, an amateur astronomer noticed a curious combination of numbers, leading to a popular theory about Charles IV. Charles is known to have been interested in numerology and astrology, and was likely aware of the significance of this date: the ninth of July at 5:31 in the morning. Written out in digits—as the year, month, day, hour, and minute—it's a numerical palindrome: 135797531. It's speculated that Charles must have chosen that precise moment (which also coincides with a favorable positioning of the earth and Saturn) to lay the foundation

stone of the bridge. Further "corroboration" of this remarkable hypothesis was provided by the discovery that the end of the bridge on the Old Town side aligns perfectly with the tomb of St. Vitus (in the cathedral across the river) and the setting sun at summer solstice. In the absence of accurate 14th-century records, this intriguing proposition has delighted the modern Czech imagination. The number "135797531" is bound to remain celebrated as the adopted birthday of Prague's most beloved structure.

Charles Bridge Reconstruction

Talked about for many years, financed by the city of Prague, and scheduled to last for more than a decade, the long-overdue reconstruction of the Charles Bridge finally began in the summer of 2007, days after the city celebrated the bridge's 650-year anniversary.

Aware of the blow that closing the entire bridge would deal to the tourist industry, the city chose a more costly and technologically challenging "chessboard" strategy. With this plan, only a small section is closed at any time, allowing people to continue using the bridge, but leading to midday crowds in the resulting bottleneck. To give everyone the opportunity to peek inside the centuries-old structure, and thus turn the bridge renovation into Prague's new attraction, the mayor requested (to the dismay of many archaeologists) that the construction site be at all times surrounded only by light, transparent fences.

The reconstruction is being carried out in two stages. In the first major stage—preceded by archaeological excavations and scheduled to be completed sometime in 2010—gas lighting will return to the bridge, and the sewage system, insulation, and pavement will be installed. In the next stage, many of the deteriorated sandstone pieces will be replaced by new ones. In the past, builders often chose poor-quality sandstone, and this is precisely the mistake current workers want to avoid. To minimize impact on the nearby areas, most of the building materials will be transported by river.

THE OLD TOWN

The magically aligned spot on the Old Town side is now occupied by the **bridge tower,** considered one of the finest Gothic gates anywhere. Contemplate the fine sculpture on the Old Town side of the tower, showing the 14th-century hierarchy of kings, bishops, and angels. Climbing the tower rewards you with wonderful views over the bridge (40 Kč, daily 10:00–19:00, as late as 22:00 in summer).

In the 17th century, there were no statues on the bridge—only a **cross,** which you can still see as part of the third sculpture on the right. The gilded Hebrew inscription from the Book of Isaiah celebrates Christ ("Holy, holy, holy is the Lord of hosts"). The inscription was paid for by a fine imposed on a Prague Jew—the result of a rivalry within the Jewish community (fellow

Jews turned him in for mocking the cross).

The bronze Baroque statue depicting **John of Nepomuk**—a saint of the Czech people—draws a crowd (look for the guy with the five golden stars around his head, near the Little Quarter end of the bridge on the right). John of Nepomuk was a 14th-century priest to whom the queen confessed all her sins. According to a 17th-century legend, the king wanted to know his wife's secrets, but Father John dutifully refused to tell. He was tortured and eventually killed by being tossed off the bridge. When he hit the water, five stars appeared. The shiny plaque at the base of the statue depicts the heave-ho. Notice the date on the inscription: This oldest statue on the

bridge was unveiled in 1683, on the supposed 300th anniversary of the martyr's death.

The reason for John of Nepomuk's immense Baroque popularity and 1729 canonization remains contested. Some historians claim that at a time when the Czechs were being forcibly converted to Catholicism, Nepomuk became the rallying national symbol ("We will convert, but our patron must be Czech"). Others argue that Nepomuk was a propaganda figure used by Catholic leaders to give locals an alternative to Jan Hus. You'll find statues like this one on squares and bridges throughout the country.

The actual spot of the much-talked-about river-toss is a few steps farther away from the castle—find a small **brass relief** depicting a floating figure with a semicircle of stars above him. This is a replica of a Baroque original that was badly damaged by a

flood in 1890, later marred by protesters in the 1920s, and finally removed by the communists. In May of 2009, this replacement was installed by the Prague archbishop as part of an attempt to revive Baroque celebrations of the saint. Devout pilgrims believe that touching the relief here on the "magic" spot will make a wish come true. According to tradition, you get only one chance in life to make this wish, so think carefully before you touch the saint.

Most of the other Charles Bridge statues date from the late 1600s and early 1700s. Today, half of them are replicas—the originals are in city museums, out of the polluted air. At the far end of

Prague's Jewish Quarter

the Charles Bridge, you reach the **Little Quarter.** For sights in this neighborhood, see The Little Quarter chapter.

▲▲▲Jewish Quarter (Josefov)

Prague's Jewish Quarter neighborhood and its well-presented, profoundly moving museum tell the story of this region's Jews. For me, this is the most interesting collection of Jewish sights in Europe, and well worth seeing. The Jewish Quarter is an easy walk from Old Town Square, up delightful Pařížská street (next to the green-domed Church of St. Nicholas).

As the Nazis decimated Jewish communities in the region, Prague's Jews were allowed to collect and archive their treasures here. While the archivists were ultimately killed in concentration camps, their work survives. Seven sights scattered over a three-block area make up the tourists' Jewish Quarter. Six of the sights—all except the Old-New Synagogue—are called "The Museum" and are covered by one admission ticket. Your ticket comes with a map that locates the sights and lists admission appointments—the times you'll be let in if it's very busy. (Ignore the times unless it's really crowded.) You'll notice plenty of security.

Cost, Hours, Tours: To visit all seven sights, you'll pay 500 Kč (300 Kč for the six sights that make up the Museum, plus 200 Kč for the Old-New Synagogue). The Museum sights are open April–Oct Sun–Fri 9:00–18:00; Nov–March Sun–Fri 9:00–16:30;

closed year-round on Sat—the Jewish Sabbath—and on Jewish holidays (Old-New Synagogue hours listed on page 73). Tel. 222-317-191, www.jewishmuseum.cz. Each sight is thoroughly and thoughtfully described in English, making a guided tour unnecessary for most visitors. Occasional guided walks in English start at the Maisel Synagogue (50 Kč, 3 hours).

Cemetery: The Old Jewish Cemetery—with its tightly packed, topsy-turvy tombstones—is, for many, the most evocative part of the experience. Unfortunately, there's no ticket just to see the cemetery, and they've closed off most free viewpoints. If the 300-Kč Museum ticket is too steep and you just want a free peek at the famous cemetery, climb the steps to the covered porch of the Ceremonial Hall (but don't rest your chin on the treacherous railing).

Planning Your Time: The most logical start (if you'll be seeing everything) is to buy your ticket at Pinkas Synagogue and visit this most powerful memorial of the museum complex first. From there, walk through the Old Jewish Cemetery, which leads to the Ceremonial Hall and Klaus Synagogue. After visiting those, head over to the Old-New Synagogue and take a coffee break (the recommended Franz Kafka Café is nearby). Next, visit the museum-like Maisel Synagogue and, finally, the Spanish Synagogue. (Note that Prague's fine Museum of Medieval Art, described on page 60, is only a few blocks from the Spanish Synagogue.)

Art Nouveau and the New Josefov: Going from sight to sight in the Jewish Quarter, you'll walk through perhaps Europe's finest Art Nouveau neighborhood. Make a point to enjoy the circa-1900 buildings with their marvelous trimmings and oh-wow entryways. While today's modern grid plan has replaced the higgledy-piggledy medieval streets of old, Široká ("Wide Street") was and remains the main street of the ghetto.

Pinkas Synagogue (Pinkasova Synagóga)

A site of Jewish worship for 400 years, this synagogue is a poignant memorial to the victims of the Nazis. The walls are covered with the handwritten names of 77,297 Czech Jews who were sent from here to the gas chambers at Auschwitz and other camps. (As you ponder this sad sight, you'll hear the somber reading of the names alternating with a cantor singing the Psalms.) Hometowns are in gold and family names are in red, followed in black by the individual's first name, birthday, and last date known to be alive.

Prague's Jewish Heritage

The Jewish people from the Holy Land (today's Israel) were dispersed by the Romans 2,000 years ago. Over the centu-

ries, their culture survived in enclaves throughout the world: "The Torah was their sanctuary which no army could destroy." Jews first came to Prague in the 10th century. The Jewish Quarter's main intersection (Maiselova and Široká streets) was the meeting point of two medieval trade routes.

During the Crusades in the 12th century, the pope declared that Jews and Christians should not live together. Jews had to wear yellow badges, and their quarter was walled in. It became a ghetto. In the 16th and 17th centuries, Prague had one of the biggest ghettos in Europe, with 11,000 inhabitants. Within its six gates, Prague's Jewish Quarter was a gaggle of 200 wooden buildings. It was said that "Jews nested rather than dwelled."

The "outcasts" of Christianity relied mainly on profits from money-lending (forbidden to Christians) and community solidarity to survive. While their money bought them protection (the kings highly taxed Jewish communities), it was often also a curse. Throughout Europe, when times got tough and Christian debts to the Jewish community mounted, entire Jewish communities were evicted or killed.

In the 1780s, Emperor Josef II, motivated more by economic concerns than by religious freedom, eased much of the discrimination against Jews. In 1848, the Jewish Quarter's walls were torn down, and the neighborhood—named Josefov in honor of the emperor who provided this small measure of tolerance—was incorporated as a district of the Old Town.

In 1897, ramshackle Josefov was razed and replaced by a new modern town—the original 31 streets and 220 buildings became 10 streets and 83 buildings. This is what you'll see today: an attractive neighborhood of pretty, mostly Art Nouveau buildings, with a few surviving historic Jewish structures. By the 1930s, Prague's Jewish community was hugely successful, thanks largely to their ability to appreciate talent— a rare quality in small Central European countries whose citizens, as the great Austrian novelist Robert Musil put it, "were equal in their unwillingness to let one another get ahead."

Of the 120,000 Jews living in the area in 1939, just 10,000 survived the Holocaust to see liberation in 1945. Today, only a few thousand Jews remain in Prague, but the legacy of their ancestors lives on.

Notice that families generally perished together. Extermination camps are listed on the east wall. Climb eight steps into the women's gallery. When the communists moved in, they closed the synagogue and erased virtually everything. With freedom, in 1989, the Pinkas Synagogue was reopened and the names were rewritten. (The names in poor condition near the ceiling are original.) Note that large tour groups may disturb this small memorial's compelling atmosphere between 10:00 and 12:00.

Upstairs is the **Terezín Children's Art Exhibit** (very well-described in English), displaying art drawn by Jewish children who were imprisoned at Terezín Concentration Camp and later perished. Terezín makes an emotionally moving day trip from Prague; it's easily accessible by local bus (see page 175) or tour bus (see page 46).

Old Jewish Cemetery (Starý Židovský Hřbitov)

From the Pinkas Synagogue, you enter one of the most wistful scenes in Europe—Prague's Old Jewish Cemetery. As you wan-

der among 12,000 evocative tombstones, remember that from 1439 until 1787, this was the only burial ground allowed for the Jews of Prague. Tombs were piled atop each other because of limited space, the sheer number of graves, and the Jewish belief that the body should not be moved once buried. With its many layers, the cemetery became a small plateau. And as things settled over time, the tombstones got crooked. The Hebrew word for cemetery means "House of Life." Many Jews believe that death is the gateway into the next world. Pebbles on the tombstones are "flowers of the desert," reminiscent of the old days when rocks were placed upon the sand gravesite to keep the body covered. Wedged under some of the pebbles are scraps of paper that contain prayers.

Ceremonial Hall (Obřadní Síň)

Leaving the cemetery, you'll find a Neo-Romanesque mortuary house built in 1911 for the purification of the dead (on the left). It's filled with a worthwhile exhibition, described in English, on Jewish medicine, death, and burial traditions. A series of

THE OLD TOWN

crude but instructive paintings (hanging on walls throughout the house) show how the "burial brotherhood" took care of the ill and buried the dead. As all are equal before God, the rich and poor alike were buried in embroidered linen shrouds similar to the one you'll see on display.

Klaus Synagogue (Klauzová Synagóga)

This 17th-century synagogue (also near the cemetery exit) is the final wing of a museum devoted to Jewish religious practices. Exhibits on the ground floor explain the Jewish calendar of festivals. The central case displays a Torah (the first five books of the Bible) and solid silver pointers used when reading—necessary since the Torah is not to be touched. Upstairs is an exhibit on the rituals of Jewish life (circumcisions, bar and bat mitzvahs, weddings, kosher eating, and so on).

Old-New Synagogue (Staronová Synagóga)

For more than 700 years, this has been the most important synagogue and the central building in Josefov. Standing like a

bomb-hardened bunker, it feels as though it has survived plenty of hard times. Stairs take you down to the street level of the 13th century and into the Gothic interior. Built in 1270, it's the oldest synagogue in Eastern Europe. Snare an attendant, who is likely to love showing visitors around. The separate, steep, 200-Kč admission keeps many away, but even if you decide not to pay, you can see the exterior and a bit of the interior. (Go ahead...pop in and crane your cheapskate neck.)

The lobby (down the stairs, where you show your ticket) has two fortified old lockers—in which the most heavily taxed community in medieval Prague stored its money in anticipation of the taxman's arrival. As 13th-century Jews were not allowed to build, the synagogue was erected by Christians (who also built the St. Agnes Convent nearby). The builders were good at four-ribbed vaulting, but since that resulted in a cross, it wouldn't work for a synagogue. Instead, they made the ceiling using clumsy five-ribbed vaulting.

The interior is pure 1300s. The Shrine of the Ark in front is the focus of worship. The holiest place in the synagogue, it holds the sacred scrolls of the Torah. The old rabbi's chair to the right remains empty (notice the thin black chain) out of respect. The red banner is a copy of the one that the Jewish community carried through town during medieval parades. Notice the yellow-pointed hat within the Star of David (on the banner), which the pope ordered all Jewish men to wear in 1215. Twelve is a popular number (e.g., windows), because it symbolizes the 12 tribes of Israel. The horizontal slit-like windows are an 18th-century addition, allowing women to view the male-only services.

Cost and Hours: The Old-New Synagogue requires a separate 200-Kč admission that includes a worthwhile 10-minute tour—ask about it. It's open Sun–Thu 9:30–18:00, Fri 9:30–17:00 or until sunset, closed Sat. Tel. 222-317-191, www.synagogue.cz. Admission also includes entry to the Art Nouveau **Jerusalem Synagogue** in the New Town (see page 82).

Maisel Synagogue (Maiselova Synagóga)

This synagogue was built as a private place of worship for the Maisel family during the 16th-century Golden Age of Prague's Jews. Maisel, the wealthy financier of the Habsburg king, lavished his riches on the synagogue's Neo-Gothic interior. In World War II, it served as a warehouse for the accumulated treasures of decimated Jewish communities, a collection that Hitler planned to use for his "Museum of the Extinct Jewish Race." The one-room exhibit shows a thousand years of Jewish history in Bohemia and Moravia. Well-explained in English, topics include the origin of the Star of David, Jewish mysticism, the history of discrimination, and the creation of Prague's ghetto. Notice the eastern wall, with the Holy Ark containing the scroll of the Torah. The central case shows the silver ornamental Torah crowns that capped the scroll.

Spanish Synagogue (Španělská Synagóga)

Displays of Jewish history through the 18th, 19th, and tumultuous 20th centuries continue in this ornate, Moorish-style synagogue built in the 1800s. The upstairs is particularly intriguing, with circa-1900 photos of Josefov, an exhibit on the fascinating story of this museum and its relationship with the Nazi regime, and life in Terezín. The Winter Synagogue (also upstairs) shows a trove of silver worshipping aids gathered from countryside Jewish neighborhoods that were depopulated in the early 1940s, thus giving a sense of what the Nazis stockpiled.

THE NEW TOWN

Nové Město

Enough of pretty, medieval Prague—let's leap into the modern era. The New Town, with Wenceslas Square as its focal point, is today's urban Prague. This part of the city offers bustling boulevards and interesting neighborhoods. The New Town is one of the best places to view Prague's remarkable Art Nouveau art and architecture, and to learn more about its recent communist past.

▲▲Wenceslas Square Self-Guided Walk

More a broad boulevard than a square (until recently, trams rattled up and down its park-like median strip), this city landmark is named for King Wenceslas—featured both on the 20-Kč coin and the equestrian statue that stands at the top of the boulevard. Wenceslas Square (Václavské Náměstí) functions as a stage for modern Czech history: The creation of the Czechoslovak state was celebrated here in 1918; in 1968, the Soviets suppressed huge popular demonstrations at the square; and, in 1989, more than 300,000 Czechs and Slovaks converged here to claim their freedom.

> • *Starting near the Wenceslas statue at the top (Metro: Muzeum), look to the building crowning the top of the square...*

National Museum (Národní Muzeum)

This museum—likely to be closed for renovation in 2011–2012—stands grandly at the top. While its collection is dull, the building offers a powerful view, and the interior is richly decorated in the Czech Revival Neo-Renaissance style that heralded the 19th-century rebirth of the Czech nation.

Prague's New Town

THE NEW TOWN

1. National Museum
2. Communist-Era Building
3. Memorial
4. Grand Hotel Evropa
5. Lucerna Gallery
6. Franciscan Garden
7. Mucha Museum
8. Jerusalem Synagogue
9. Municipal House
10. Museum of Communism
11. National Theater
12. Dancing House
13. Greek Orthodox Church
14. Charles Square

The light-colored patches in the museum's columns fill holes where Soviet bullets hit during the crackdown against the 1968 Prague Spring uprising. Masons—defying their communist bosses, who wanted the damage to be forgotten—showed their Czech spirit by intentionally mismatching their patches. The museum's skippable collection is basically halls of Czech fossils and animals (150 Kč, daily May–Sept 10:00–18:00, Oct–April 9:00–17:00, periodic closures year-round, tel. 224-497-111, www.nm.cz).

The nearby Metro stop (Muzeum) is the crossing point of two Metro lines built with Russian know-how in the 1970s.

• *To the left of the National Museum (as you face it) is an ugly...*

Communist-Era Building

This structure housed the rubber-stamp Parliament back when it voted with Moscow. A Socialist Realist statue showing trium-

phant workers still stands at its base. Between 1994 and 2008, this building was home to Radio Free Europe. After communism fell, RFE lost some of its funding and could no longer afford its Munich headquarters. In gratitude for its broadcasts—which had kept the people of Eastern Europe in touch with real news—the Czech government offered this building to RFE for 1 Kč a year. But as RFE energetically beamed its American message deep into Islam from here, it drew attention—and threats—from Al-Qaeda. So in 2009, RFE moved to a new purpose-built, fortress-like headquarters at an easier-to-defend locale near Franz Kafka's grave, at the Želivského Metro station.

Today, this building's long interior can be viewed with a guided tour that takes you step-by-step through this fascinating stage of recent Czech—and journalistic—history (80 Kč, daily 10:00–18:00, tours in Czech leave on the hour on weekdays, every half-hour on weekends, English audioguide provided, tel. 224-497-430, www.nm.cz). The National Museum, which now administers this building, uses part of the space for temporary exhibits.

• *In front of the National Museum is the equestrian...*

St. Wenceslas Statue

Wenceslas (Václav) is the "good king" of Christmas-carol fame. He was the wise and benevolent 10th-century Duke of Bohemia. A rare example of a well-educated and literate ruler, King Wenceslas I was credited by his people for Christianizing his nation and lifting the culture. He astutely allied the Czechs with Saxony, rather than Bavaria, giving the Czechs a vote when the Holy Roman Emperor was selected (and therefore more political clout).

After his murder in 929, Wenceslas was canonized as a saint. He became a symbol of Czech nationalism and statehood, and remains an icon of Czech unity whenever the nation has to rally. Supposedly, when the Czechs face their darkest hour, Wenceslas will come riding out of Blaník Mountain (east of Prague) with an army of knights to rescue the nation. In 1620, when Austria stripped the Czechs of their independence, many people went to Blaník Mountain to see whether it had opened up. They did the same at other critical points in their history (in 1938, 1948, and 1968), but Wenceslas never emerged. Although the Czech Republic is now safely part of NATO and the EU, Czechs remain realistic: If Wenceslas hasn't come out yet, the worst times must still lie ahead...

Study the statue. Wenceslas, on the horse, is surrounded by the four other Czech patron saints. Notice the focus on books. A small nation without great military power, the Czech Republic chose national heroes who enriched the culture by thinking, rather than fighting. This statue is a popular meeting point. Locals say, "I'll see you under the tail."

• *Now begin walking down the square. Thirty yards below the big horse is a small garden with a low-key...*

Memorial

This commemorates victims of communism, such as Jan Palach. In 1969, a group of patriots decided that an act of self-immolation would stoke the fires of independence. Palach, a philosophy student who loved life—but wanted to live in freedom—set himself on fire on the steps of the National Museum for the cause of Czech independence. He died a few days later in a hospital ward. Czechs are keen on anniversaries, and huge demonstrations swept the city on the 20th anniversary of Palach's death. These protests led, 10 months later, to the overthrow of the Czech communist government in 1989.

This grand square is a gallery of modern architectural styles. As you wander downhill, notice the fun mix, all post-1850: Romantic Neo-Gothic, Neo-Renaissance, and Neo-Baroque from the 19th century; Art Nouveau from about 1900; ugly Functionalism from the mid-20th century (the "form follows function" and "ornamentation is a crime" answer to Art Nouveau); Stalin Gothic from the 1950s "communist epoch" (a good example is the Jalta building, halfway downhill on the right); and the glass-and-steel buildings of the 1970s.

• *Walk a couple of blocks downhill through the real people of Prague (not tourists) to* **Grand Hotel Evropa**, *with its dazzling Art Nouveau exterior and plush café interior full of tourists. Stop for a moment to consider the events of...*

November 1989

This huge square was filled every evening with more than 300,000 ecstatic Czechs and Slovaks who believed freedom was at hand. Assembled on the balcony of the building opposite Grand Hotel Evropa (look for the *Marks & Spencer* sign) were a priest, a rock star (famous for his unconventional style, which constantly unnerved the regime), Alexander Dubček (hero of the 1968 revolt), and Václav Havel (the charismatic playwright, newly released from prison, who was every freedom-loving Czech's Nelson Mandela). Through a sound system provided by the rock star, Havel's voice boomed over the gathered masses, announcing the resignation of the Politburo and saying that the Republic of Czechoslovakia's freedom was imminent. Picture that cold November evening, with thousands of Czechs jingling their key chains in solidarity, chanting at the government, "It's time to go now!" (To quell this revolt, government tanks could have given it the Tiananmen Square treatment, which had spilled patriotic blood in China just six months earlier. Locals believe that the Soviet head of state, Mikhail Gorbachev, must have made a phone call recommending a nonviolent response.) For more on the events leading up to this climactic rally, see "The Velvet Revolution of 1989" sidebar on page 85.

• *Immediately opposite Grand Hotel Evropa is the Lucerna Gallery (use entry marked* Pasáz Rokoko *and walk straight in).*

THE NEW TOWN

Lucerna Gallery

This grand mall retains some of its Art Deco glamour from the 1930s, with shops, theaters, a ballroom in the basement, and the fine Lucerna Café upstairs. You'll see a sculpture—called *Wenceslas Riding an Upside-Down Horse*—hanging like a swing from a glass dome. David Černý, who created the statue in 1999, is one of the Czech Republic's most original contemporary artists. Always aspiring to provoke controversy, Černý has painted a menacing Russian tank pink, attached crawling babies to the rocket-like Žižkov TV tower, defecated inside the National Gallery to protest the policies of its director, and sunk a shark-like Saddam Hussein inside an aquarium. His art hoax *Entropa* was created to commemorate the Czech presidency of the European Union in 2009. But when it was unveiled in Brussels, it insulted many EU nations with its satirical symbolism (Bulgaria was represented by squat toilets, Germany consisted of twisted autobahns hinting at a swastika, and so on).

Inside the gallery, you'll also find a **Ticketpro box office** (with all available tickets, daily 9:30–18:00), a lavish 1930s Prague cinema (under the upside-down horse, shows artsy films in Czech with English subtitles or vice versa, 110 Kč), and the popular **Lucerna Music Bar** in the basement (disco themes from the '70s, '80s, and '90s, 100 Kč, nightly from 21:00, described in the Entertainment in Prague chapter).

Directly across busy Vodičkova street (with a handy tram stop) is the Světozor mall. Inside you'll find the **World of Fruit Bar Světozor,** every local's favorite ice-cream joint. True to its name, the bar tops its ice cream with every variety of fruit. They sell cakes and milkshakes, too. Ask at the counter for an English menu.

• *Farther down the mall on the left is the entrance to the peaceful...*

Franciscan Garden (Františkánská Zahrada)

Its white benches and spreading rosebushes are a universe away from the fast beat of the city, which throbs behind the buildings that surround the garden.

Back on Wenceslas Square, if you're in the mood for a mellow hippie teahouse, consider a break at the recommended **Dobrá Čajovna** ("Good Teahouse") near the bottom of the square (#14). Or, if you'd like an old-time wine bar, pop in to the plain **Šenk Vrbovec** (nearby at #10); it comes with a whiff of the communist days, embracing the faintest bits of genteel culture from an age when refinement was sacrificed for the good of the working class. They serve traditional drinks, Czech keg wine, Moravian wines (listed on blackboard outside), *becherovka* (the 13-herb liqueur), and—only in autumn—*burčák* (this young wine tastes like grape juice turned halfway into wine).

The bottom of Wenceslas Square is called **Můstek,** which means "Bridge"; a bridge used to cross a moat here, allowing entrance into the Old Town (you can still see the original Old Town entrance down in the Metro station).

• *Running to the right from the bottom of Wenceslas Square is the street called Na Příkopě.*

Na Příkopě: Art Nouveau Prague

Meaning "On the Moat," this busy boulevard follows the line of the Old Town wall, leading to one of the wall's former gates,

Art Nouveau

Prague is the best Art Nouveau town in Europe, with fun facades gracing streets all over town. Art Nouveau, born in Paris, is "nouveau" because it wasn't inspired by Rome. It's neo-nothing...a fresh answer to all the revival styles of the

later 19th century and an organic response to the Eiffel Tower art of the Industrial Age. The style liberated the artist in each architect. Notice the unique curves and motifs expressing originality on each Art Nouveau facade. Artists such as Alfons Mucha believed that the style should include all facets of daily life. They designed everything from buildings and furniture to typefaces and cigarette packs.

Prague's three top Art Nouveau architects are Jan Koula, Josef Fanta, and Osvald Polivka (whose last name sounds like the Czech word for "soup"). Think "Cola, Fanta, and Soup"—easy to remember and a good way to impress your local friends.

Prague's Art Nouveau highlights include the facades lining the streets of the Jewish Quarter, the Jerusalem Synagogue, the Mucha window in St. Vitus Cathedral, and the Grand Hotel Evropa on Wenceslas Square. The top two sights for Art Nouveau fans are the Mucha Museum and the Municipal House.

the Powder Tower. Along the way, it passes the Museum of Communism and a couple of Art Nouveau sights. City tour buses (see page 46) leave from along this street, which offers plenty of shopping temptations (such as these malls: Slovanský Dům at Na Příkopě 22, and Černá Růže at Na Příkopě 12, next door to Mosers, which has a crystal showroom upstairs).

Stroll up Na Příkopě to take in two of Prague's best Art Nouveau sights: the Mucha Museum and the Municipal House. The first is on the street called Panská (turn right up the first street you reach as you walk up Na Příkopě from Wenceslas Square); the second is two blocks farther up Na Příkopě, next to the big, Gothic Powder Tower.

▲▲**Mucha Museum**—This is one of Europe's most enjoyable little museums. I find the art of Alfons Mucha (MOO-kah, 1860–1939) insistently likeable. See the crucifixion scene he painted as an eight-year-old boy. Read how this popular Czech artist's posters, filled with Czech symbols and expressing his people's ideals and aspirations, were patriotic banners that aroused the national spirit.

And check out the photographs of his models. With the help of an abundant supply of slinky models, Mucha was a founding father of the Art Nouveau movement. Partly overseen by Mucha's grandson, the museum is two blocks off Wenceslas Square and wonderfully displayed on one comfortable floor (120 Kč, daily 10:00–18:00, good English descriptions, Panská 7, tel. 224-233-355, www .mucha.cz). The included 30-minute video is definitely worthwhile (in English, generally at :15 and :45 past the hour—ask for the starting time); it describes the main project of Mucha's life—the *Slav Epic,* currently on display in the town of Moravský Krumlov (described in the Moravský Krumlov chapter), though there is talk of moving it to Prague.

• *Coming back to Na Příkopě and continuing toward the Powder Tower, notice the Neo-Renaissance* **UniCredit Bank** *building (formerly Živnostenská Banka, Prague's oldest banking institution) on the corner of Nekázanka. It houses a modern bank with classy circa-1900 ambience (enter and peek into the main hall upstairs).*

Consider a several-block detour down Nekázanka to visit another of Prague's Art Nouveau buildings—the Jerusalem Synagogue. Follow Nekázanka to Jindřišská street, turn left, then turn right onto Jeruzalémská street. About halfway down on your left is the...

Jerusalem Synagogue (Jeruzalémské Synagóga)—This colorful synagogue, also known as the Jubilee Synagogue, is a fascinating combination of Moorish Renaissance and Viennese Art Nouveau styles. It was built from 1905 to 1906 in commemoration of the first 50 years of Franz Josef's liberal rule. Recently restored, still serving the Prague Jewish community, and sparsely visited, this is the most contemplative as well as visually stunning of Prague's synagogues (200-Kč admission includes entry to Old-New Synagogue in the Jewish Quarter—see page 73, April–Oct Sun–Fri 13:00–17:00, closed Sat, closed in winter and on Jewish holidays, between Powder Tower and Main Train Station at Jeruzalémská 7, tel. 222-319-002, www.synagogue.cz/Jerusalem).

• *Return to Jindřišská street and go left, passing the Jindřišská gate, then take a right on Senovážná street, which leads you to the...*

▲▲Municipal House (Obecní Dům)—The Municipal House is the "pearl of Czech Art Nouveau." Financed by cultural and artistic leaders, it was built (1905–1911) as a ceremonial palace to reinforce the self-awareness of the Czech nation. It features Prague's largest concert hall, a recommended Art Nouveau café (Kavárna Obecní Dům), and two other restaurants. Pop in and wander around the lobby of the concert hall. Walk through to the ticket office on the ground floor. For the best look, including impressive halls and murals you won't see otherwise, take one of the regular hour-long **tours** (open daily 10:00–18:00; tours—150 Kč; generally at 10:15, 12:00, 14:00, and 16:00; 2/day in English, buy ticket from ground-

THE NEW TOWN

Prague: Pre-1989

It's hard to imagine the gray and bleak Prague of the communist era. Before 1989, the city was a wistful jumble of possibility. Cobbled lanes were shadowed by decrepit, crusty buildings. Timbers—strung across the lanes like laundry lines—held crumbling buildings apart. Consumer goods were plain and uniform, stacked like Legos on thin shelves in shops where customers waited in line for a tin of pineapples or a bottle of ersatz Coke. The Charles Bridge and its statues were black with soot, and there was no commerce, except for a few shady characters trying to change money. Hotels had two price schedules: one for people from the Warsaw Pact nations, and another (6–8 times more expensive) for capitalists. This made the run-down, Soviet-style hotels as expensive as fine Western ones. At the train station, frightened but desperate folks would meet arriving foreigners and offer to rent them a room in their apartment, hoping to earn enough Western cash to buy batteries or Levi's at one of the hard-currency stores.

floor shop where tour departs; tel. 222-002-101, www.obecni dum.cz).

Standing in front of the Municipal House, you can survey four different styles of architecture. First, enjoy the colorful facade of the Municipal House itself—a mixture of Neo-Baroque and Art Nouveau. Featuring a goddess-like Praha presiding over a land of peace and high culture, the *Homage to Prague* mosaic on the building's striking facade stoked cultural pride and nationalist sentiment. Across the street, the classical fixer-upper from 1815 was the customs house, which has recently been turned into a giant stage for Broadway-style musicals.

The stark national bank building (Česká Národní Banka) is textbook Functionalism from the 1930s. Farther away, across the square, former Neo-Romanesque barracks have been transformed into central Prague's biggest shopping mall and underground parking lot.

Powder Tower: The big, black Powder Tower (not worth touring inside) was the Gothic gate of the town wall, built to house the city's gunpowder. The decoration on the tower, portraying Czech kings, is the best 15th-century sculpture in town. If you go through the tower, you'll reach Celetná street, which leads past a few sights to the Old Town Square (see page 52).

Národní Třída: Communist Prague

From Můstek at the bottom of Wenceslas Square, you can head west on Národní Třída (in the opposite direction from Na Příkopě and the Art Nouveau sights) for an interesting stroll through urban Prague to the National Theater and the Vltava River. But first, consider dropping into the Museum of Communism, a few steps down Na Příkopě (on the right).

▲▲**Museum of Communism**—This museum traces the story of communism in Prague: the origins, dream, reality, and nightmare; the cult of personality; and, finally, the Velvet Revolution. Along the way, it gives a fascinating review of the Czech Republic's 40-year stint with Soviet economics, "in all its dreariness and puffed-up glory." You'll find propaganda posters, busts of communist All-Stars (Marx, Lenin, Stalin), and a photograph of the massive stone Stalin that overlooked Prague until 1962. Slices of communist life are re-created here, from a bland store counter to a typical classroom (with textbooks using Russia's Cyrillic alphabet—no longer studied—and a poem on the chalkboard that extols the virtues of the tractor). Don't miss the Jan Palach exhibit and the 20-minute video (plays continuously, English subtitles) that shows how the Czech people chafed under the big Red yoke from the 1950s through 1989 (180 Kč, daily 9:00–21:00, Na Příkopě 10, above a McDonald's and next to a casino—Lenin is turning over in his grave, tel. 224-212-966, www.muzeumkomunismu.cz).

• *Now head for the river (with your back to Wenceslas Square, go left down 28 Října to Národní Třída). Along the way, Národní Třída has a story to tell.*

Národní Třída and the Velvet Revolution—Národní Třída (National Street) is where you feel the pulse of the modern city. The street, which connects Wenceslas Square with the National Theater and the river, is a busy thoroughfare running through the heart of urban Prague. In 1989, this unassuming boulevard played host to the first salvo of a Velvet Revolution that would topple the communist regime.

Make your way down Národní Třída until you hit the tram tracks (just beyond the Tesco department store). On the left, look for the photo of Bill Clinton playing saxophone,

THE NEW TOWN

The Velvet Revolution of 1989

On the afternoon of November 17, 1989, 30,000 students gathered in Prague's New Town to commemorate the 50th anniversary of the suppression of student protests by the Nazis, which had led to the closing of Czech universities through the end of World War II. The 1989 demonstration—initially planned by the Communist Youth as a celebration of the communist victory over fascism—spontaneously turned into a protest *against* the communist regime. "You are just like the Nazis!" shouted the students. The demonstration was supposed to end in the National Cemetery at Vyšehrad (the hill just south of the New Town). But when the planned events concluded in Vyšehrad, the students decided to march on toward Wenceslas Square, making history.

As they worked their way north along the Vltava River toward the New Town's main square, the students were careful to keep their demonstration peaceful. Any hint of violence, the demonstrators knew, would incite brutal police retaliation. Instead, as the evening went on, the absence of police became conspicuous. (In the 1980s, the police never missed a chance to participate in any demonstration...preferably outnumbering the demonstrators.) At about 20:00, as the students marched down this very stretch of street toward Wenceslas Square, three rows of policemen suddenly blocked the demonstration at the corner of Národní and Spálená streets. A few minutes later, military vehicles with fences on their bumpers (having crossed the bridge by the National Theater) appeared behind the marching students. This new set of cops compressed the demonstrators into the stretch of Národní Třída between Voršilská and Spálená. The end of Mikulandská street was also blocked, and policemen were hiding inside every house entry. The students were trapped.

At 21:30, the "Red Hats" (a special anti-riot commando force known for its brutality) arrived. The Red Hats lined up on both sides of this corridor. To get out, the trapped students had to run through the passageway as they were beaten from the left and right. Police trucks ferried captured students around the corner to the police headquarters (on Bartolomějská) for interrogation.

The next day, university students throughout Czechoslovakia decided to strike. Actors from theaters in Prague and Bratislava joined the student protest. Two days later, the students' parents—shocked by the attacks on their children—marched into Wenceslas Square. Sparked by the events of November 17, 1989, the wave of peaceful demonstrations ended later that year on December 29, with the election of Václav Havel as the president of a free Czechoslovakia.

with Václav Havel on the side (this is the entrance to **Reduta,** Prague's best jazz club—see the Entertainment in Prague chapter; next door are two recommended eateries, **Café Louvre** and **Le Patio**). Just beyond that, you'll come to a short corridor with white arches. Inside this arcade is a simple memorial to the hundreds of students injured here by the police on November 17, 1989. For the fascinating story, see "The Velvet Revolution of 1989" sidebar.

Along the Vltava River

I've listed these sights from north to south, beginning at the grand, Neo-Renaissance National Theater, which is five blocks south of Charles Bridge and stands along the riverbank at the end of Národní Třída.

National Theater (Národní Divadlo)—Opened in 1883 with Smetana's opera *Libuše,* this theater was the first truly Czech venue in Prague. From the very start, it was nicknamed the "Cradle of

Czech Culture." The building is a key symbol of the Czech national revival that began in the late 18th century. In 1800, "Prag" was predominantly German. The Industrial Revolution brought Czechs from the countryside into the city, their new urban identity defined by patriotic teachers and priests. By 1883, most of the city spoke Czech, and the opening of this theater represented the birth of the modern Czech nation. It remains an important national icon: The state annually pours more subsidies into this theater than into all of Czech film production. It's the most beautiful venue in town for opera and ballet, often with world-class singers (for more details on performances, see the Entertainment in Prague chapter).

Next door (just inland, on Národní Třída) is the boxy, glassy facade of the **Nová Scéna.** This "New National Theater" building, dating from 1983 (the 100th anniversary of the original National Theater building), reflects the bold and stark communist aesthetic.

Across the street from the National Theater is the former haunt of Prague's intelligentsia, the recommended **Grand Café Slavia,** a Viennese-style coffeehouse that is fine for a meal or drink with a view of the river.

• *Just south of the National Theater in the Vltava, you'll find...*

THE NEW TOWN

Prague's Islands—From the National Theater, the Legions' Bridge (Most Legií) leads across the island called **Střelecký Ostrov.** Covered with chestnut trees, this island boasts Prague's best beach (on the sandy tip that points north to Charles Bridge). You might see a fisherman pulling out trout from a river that's now much cleaner than it used to be. Bring a swimsuit and take a dip just a stone's throw from Europe's most beloved bridge. In summer, the island hosts open-air movies (most in English or with English subtitles, nightly mid-July–early Sept at about 21:00, www.strelak.cz).

In the mood for boating instead of swimming? On the next island up, **Slovanský Ostrov,** you can rent a boat (40 Kč/hr for rowboats, 60 Kč/hr for paddleboats, bring a picture ID as deposit). A lazy hour paddling around Střelecký Ostrov—or just floating sleepily in the middle of the river surrounded by this great city's architectural splendor—is a delightful experience on a sunny day. It's cheap, easy fun (and it's good for you).

• *A 10-minute walk (or one stop on tram #17) south from the National Theater, beyond the islands, is Jirásek Bridge (Jiráskův Most), where you'll find the...*

Dancing House (Tančící Dům)—If ever a building could get your toes tapping, it would be this one, nicknamed "Fred and

Ginger" by American architecture buffs. This metallic samba is the work of Frank Gehry (who designed the equally striking Guggenheim Museum in Bilbao, Spain, and Seattle's Experience Music Project). Eight-legged Ginger's wispy dress and Fred's metal mesh head are easy to spot. The building's top-floor restaurant, La Perle de Prague, is a fine place for a fancy French meal (VIPs often eat and drink here, reservation needed even to get into the elevator, tel. 221-984-160).

Of course, most Czechs have never heard of Fred and Ginger. Some prefer to think that the two "figures" represent the nation's greatest 20th-century heroes, the WWII paratroopers Jozef Gabčík and Jan Kubiš. Their 1942 assassination of SS second-in-command Reinhard Heydrich, who controlled the Nazi-occupied Czech lands and was one of the main architects of the Holocaust, was the most significant act of Czech resistance. German retaliation was violent. Hundreds of Czechs were executed, and two villages—Lidice and Ležáky—were summarily razed to the ground.

In the weeks following the assassination, the two paratroopers hid along with other freedom fighters in the crypt of the **Greek**

Orthodox Church on Resslova street, one block up from the Dancing House. One soldier betrayed the others. The Gestapo surrounded the church. To escape capture, each man inside the church saved his last bullet for himself. Today, the church crypt shelters a modest exhibition on the history of the Czech resistance movement. The pub **U Parašutistů** ("By the Paratroopers"), directly across the street at #7, is a great place to toast to the memory of the men who fought and died in the crypt (tel. 224-922-267).

• *Three blocks up Resslova street is...*

Charles Square (Karlovo Náměstí)—Prague's largest square is covered by lawns, trees, and statues of Czech writers. It's a quiet antidote to the bustling Wenceslas and Old Town squares. The Gothic New Town Hall at the top-left corner of the square has excellent views and labeled panoramic photographs that help you orient yourself to what you see. The little parlor across the street has some of the best gelato in town.

THE NEW TOWN

THE LITTLE QUARTER

Malá Strana

This charming neighborhood, huddled under the castle on the west bank of the river, is low on blockbuster sights but high on ambience. The most enjoyable approach from the Old Town is across Charles Bridge. From the end of the bridge (TI in tower), Mostecká street leads two blocks up to the Little Quarter Square (Malostranské Náměstí) and the huge Church of St. Nicholas. But before you head up there, consider a detour to Kampa Island.

Between Charles Bridge and Little Quarter Square

Kampa Island

One hundred yards before the castle end of the Charles Bridge, stairs on the left lead down to the main square of Kampa Island

(mostly created from the rubble of the Little Quarter, which was destroyed in a 1540 fire). The island features relaxing pubs, a breezy park, hippies, lovers, a fine contemporary art gallery, and river access. From the main square, Hroznová lane (on the right) leads to a bridge. Behind the **old mill wheel,** notice the high-water marks from the flood of 2002. The water wheel is the last survivor of many that once lined the canal here. Each mill had its own protective water spirit *(vodník)*. Today, only one wheel—and one spirit (Mr. Kabourek)—remains.

• *Fifty yards beyond the bridge (on the right, under the trees) is the...*

Lennon Wall (Lennonova Zeď)

While Lenin's ideas hung like a water-soaked trench coat upon the Czech people, rock singer John Lennon's ideas gave many locals hope and a vision. When Lennon was killed in 1980, a large wall was spontaneously covered with memorial graffiti. Night after night, the police would paint over the "All You Need Is Love" and "Imagine" graffiti. And day after day, it would reappear. Until independence came in 1989, travelers, freedom-lovers, and local hippies gathered here. Silly as it might seem, this wall is remembered as a place that gave hope to locals craving freedom. Even today, while the tension and danger associated with this wall are gone, people come here to imagine. *"John žije"* is Czech for "John lives." In the left-hand corner of the wall, a small gate leads to a quiet courtyard with the recommended John & George Café.

• *From here, you can continue up to the Little Quarter Square.*

On or near Little Quarter Square

The focal point of this neighborhood, the Little Quarter Square (Malostranské Náměstí) is dominated by the huge Church of St. Nicholas. Note that there's a handy Via Musica ticket office across from the church.

Church of St. Nicholas (Kostel Sv. Mikuláše)—When the Jesuits came to Prague, they found the perfect piece of real estate for their church and its associated school—right on Little Quarter Square. The church (built 1703–1760) is the best example of High Baroque in town. It's giddy with curves and illusions. The altar features a lavish gold-plated Nicholas, flanked by the two top Jesuits: the founder, St. Ignatius Loyola, and his missionary follower, St. Francis Xavier. Climb up the **gallery** through the staircase in the left transept for a close-up look at a collection of large canvases and illusionary frescoes by Karel Škréta, who is considered the greatest Czech Baroque painter. Notice that at first glance the canvases are utterly dark, but as sunbeams shine through the window, various parts of the painting brighten up. Like a looking-glass, the image reflects the light, creating a play of light and dark. This painting technique represents a central Baroque belief: The world is full of darkness, and the only hope that makes it come alive comes from God. The church walls seem to nearly fuse with the sky, suggesting that happenings on earth are closely connected to heaven. Find St. Nick with his bishop's

Prague's Little Quarter

Letenské Park

Letenské Park

1. Kampa Island & Old Mill Water Wheel
2. Lennon Wall
3. Church of St. Nicholas
4. Wallenstein Palace Garden (Entrance)
5. Vrtba Garden
6. Church of St. Mary the Victorious
7. Monument to Victims of Communism Who Survived
8. Hungry Wall
9. Petřín Tower & Museum of Jára Cimrman
10. Mirror Maze
11. US Embassy

200 Meters

200 Yards

miter in the center of the ceiling, on his way to heaven (60 Kč, church open daily 9:00–17:00, opens at 8:30 for prayer).

Tower Climb: For a good look at the city and the church's 250-foot dome, climb 215 steps up the bell tower (50 Kč, April–Oct daily 10:00–18:00, closed Nov–March, tower entrance is outside the right transept).

Concerts: The church is also an evening concert venue; tickets are usually on sale at the door (450 Kč, generally nightly, except Tue, at 18:00, www.psalterium.cz).

Czechs After Communism

Czech survivors of communist prisons (honored by the Monument to Victims of Communism Who Survived, described at the end of this chapter) feel a sense of injustice. Following World War II, many of the Czechs who collaborated with the Nazis were brought to justice. In contrast, after communism fell in 1989, few individuals responsible for the crimes committed by the communist regime faced retribution. In fact, when the country's industrial infrastructure was privatized in the early 1990s, the former Communist Party big shots used their connections to take control of some of the country's new capitalist enterprises. Many of the old Party leaders morphed into the bosses of the new Czech economy.

The Czech Republic was the first post-communist country to ban informants of the secret police from public office (a policy called *lustrace*, or "lustration"). They were also the first to outlaw the propagation of communism (and other totalitarian ideologies). Even so, efforts to enforce this legislation have been less than successful. Many former agents have destroyed evidence, while others contend that they were not aware of their own cooperation.

In the early 1990s, stalwart members of the Communist Party fended off attempts at reform and preserved a fossil of an institution that still draws about 15 percent of votes in national elections. Today's "vanguards of progress" no longer preach class warfare, but instead they blend empty rhetoric ("We have

THE LITTLE QUARTER

• *From here, you can hike 10 minutes uphill to the castle (and five more minutes to the Strahov Monastery). For information on these sights, see the next chapter. If you're walking up to the castle, consider going via...*

Nerudova Street—This steep, cobbled street, leading from Little Quarter Square to the castle, is named for Jan Neruda, a gifted 19th-century journalist (and somewhat less-talented fiction writer). It's lined with old buildings still sporting the characteristic doorway signs (e.g., the lion, three violinists, house of the golden suns) that once served as street addresses. The surviving signs are carefully restored and protected by law. They represent the family name, the occupation, or the various passions of the people who once inhabited the houses. (If you were to replace your house number with a symbol, what would it be?) In 1777, in order to collect taxes more effectively, Habsburg empress Maria Theresa decreed that numbers be used instead of these quaint house names. This neighborhood is filled with old noble palaces, now generally used as foreign embassies and offices of the Czech Parliament.

a solution") with vague finger-pointing ("Who took away our hard-won securities?"). To become more palatable to a wider public and to hide their Stalinist roots, they altered their symbol, exchanging the unsavory red star for a far more innocuous pair of cherries (allegedly to recall the Paris Commune of 1871).

Their nostalgic-about-the-good-old-times message registers mainly with Czechs who find it difficult to adapt to a more complex and risk-prone society. Many of them (including members of the younger generation) find communism's ordered worldview—familiar since childhood—to be the most easily comprehensible. Today, they read the newspapers for reassurance that capitalism is responsible for many social ills, that the European Union is German imperialism in disguise, and—in some extreme cases—that China is pairing up with Russia to defend humanity.

The idealistic Velvet Revolutionaries of 1989 thought that communism would naturally disappear over time—but they failed to realize how deeply the years of authoritarian rule affected everyone, even its opponents. Today, the sight of familiar communist faces in Parliament is a reminder for the Czechs of how little they'd reflected on their recent past. And visitors surprised by the communist presence in a newly free Czech Republic can take it as a reminder that difficult experiences, individual as much as collective ones, take lifetimes to process—especially if kept buried inside.

North of Little Quarter Square, near Malostranská Metro Station

Twenty yards from the Malostranská Metro station (go left from the top of the escalator and turn right when you get outside), a few blocks north of Little Quarter Square, is a lovely palace and garden. If you want to reach Little Quarter Square from here, follow Valdštejnská street.

Wallenstein Palace Garden (Valdštejnská Palac Zahrada)—Of the neighborhood's many impressive palace gardens, this is by far the largest and most beautiful. The complex—consisting of a palace (generally closed) and the surrounding garden (generally open)—was commissioned during the Thirty Years' War by the Habsburg general and Czech nobleman Albrecht z Valdštejna (or, in German, Albrecht von Wallenstein). It's a testimony to how war can be such a great business for the unscrupulous. For 16 years (1618–1634), the mercenary Albrecht conspired with all sides involved in the war. He was the banker of the Czech Estates Uprising until he ran off to Vienna with the

Jára Cimrman:
When Optimists Should Be Shot

"I am such a complete atheist that I am afraid God will punish me." Such is the pithy wisdom of Jára Cimrman, the man overwhelmingly voted the "Greatest Czech of All Time" in a 2005 national poll. Who is Jára Cimrman? A philosopher? An explorer? An inventor? He is all of these things, yes, and much more. Today, a museum celebrates his life (see the Museum of Jára Cimrman, at the end of this chapter).

Born in the mid-19th century to a Czech tailor of Jewish descent and an Austrian actress, Cimrman studied in Vienna before starting off on his journeys around the world. He traversed the Atlantic in a steamboat he designed himself, taught drama to peasants in Peru, and drifted across the Arctic Sea on an iceberg. Other astounding feats soon followed. Cimrman was the first to come within 20 feet of the North Pole. He was the first to invent the light bulb (unfortunately, Edison beat him to the patent office by five minutes). It was he who suggested to the Americans the idea for a Panama Canal, though, as usual, he was never credited. Indeed, Cimrman surreptitiously advised many of the world's greats: Eiffel on his tower, Einstein on his theories of relativity, Chekhov on his plays. ("You can't just have *two* sisters," Cimrman told the playwright. "How about three?") In 1886, long before the world knew of Sartre or Camus, Cimrman was writing tracts such as *The Essence of the Existence,* which would become the foundation for his philosophy of "Cimrmanism," also known as "non-existentialism." (Its central premise: "Existence cannot not exist.")

This man of unmatched genius would have won the honor of "Greatest Czech of All Time" if not for the bureaucratic narrow-mindedness of the poll's sponsors, who had a single objection to Cimrman's candidacy: He's not real. Jára Cimrman is the brainchild of two Czech humorists—Zdeněk Svěrák and Jiří Šebánek—who brought their patriotic Renaissance Man to life in 1967 in a satirical radio play. So, even though Cimrman handily won the initial balloting in January of 2005, Czech TV officials—blatantly biased against his non-existentialism—refused to let him into the final rounds of the competition.

money to join the Habsburgs. Plundering territories in the name of the Catholic faith, Albrecht followed his own simple rule: half for the emperor, half for me. When Habsburg favors waned, Albrecht secretly negotiated with the Swedes. When desperate Habsburgs put him in charge of their armies once again, he continued to play both sides. Finally, somebody had enough: Albrecht was murdered in his bedroom in 1634.

The inconspicuous entry to the palace's Wallenstein Garden is by the Malostranská Metro station. The garden, renovated in the

How should we interpret the fact that the Czechs would rather choose a fictional character as their greatest countryman over any of their flesh-and-blood national heroes—say, Charles IV (the 14th-century Holy Roman Emperor who established Prague as the cultural and intellectual capital of Europe), Jan Hus (the 15th-century religious reformer who challenged the legitimacy of the Catholic Church), Comenius (a 17th-century educator and writer, considered one of the fathers of modern education), or Martina Navrátilová (someone who plays a sport with bright green balls)? The more cynically inclined—many Czechs among them—might point out that the Czech people have largely stayed behind their mountains for the past millennia, with little interest in, or influence on, happenings elsewhere in the world. Perhaps Cimrman is so beloved because he embodies that most prickly of ironies: a Czech who was greater than all the world's greats, but who for some hiccup of chance has never been recognized for his achievements.

Personally, I like to think that the vote for Cimrman says something about the country's rousing enthusiasm for blowing raspberries in the face of authority. Throughout its history—from the times of the Czech kings who used crafty diplomacy to keep the German menace at bay, to the days of Jan Hus and his questioning of the very legitimacy of any ruler's power, to the flashes of anti-communist revolt that at last sparked the Velvet Revolution in 1989—the Czechs have maintained a healthy disrespect for those who would tell them what is best or how to live their lives. Other countries soberly choose their "Greatest" from musty tomes of history, but the Czechs won't play this silly game. Their vote for a fictional personage, says Cimrman's co-creator Svěrák, shows two things about the Czech nation: "That it is skeptical about those who are major figures and those who are supposedly the 'Greatest.' And that the only certainty that has saved the nation many times throughout history is its humor."

Cimrman would agree. A man of greatness, he was always a bit skeptical of those who saw themselves as great, or who marched forward under the banner of greatness. As Cimrman liked to say, "There are moments when optimists should be shot."

late 1990s, features a large pool surrounded by peacocks. The statues that line the central walkway (inspired by Greek mythology) were created by the Danish artist Adrian de Vries—arguably the best Renaissance sculptor outside of Italy. Notice the elegant classical shapes, a sharp contrast to the chubbiness of the Baroque figures on the Charles Bridge and elsewhere in the city. The original statues were stolen by invading Swedish armies in 1648, and are still in Sweden; the present replicas were cast in the early 1900s.

The Renaissance garden and the palace were built by Italian

architects, just like most of the Little Quarter. The theatrical loggia—the *sala terena*—is a drama and music stage inspired by Greek amphitheaters. Notice the unusual pairing of columns—at the time, a trendy invention of the Italian architect Andrea Palladio. Inside, the gory depictions of the Trojan War tell you about the taste and character of the owner. (A handy WC is to the left of the amphitheater.) The bizarre grotto wall farther on the left was an expression of an uncertain age. It creates the illusion of caves and holes, stalagmites and stalactites, interspersed with partially hidden stone goblins, frogs, and snakes (count how many you can find). The wall continues into a cage with live owls, completing the transition from dead to living nature. The twisted cries of the owls deepen the surreal sensation of the place. Exit through the door in the right corner of the garden by the *sala terena*. You'll pass into a small courtyard surrounded by what once was the residential part of the palace. Today, the upper chamber of the Czech Parliament meets inside.

Cost and Hours: Garden—free, April–Oct daily 10:00–18:00, closed Nov–March. Palace—usually closed to the public.

Near the Garden: For a terraced Baroque garden to compare to this Renaissance one, visit the **Vrtba Garden** (Vrtbovská Zahrada, 100 Kč, daily 10:00–18:00; just south of Little Quarter Square, on Karmelitská before the Church of St. Mary the Victorious—described next).

South of Little Quarter Square, to Petřín Hill

Karmelitská street, leading south (along the tram tracks) from Little Quarter Square, is home to these sights.

Church of St. Mary the Victorious (Kostel Panny Marie Vítězné)—This otherwise ordinary Carmelite church displays Prague's most worshipped treasure, the Infant of Prague (Pražské Jezulátko). Kneel at the banister in front of the tiny lost-in-gilded-Baroque altar, and find the prayer in your language (of the 13 in the folder). Brought to Czech lands during the Habsburg era by a Spanish noblewoman who came to marry a Czech nobleman, the Infant has become a focus of worship and miracle tales in Prague and Spanish-speaking countries. South Americans come on pilgrimage to Prague just to see this one statue. An exhibit upstairs shows tiny embroidered robes given to the Infant, including robes from Habsburg Empress Maria Theresa of Austria (1754) and Vietnam (1958), as well as a video showing a nun lovingly dressing the doll-like sculpture (free, Mon–Sat 9:30–17:30, Sun 13:00–17:00, English-language Mass Sun at 12:00, Karmelitská 9, www.pragjesu.com).

• *Continue a few more blocks down Karmelitská to the south end of the Little Quarter (where the street is called Újezd, roughly across the*

Legions' Bridge from the National Theatre). Here you find yourself at the base of...

Petřín Hill—This hill, topped by a replica of the Eiffel Tower, features several unusual sights.

The figures walking down the steps in the hillside make up the **Monument to Victims of Communism Who Survived.** The monument's figures are gradually atrophied by the totalitarian regime. They do not die but slowly disappear, one limb at a time. The statistics say it all: In Czechoslovakia alone, 205,486 people were imprisoned, 248 were executed, 4,500 died in prison, 327 were shot attempting to cross the border, and 170,938 left the country. To the left of the monument is the **Hungry Wall,** Charles IV's 14th-century equivalent of FDR's work-for-food projects. On the right (50 yards away) is the base of a handy **funicular**—hop on to reach Petřín Tower (uses tram/Metro ticket, runs daily, every 10–15 min from 8:00–22:00).

The summit of Petřín Hill is considered the best place in Prague to take your date for a romantic city view. Built for an exhibition in 1891, the 200-foot-tall **Petřín Tower** is a fifth the height of its Parisian big brother, which was built two years earlier. But, thanks to this hill, the top of the tower sits at the same elevation as the real Eiffel Tower. Climbing the 400 steps rewards you with amazing views of the city. Local wives drag their men to Petřín Hill each May Day to reaffirm their love with a kiss under a blooming sour-cherry tree.

In the tower's basement is the funniest sight in Prague, the **Museum of Jára Cimrman, Genius Who Did Not Become Famous.** The museum traces Cimrman's (fictional) life, including pictures and English descriptions of the thinker's overlooked inventions (50 Kč includes tower and Cimrman museum, daily 10:00–22:00). For more on the mysterious Cimrman, see the sidebar on page 94.

The **mirror maze** next door is nothing special, but fun to wander through quickly since you're already here (50 Kč, daily 10:00–22:00).

THE CASTLE QUARTER

Hradčany

Looming above Prague, dominating its skyline, is the Castle Quarter. Prague Castle and its surrounding sights are packed with Czech history, as well as with tourists. In addition to the castle, I enjoy visiting the nearby Strahov Monastery—which has a fascinating old library and beautiful views over all of Prague.

Castle Square (Hradčanské Náměstí)—right in front of the castle gates—is at the center of this neighborhood. Stretching along the promontory away from the castle is a regal neighborhood that ends at the Strahov Monastery. Above the castle are the Royal Gardens, and below the castle are more gardens and lanes leading down to the Little Quarter (see previous chapter).

Getting to Prague Castle

If you're not up for a hike, the tram offers a sweat-free ride up to the castle. Taxis are expensive, as they have to go the long way around (200 Kč).

By Foot: Begin in the Little Quarter, just across Charles Bridge from the Old Town. Hikers can follow the main cobbled road (Mostecká) from Charles Bridge to Little Quarter Square, marked by the huge, green-domed Church of St. Nicholas. (The nearest Metro stop is Malostranská, from which Valdštejnská street leads down to Little Quarter Square.) From Little Quarter Square, hike uphill along Nerudova street (described on page 92). After about 10 minutes, a steep lane on the right leads to the castle. (If you continue straight, Nerudova becomes Úvoz and climbs to the Strahov Monastery.)

By Tram: Tram #22 takes you up to the castle (see page 47 for my self-guided tram tour, which ends at the castle). While you can catch the tram in various places, these three stops are particularly convenient: at the Národní Třída Metro stop (between

Wenceslas Square and the National Theater in the New Town); in front of the National Theater (Národní Divadlo, on the riverbank in the New Town); and at Malostranská (the Metro stop in the Little Quarter). After rattling up the hill, the tram makes three stops near the castle: Get off at **Královský Letohrádek** for the scenic approach to the castle (through the Royal Gardens); stay on one more stop to get off at **Pražský Hrad** (most direct but least interesting—simply walk along U Prašného Mostu over the bridge into the castle); or go yet two more stops—passing the Brusnice stop—to **Pohořelec** to visit the Strahov Monastery before hiking down to the castle (explained on page 100).

Tram Tips: When you're choosing which of the castle's three tram stops to get off at, consider the time of day. The castle is plagued with crowds. If you're visiting in the morning, use the Pražský Hrad tram stop for the quickest commute to the castle. Be at the door of St. Vitus Cathedral when it opens at 9:00 (except on Sunday mornings, when it's closed for Mass). If you arrive just 10–15 minutes later, it'll be swamped with tour groups. See the castle sights quickly, then move on to the Strahov Monastery. I'd avoid the castle entirely mid-morning, but by mid-afternoon, the tour groups are napping and the grounds are (relatively) uncrowded. If you're going in the afternoon, take the tram to the Pohořelec stop, see the Strahov Monastery, then wander down to the castle.

Sights Above the Castle, near the Královský Letohrádek Tram Stop

These sights, above Prague Castle, are only worth visiting if you get off tram #22 at Královský Letohrádek (the Royal Summer Palace is across the street from this stop, WC at gate).

Royal Summer Palace (Královský Letohrádek)—This gift of love is like a Czech Taj Mahal, presented by Emperor Ferdinand I to his beloved Queen Anne. It's the purest Renaissance building in town. You can't go inside, but the building's detailed reliefs are worth a close look. In good Renaissance style, they're based on classical, rather than Christian, stories. The one depicted here is Virgil's *Aeneid*. The fountain in front of the palace features the most elaborate bronze-work in the country. (For a trip to Tibet, stick your head under the bottom of the fountain. The audio rainbow you hear is the reason it's called the Singing Fountain.)

• *From here set your sights on the cathedral's lacy, black spires marking the castle's entrance and stroll through the...*

Royal Gardens (Královská Zahrada)—Once the private grounds and residence (you'll see the building) of the communist presidents, these were opened to the public with the coming of freedom under Václav Havel (free, April–Oct daily 10:00–18:00,

Prague's Castle Quarter

Sights

1. Castle Square & Plague Column
2. Schwarzenberg Palace
3. Archbishop's Palace
4. Sternberg Palace
5. Castle Gate
6. Tickets & Information (2)
7. St. Vitus Cathedral
8. Old Royal Palace
9. Basilica & Convent of St. George
10. Golden Lane
11. Lobkowicz Palace & Panoramic Café
12. Toy & Barbie Museum
13. Steps to Terraced Gardens
14. Royal Summer Palace
15. Royal Gardens
16. Strahov Monastery & Library
17. Museum of Miniatures
18. Loreta Church
19. Černín Palace

Eateries

20. U Sedmi Švábů & U Osla v Kolébce
21. U Hrocha Pub
22. To Restaurace Rybářský Klub
23. Villa Richter Eateries
24. Klášterní Pivovar
25. Bellavista Restaurant
26. Restaurace Nad Úvozem
27. Hostinec u Černého Vola Pub
28. Malý Buddha Veggie Rest.
29. Espresso Kajetánka
30. Na Baště Café
31. Restaurace David & Baráčnická Rychta

closed Nov–March). Walk through these gardens (with lovely views of St. Vitus Cathedral) to the gate, which leads you over the moat and into Castle Square, the entrance to the vast castle complex.

▲Strahov Monastery and Library, near the Pohořelec Tram Stop

Twin Baroque domes high above the castle mark the Strahov Monastery. This complex is best reached from the Pohořelec stop on tram #22 (from the stop, follow the tram tracks uphill for 50 yards, enter the fancy gate on the left near the tall red-brick wall, and you'll see the twin spires of the monastery; the library entrance is in front of the church on the right). If you're coming on foot from the Little Quarter, allow 15 minutes for the uphill hike. After seeing the monastery, hike down to the castle (a 5-min walk).

Monastery: The monastery (Strahovský Klášter Premonstrátů) had a booming economy of its own in its heyday, with vineyards, a brewery, and a sizeable beer hall—all still open. Its main church, dedicated to the Assumption of St. Mary, is an originally Romanesque structure decorated by the monks in textbook Baroque (usually closed, but look through the window inside the front door to see its interior).

Library: The adjacent library (Strahovská Knihovna) offers a peek at how enlightened thinkers in the 18th century influenced learning (80 Kč, daily 9:00–11:45 & 13:00–17:00). Cases in the library gift shop show off illuminated manuscripts (described in English). Some are in old Czech, but because the Enlightenment promoted the universality of knowledge, there was little place for vernaculars—therefore, few books here are in the Czech language. Two rooms (seen only from the door) are filled with 10th- to 17th-century books, shelved under elaborately painted ceilings. The theme of the first and bigger hall is philosophy, with the history of man's pursuit of knowledge

painted on the ceiling. The other hall focuses on theology. Notice the gilded, locked case containing the *libri prohibiti* (prohibited books) at the end of the room. Only the abbot had the key, and you had to have his blessing to read these books—by writers such as Nicolas Copernicus and Jan Hus, and even including the French encyclopedia. As the Age of Enlightenment began to take hold in Europe at the end of the 18th century, monasteries still controlled the books. The hallway connecting these two library rooms was filled with cases illustrating the new practical approach to natural sciences. Find the dried-up elephant trunks, baby dodo bird (which became extinct in the 17th century), and one of the earliest models of an electricity generator.

Nearby Views: Just downhill from the monastery, past the venerable linden trees (a symbol of the Czech people) and through the gate, the views from the **monastery garden** are among the best in Prague. From the public perch beneath the tables, you can see St. Vitus Cathedral (the heart of the castle complex), the green dome of the Church of St. Nicholas (marking the center of the Little Quarter), the two dark towers fortifying both ends of Charles Bridge, and the fanciful black spires of the Týn Church (marking the Old Town Square). On the horizon is the modern **Žižkov TV and radio tower** (conveniently marking the liveliest nightlife zone in town—see "In Žižkov" in the Entertainment in Prague chapter). Begun in the 1980s, it was partly meant to jam Radio Free Europe's broadcast from Munich. By the time it was finished, communism was dead, and Radio Free Europe's headquarters had moved to Prague.

Getting to the Castle: To reach the castle from Strahov Monastery, take Loretánská (the upper road, passing Loreta Square—described later); this is a more interesting route than the lower road, Úvoz, which takes you down a steep hill, below Castle Square.

Or, for one more little sight, consider visiting the Museum of Miniatures. From the monastery garden viewpoint, backtrack through the gate to the big linden trees and leave through a passage on your right. At the door is the miniscule...

Museum of Miniatures: You'll see 40 teeny exhibits, each under a microscope, crafted by an artist from St. Petersburg. Yes, you could fit the entire museum in a carry-on-size suitcase, but good things sometimes come in very, very small packages—it's fascinating to see minutiae such as a padlock on the leg of an ant. An English flier explains it all (50 Kč, kids-20 Kč, daily 9:00–17:00).

On Loreta Square, Between Strahov Monastery and Castle Square

From the monastery, take Loretánská street to Loreta Square (Loretánské Náměstí). As you wander this road, you'll pass several mansions and palaces and an important pilgrimage church.

Loreta Church—This church has been a hit with pilgrims for centuries, thanks to its dazzling bell tower, peaceful yet plush

cloister, sparkling treasury, and much-venerated Holy House (110 Kč, Tue–Sun 9:00–12:15 & 13:00–16:30, closed Mon).

Once inside, follow the one-way clockwise route. While you stroll along the cloister, notice that the ceiling is painted with the many places Mary has miraculously appeared to the faithful in Europe.

In the garden-like center of the cloister stands the ornate **Santa Casa (Holy House),** considered by some pilgrims to be part of Mary's home in Nazareth. Because many pilgrims returning from the Holy Land docked at the Italian port of Loreto, it's called the

Loreta Shrine. The Santa Casa is the "little Bethlehem" of Prague. It is the traditional departure point for Czech pilgrims setting out on the long, arduous journey to Europe's most important pilgrimage site, Santiago de Compostela, in northwest Spain. Inside, on the left wall, hangs what some consider to be an original beam from the house of Mary. It's overseen by a much-venerated statue of the Black Virgin. The Santa Casa itself might seem like a bit of a letdown, but consider that you're entering the holiest spot in the country for generations of believers.

The small Baroque church behind the Santa Casa is one of the most beautiful in Prague. The decor looks rich—but the marble and gold is all fake (tap the columns). From the window in the back, you can see a stucco relief on the Santa Casa that shows angels rescuing the house from a pagan attack in Nazareth and making a special delivery to Loreto in Italy.

Continue around the cloister. In the last corner is "St. Bearded Woman" (Svatá Starosta). This patron saint of unhappy marriages is a woman whose family arranged for her to marry a pagan man.

European Flags Fly in the Czech Republic

Today, the blue flag of the European Union flies alongside the Czech flag on the roof of government buildings, such as the Černín Palace (housing the Ministry of Foreign Affairs). The Czech Republic entered the EU along with nine other countries on May 1, 2004. Most Czechs are disappointed they weren't admitted much earlier.

The former president of the Czech Republic, Václav Havel, said the EU offers Europe the historic chance to finally get together and resolve issues over a table, rather than on the battlefield. But there are Euro-skeptics, including the right wing, the communists, and the current Czech president, Václav Klaus, who argues that the country is surrendering too much of its autonomy to Brussels. Still, most Czechs are optimistic about their future in the EU, and the majority of the government feels that membership will benefit the country. The year following Czech entry into the EU saw the largest GDP growth since 1989, as well as growing foreign investment. Japanese and Korean companies now find it advantageous to produce goods in the Czech Republic (or Slovakia), since assembling their final products within these member countries exempts them from EU tariffs.

During the first half of 2009, the Czech Republic assumed the rotating presidency of the European Union. Halfway through its term, however, the opposition pushed through a nonconfidence vote, forcing the administration to step down.

The Czech Republic currently has no plans to adopt the euro: The recent financial downturn seems to support those economists who argue that using the euro is actually a disadvantage for the small-country economies of Central and Eastern Europe.

She prayed for an escape, sprouted a beard...and the guy said, "No way." While she managed to avoid the marriage, it angered her father, who crucified her. The many candles here are from people suffering through unhappy marriages.

Take a left just before the exit and head upstairs, following signs to the treasury—a room full of jeweled worship aids (well-described in English). The highlight here is a monstrance (Communion wafer holder) from 1699, with more than 6,000 diamonds.

Enjoy the short carillon concert at the top of the hour; from the lawn in front of the main entrance, you can see the racks of bells being clanged. (At the exit, you'll see a schedule of English-language Masses and upcoming *pout'*—pilgrimages—departing from here.)

• *On the opposite side of the square is...*

Černín Palace—This palace once belonged to one of the most cosmopolitan Czech families, and so, in 1918, it was turned into the Ministry of Foreign Affairs. In May 2005, a memorial to the first secretary of state of Czechoslovakia, Edvard Beneš, was unveiled in front of the Ministry. This second president of Czechoslovakia, who led the country from exile in London during World War II, is highly controversial these days (see sidebar on page 194). The tiny size of the statue expresses the nation's present uncertainty about the legacy of the man.

Beneš faces the bronze portrait bust of Hana Benešová, Edvard's wife, on the nearby house where she lived for a brief period. Hana has long been regarded as the force behind many of Edvard's crucial decisions. Czechs typically measure statesmen by their wives, since many Czechs regard men as pathologically ambitious and imprudent creatures, whose success and apparent political wisdom are due to the out-of-sight, sensible judgment of their better halves.

Castle Square (Hradčanské Náměstí)

This is the central square of the Castle Quarter. Enjoy the awe-

some city view and the two entertaining bands that play regularly at the gate. (If the Prague Castle Orchestra is playing, say hello to friendly, mustachioed Josef, and consider getting the group's terrific CD.) The recommended **Espresso Kajetánka** café, with dramatic city views, hides a few steps down (immediately to the right as you face the castle). From the café, stairs lead down to the Little Quarter.

Castle Square was a kind of medieval Pennsylvania Avenue—the king, the most powerful noblemen, and the archbishop lived here. Look uphill from the gate. The Renaissance **Schwarzenberg Palace** (on the left, with the big rectangles scratched on the wall) was where the Rožmberks "humbly" stayed when they were in town from their Český Krumlov estates. The Schwarzenberg family inherited the Krumlov estates and aristocratic prominence in Bohemia and stayed in the palace until the 20th century. The palace now houses the National Gallery's collection of Czech Baroque paintings, displayed in recently restored rooms that also have great views of the city (150 Kč, Tue–Sun 10:00–18:00, cheaper after 16:00, closed Mon).

The archbishop still lives in the yellow Rococo **palace** across

Tomáš Garrigue Masaryk
(1850–1937)

Tomáš Masaryk was the George Washington of Czechoslovakia. He founded the first democracy in Eastern Europe at the end of World War I, uniting the Czechs and the Slovaks to create

Czechoslovakia. Like Václav Havel 70 years later, Masaryk was a politician whose vision extended far beyond the mountains enclosing the Bohemian basin.

Masaryk was born into a poor servant family in southern Moravia. After finishing high school, the village boy set off to attend university in Vienna. Masaryk earned his Ph.D. in sociology just in time for the opening of the Czech-language university in Prague. By then, he was married to an American music student named Charlotta Garrigue, who came from a prominent New York family. (The progressive Tomáš actually took her family name as part of his own.) Charlotta opened the doors of America's high society to Masaryk. Among the American friends he made was a young Princeton professor named Woodrow Wilson.

Masaryk was greatly impressed with America, and his admiration for its democratic system became the core of his gradually evolving political creed. He traveled the world and went to Vienna to serve in the parliament. By the time World War I broke

the square (with the three white goose necks in the red field—the coat of arms of Prague's archbishops).

Through the portal on the left-hand side of the palace, a lane leads to the **Sternberg Palace** (Šternberský Palác), filled with the National Gallery's skippable collection of European paintings—including minor works by Albrecht Dürer, Peter Paul Rubens, Rembrandt, and El Greco (150 Kč, Tue–Sun 10:00–18:00, closed Mon).

The black Baroque sculpture in the middle of the square is a **plague column,** erected as a token of gratitude to the saints who saved the population from the epidemic and an integral part of the main square of many Habsburg towns.

The statue marked *TGM* honors **Tomáš Garrigue Masaryk**

out, in 1914, Masaryk was 64 years old and—his friends thought—ready for retirement. But while most other Czech politicians stayed in Prague and supported the Habsburg Empire, Masaryk went abroad in protest and formed a highly original plan: to create an independent, democratic republic of Czechs and Slovaks. Masaryk and his supporters recruited an army of 100,000 Czech and Slovak soldiers who were willing to fight with the Allies against the Habsburgs, establishing a strong case to put on his friend Woodrow Wilson's Oval Office desk.

On the morning of October 28, 1918, news of the unofficial capitulation of the Habsburgs reached Prague. Local supporters of Masaryk's idea quickly took control of the city and proclaimed the free republic. As the people of Prague tore down double-headed eagles (a symbol of the Habsburgs), Czechoslovakia was born.

On November 11, 1918, four years after he had left the country as a political unknown, Masaryk arrived in Prague as the greatest Czech hero since the revolutionary priest Jan Hus. The dignified old man rode through the masses of cheering Czechs on a white horse. He told the jubilant crowd, "Now go home—the work has only started." Throughout the 1920s and 1930s, Masaryk was Europe's most vocal defender of democratic ideals against the rising tide of totalitarian ideologies.

In 2001, the US government honored Masaryk's dedication to democracy by erecting a monument to him in Washington, DC. He is one of only three foreign leaders (along with Gandhi and Churchill) to have a statue in the American capital.

(1850–1937), a university prof and a pal of Woodrow Wilson. At the end of World War I, Masaryk united the Czechs and the Slovaks into one nation and became its first president.

▲▲ Prague Castle (Pražský Hrad)

For more than a thousand years, Czech leaders have ruled from Prague Castle. Today, Prague's Castle is, by some measures, the biggest on earth. Four stops stand out, and all are explained here:

St. Vitus Cathedral, Old Royal Palace, Basilica of St. George, and the Golden Lane.

Hours: Castle sights are open daily April–Oct 9:00–17:00, Nov–March 9:00–16:00, last entry 15 minutes before closing; grounds are open daily 5:00–23:00. St. Vitus Cathedral is closed Sunday mornings for Mass. Be warned that the cathedral can be closed unexpectedly due to special services—consider calling ahead to confirm (tel. 224-373-368 or 224-372-434). If you're not interested in entering the museums, you could try a nighttime visit—the castle grounds are safe, peaceful, floodlit, and open late.

Tickets: The cathedral is free. For the other castle sights, rather than buying the comprehensive long-tour ticket (350 Kč), I recommend getting the short-tour ticket (250 Kč, covers the Old Royal Palace, Basilica of St. George, and the Golden Lane; buy in palace, Basilica, or the ticket offices on the two castle courtyards). To save time, skip the packed Golden Lane during the day, and return at night for a romantic, crowd-free visit (free before 9:00 and after 18:00, or after 17:00 in winter).

Tours: Hour-long tours in English depart from the main ticket office across from the cathedral entrance about three times a day, but they cover only the cathedral and Old Royal Palace (100 Kč plus entry ticket, tel. 224-373-368). You can rent an **audioguide** for 200 Kč (good all day)—pick it up at the main desk, and show this book for this rate (promised through 2011 by the manager Tomáš Kuha). The audioguide also entitles you to priority entrance at the cathedral—when the line in front of the entrance is long, walk to the exit door on the right and show the audioguide to the guard to be let in.

Crowd-Beating Tips: Huge throngs of tourists turn the castle grounds into a sea of people during peak times (9:30–12:30). St. Vitus Cathedral is the most crowded part of the castle complex. If you're visiting in the morning, be at the cathedral entrance promptly at 9:00, when the doors open. For 10 minutes you'll have the sacred space to yourself (after about 9:15, tour guides jockeying unwieldy groups from tomb to tomb turn the church into a noisy human traffic jam). Late afternoon is least crowded.

Castle Gate and Courtyards

Begin at Castle Square. From here, survey the castle—the tip of a 1,500-foot-long series of courtyards, churches, and palaces. The guard changes on the hour (5:00–23:00), with the most ceremony and music at noon.

Walk under the fighting giants, under an arch, through the passageway, and into the courtyard. The modern green awning with the golden-winged cat (just past the ticket office) marks the offices of the Czech president,

The Battle Between Church and State for St. Vitus Cathedral

There's no question that St. Vitus Cathedral is close to the hearts of Czechs. But in recent years controversy has erupted over just what aspect of the national spirit the cathedral embodies.

The cathedral was nationalized in the 1950s, and was managed by the Czech government for the next several decades. But in 1993—after the fall of communism—the Church began vying with the state for property rights. Since this building holds such symbolic value for the Czechs, it's not just the keys to the country's most precious artwork at stake. Those who wanted the cathedral to remain state-owned argued that it was the king, not the Church, who commissioned the cathedral, and that its completion in the 19th century was inspired more by patriotism than by religious fervor. The Church, however, pointed out the cathedral's role as a pilgrimage site, claiming that it should be dedicated to prayer. In 2006, the Czech courts ruled in the Church's favor (and against public opinion).

The Church has been cash-strapped since the fall of communism. While the state returned thousands of deteriorating chapels throughout the country to the Church, it didn't return ownership of the lands that once provided the revenue for maintenance. So, perhaps understandably, once the keys changed hands, the Church looked for an easy source of cash. Hoping that the throngs of cathedral visitors would help them bring new life to neglected rural chapels, Church leaders immediately imposed a 100-Kč entrance fee. Some accused them of greediness. But in 2008, before the coins had filled a single coffer, the Supreme Court overruled the decision and returned the cathedral to the state (which made the entrance free).

who is elected by the parliament rather than by popular vote and serves as more of a figurehead than a power broker. The current president is Václav Klaus. His consistent politics have brought him popularity from like-minded Czechs, but bitter resentment from those who see him as incapable of considering points of view other than his own. Outside the Czech Republic, Klaus is known for his unconstructive criticism of the European Union and denunciation of the campaign against global warming (the reality of which he denies). In the fall of 2007, Klaus—who in his most recent book argues that "environmental hysteria" fundamentally endangers the freedom of the individual—became the face of an ExxonMobil-sponsored campaign in the American media that preceded a UN conference on global warming.

• *As you walk through another passageway, you'll find yourself facing...*

▲▲▲St. Vitus Cathedral (Katedrála Sv. Víta)

The Roman Catholic cathedral symbolizes the Czech spirit—it contains the tombs and relics of the most important local saints and kings, including the first three Habsburg kings.

Cathedral Facade: Before entering, check out the facade. What's up with the guys in suits carved into the facade beneath

the big, round window? They're the architects and builders who finished the church. Started in 1344, construction was stalled by wars and plagues. But, fueled by the 19th-century rise of Czech nationalism, Prague's top church was finished in 1929 for the 1,000th anniversary of the death of St. Wenceslas. While it looks all Gothic, it's actually two distinct halves: the original 14th-century Gothic around the high altar, and the modern Neo-Gothic nave. For 400 years, a temporary wall sealed off the functional, yet unfinished, cathedral.

Mucha Stained-Glass Window: Enter through the gate on the left with the fenced-off queuing area and find the third window on the left. This masterful 1931 Art Nouveau window is by Czech artist Alfons Mucha (if you like this, you'll love the Mucha Museum in the New Town—see page 81; also see Mucha's masterpiece, *Slav Epic,* described on page 233).

Notice Mucha's stirring nationalism: Methodius and Cyril,

widely considered the fathers of Slavic-style Christianity, are top and center. Cyril—the monk in black holding the Bible—brought the word of God to the Slavs. They had no written language in the ninth century, so he designed the necessary alphabet (Glagolitic, which later developed into Cyrillic). Methodius, the bishop, is shown baptizing a mythic, lanky, long-haired Czech man—a reminder of how he brought Christianity to the Czech people. Scenes from the life of Cyril on the left, and scenes from the life of Methodius on the right, bookend the stirring and epic Slavic scene. In the center are a kneeling boy and a proph-esying elder—that's young St. Wenceslas and his grandmother, St. Ludmila. In addition to being specific historical figures, these characters are also symbolic: The old woman, with closed eyes, stands for the past and memory; the young boy, with a penetrat-ing stare, represents the hope and future of a nation. Notice how master designer Mucha draws your attention to these two figures through the use of colors—the dark blue on the outside gradually turns into green, then yellow, and finally the gold of the woman and the crimson of the boy in the center. In Mucha's color lan-guage, blue stands for the past, gold for the mythic, and red for the future. Besides all the meaning, Mucha's art is simply a joy to behold. (And on the bottom, the tasteful little ad for *Banka Slavie,* which paid for the work, is hardly noticeable.)

Habsburg Emperor's Tomb: Continue circulating around the apse. The big royal tomb (within the black iron fence) is of the first Habsburg emperor. It dates from 1590, when Prague was a major Habsburg city.

Relief of Prague: As you walk around the high altar, study the fascinating carved-wood relief of Prague. It depicts the vic-torious Habsburg armies entering the castle after the Battle of White Mountain, while the Protestant King Frederic escapes over the Charles Bridge (before it had any statues). Carved in 1630, 10 years after the famous event occurred, the relief also gives you a peek at Prague in 1620, stretching from the Týn Church to the cathedral (half-built at that time, up to where you are now). Notice that back then, the Týn Church was Hussite, so the centerpiece of its facade is not the Virgin Mary, but a chalice, symbol of Jan Hus' ideals. The old city walls—now replaced by the main streets of the city—stand strong. The Jewish Quarter (the slummy, muddy zone along the riverside below the bridge on the left) fills land no one else wanted.

Apse: Circling around the high altar, you pass graves of bishops, including the tomb of St. Vitus (behind the chair of the bishop). The stone sarcophagi contain kings from the Přemysl dynasty (12th–14th centuries). Locals claim the gigantic, shiny tomb of St. John of Nepomuk has more than a ton of silver (for more on St. John of Nepomuk, see page 68). After the silver tomb, look up at the royal box from where the king would attend Mass in his jammies (an elevated corridor connected his private apartment with his own altar-side box pew).

Look for the finely carved wood panel that gives a Counter-Reformation spin on the Wars of Religion. It shows the "barbaric" Protestant nobles destroying the Catholic icons in the cathedral after their short-lived victory.

Wenceslas Chapel: A fancy roped-off chapel (right transept)

The Catholic Church in Prague

In stark contrast to Poland, the powerful Catholic Church —traditionally closely allied with the Habsburgs and Austria— was never the favorite institution of the freedom-loving Czechs. The communists took advantage of this popular sentiment, and in their Marxist zeal did everything short of banning the Church to uproot the faith of the relatively few practicing Catholics. In the early 1950s, most monks and priests, including the archbishop, were arrested and sent to prisons,

from which they were not released until the thawing that came with the Khrushchev era. A wise old priest remembers his 13 years in a labor camp as "a fascinating, well-spent time in the company of some truly great minds."

During the communist era, Church property was confiscated, churches quickly deteriorated, churchgoers were persecuted, and many priests had to become confidants of the secret police in order to continue their service. Ironically, by persecuting Catholics, the communists gave the Church the opportunity to improve its reputation with the Czechs. In the 1980s, the charismatic archbishop of Prague, Cardinal Tomášek, became a local hero by frequently standing up to the regime. By 1989, Tomášek was a main symbol of anti-communist opposition (along with Václav Havel).

After 1989, many Czechs returned to the Catholic faith. The trend peaked in 1992 when Tomášek died (he's now buried under the Mucha window in St. Vitus Cathedral). Since then, the Church's hold has steadily declined, for various reasons. The media depict the Church as greedy; questions have arisen about the status of former Church property (see sidebar on page 109); and the new archbishop—named Vlk (Wolf), which his critics find fitting—is uninspiring.

These days, "new" and fashionable spiritual movements, such as Buddhism, are drawing Czechs in increasing numbers. The Dalai Lama has been a frequent visitor to Prague.

houses the tomb of St. Wenceslas, surrounded by precious 14th-century murals showing scenes of his life (see description on page 77), and a locked door leading to the crown jewels. The Czech kings used to be crowned right here in front of the coffin, draped in red. The chapel is roped off because the wallpaper is encrusted with precious and semiprecious stones. (Lead us not into temptation.) You can view the chapel from either door (if the door facing the nave is crowded, duck around to the left to find a door that is most likely open).

Spire: You can climb 287 steps up the spire for one of the best views of the whole city (may be closed for reconstruction, otherwise April–Oct daily 9:00–17:00 except Sun morning, Nov–March until 16:00, last entry 45 min before closing).

Back Outside the Cathedral: Leaving the cathedral, turn left (past the public WC). The **obelisk** was erected in 1928—a single piece of granite celebrating the 10th anniversary of the establishment of Czechoslovakia and commemorating the soldiers who fought for its independence. It was originally much taller, but broke in transit—an inauspicious start for a nation destined to last only 70 years. Up in the fat, green tower of the cathedral is the Czech Republic's biggest bell, nicknamed "Zikmund." In June 2002, it cracked, and two months later, the worst flood in recorded history hit the city—the locals saw this as a sign. As a nation sandwiched between great powers, Czechs are deeply superstitious when it comes to the tides of history. Often feeling unable to influence the course of their own destiny, they helplessly look at events as we might look at the weather and other natural phenomena—trying to figure out what fate has in store for them next.

Find the 14th-century **mosaic** of the Last Judgment outside on the right transept. It was commissioned in the Italian style by King Charles IV, who was modern, cosmopolitan, and ahead of his time. Jesus oversees the action, as some go to heaven and some go to hell. The Czech king and queen kneel directly beneath Jesus and the six patron saints. On coronation day, they would walk under this arch, which would remind them (and their subjects) that even those holding great power are not above God's judgment. The royal crown and national jewels are kept in a chamber (see the grilled windows) above this entryway, which was the cathedral's main entry for centuries while the church remained uncompleted.

Across the square and 20 yards to the right, a door leads into the Old Royal Palace (in the lobby, there's a WC with a window shared by the men's and women's sections—meet your partner to enjoy the view).

Old Royal Palace (Starý Královský Palác)

Starting in the 12th century, this was the seat of the Bohemian princes. While extensively rebuilt, the **large hall** is late Gothic, designed as a multipurpose hall for the old nobility. It's big enough for jousts—even the staircase was designed to let a mounted soldier gallop in. It was filled with market stalls, giving nobles a chance to shop without actually going into town. In the 1400s, the nobility met here to elect their king. The tradition survived until modern times, as the parliament crowded into this room until the late 1990s to elect the Czechoslovak (and later Czech Republic) president. (The last three elections happened in another, far more lavish hall in the castle.) Look up at the flower-shaped, vaulted ceiling.

On your immediate right, enter the two small Renaissance rooms known as the **"Czech Office."** From these rooms (empty today except for their 17th-century porcelain heaters), two governors used to oversee the Czech lands for the Habsburgs in Vienna. In 1618, angry Czech Protestant nobles poured into these rooms and threw the two Catholic governors out of the window. An old law actually permits defenestration—throwing people (usually bad politicians) out of windows when necessary. Old prints on the wall show the second of Prague's many defenestrations. The two governors landed—fittingly—in a pile of horse manure. Even though they suffered only broken arms and bruised egos, this event kicked off the huge and lengthy Thirty Years' War.

Look down on the chapel from the end, and go out on the balcony for a sweeping view of Prague. Is that Paris' Eiffel Tower in the distance? No, it's Petřín Tower, a fine place for a relaxing day at the park, offering sweeping views over Prague (see previous chapter).

As you exit through the side door, pause at the door to consider the subtle yet racy little Renaissance knocker. Go ahead—play with it for a little sex in the palace (be gentle).

• *Across from the palace exit is the...*

Basilica and Convent of St. George (Bazilika Sv. Jiří)

Step into the beautiful-in-its-simplicity Basilica of St. George to see Prague's best-preserved Romanesque church. Notice the characteristic double windows on the gallery, as well as the walls made of limestone (the rock that Prague rests on). In those early years, the building techniques were not yet advanced, and the ceiling is made of wood, rather than arched with stone. St. Wenceslas' grandmother, St. Ludmila, who established this first Bohemian convent, was reburied here in 973. Look for Gothic frescoes depicting this cultured woman (to the right of the altar space). The Baroque front—which dates from much later—was added on the exterior at the same time as the St. John of Nepomuk chapel (through which you exit the church). The scary-looking bones under the chapel altar are replicas—neither St. John's nor real.

Today, the **convent** next door houses the National Gallery's collection of 19th-century Czech paintings (150 Kč, Tue–Sun 10:00–18:00, closed Mon).

• *Continue walking downhill through the castle grounds. Turn left on the first street, which leads into the...*

Golden Lane (Zlatá Ulička)

This street of old buildings, which originally housed goldsmiths, is jammed with tourists dur-ing the day and lined with overpriced gift shops. Franz Kafka lived briefly at #22. There's a deli/bistro at the top. In the morning (before 9:00) and at night (after 18:00 in summer, after 17:00 in winter), the tiny street is empty and romantic. Exit the lane through a corridor at the last house (#12).

Lobkowicz Palace (Lobkowiczký Palác)

At the bottom of the castle complex just after you leave the Golden Lane, this palace displays the private collection of a prominent Czech noble family, including paintings, ceramics, and musical scores. The Lobkowiczes' property was confiscated twice in the 20th century: first by the Germans, and then by the communists. In 1990, William Lobkowicz, then a Boston investment banker, returned to Czechoslovakia to fight a legal battle to reclaim his family's property and, eventually, to restore the castles and palaces to their former state.

A conscientious host, William himself narrates the audio-guide. As you pass by the portraits of his ancestors, listen to their stories, including that of Polyxena, whose determination saved the two Catholic governors defenestrated next door (according to family legend, she hid the bruised officials under the folds of her skirt). The museum's highlights are Peter Brueghel the Elder's magnificently preserved *Haymaking,* one of the earliest landscape paintings in Europe, and the manuscript of Beethoven's *Heroica* (dedicated to his sponsor, Count Lobkowicz), displayed alongside Mozart's annotation of Handel's *Messiah*. While the National Gallery may seem a more logical choice for the art enthusiast, the obvious care that went into creating this museum, the collection's variety, and the personal insight that it opens into the past and present of Czech nobility make the Lobkowicz worth a half-hour visit (275 Kč, includes audioguide, not included in any castle tickets, Tue–Sun 10:30–18:00, last entry one hour before closing, closed Mon, tel. 233-312-925, www.lobkowiczevents.cz). The **Panoramic Café** by the exit has a creative cosmopolitan menu and stunning views of the city (daily 10:00–18:00).

Toy and Barbie Museum (Muzeum Hraček)

Across the street from Lobkowicz Palace, a courtyard and a long wooden staircase lead to two entertaining floors of old toys and dolls, thoughtfully described in English. You'll see a century of teddy bears, some 19th-century model train sets, and an incredible Barbie collection (the entire top floor). Find the buxom 1959 first edition, and you'll understand why these capitalistic sirens of material discontent weren't allowed here until 1989 (70 Kč, 120 Kč family ticket, not included in any castle tickets, daily 9:30–17:30, WC next to entrance).

After Your Castle Visit...

Tourists squirt slowly through a fortified door at the bottom end of the castle. From there, you can follow the steep lane directly back to the riverbank...or turn right about halfway down the steps to visit the recently reopened **Fürstenberg Gardens,** with 3,500 flowering plants and 2,200 rose bushes (80 Kč, April–Oct daily from 10:00 until one hour before sunset). Either way, you'll end up at the Malostranská Metro station.

Or, as you walk out of the castle gate, you can take a hard right and stroll through the long, delightful park. Along the way, notice the Modernist design of the **Na Valech Garden,** which was carried out by the court architect of the 1920s, Jože Plečnik of Slovenia.

Halfway through the long park is a viewpoint overlooking the terraced **Pálffy Gardens;** you can zigzag down through these gardens into the Little Quarter (80 Kč, April–Oct daily 10:00–18:00, closed Nov–March).

If you continue through the park all the way to Castle Square, you'll find two more options: a staircase leading down into the Little Quarter, or a cobbled street taking you to historic Nerudova street (described in the previous chapter).

Congratulations. You've conquered the castle.

THE CASTLE QUARTER

SLEEPING IN PRAGUE

Peak season for hotels in Prague is May, June, and September. Easter and New Year's are the most crowded times, when prices are jacked up a bit. I've listed peak-time prices—if you're traveling in July or August, you'll find rates generally 15 percent lower, and from November through March, about 30 percent lower.

Room-Booking Services

Prague is awash with fancy rooms on the push list; private, small-time operators with rooms to rent in their apartments; and roving agents eager to book you a bed and earn a commission. You can save about 30 percent by showing up without a reservation and finding accommodations upon arrival. However, it can be a hassle, and you won't necessarily get your ideal choice. If you're coming in by train or car, you'll encounter booking agencies. They can almost always find you a reasonable room, and, if it's in a private guest house, your host can even come and lead you to the place.

Athos Travel has a line on 200 properties (ranging from hostels to five-star hotels), 90 percent of which are in the historical center. To book a room, call them or use their handy website, which allows you to search for a room, based on various criteria (best to arrange in advance during peak season, can also help with last-minute booking off-season, tel. 241-440-571, fax 241-441-697, www.a-prague.com, info@a-prague.com). Readers report that Athos is aggressive with its business policies—although there's no fee to cancel well in advance, they strictly enforce penalties on cancellations within 48 hours.

Touristpoint, at the main train station (Hlavní Nádraží), is another booking service (daily 8:00–22:00). They have a slew of hotels and small pensions available (2,000-Kč pension doubles in old center, 1,500-Kč doubles a Metro ride away). You can reserve

Sleep Code

(18 Kč = about $1, country code: 420)
S = Single, **D** = Double/Twin, **T** = Triple, **Q** = Quad, **b** = bathroom,
s = shower only. Unless otherwise noted, credit cards are
accepted, and breakfast and tax are included. Everyone listed
here speaks English.

   To help you sort easily through these listings, I've divided
the rooms into three categories based on the price for a
standard double room with bath:

$$$ Higher Priced—Most rooms 3,500 Kč or more.
 $$ Moderately Priced—Most rooms between
                2,500–3,500 Kč.
  $ Lower Priced—Most rooms 2,500 Kč or less.

by email, using your credit card as a deposit (tel. 224-946-010,
www.touristpoint.cz, info@touristpoint.cz), or just show up at the
office and request a room. Be clear on the location before you make
your choice.

Lída Jánská's **Magic Praha** can help with accommodations (mobile 604-207-225, www.magicpraha.cz, magicpraha @magicpraha.cz; see "Helpful Hints" on page 38). Lída rents a well-located apartment with a river view near the Jewish Quarter.

Web-booking services, such as Priceline.com and Bidding fortravel.com, enable budget travelers to snare fancy rooms on the push list for half the rack rate. It's not unusual to find a room in a four-star hotel for 1,300 Kč—but keep in mind that many of these international business-class hotels are far from the city center.

Old Town Hotels and Pensions

You'll pay higher prices to stay in the Old Town, but for many travelers, the convenience is worth the expense. These places are all within a 10-minute walk of the Old Town Square.

$$$ Hotel Metamorphis is a splurge, with solidly renovated rooms in Prague's former caravanserai (hostel for foreign merchants). Its breakfast room is in a spacious medieval cellar with modern artwork. Some of the street-facing rooms, located above two popular bars, are noisy at night (Db-4,800 Kč, significant discounts available based on demand—check the website, Malá Štupartská 5, tel. 221-771-011, fax 221-771-099, www.metamorphis .cz, hotel@metamorphis.cz).

$$$ Hotel Maximilian is a sleek, mod, 70-room place with Art Deco black design; big, plush living rooms; and all the business services and comforts you'd expect in a four-star hotel. It faces a church on a perfect little square just a short walk from the

Hotels in Prague's Old Town

1. Hotel Metamorphis
2. Hotel Maximilian & Hotel Haštal
3. Residence Masná
4. Pension u Medvídků
5. Hotel u Klenotníka
6. Green Garland Pension
7. Old Prague Hostel
8. Hostel Týn
9. Launderettes (2)

250 Meters
250 Yards

action (Db-4,000 Kč, extra bed-1,500 Kč, 20 percent discount on weekends, 15 percent discount if you stay three nights or more, check online for lower rates, Internet access, Haštalská 14, tel. 225-303-111, fax 225-303-110, www.maximilianhotel.com, reservation @maximilianhotel.com).

$$ Residence Masná rents 12 apartments in an elegant 1930s building with a marble staircase. Apartments vary somewhat in size, but all have hardwood floors, a kitchen, basic furniture, and a few plants (Db-3,125 Kč, extra person-125 Kč, 25 percent discount with this book, breakfast in room or in ultra-modern café next door, Masná 9, tel. 222-311-244, mobile 724-744-395, www.heart ofprague.cz, info@heartofprague.cz).

$$ Pension u Medvídků has 31 comfortably renovated rooms in a big, rustic, medieval shell with dark wood furniture. Upstairs, you'll find lots of beams—or, if you're not careful, they'll find you (Sb-2,000 Kč, Db-3,000 Kč, Tb-4,000 Kč, extra bed-500 Kč, "historical" rooms 10 percent more, apartment for 20 percent more, manager Vladimír promises readers of this book a 10 percent discount with cash if you book direct, Internet access, Na Perštýně 7, tel. 224-211-916, fax 224-220-930, www.umedvidku.cz, info @umedvidku.cz). The pension runs a popular beer-hall restaurant with live music most Fridays and Saturdays until 23:00—request an inside room for maximum peace.

$$ Hotel u Klenotníka ("At the Jeweler"), with 11 modern, comfortable rooms in a plain building, is three blocks off the Old Town Square (Sb-2,000 Kč, small double-bed Db-2,750 Kč, bigger twin-bed Db-3,300 Kč, Tb-3,750 Kč, 10 percent off with this book, Wi-Fi, Rytířská 3, tel. 224-211-699, fax 224-221-025, www .uklenotnika.cz, info@uklenotnika.cz, Marie and Helena).

$ Green Garland Pension (U Zeleného Věnce), on a central but delightfully quiet cobbled lane, has a warm and personal feel rare for the Old Town. Located in a thick 14th-century building with open beams, it has a blond-hardwood charm decorated with a woman's touch. Its nine rooms are clean and simply furnished (big Sb-1,700 Kč, Db-2,200 Kč, bigger Db-2,500 Kč, Tb-2,800 Kč, family suite, Wi-Fi, Řetězová 10, tel. 222-220-178, fax 224-248-791, www.uzv.cz, pension@uzv.cz).

$ Hotel Haštal is next to Hotel Maximilian (listed earlier) on the same quiet, hidden square in the Old Town. A popular hotel back in the 1920s, it has been renovated to complement the neighborhood's vibrant circa-1900 architecture. Its 24 rooms are comfortable, but the walls are a bit thin (Sb-1,500 Kč, Db-2,000 Kč, extra bed-550 Kč, book by email to avoid online booking fee, air-con, Wi-Fi, Haštalská 16, tel. 222-314-335, www.hastal.com, info@hastal.com). The hotel's small restaurant is understandably

Hotels & Restaurants in the Little Quarter

1 Vintage Design Hotel Sax
2 Hotel Julián
3 Dům u Velké Boty
4 Petřínské Terasy & Nebozízek Rests.
5 John & George Café
6 U Sedmi Švábů & U Osla v Kolébce
7 U Hrocha Pub
8 Restaurace Rybářský Klub
9 Klášterní Pivovar (Brewery)
10 Bellavista Restaurant
11 Restaurace David & Baráčnická Rychta Music Club

popular with locals for its reasonably priced lunch specials and draft beer.

Under the Castle, in the Little Quarter

The first and third listings below are buried on quiet lanes deep in the Little Quarter, among cobbles, quaint restaurants, rummaging tourists, and embassy flags. Hotel Julián is a 10-minute walk up the river on a quiet and stately street, with none of the intense medieval cityscape of the others.

SLEEPING

$$$ Vintage Design Hotel Sax recently remodeled its 22 rooms in a retro, meet-the-Jetsons fashion. With a fruity atrium and a distinctly modern, stark feel, this is a stylish, no-nonsense place (Sb-3,800–4,300 Kč, Db-3,800–4,500 Kč, Db suite-5,000 Kč, extra bed-750 Kč, 10 percent off with this book, elevator, Internet access, Jánský Vršek 3, tel. 257-531-268, fax 257-534-101, www.sax.cz, hotel@sax.cz).

$$$ Hotel Julián is an oasis of professional, predictable decency in an untouristy neighborhood. Its 32 spacious, fresh, well-furnished rooms and big, homey public spaces hide behind a noble Neoclassical facade. The staff is friendly and helpful (Sb-3,680 Kč, Db-3,980 Kč, Db suite-4,800 Kč, extra bed-900 Kč, check website for lower rates, 15 percent discount off rack rate with this book, free tea and coffee in room, air-con, Wi-Fi, elevator, plush and inviting lobby, summer roof terrace has view of Prague Castle, parking lot; Metro: Anděl, then an 8-min walk, or take tram #6, #9, #12, #20, or #58 for two stops; Elišky Peškové 11, Praha 5, reservation tel. 257-311-150, reception tel. 257-311-145, fax 257-311-149, www.julian.cz, info@julian.cz). Free lockers and a shower are available for those needing a place to stay after check-out (for example, while waiting for an overnight train). Mike's Chauffeur Service, based here, is reliable and affordable (see page 161).

$$ Dům u Velké Boty ("House at the Big Boot"), on a quiet square in front of the German Embassy, is the rare quintessential family hotel in Prague: homey, comfy, and extremely friendly. Charlotta, Jan, and their two sons treat every guest as a (thirsty) friend, and the wellspring of their stories never runs dry. Each of their 12 rooms is uniquely decorated, most in tasteful 19th-century Biedermeier style (tiny S-2,100 Kč, two D rooms that share a bathroom-2,250 Kč each, Db-2,900–3,600 Kč, extra bed-725 Kč, 10 percent off with advance reservation and this book, prices can be soft when slow, cash only, children up to 10 free—toys provided, free Internet access and Wi-Fi, Vlašská 30, tel. 257-532-088, www.bigboot.cz, info@bigboot.cz). There's no hotel sign on the house—look for the splendid geraniums that Jan nurtures in the windows.

Away from the Center

Moving just outside central Prague saves you money—and gets you away from the tourists and into some more workaday residential neighborhoods. The following listings are great values compared with the downtown hotels listed previously, and are all within a 5- to 15-minute tram or Metro ride from the center.

Beyond Wenceslas Square

These hotels are in urban neighborhoods on the outer fringe of the New Town, beyond Wenceslas Square. But they're still within

Hotels & Restaurants in the New Town & Beyond

1. To Sieber Hotel
2. Hotel 16
3. To Hotel Anna
4. To Hostel Elf
5. Restaurace u Pinkasů
6. Hospoda u Nováka
7. Pivovarský Dům
8. Le Patio & Café Louvre
9. Dobrá Čajovna Teahouse
10. Čajový Klub Cha Dao
11. Restaurant Červená Tabulka
12. Café Medúza
13. Hlučná Samota
14. To Restaurace u Sadu, Hospůdka nad Viktorkou & Palác Akropolis Club

several minutes' walk of the sightseeing zone, and are well-served by trams.

$$$ Sieber Hotel, with 20 rooms, is a quality four-star, business-class hotel in an upscale circa-1900 residential neighborhood (Vinohrady) that has recently become popular with Prague's expat community. They do a good job of being homey and welcoming (Sb-4,480 Kč, Db-4,780 Kč, extra bed-990 Kč, fourth night free, 20 percent discount with this book, 30 percent discount for last-minute reservations, air-con, elevator, Internet access, 3-min walk to Metro: Jiřího z Poděbrad, or tram #11, Slezská 55, Praha 3, tel. 224-250-025, fax 224-250-027, www.sieber.cz, reservations@sieber.cz).

$$ Hotel 16 is a sleek and modern business-class place with an intriguing Art Nouveau facade, polished cherry-wood elegance, high ceilings, and 14 fine rooms (Sb-2,800 Kč, Db-3,500 Kč, bigger Db-3,700 Kč, Tb-4,400 Kč, 10 percent discount with this book, check website for last-minute rates, triple-paned windows, back rooms facing the garden are quieter, air-con, elevator, Internet access, 10-min walk south of Wenceslas Square, Metro: I.P. Pavlova, Kateřinská 16, Praha 2, tel. 224-920-636, fax 224-920-626, www.hotel16.cz, hotel16@hotel16.cz).

$ Hotel Anna offers 24 bright, simple, pastel rooms and basic service. It's a bit closer—just 10 minutes by foot east of Wenceslas Square (Sb-1,600 Kč, Db-1,900 Kč, Tb-2,100 Kč, special online offers, elevator, Budečská 17, Praha 2, Metro: Náměstí Míru, tel. 222-513-111, fax 222-515-158, www.hotelanna.cz, sales@hotelanna.cz). They run a similar hotel (same standards and prices) nearby.

The Best Values, Farther from the Center

These accommodations are a 10- to 20-minute tram ride from the center, but once you make the trip, you'll see it's no problem—and you'll feel pretty smug saving $50–100 a night per double by not sleeping in the Old Town. Hotel u Šemíka and Guest House Lída are within a stone's throw of peaceful Vyšehrad Park, with a legendary castle on a cliff overlooking the Vltava River. Hotel Adalbert is on the grounds of an ancient monastery, and Pension Větrník is adjacent, with two of Prague's best-preserved natural areas (Star Park and Šárka) just a short walk away.

$$ Hotel Adalbert occupies an 18th-century building in the Břevnov Monastery (one of the Czech Republic's oldest monastic institutions, founded in 993). Meticulously restored after the return of the Benedictine monks in the 1990s, the monastery complex is the ultimate retreat for those who come to Prague for soul-searching or just wanting a quiet place away from the bustle. Join the monks for morning (7:00) and evening (18:00) Mass in the St. Margaret Basilica, a large and elegant Baroque church decorated with unusual simplicity. You can help yourself in the monastery fruit orchard and eat in the atmospheric monastery pub (Klášterní Šenk). The hotel itself caters primarily to business clientele and takes ecology seriously: recycling, water conservation, and free tram tickets for guests. I prefer the first-floor rooms, as some of the attic rooms—room numbers in the 200s—feel a bit cramped (Sb-2,300 Kč, Db-3,200 Kč, extra bed-1,050 Kč, less on weekends, ask for 15 percent Rick Steves discount when you reserve, Wi-Fi, free parking, halfway between city and airport at Markétská 1, Praha 6, tram #22 to Břevnovský Kláster; 5 min by tram beyond the castle, 20 min from Old and New Towns; tel. 220-406-170, fax 220-406-190, www.hoteladalbert.cz, info@hoteladalbert.cz).

$$ Hotel u Šemíka, named for a heroic mythical horse, offers 25 rooms in a quiet residential neighborhood just below Vyšehrad Castle and the Slavín cemetery where Dvořák, Mucha, and Čapek are buried. It's a 10-minute tram ride south of the Old Town (Sb-2,000 Kč, Db-2,650 Kč, apartment-3,350–3,700 Kč for 2–4 people, extra bed-600 Kč, ask for the "direct booking" Rick Steves 10 percent discount, Internet access; from the center, take tram #3, #17, or #21 to Výtoň, go under rail bridge, and walk 3 blocks uphill to Vratislavova 36; Praha 2, tel. 224-920-736, fax 224-911-602, www .usemika.cz, usemika@usemika.cz).

$ Pension Větrník fills an attractive white-and-orange former 18th-century windmill in one of Prague's most popular residential areas, right next to the Břevnov Monastery and midway between the airport and the city. The talkative owner, Miloš Opatrný, is a retired prizewinning Czech chef whose culinary work took him as far as Japan. On request, he will gladly prepare a meal you won't forget. The six rooms here are the pride of the Opatrný family, who live on the upper floors. The garden has a red-clay tennis court—rackets and balls are provided (Db-2,200 Kč, suite-3,300 Kč, extra bed-550 Kč, Internet access, U Větrníku 1, Praha 6; airport bus #179 stops near the house, tram #18 goes straight to Charles Bridge, both take 20 min; tel. 220-612-404, fax 220-513-390, www.vetrnik1722.cz, pension@vetrnik1722.cz).

$ Guest House Lída, with 12 homey and spacious rooms, fills a big house in a quiet residential area farther inland, a 15-minute tram ride from the center. Jan, Jiří, and Jitka Prouza, who run the place, are a wealth of information and know how to make people feel at home (Sb-1,380 Kč, small Db-1,440 Kč, Db-1,760 Kč, Tb-2,110 Kč, Qb-2,530 Kč, cash only, family rooms, top-floor family suite with kitchenette, Internet access, parking garage-200 Kč/day, Metro: Pražského Povstání; exit Metro and turn left on Lomnického between the Metro station and big blue-glass ČSOB building, follow Lomnického for 500 yards, then turn left on Lopatecká, go uphill and ring bell at Lopatecká #26, no sign outside; Praha 4, tel. & fax 261-214-766, www.lidabb.eu, lidabb@seznam.cz). The Prouza brothers also rent four **apartments** across the river, an equal distance from the center (Db-1,600 Kč, Tb-1,900 Kč, Qb-2,100 Kč).

Hostels in the Center

It's tough to find a double for less than 2,500 Kč in the old center. But Prague has an abundance of fine hostels—each with a distinct personality, and each excellent in its own way for anyone wanting a 300–500-Kč dorm bed or an extremely simple twin-bedded room for about 1,300 Kč. With travelers seeking cheaper options these days, it's good to keep in mind that hostels are no longer the exclusive domain of backpackers. The first two hostels are centrally located; the last two are found in workaday neighborhoods and have atmospheric interiors.

$ Old Prague Hostel is a small and friendly place with 70 beds on the second and third floors of an apartment building on a back alley near the Powder Tower. The spacious rooms were once apartment bedrooms, so it feels less institutional than most hostels. You can hang out in the comfy TV lounge/breakfast room. Older travelers would feel comfortable in this mellow place (D-1,400 Kč, bunk in 4- to 8-person room-400–500 Kč; includes breakfast, sheets, towels, lockers, and free Internet access; in summer reserve 2 weeks ahead for doubles, a few days ahead for bunks; Benediktská 2, see map on page 119 for location, tel. 224-829-058, fax 224-829-060, www.oldpraguehostel.com, oldpraguehostel@seznam.cz).

$ Hostel Týn is hidden in a silent courtyard two blocks from the Old Town Square. Because the management is aware of its value, they don't bother being too friendly (D-1,240 Kč, T-1,410 Kč, bunk in 4- to 5-bed co-ed room-420 Kč, lockers, Internet access, kitchen, no breakfast, reserve one week ahead, Týnská 19, see map on page 119, tel. 224-828-519, mobile 776-122-057, www.hosteltyn.com, roomservice@seznam.cz).

$ Sir Toby's is in a 1930s working-class neighborhood—a newly popular residential and dining-out area that's a 12-minute tram ride from the center. The owners have taken great pains to stamp the place with character: restored hardwood floors, a back garden with tables made out of sewing machines, and rooms filled with vintage 1930s furniture and photographs. Amenities include self- and full-service laundry, an on-site pub, and a friendly staff (120 beds, S-1,200 Kč, Db-1,640 Kč, Tb-1,840 Kč, bunk in 4- to 6-bed co-ed room-480 Kč, bunk in 8- to 10-bed co-ed room-340 Kč, take tram #5 from the main train station or tram #3 from the middle of Wenceslas Square to Dělnická, at Dělnická 24, Praha 7, tel. 246-032-610, www.sirtobys.com). They also run two contemporary-design hostels in Vinohrady.

$ Hostel Elf, a 10-minute walk from the main train station, or one bus stop from the Florenc Metro station, is fun-loving; ramshackle; covered with noisy, self-inflicted graffiti; and the wildest of these hostels. They offer cheap, basic beds, a helpful staff, and lots of creative services—kitchen, free luggage room, free Internet access, laundry, no lockout, free tea, cheap beer, a terrace, and lockers (120 beds, D-1,100 Kč, bunk in 6- to 11-person room-320 Kč, includes sheets and breakfast, cash only, reserve four days ahead, Husitská 11, Praha 3, take bus #133 or #207 from Florenc Metro station for one stop to U Památníku, tel. 222-540-963, www .hostelelf.com, info@hostelelf.com).

EATING IN PRAGUE

A big part of Prague's charm is found in wandering aimlessly through the city's winding old quarters, marveling at the architecture, watching the people, and sniffing out fun restaurants. You can eat well here for very little money. What you'd pay for a basic meal in Vienna or Munich will get you a feast in Prague. In addition to meat-and-potatoes Czech cuisine (see "Czech Food" on page 22), you'll find trendy, student-oriented bars and lots of fine ethnic eateries. For ambience, the options include traditional, dark Czech beer halls; elegant Art Nouveau dining rooms; and hip, modern cafés.

Watch out for scams. Many restaurants put more care into ripping off green tourists (and even locals) than into their cooking. Tourists are routinely served cheaper meals than what they ordered, given a menu with a "personalized" price list, charged extra for things they didn't get, or shortchanged. Speak Czech. Even saying "Hello" in Czech (see "Czech Survival Phrases" on page 307) will get you better service. Avoid any menu without clear and explicit prices. Be careful of waiters padding the tab. Closely examine your itemized bill and understand each line (a 10 percent service charge is sometimes added—in that case, there's no need to tip extra). Tax is always included in the price, so it shouldn't be tacked on later. Part with very large bills only if necessary, and deliberately count your change. Never let your credit card out of your sight. Make it a habit to get cash from an ATM to pay for your meals. (Credit cards can cost merchants as much as 10 percent.) Remember, there are two parallel worlds in Prague: the tourist town and the real city. Generally, if you walk two minutes away from the tourist flow, you'll find better value, atmosphere, and service. (For more on scams, see "Rip-Offs in Prague" on page 38.)

Czech Beer

Czechs are among the world's most enthusiastic beer (pivo) drinkers—adults drink an average of 80 gallons a year. The pub is a place to have fun, complain, discuss art and politics, talk hockey, and chat with locals and visitors alike. The pivo that was drunk in the country before the Industrial Revolution was much thicker, providing the main source of nourishment for the peasant folk. Even today, it doesn't matter whether you're in a restaurace (restaurant), a hostinec (pub), or a hospoda (bar)—a beer will land on your table upon the slightest hint to the waiter, and a new pint will automatically appear when the old glass is almost empty. (You must tell the waiter not to bring more.) Order beer from the tap (točené means "draft," sudové pivo means "keg beer"). A pivo is large (0.5 liter, or

17 oz); a malé pivo is small (0.3 liter, or 10 oz). Men invariably order the large size. Pivo for lunch has me sightseeing for the rest of the day on Czech knees.

The Czechs invented Pilsner-style lager in nearby Plzeň ("Pilsen" in German), and the result, Pilsner Urquell, is on tap in many local pubs. But be sure to venture beyond this famous beer. The Czechs produce plenty of other good beers, including Krušovice, Gambrinus, Staropramen, and Kozel. Budvar, from the town of Budějovice ("Budweis" in German), is popular with Anheuser-Busch's attorneys. (The Czech and the American breweries for years disputed the "Budweiser" brand name. The solution: The Czech Budweiser

is sold under its own name in Europe, China, and Africa, while in America it is marketed as Czechvar.)

The big degree symbol on bottles does not indicate the percentage of alcohol content. Instead, it is a measurement used by brewers to track the density of certain ingredients. As a rough guide, 10 degrees is about 3.5 percent alcohol, 12 degrees is about 4.2 percent alcohol, and 11 and 15 degrees are dark beers. The most popular Czech beers are about as potent as German beers and only slightly stronger than typical American beers.

Each establishment has only one kind of beer on tap; to try a particular brand, look for its sign outside. A typical pub serves only one brand of 10-degree beer, one brand of 12-degree beer, and one brand of dark beer. Czechs do not mix beer with anything, and they do not hop from pub to pub (in one night, it is said, you must stay loyal to one woman and to one beer). Na zdraví means "to your health" in Czech.

I've listed these eating and drinking establishments by neighborhood. The most options—and highest prices—are in the Old Town. If you want a memorable splurge, see the "Dining with Style" section. For a light meal, consider one of Prague's many cafés (see the "Cafés" section). Many of the places listed here are handy for an efficient lunch, but may not offer fine evening dining. Others make less sense for lunch, but are great for a slow, drawn-out dinner. Read the descriptions to judge which is which.

Fun, Touristy Neighborhoods: Several areas are pretty and well-situated for sightseeing, but lined only with touristy restaurants. While these places are not necessarily bad values, I've listed only a few of your many options—just survey the scene in these spots and choose whatever looks best. Kampa Square, just off the Charles Bridge, feels like a small-town square. Havelská Market is surrounded by colorful little eateries, any of which offer a nice perch for viewing the market scene while you munch. The massive Old Town Square is *the* place to nurse a drink or enjoy a meal while watching the tide of people, both tourists and locals, sweep back and forth. There's often some event on this main square, and its many restaurants provide tasty and relaxing vantage points.

Dining with a View: For great views, consider these options: **Restaurant u Prince Terrace** (rooftop dining above a fancy hotel, completely touristy but with awesome views, described on page 136); **Villa Richter** (next to Prague Castle, above Malostranská Metro stop, described on page 139); the **Bellavista Restaurant** at Strahov Monastery; **Petřínské Terasy** and **Nebozízek** next to the funicular stop halfway up Petřín Hill; and the many overpriced but elegant places serving scenic meals along the riverbanks. For the best cheap riverside dinner, have a picnic on a paddleboat (see page 47). There's nothing like drifting down the middle of the Vltava River as the sun sets, while munching on a picnic meal and sipping a beer with your favorite travel partner.

In or near the Old Town
Characteristically Czech Places

With the inevitable closing of cheap student pubs (replaced by shops and hotels that make more money), it's getting difficult to find a truly Czech pub in the historic city center. Most Czechs no longer go to "traditional" eateries, preferring the cosmopolitan taste of the world to the mundane taste of sauerkraut. As a result, ancient institutions with "authentic" Czech ambience have become touristy—but they're still great fun, a good value, and respected by locals. Expect wonderfully rustic spaces, smoke, surly service, and reasonably good, inexpensive food. Understand every line on your bill.

Restaurants in the Old Town

1. Restaurace u Provaznice
2. U Medvídků Beer Hall
3. U Zlatého Tygra Pub
4. Restaurace u Betlémské Kaple
5. Česká Kuchyně
6. Restaurace Mlejnice
7. Country Life Vegetarian Rest.
8. Lehká Hlava Vegetarian Rest.
9. Restaurace Maitrea
10. Beas Vegetarian Restaurant
11. Klub Architektů
12. Chez Marcel
13. Amici Miei Restaurant
14. Aldente Trattoria
15. Ariana Afghan Rest.
16. Indian Jewel
17. Orange Moon
18. Molly Malone's Irish Pub
19. La Casa Blů
20. Bohemia Bagel
21. Restaurant u Prince Terrace
22. Municipal House Eateries
23. Grand Café Slavia
24. Grand Café Orient
25. Café Montmartre & Ebel Coffee House
26. Havelská Market

Restaurace u Pinkasů, with a menu that reads like a 19th-century newspaper, is a Prague institution, founded in 1843. It's best in summer, when you sit in the garden behind the building, in the shade of the Gothic buttresses of the St. Mary of the Snows Church. But its waiters could win the award for the rudest service in town (daily 9:00–24:00, tucked in a courtyard near the bottom of Wenceslas Square, on the border between Old and New towns—for location see map on page 123, Jungmannovo Náměstí 16, tel. 221-111-150).

Restaurace u Provaznice ("By the Ropemaker's Wife") has all the Czech classics, peppered with the story of a once-upon-a-time-faithful wife. (Check the menu for details of the gory story.) It's less touristy and less expensive than the other restaurants in this area. Natives congregate here for their famously good "pig leg" with horseradish and Czech mustard (daily 11:00–24:00, a block into the Old Town from the bottom of Wenceslas Square at Provaznická 3, tel. 224-232-528).

U Medvídků ("By the Bear Cubs"), which started out as a brewery in 1466, is now a flagship beer hall of the Czech Budweiser. The one large room is bright, noisy, touristy, and a bit smoky (daily 11:30–23:00, a block toward Wenceslas Square from Bethlehem Square at Na Perštýnì 7, tel. 224-211-916). The small beer bar next to the restaurant (daily 16:00–3:00 in the morning) is used by university students during emergencies—such as after most other pubs have closed.

U Zlatého Tygra ("By the Golden Tiger") has long embodied the proverbial Czech pub, where beer turns strangers into kindred spirits, who cross the fuzzy line between memory and imagination as they tell their hilarious life stories to each other. Today, "The Tiger" is a buzzing shrine to one of its longtime regulars, the writer Bohumil Hrabal, whose fictions immortalize many of the colorful characters that once warmed the wooden benches here. Only regulars have reserved tables. If you find a rare empty spot, you'll be treated as a surprise guest rather than a customer (daily 15:00–23:00, just south of Karlova at Husova 17, tel. 222-221-111).

Hospoda u Nováka, behind the National Theater (i.e., not so central), is emphatically Czech, with few tourists. It takes good care of its regulars (you'll see the old monthly beer tabs in a rack just inside the door). Nostalgic communist-era signs are everywhere. During that time, pubs like this were close-knit communities where regulars escaped from the depression of daily life. Today, the U Nováka is a bright and smoky hangout where you can still happily curse whatever regime you happen to live under. While the English menu lists the well-executed Czech classics, it doesn't list the cheap daily specials (daily 10:00–23:00, V Jirchářích 2—see map on page 123, tel. 224-930-639).

Pivovarský Dům ("The Brewhouse"), on the corner of Ječná and Lípová in the New Town, is popular with locals for its rare variety of fresh beers (yeast, wheat, and fruit-flavored), fine classic Czech dishes, and an inviting interior that mixes traditonal and modern (daily 11:00–23:00, reservations recommended in the evenings; walk up Štěpánská street from Wenceslas Square for 10 minutes, or take tram #22 for two stops from Národní to Štěpánská; Lípová 15—see map on page 123, tel. 296-216-666, variety of beer mugs sold).

Restaurace u Betlémské Kaple, behind Bethlehem Chapel, is not "ye olde" Czech. It has light wooden decor, cheap lunch deals, and fish specialties that attract natives and visitors in search of a good Czech bite for good Czech prices (daily 11:00–23:00, Betlémské Náměstí 2, tel. 222-221-639).

Česká Kuchyně ("Czech Kitchen") is a blue-collar cafeteria serving steamy old Czech cuisine to a local clientele. It's fast, practical, cheap, and traditional as can be. There's no English inside, so if you want apple charlotte, but not tripe soup be sure to review the small English menu in the window outside before entering. Note the numbers of your preferred dishes (they correspond to the Czech menu inside), pick up your tally sheet as you enter, grab a tray, point to whatever you'd like, and keep the paper to pay as you exit. It's extremely cheap...unless you lose your paper (daily 9:00–20:00, very central, across from Havelská Market at Havelská 23, tel. 224-235-574).

Restaurace Mlejnice ("The Mill") is a fun little pub strewn with farm implements and happy eaters, located just out of the tourist crush two blocks from the Old Town Square. They serve hardy traditional and modern Czech plates for 150–180 Kč. Reservations are smart in the evening (daily 11:00–24:00, between Melantrichova and Železná at Kožná 14, tel. 224-228-635).

Hip Restaurants

Country Life Vegetarian Restaurant is a bright, easy, non-smoking cafeteria with a well-displayed buffet of salads and hot veggie dishes. It's midway between the Old Town Square and the bottom of Wenceslas Square. They're serious about their vegetarianism, serving only plant-based, unprocessed, and unrefined food. Its dining area is quiet and elegantly woody for a cafeteria, with three tables and wicker chairs outside in the courtyard (Sun–Thu 9:00–20:30, Fri 9:00–17:00, closed Sat, through courtyard at Melantrichova 15/Michalská 18, tel. 224-213-366).

Lehká Hlava Vegetarian Restaurant ("Clear Head"), tucked away on a cul-de-sac, has a mission to provide a "clear atmosphere for enjoying food." Sitting in an enchanted-forest setting, diners enjoy dishes from around the world. Reserve in advance for evenings (100–150-Kč plates, two-course 90-Kč daily special, no eggs, no smoke, lots of vegan dishes, daily 11:30–23:30, between Bethlehem Chapel and the river at Boršov 2, tel. 222-220-665).

Restaurace Maitrea, just off the Old Town Square alongside the Týn Church, builds on the success of its older sibling, Lehká Hlava (listed earlier). Every inch of the modern interior is curved to ensure the "unobstructed flow of energy." None of the imaginative vegetarian dishes duplicates those served at Lehká Hlava. The 105-Kč lunch special is a great value (Mon–Fri 11:30–23:30, Sat–Sun 12:00–23:30, Týnská ulička 6, tel. 221-711-631).

Beas is a cheap vegetarian restaurant ruled by a Punjabi chef who concocts mild *thalis* (mixed platters in the style of the north Indian plains) and *dosas* (south Indian crêpes). Tucked away in a courtyard behind the Týn Church, this place is popular with university students (Mon–Sat 9:30–20:00, Sun 10:00–18:00, Týnská 19, mobile 608-035-727).

Klub Architektů, next to Bethlehem Chapel, is a modern hangout in a medieval cellar that serves excellent original dishes, hearty salads, Moravian wines, and Slovak beer (daily, Betlémské Náměstí 169, tel. 224-401-214).

At **Le Patio,** on the big and busy Národní Třída, the first things you'll notice are the many lanterns suspended from the ceiling—and the big ship moored out back (OK, just its hulking bow). Le Patio has a hip, continental feel, but for a place that also sells furniture (head straight back and down the stairs), it definitely needs comfier dining chairs. The atmosphere is as pleasant and carefully designed as the dishes, with international fare from India, France, and points in between. There's always a serious vegetarian option available (200–350-Kč plates, daily 8:00–23:00, Národní 22—see map on page 123, tel. 224-934-375). Diners enjoy live music on Friday and Saturday nights (19:30–22:30).

Ethnic Eateries and Bars near Dlouhá Street

Dlouhá, the wide street leading away from the Old Town Square behind the Jan Hus Memorial (left of Týn Church), is lined with ethnic restaurants catering mostly to cosmopolitan locals. Within a couple of blocks, you can eat your way around the world. From Dlouhá, wander the Rámová/Haštalská/Vězeňská area to survey a United Nations of eateries: You'll find French (**Chez Marcel** at Haštalská 12 is understandably popular—with a fun-loving waitstaff, cash only); Italian (**Amici Miei** at Vězeňská 5 prides itself on fresh *pesci* and *frutti di mare,* while the **Aldente Trattoria,** directly across the street, has a genuinely rustic Italian feel); and Afghan (**Ariana** at Rámová 6 serves up a taste of Central Asia at Czech prices). These five deserve special consideration:

Indian: **Indian Jewel,** in the Ungelt courtyard behind the

Týn Church, is the best place in Prague to find a full Indian menu that actually tastes Indian. Located in a pleasant, artfully restored courtyard, this is my choice for outdoor dining, with seriously executed subcontinental classics and good-value lunch specials (daily 11:00–23:00, Týn 6, tel. 222-310-156).

Thai: **Orange Moon** specializes in Thai curries, but you'll also find dishes from Myanmar (Burma) and India, served in a space delightfully decorated with artwork from Southeast Asia. This restaurant attracts a mixture of locals, expats, and tourists—as well as a mixture of wait-staff attitudes (daily 11:30–23:30, reservations recommended, Rámová 5, tel. 222-325-119).

Irish: **Molly Malone's Irish Pub,** hidden in a forgotten corner of the Jewish Quarter, may seem like a strange recommendation in Prague—home of some of the world's best beer—but it has the kind of ambience that locals (and few tourists) seek out. Molly Malone's has been the expat and local favorite for Guinness ever since the Velvet Revolution enabled the Celts to return to one of their homelands. Worn wooden floors, dingy walls, and the Irish manager transport you right into the heart of blue-collar Dublin— which is, after all, a popular place for young Czechs to find jobs in the high-tech industry (Sun–Thu 11:00–1:00 in the morning, Fri–Sat 11:00–2:00 in the morning, U Obecního Dvora 4, tel. 224-818-851).

Latin American: **La Casa Blů,** with cheap lunch specials, Mexican plates, Staropramen beer, and greenish *mojitos,* is your own little pueblo in Prague. It's one of the last student bastions in the Old Town—and one of the first bars in the city to go non-smoking. Painted in warm oranges and reds and guarded by creatures from Mayan mythology, La Casa Blů is packed nightly with guitar music and a fusion of Czechs and Chileans (Mon–Sat 11:00–23:00, Sun 14:00–23:00, on the corner of Kozí and Bílkova, tel. 224-818-270).

North American: **Bohemia Bagel** is hardly authentic— exasperated Czechs insist that bagels have nothing to do with Bohemia. Owned by an American, this practical café caters mostly to youthful tourists, with good sandwiches (100–125 Kč), a little garden out back, and Internet access (1.50 Kč/min). If homesick, you'll love the menu, with everything from Philly cheesesteaks to bacon and eggs (daily 7:00–24:00, Masná 2, tel. 224-812-560).

In the Jewish Quarter

These three eateries are well-located to break up a demanding tour of the Jewish Quarter—all within two blocks of each other on or near Široká (see map on page 69). Also consider the nearby ethnic eateries listed above.

Kolkovna, the flagship of a franchise owned by Pilsner

EATING

Urquell, is big and woody, yet modern, serving a fun mix of Czech and international cuisine—ribs, salads, cheese plates, and good beer (a bit overpriced but good energy, daily 11:00–24:00, across from Spanish Synagogue at V Kolkovně 8, tel. 224-819-701).

Franz Kafka Café, with a cool, dark, and woody interior strewn with historic photos of the ghetto and a few good sidewalk tables, is great for a relaxing salad, sandwich, snack, or drink (150-Kč salads, daily 10:00–21:00, one block from the cemetery at Široká 12).

Restaurace U Knihovny ("By the Library"), situated steps away from the City and National Libraries as well as the Pinkas Synagogue, is a favorite lunch spot for locals who work nearby. Their cheap daily lunch specials consist of seven imaginative variations on traditional Czech themes. The service is friendly and the stylish red-brick interior is warm. Smoking is not permitted during lunch (daily 11:00–23:00, on the corner of Veleslavínova and Valentinská, mobile 732-835-876).

Dining with an Old Town Square View

Restaurant u Prince Terrace, in the five-star U Prince Hotel facing the Astronomical Clock, is designed for foreign tourists. A sleek elevator takes you to its rooftop, where every possible inch is used to serve good food (international with plenty of fish) from their open-air grill. The view is arguably the best in town—especially at sunset. The menu is a fun but overpriced mix, with photos that make ordering easy. Being in such a touristy spot, waiters are experts at nicking you with confusing menu charges; don't be afraid to confirm exact prices before ordering. This place is also great for a drink at sunset or late at night (fine salads, 240–300-Kč plates, daily until 24:00, brusque staff, outdoor heaters when necessary, Staroměstské Náměstí 29, tel. 224-213-807—but no reservations possible).

Art Nouveau Splendor in the Municipal House

The Municipal House (Obecní Dům), the sumptuous Art Nouveau concert hall, has three restaurants: a café, a French restaurant, and a beer cellar (all at Náměstí Republiky 5). The dressy café, **Kavárna Obecní Dům,** is drenched in chandeliered, Art Nouveau elegance and offers the best value and experience here. Light, pricey meals and drinks come with great atmosphere and bad service (250-Kč three-course special daily for lunch or dinner, open daily 7:30–23:00, live piano or jazz trio 16:00–20:00, tel. 222-002-763). The fine and formal French restaurant in the next wing oozes Mucha elegance (700–1,000-Kč meals, daily 12:00–16:00 & 18:00–23:00, tel. 222-002-777). The beer cellar is overpriced and touristy (daily 11:30–23:00).

Cafés

Dripping with history, these places are as much about the ambience as they are about the coffee. Most cafés also serve sweets and light meals.

Grand Café Slavia, across from the National Theater (facing the Legií Bridge on Národní street), is a fixture in Prague, famous as a hangout for its literary elite. Today, it's tired and clearly past its prime, with an Art Deco interior, lousy piano entertainment, and celebrity photos on the wall. But its iconic status makes it a fun stop for a coffee—skip the food (daily 8:00–23:00, sit as near the river as possible, tel. 224-218-493). Notice the *Drinker of Absinthe* painting on the wall (and on the menu for 55 Kč)—with the iconic Czech writer struggling with reality.

Café Louvre is a longtime elegant favorite (opened in 1902) that still draws an energetic young crowd. From the big and busy Národní street, you walk upstairs into a venerable world of newspapers on sticks (including English) and waiters in vests and aprons. The back room has long been *the* place for billiard tables (100 Kč/hr). An English flier tells its history (200-Kč plates, 120-Kč two-course lunch offered 11:00–15:00, open daily 8:00–23:30, Národní 22—see map on page 123, tel. 224-930-949).

Grand Café Orient is just one flight up off busy Celetná street, yet a world away from the crush of tourism below. Located in the Black Madonna House, the café is upstairs, above the entrance to the Museum of Czech Cubism and fittingly decorated with a Cubist flair. With its stylish, circa-1910 decor toned to dark green, this space is full of air and light—and a good value as well (salads, sandwiches, great balcony seating, Mon–Fri 9:00–22:00, Sat–Sun 10:00–22:00, Ovocný Trh 19, at the corner of Celetná near the Powder Tower, tel. 224-224-240).

Café Montmartre, on a small street parallel to Karlova, combines Parisian ambience with unbeatable Czech prices for coffee (no food served). Dreamy Czech minds found their quiet asylum here after Grand Café Slavia (listed earlier) and other longtime favorites either closed down or became stuck in their past. The main room is perfect for discussing art and politics; the intimate room behind the courtyard is where you recite poetry to your date (Mon–Fri 9:00–23:00, Sat–Sun 12:00–23:00, Retězová 7, tel. 222-221-244).

Ebel Coffee House, next door to Café Montmartre, prides itself on its wide assortment of fresh brews from every coffee-bean-growing country in the world, inviting cakes, and a colorful setting that delights the mind as much as the caffeine (daily 9:00–22:00, Řetězová 3, tel. 224-895-788).

John & George Café, in the courtyard on the other side of the Lennon Wall, is a secluded spot serving raspberry drinks, fresh sandwiches, and Italian coffee next to a flower garden, an English lawn, and one of the oldest trees in Prague (daily 11:00–22:00, Velkopřevorské Náměstí 4, look for small gate at left end of Lennon Wall, entrance to indoor seating area is another 20 yards to the left, see map on page 100, tel. 257-217-736).

Teahouses

Many Czech people are bohemian philosophers at heart and prefer the mellow, smoke-free environs of a teahouse to the smoky, traditional beer hall. Young Czechs are much more interested in traveling to exotic destinations like Southeast Asia, Africa, or Peru than to Western Europe, so the Oriental teahouses set their minds in vacation mode.

While there are teahouses all over town, a fine example in a handy locale is Prague's original one, established in 1991. **Dobrá Čajovna** ("Good Teahouse"), just a few steps off the bustle of Wenceslas Square, takes you into a very peaceful world that elevates tea to an almost religious ritual. At the desk, you'll be given an English menu and a bell. Grab a seat and study the menu, which lovingly describes each tea. The menu lists a world of tea (very fresh, prices by the small pot), "accompaniments" (such as Exotic Miscellany), and light meals "for hungry tea drinkers." When you're ready to order, ring your bell to beckon a tea monk—likely a member of the Lovers of Tea Society (Mon–Sat 10:00–21:30, Sun 14:00–21:30, near the base of Wenceslas Square, opposite McDonald's at Václavské Náměstí 14, tel. 224-231-480).

For an actual taste of tea from Prague's newly emerging Chinese middle class (rather than from some Czech's dreams of the Orient), head to **Čajový Klub** ("Tea Club") **Cha Dao,** just opposite the Jerusalem Synagogue. Creatively run by a cultured man from Beijing, here you'll find red cherry-wood decor, expertly served tea, and the freshest green leaves in town (Mon–Fri 10:00–21:00, Sat 11:00–21:00, closed Sun, Jeruzalémská 10, tel. 222-721-072).

In the Little Quarter

These characteristic eateries are handy for a bite before or after your Prague Castle visit. For locations, see the map on page 100.

U Sedmi Švábů ("By the Seven Roaches") is an ever-more-touristy den where even the cuisine is medieval. Since America had not yet been discovered in the Middle Ages, you won't find any corn, potatoes, or tomatoes on the menu. The salty yellow things that come with the Krušovice beer are chickpeas. Carnivores thrive here: Try the skewered meats *(špíz u Sedmi Švábů)*, flaming beef *(flambák)*, or pork knuckle (daily 11:00–23:00, Janský Vršek 14, tel. 257-531-455).

U Osla v Kolébce ("By the Donkey in the Cradle") fills a peaceful courtyard just a minute off the touristy hubbub of Nerudova. The laid-back scene consists of two restaurants with nearly identical simple menus, dominated by tasty sausages and salads (daily 10:00–22:00, Jánský Vršek 8, below Nerudova, next door to U Sedmi Švábů, mobile 731-407-036).

U Hrocha ("By the Hippo"), a very authentic little pub packed with beer-drinkers and smoke, serves simple, traditional meals— basically meat starters with bread. Just below the castle near Little Quarter Square (Malostranské Náměstí), it's actually the haunt of many members of Parliament, which is located around the corner (daily 12:00–23:00, chalkboard lists daily meals in English, Thunovská 10, tel. 257-533-389).

Restaurace Rybářský Klub, on Kampa Island overlooking the river, is run by the Society of Czech Fishermen and serves one of the widest selections of freshwater fish in Prague. Dine on fish-cream soup, pike, trout, carp, or catfish under the imaginative artwork of Little Quarter painter Mr. Kuba. On warm evenings, late May through October, the Society fills its dock with tables—my choice for the best riverside dining in town (three-course meal for around 500 Kč, riverside menu not as extensive as indoor restaurant menu, daily 12:00–23:00, U Sovových Mlýnů 1, tel. 257-534-200).

In the Castle Quarter

To locate the following restaurants, see the map on page 100.

Villa Richter, at the end of the castle promontory and surrounded by newly replanted vineyards, consists of three classy restaurants: the ground-floor Piano Terra, with a menu built on Czech cooking (200–300-Kč entrées); the first-floor Piano Nobile, inspired by French and Italian cuisine (700-Kč entrées); and the outdoor Panorama Pergola, with superb views and ideal for an after-castle Caesar salad and glass of wine (all three open daily 10:00–23:00, Staré Zámecké Schody 6, tel. 257-219-079). Walk out of the castle gate near the Golden Lane, then turn left onto the path between the vines.

Klášterní Pivovar ("Monastery Brewery"), founded by an abbot in 1628 and reopened in 2004, has two large rooms, a pleasant courtyard, and typically unpleasant staff. This is the place to taste rare unpasteurized yeast beer, brewed on the premises. The wooden decor and circa-1900 newspaper clippings (including Habsburg Emperor Franz Josef's "Proclamation to My Nations," announcing the beginning of the First World War) evoke the era when Vienna was Europe's artistic capital, Prague was building its faux Eiffel Tower, and life moved much slower. To accompany the beer, try the beer-flavored cheese served on toasted black-yeast bread (daily 10:00–22:00, Strahovské Nádvoří 301, tel. 233-353-155). It's directly across from the entrance to the Strahov Library (not to be confused with the enormous, group-oriented Klášterní Restaurace next door, to the right).

Restaurace Nad Úvozem is hidden in the middle of a stair-case that connects Loretánská and Úvoz streets. This secret spot, which boasts super views of the Little Quarter and Petřín Hill, is one of the few places in the area for decent—but by no means exceptional—food in a secluded space. Try the roast beef in plum sauce (170 Kč). The service is slower when the restaurant is full, as the kitchen has limited space. Check your bill for "special charges" before you pay (daily 12:00–21:00; as you go down Loretánská watch for pans, scoops, and spoons hanging on chains on your right at #15; tel. 220-511-532). To discourage pub-goers from min-gling with diners, the beer here is terribly overpriced (69 Kč).

Hostinec u Černého Vola ("By the Black Ox") is a smoky, dingy old-time pub—its survival in the midst of all the castle splendor and tourism is a marvel. It feels like a kegger on the banks of the river Styx, with classic bartenders serving up Kozel beer (traditional "Goat" brand with excellent darks) and beer-friendly light meals. The pub is located on Loretánská (no sign outside, sniff for cigarette smoke and look for the only house on the block without an arcade, daily 10:00–22:00, English menu on request, tel. 220-513-481).

Malý Buddha ("Little Buddha") serves delightful food—especially vegetarian—and takes its theme seriously. You'll step into a mellow, low-lit escape of bamboo and peace, where you'll be served by people with perfect complexions and almost no pulse (Tue–Sun 13:00–22:30, closed Mon, non-smoking, between the castle and Strahov Monastery at Úvoz 46, tel. 220-513-894).

Espresso Kajetánka, just off Castle Square, has magnificent city views. It's a good, though overpriced, place for a drink or snack as you start or end your castle visit (daily 10:00–20:00, Ke Hradu, tel. 257-533-735).

Na Baště, more convenient but not as scenic, is in a garden through the gate to the left of the main castle entry. The outdoor seating, among Jože Plečnik's ramparts and obelisks, is the castle at its most peaceful (Sun–Thu 11:00–23:00, Fri–Sat 11:00–24:00, tel. 281-933-010).

Dining with Style

In Prague, a fancy candlelit dinner with fine wines and connois-seur-approved dishes costs more than most locals can afford—but it's still a bargain compared with similar restaurants in Paris or Dallas. I list only two such splurges: one aristocratic, Old World, and under the castle; one more modern, untouristy, and near the Old Town Square.

Restaurace David, with two little 18th-century rooms hiding on a small cobblestone street opposite the American Embassy in the Little Quarter, is my choice for a romantic splurge. The exquisite cuisine—a modern incarnation of traditional Czech dishes with French and European influences—ranges from game to roasted duck and liver. Your meal comes with the gourmet quotient of knives and fancy glasses and measured, no-nonsense service (most meals 600–1,000 Kč, open daily, Tržiště 21—see map on page 100, tel. 257-533-109).

Restaurant Červená Tabulka ("Red Chalkboard") is in a low, nondescript townhouse in a quiet neighborhood outside of the tourist circus. Sit in the dressy candlelit interior or on the quiet, breezy cobbled courtyard. Either way, there's not a dumpling in sight. The menu features modern international dishes with a focus on fish (fine 300-Kč plates and gourmet presentation). The wines are excellent and a great value (daily 11:30–23:00, Lodecká 4, tel. 224-810-401). To get to the restaurant from the Municipal House, cross Náměstí Republiky and turn right onto Truhlářská; it's 200 yards down the street on the corner of quiet Petrské Náměstí Square (see map on page 123).

Rubbing Elbows with Hip Locals Away from the Center, in Vinohrady and Žižkov

To locate the next four listings, see the map on page 123.

Café Medúza ("Café Jellyfish"), an authentic between-the-World-Wars café with plush sofas and pictures of 1930s movie stars, draws a crowd of dreamy young Czechs enjoying coffee, cigarettes, dark Svijany beer, and cheap lunch specials (daily 11:00–24:00, Belgická 17, Metro: Náměstí Míru; from Metro stop, walk down the street a bit and look for Belgická on your left; tel. 222-515-107).

At **Hlučná Samota** ("Loud Solitude"), the wooden floor and brick walls are dedicated to the great Czech writer Bohumil Hrabal. Though he never visited here, Hrabal would surely be inspired by the rich mix of Czech and Italian cuisine (including honey duck, spinach salmon, and Prague's own Staropramen beer). On a nice day, the good sidewalk seating is a pleasure (daily 11:00–23:00, Záhřebská 14, tel. 222-522-839).

Restaurace u Sadu, dark and dingy, is decorated with old typewriters, radios, meat grinders, skis, and sledges. It serves cheap beer and decent food indoors on aged green tablecloths or outside on wooden tables. The way that Czechs of all generations drink beer in this classic blue-collar pub hasn't changed a beat since the 1920s (daily 10:00–4:00 in the morning, on Škroupa Square below TV tower at Škroupovo Náměstí 5, tel. 222-727-072). The restaurant up in the TV tower itself is expensive, but it comes with a Sputnik's-eye view.

Hospůdka nad Viktorkou, named for this neighborhood's soccer team, is around the corner on Bořivojova street. This quintessential Žižkov pub features occasional live performances by local bands, a warm glassed-in terrace in the winter, and a little courtyard with a shady canopy of chestnut trees in the summer (Mon–Fri 15:00–1:00 in the morning, Sat–Sun 17:00–1:00 in the morning, English menu available, Bořivojova 79, tel. 222-722-557).

SHOPPING IN PRAGUE

Prague's entire Old Town seems designed to bring out the shopper in visitors. Puppets, glass, and ceramics are traditional. For information on VAT refunds (for purchases of more than 2,000 Kč—about $110) and customs regulations, see page 15.

Shopping Streets and Squares

Shop your way from the Old Town Square up Celetná street to the Powder Tower, then along Na Příkopě to the bottom of Wenceslas Square (Václavské Náměstí). The city center is tourist-oriented—most locals do their serious shopping in the suburbs.

Celetná is lined with big stores selling all the traditional Czech goodies. Tourists wander endlessly here, mesmerized by the window displays. Celetná Crystal, about midway down the street, offers the largest selection of affordable crystal. You can have the glass safely shipped home directly from the shop.

Náměstí Republiky (Republic Square) boasts Prague's newest and biggest mall, Palladium (Sun–Wed 9:00–21:00, Thu–Sat 9:00–22:00). It's hidden behind a pink Neo-Romanesque facade and the brown steel-and-glass 1980s department store Kotva (Anchor), an obsolete beast on the verge of extinction (Mon–Fri 9:00–20:00, Sat–Sun 10:00–18:00).

Na Příkopě has a couple of good modern malls. The best is Slovanský Dům (daily 10:00–20:00, Na Příkopě 22), where you'll wander deep past a 10-screen multiplex into a world of classy restaurants and designer shops surrounding a peaceful, park-like inner courtyard. Another modern mall is Černá Růže (daily 10:00–20:00, Na Příkopě 12), with a great Japanese restaurant around a small garden. Next door is Moser, which has a museum-like crystal showroom upstairs. The Galerie Myslbek, directly across the street, has fancy stores in a space built to Prague's scale.

Czech Puppets

The first puppets were born on the Indian subcontinent and soon found their way to Europe and Southeast Asia. Czechs have treasured the art of puppets for centuries; at times of heavy German influence in the 18th century, traveling troupes of puppeteers kept the Czech language and humor alive in the countryside. While the language of "legitimate theater" had to be German, Czech was tolerated if it came out of a puppet's mouth.

Until recently, most grandfathers felt obliged to bequeath to their grandsons an assembly of their own linden-wood-carved designs. The power of puppetry peaked between 1938 and 1989, when the Czechs were ruled by a series of puppet governments. Today, Špejbl and Hurvínek, who have their own permanent stage in Prague, are the greatest Czechs for kids from Japan to Patagonia. Filmmaker Jan Švankmajer (see page 301) is turning wooden characters into Oscar-winning film stars.

Most marionettes sold in the tourist shops in Prague and Český Krumlov are meant as souvenirs. It takes a rare artist to turn pieces of wood into nimble puppets, and prices for these can reach into the thousands of dollars. But given that puppets have a glorious past and vibrant present in the Czech Republic, even a simple jester, witch, or Pinocchio can make a thoughtful memento of your Czech adventure.

Národní Třída (National Street) is less touristy and lined with some inviting stores. The big Tesco department store in the middle sells anything you might need, from a pin for a broken watchband to a swimsuit (generally daily 9:00–21:00, Národní Třída 26).

Crystal and Garnets

Crystal: Along with shops on Celetná and Na Příkopě, a small square just off the Old Town Square, Malé Náměstí, is ringed by three major crystal retailers (generally open daily 10:00–20:00): Moser, Rott Crystal, and Crystalex (which claims to have "factory-direct" prices, at #6 on the square).

Garnets: This extraordinary stone of fiery red color, with unique refractive—some claim even curative—properties, is found only in Bohemia. The characteristic design of garnet jewelry, with the gems overwhelming the metal setting, became popular in the 1890s and remains so today. Although garnet jewelry is sold in most crystal shops, the Turnov Granát Co-op has the largest selection (with shops at Dlouhá 30 and Panská 1, www.granat.eu). It oversees its own mining and represents more than 300 traditional goldsmiths and jewelers. If you buy garnet jewelry, make sure to ask your vendor for a certificate of authenticity—many shops sell glass imitations.

Bookstores

Anagram Bookshop, in the Ungelt courtyard behind the Týn Church, professes that of all the ways of acquiring books, writing them yourself is the most praiseworthy. While you won't be asked to leave a bit of yourself here, you will find books in English on a wide range of topics (Mon–Sat 10:00–20:00, Sun 10:00–19:00, Týn 4, tel. 224-895-737).

V Ráji, next to Maisel Synagogue in the Jewish Quarter, is the flagship store of a small publishing house dedicated to books about Prague. They offer an assortment of photo publications, fairy tales, and maps (Maiselova 12, tel. 222-326-925).

Kiwi Map Store, near Wenceslas Square, is one of Prague's best sources for maps (Mon–Fri 9:00–19:00, Sat 9:00–14:00, closed Sun, Jungmanova 23, tel. 224-948-455).

For CDs and DVDs, see the next chapter.

SHOPPING

ENTERTAINMENT IN PRAGUE

Prague booms with live and inexpensive theater, classical music, jazz, and pop entertainment. Everything is listed in several monthly cultural events programs (free at TIs) and in the *Prague Post* newspaper (60 Kč at newsstands).

You'll be tempted to gather fliers as you wander through the town. Don't bother. To really understand all your options (the street Mozarts are pushing only their concerts), drop by a **Via Musica** box office. There are two: One is next to Týn Church on the Old Town Square (daily 10:30–19:30, tel. 224-826-969), and the other is in the Little Quarter across from the Church of St. Nicholas (daily 10:30–18:00, tel. 257-535-568). The event schedule posted

on the wall clearly shows everything that's playing today and tomorrow, including tourist concerts, Black Light Theater, and marionette shows, with photos of each venue and a map locating everything (www.viamusica.cz).

Ticketpro sells tickets for the serious concert venues and most music clubs (daily 8:00–12:00 & 12:30–16:30, Rytířská 31, between Havelská Market and Estates Theater; also has a booth in Tourist Center at Rytířská 12, daily 9:00–20:00; English-language reservations tel. 296-329-999).

Consider buying concert tickets directly from the actual venues. You won't save money, but more of your money will go to the musicians.

Locals dress up for the more "serious" concerts, opera, and

Entertainment in Prague

ENTERTAINMENT

❶ Via Musica Box Office
❷ Ticketpro
❸ Ta Fantastika Theater
❹ Image Theater
❺ National Theater &
   Laterna Magica
❻ Estates Theater
❼ To State Opera
❽ St. Martin in the Wall
❾ Church of St. Nicholas
❿ Klementinum (Chapel of Mirrors)
⓫ Rudolfinum
⓬ Municipal House (Smetana Hall)
⓭ Roxy Club
⓮ Agharta Jazz Club
⓯ Lucerna Music Bar
⓰ Reduta Jazz Club
⓱ Bontonland CD Shop
⓲ Terryho Ponožky DVD Shop

Mozart, Smetana, Dvořák, and More

The three major composers connected with Prague—Mozart, Smetana, and Dvořák—all have museums dedicated to their lives and work in the city.

During his frequent visits to Prague, Austrian **Wolfgang Amadeus Mozart** (1756–1791) stayed with his friends in the beautiful, small Neoclassical Villa Bertramka, now the Mozart Museum. Surrounded by a peaceful garden, the villa preserves the time when the Salzburg prodigy felt more appreciated in Prague than in Austria. Intimate concerts are held some afternoons and evenings, either in the garden or in the small concert hall (110 Kč, daily April–Oct 9:30–18:00, Nov–March 9:30–17:00, Mozartova 169, Praha 5; from Metro: Anděl, it's a 10-min walk—head to Hotel Mövenpick and then go up alley behind hotel; tel. 257-317-465, www.bertramka.cz).

A statue of **Bedřich Smetana** (1824–1884), the father of Czech classical music, is seated in front of his museum, listening intently to the rapids of the Vltava River near the Charles Bridge (50 Kč, Wed–Mon 10:00–17:00, closed Tue, Novotného Lávka, Praha 1, tel. 224-229-075). Like Richard Wagner in Germany, Smetana aimed to stir the Romantic nationalist spirit of the Czechs. His finest work, the cycle of symphonic poems called *My Country (Má Vlast),* was inspired by places and myths important to the Czech people. *Vltava,* the most beautiful of the poems, is played to get your attention as trains arrive in stations.

Antonín Dvořák (1841–1904) is the Czech Republic's best-

ballet, but many tourists wear casual clothes—as long as you don't show up in shorts, sneakers, or flip-flops, you'll be fine.

Black Light Theater

A kind of mime/modern dance variety show, Black Light Theater has no language barrier and is, for many, more entertaining than a classical concert. Unique to Prague, Black Light Theater originated in the 1960s as a playful and mystifying theater of the absurd. These days, aficionados and critical visitors lament that it's becoming a cheesy variety show, while others are uncomfortable with the sexual flavor of some acts. Still, it's an unusual theater experience that most enjoy. Shows last about an hour and a half. Avoid the first four rows, which get you so close that it ruins the illusion. Each theater has its own spin on what Black Light is supposed to be:

Ta Fantastika is traditional and poetic, with puppets and a little artistic nudity (*Aspects of Alice* nightly at 21:30, 650 Kč, reserved seating, near east end of Charles Bridge at Karlova 8, tel. 222-221-366, www.tafantastika.cz).

known composer. For three years, Dvořák directed the National Conservatory in New York, during which time he composed his most famous work, the *New World Symphony (Z Nového Světa)*. Dvořák's advice to his students was to look for inspiration in America's authentic melodies (African American spirituals and Native American music) rather than in European models. Dvořák's gentle opera of a water nymph, *Rusalka,* is considered by many to be the best Czech opera and is often performed in Prague's National Theater. The Dvořák Museum is located in Villa America. Designed by Prague's most prolific Baroque architect, K. I. Dientzenhofer, Villa America—the first of his structures to be built in the city—was purchased by the Dvořák Society in 1932 (50 Kč, Tue–Sun 10:00–17:00, closed Mon, Ke Karlovu 20, Praha 2, see map on page 76, tel. 224-923-363).

Two other important composers from Czech lands are the moderns Mahler and Janáček. **Gustav Mahler** (1860–1911), a Jew from Jihlava (see page 221), was a pioneer of atonal music. His best works are *Symphony No. 1: Titan* and *The Song of the Earth,* both inspired by the sounds of the Moravian woods and fields. **Leoš Janáček** (1854–1928), arguably the most original and least accessible Czech composer, was stimulated by language—its flow and abrupt pauses. He's known for his *Symphonietta* and *Lachian Dances (Lašské Tance),* as well as the operas *Cunning Little Vixen (Příhody Lišky Bystroušky)* and my favorite, *Jenůfa*—both perennials in the National Theater's repertoire.

Image Theater has more mime and elements of the absurd, with shows including *Clonarium, Fiction,* and *The Best of Image:* "It's precisely the fact that we are all so different that unites us" (shows nightly at 18:00 and 20:00, 480 Kč, open seating—arrive early to grab a good spot, just off Old Town Square at Pařížská 4, tel. 222-314-448, www.imagetheatre.cz).

Laterna Magica, in the big, glassy building next to the National Theater, mixes Black Light techniques with film projection into a multimedia performance that draws Czech audiences (*Wonderful Circus, Rendezvous, Graffiti,* shows Mon–Sat at 20:00, no shows on Sun, 680 Kč, tel. 224-931-482, www.laterna.cz).

The other Black Light theaters advertised around town aren't as good.

Concerts

Each day, six to eight classical concerts designed for tourists fill delightful Old World halls and churches with music of the crowd-pleasing sort: Vivaldi, Best of Mozart, Most Famous Arias, and works by the famous Czech composer Antonín Dvořák. Concerts typically cost 400–1,000 Kč, start anywhere from 13:00 to 21:00, and last about an hour. Typical venues include two buildings on the Little Quarter Square (the Church of St. Nicholas and the Prague Academy of Music in Liechtenstein Palace), the Klementinum's Chapel of Mirrors, the Old Town Square (in a different Church of St. Nicholas), and the stunning Smetana Hall in the Municipal House (see below). The artists vary from excellent to amateurish.

A sure bet is the jam session held every Monday at 17:00 at **St. Martin in the Wall,** where some of Prague's best musicians gather to tune in and chat with one another (400 Kč, Martinská street, just north of the Tesco department store in the Old Town).

The **Prague Castle Orchestra,** one of Prague's most entertaining acts, performs regularly on Castle Square. This trio—Josef on flute, Radek on accordion, and Zdeněk on bass—plays a lively Czech mélange of Smetana, swing, old folk tunes, and 1920s cabaret songs. Look for them if you're visiting the castle (see page 107), and consider picking up their fun CD. They're also available for private functions (mobile 603-552-448, josekocurek@volny.cz).

Serious music-lovers should consider Prague's two top ensembles: The **Czech Philharmonic,** which performs in the classical Neo-Renaissance Rudolfinum (on Palachovo Náměstí, in the Jewish Quarter on the Old Town side of Mánes Bridge); and the **Prague Symphony Orchestra,** based in the gorgeous Art Nouveau Municipal House. Both orchestras perform in their home venues about five nights a month from September through June. Most other nights these spaces are rented to agencies that organize tourist concerts of varying quality for double the price (as described earlier). Check first whether your visit coincides with either ensemble's performance.

One advantage of a tourist concert is that it allows you to experience music in one of Prague's best venues on the night of your choice. This is especially worth considering if you want to enjoy classical music in the Municipal House when the Symphony Orchestra isn't in town—but make sure your concert takes place in the building's Smetana Hall rather than in the much smaller Grégr Hall.

The Czech Philharmonic ticket office is at the Rudolfinum, on the right side under the stairs (250–1,000 Kč, open Mon–Fri 10:00–18:00, and until just before the show starts on concert days, tel. 227-059-352, www.ceskafilharmonie.cz, info@cfmail.cz).

The Prague Symphony Orchestra ticket office is on the right side of the Municipal House, on U Obecního Domu street opposite Hotel Paris (Mon–Fri 10:00–18:00, tel. 222-002-336, www .fok.cz, pokladna@fok.cz). A smaller selection of tickets is also available in the information office inside the Municipal House.

You'll find tickets for tourist concerts advertised and sold on the street in front of these buildings. Both the Rudolfinum and the Municipal House also act as chief venues for the Prague Spring, Prague Proms, and Dvořák's Prague music festivals (see "Festivals," later).

Opera and Ballet

The **National Theater** (Národní Divadlo, on the New Town side of Legií Bridge)—with a must-see Neo-Renaissance interior (see page 86)—is best for opera and ballet (shows from 19:00, 300–1,000 Kč, tel. 224-912-673, www.nationaltheatre.cz). The **Estates Theater** (Stavovské Divadlo) is where Mozart premiered and personally directed many of his most beloved works (see page 61). *Don Giovanni, The Marriage of Figaro,* and *The Magic Flute* are on the program a couple of times each month (shows from 20:00, 800–1,400 Kč, between the Old Town Square and the New Town on a square called Ovocný Trh, tel. 224-214-339, www.estates theatre.cz). A handy ticket office for both of these theaters is in the little square (Ovocný Trh) behind the Estates Theater, next to a pizzeria.

The **State Opera** (Státní Opera) operates on a smaller budget and is also not as architecturally rewarding as the National Theater (shows at 19:00 or 20:00, 400–1,200 Kč, buy tickets at the theater, 101 Wilsonova, on the busy street between the main train station and Wenceslas Square, see map on page 76, tel. 224-227-693, www .opera.cz).

Festivals

World-class musicians are in town during these musical festivals: **Prague Spring** (last three weeks of May, www.festival.cz), **Prague Proms** (July–Aug, www.pragueproms.cz), and the newer **Dvořák's Prague** (Aug–Sept, www.dvorakovapraha.cz).

Music Clubs

Young locals keep Prague's many music clubs in business. Most clubs are neighborhood institutions with decades of tradition, generally holding only 100–200 people. Live rock and Bob Dylan–style folk are what younger generations go for. A number of good jazz clubs attract a diverse audience, from ages 18 to 80. In the last decade, ethnic music has also become hugely popular: Roma (Gypsy) bands, Moravian poets, African drummers, Cuban boleros, and Moroccan divas often sell out even the largest venues. You can buy tickets at the club, or, for most places, at the Ticketpro offices (see page 146). If you like jazz, I've listed some fine options; avoid the Jazzboat (advertised by commission-hungry hotels), which has mediocre musicians and high prices.

Buying Czech CDs and DVDs

While the most convenient places to get CDs of classical music are the shops in the **Via Musica** and **Rudolfinum** ticket offices, you'll find a larger selection and other genres at the huge **Bontonland** music and video store, at the bottom of Wenceslas Square (enter from the mall with the big *Kenvelo* sign on the outside). In the classical music section, you'll find many interpretations of Czech works. For the best renditions, look for music performed by the Czech Philharmonic.

For contemporary, lighter music, get a CD by Čechomor (*Metamorphosis* is their best). This band, which began by playing traditional Czech music at weddings and funerals, synthesized the sound of folk ballads and has since become one of the most popular groups in the country. Jiří Pavlica and Hradišťan keep the music of Moravia alive; Věra Bíla and Ida Kellarová capture the lively spirit of the Roma (Gypsies). Some cool Czech contemporary groups are Psí Vojáci, Neočekávaný Dýchánek, and Už Jsme Doma.

A handy place to get DVDs of Czech and European films is the tiny **Terryho Ponožky** shop in the Světozor mall just off Wenceslas Square (Mon–Sat 10:00–20:00, closed Sun; enter from Vodičkova 41, the store is on the right next to the Světozor Cinema; tel. 224-946-829, www.terryhoponozky .cz). Be warned that many European discs don't work on American DVD players (though they usually play on computers just fine).

In the Old Town

Roxy, a few blocks from the Old Town Square, features live bands from outside the country twice a week—anything from Irish punk to Balkan brass. On other nights, the floor is taken over by experimental DJs spinning a healthy dose of Japanese pop (concerts start at 20:00, disco at 22:00, cover from 100 Kč, Mon free, easy to book online and pick up tickets at the door, Dlouhá 33, tel. 224-826-296, www.roxy.cz).

Agharta Jazz Club, which showcases some of the best Czech and Eastern European jazz, is just steps off the Old Town Square in a cool Gothic cellar. Inside they also sell a wide selection of Czech jazz CDs (shows start nightly at 21:00, 200-Kč cover, Železná 16, tel. 222-211-275, www.agharta.cz).

In the New Town

Lucerna Music Bar, at the bottom of Wenceslas Square, is popular for disco nights. Friday and Saturdays are the "1980s Party," featuring the silly pop songs of the last years under communism, when spineless Czech pop stars took the easy route to success instead of coming up with thoughtful lyrics that could have furthered the cause of freedom. The scene is a big, noisy dance hall with a giant video screen. Young and trendy, the Lucerna is cheap, and even older tourists mix in easily (music nightly from 21:00, about 100-Kč cover, in the basement of Lucerna Gallery, Vodičkova 36, tel. 224-217-108).

The small **Reduta Jazz Club,** with cushioned brown sofas stretching along mirrored walls, will launch you straight into the 1960s classic jazz scene. The top Czech jazzmen—Stivín and Koubková—regularly perform. Bill Clinton played the sax here (live jazz every night from 21:00, on Národní street next to Café Louvre, tel. 224-933-486, www.redutajazzclub.cz).

In the Little Quarter
Baráčnická Rychta, with a gymnasium-like hall, saw many great polka parties in the 1920s. Since then, rock has replaced waltz, but the place still feels like a village dancehall, complete with flags of bakers' and butchers' guilds and black-and-white photos of the proud Austro-Hungarian landlords. It's a great scene if the hall is full, but less popular bands look a bit lost in the large space. Try the yeasty and strong Svijany beer here (3 shows weekly starting at 20:00 or 21:00, arrive earlier to get a seat at a table, 150-Kč cover, on Tržiště, tucked away from tourists and out-of-town Czechs in a small courtyard directly across from the US Embassy, see map on page 100, tel. 257-532-461, www.baracnickarychta.cz).

In Žižkov
This hip neighborhood, below the Žižkov TV tower (Metro: Jiřího z Poděbrad), has Prague's highest concentration of cool pubs.

Palác Akropolis is *the* home of Czech independent music. Originally a 1920s movie theater, in the 1990s it was turned into a chill-out lounge, a literary café, and two halls that offer a mix of concerts, disco, and theater (advance ticket sales at café, Mon–Fri 10:00–24:00, Sat–Sun 16:00–24:00, corner of Kubelíkova and Fibichova, under TV tower, Metro: Jiřího z Poděbrad, see map on page 123, tel. 296-330-913, www.palacakropolis.cz).

Sports
Prague's top sports are soccer (that's "football" here) and hockey. Surprisingly, the Czechs are a world power in both. You'll find the latest schedules for games in the *Prague Post* newspaper (soccer—usually late Sat, Sun, or Mon afternoons Feb–May and Aug–Nov; hockey—Tue, Fri, and Sun nights Sept–April). With the exception of matches between the top two Czech soccer teams (Sparta and Slavia), both soccer and hockey games are rarely sold out—just show up at the stadium 15 minutes before the game starts.

Soccer

The Czech national soccer team reached the finals of the 1996 European Cup and the semifinals of the 2004 European Cup, but they were eliminated in the first round of the 2006 World Cup and lost to Turkey in the final first round of the 2008 European Cup (Turkey scored 3 goals in the last 10 minutes of play).

Within the Czech Republic, the two oldest and by far most successful soccer clubs are the bitter Prague rivals Sparta and Slavia. Sparta's 1970s-era stadium is at Letná (behind the giant Metronome ticking above the river in Letenské Park). Slavia's brand-new stadium is in Vršovice (12 stops from the National Theater on tram #22). While Sparta has historically harvested more trophies, Slavia won the last two league titles. Neither team has, however, qualified for Europe's top club competition—the Champions League—in the last three years, having to settle for the less prestigious and less profitable Europa League. The clubs' mounting losses highlight the degree to which the Czech Republic lacks—in professional sports as much as in other sectors of the economy—the financial muscle to challenge the European biggies. Elimination from the Champions League means a huge economic loss, invariably solved by the sale of the team's most promising player to a big club abroad days after the defeat.

The other Prague team in the top Czech league is the Bohemians. Although the club operates on a fraction of the budget of the two big S's, its fans make up for the lack of skill on the pitch with a die-hard attitude in the stands and beyond—several years ago, fans donated enough money to save the club from bankruptcy.

Hockey

Between 1996 and 2005, the Czech national hockey team won five annual world championships. In 1998, it won the gold medal at the Olympic Games in Nagano, Japan. However, the golden generation is retiring—though Dominik Hašek, now in his 40s, still plays for his hometown team—and younger players have been slow to fill the gap. In each of the last three world championships, the Czech team lost in the quarterfinals.

Currently, more than 50 Czech players take the ice in America's NHL. Think of Jaromír Jágr, one of the NHL's all-time leading scorers. (In a "Beckham move," Jágr switched in 2008 from the New York Rangers to the newly founded, Russian oil–fueled Continental Hockey League, with a contract that ensures he remains the world's best-paid hockey player and the league's most coveted star.)

Sparta and Slavia, the traditional Czech soccer powers, also have hockey teams, but the rivalry is less intense, as the teams from smaller towns are more than their equals. Slavia plays in the state-of-the-art Sazka Arena built for the 2004 World Hockey Championships (right at the Českomoravská Metro stop).

Back in the old days, ice hockey was the only battleground on which Czechoslovaks could seek revenge on their Russian oppressors (ice hockey is also the most popular sport in Slovakia). The hockey rink is still where Czechs are proudest about their nationality. If you are in town in May during the hockey championships, join locals cheering their team in front of a giant screen on the Old Town Square, as well as on other main squares around the country.

Sports on the Old Town and Wenceslas Squares

ENTERTAINMENT

When there are sporting events of great interest (such as hockey and soccer championships), the Old Town Square plays host to

huge TV screens, beer and bratwurst stands, and thousands of Czechs. The warm and friendly scene is like a big family gathering. Some fans lie on the cobblestones up front and focus on the game, while others mill around in the back and just enjoy the party.

Major running and biking events (such as the Prague International Marathon at the beginning of May) finish in the Old Town Square. The two biggest sporting events on Wenceslas Square are the Prague Pole Vault and a cycling competition that uses the square as a lap. The bottom of Wenceslas Square is sometimes set up for soccer, basketball, and beach volleyball tournaments. Both squares are also used for pop and folk concerts and for political rallies. These events are fine opportunities to feel the pulse of the Czech capital.

PRAGUE CONNECTIONS

Centrally located Prague is a logical gateway between Western and Eastern Europe. It's also the hub for trains and buses in the Czech Republic—from here, rail lines and expressways fan out like spokes on a wheel. This chapter covers arrivals and departures by train, bus, plane, and car.

By Train

Prague has two international train stations. The **Main Station** (Hlavní Nádraží) serves trains from Frankfurt, Munich, Salzburg, Vienna, and Kraków; most trains within the Czech Republic, including the high-speed SC Pendolino trains; and the DB-ČD bus from Nürnberg. The secondary **Holešovice Station** (Nádraží Holešovice, located north of the river) handles all trains from Berlin and Budapest—though these may move to the Main Station as early as 2010.

Upon arrival, get money. Both stations have ATMs (best rates) and an exchange bureau (rates are generally bad; consider waiting until you can get to a bank in town to exchange money). Then buy a good map and confirm your departure plans.

Main Train Station (Hlavní Nádraží)

The station's creepy two-floor hall is the work of communist architects who expanded a classy building to make it big, then painted it the compulsory dreary gray with reddish trim. Originally named for Emperor Franz Josef, the station was later renamed for President Woodrow Wilson (see the commemorative plaque in the main exit hall leading away from the tracks), because his promotion of self-determination led to the creation of the free state of Czechoslovakia in 1918. Under the communists (who weren't big fans of Wilson), it was bluntly renamed Hlavní Nádraží—"Main Station." But a renovation is underway: Drunks and homeless people are being pushed out, and an Italian firm is currently refitting the station to Western European standards, filling every empty space with shiny clothing boutiques and convenience stores.

Three parallel tunnels connect the tracks to the arrival hall. The first area you reach (with low ceilings) has an exchange office and signs pointing to the "official" taxi stand to the right (avoid these rip-off cabbies—explained later). If you turn around and go up another floor, you'll find the **Fantova Kavárna,** a decrepit Art Nouveau cupola café. Outside is the stop for the **AE bus** to the airport (buy 50-Kč ticket from driver, runs every half-hour daily 5:35–22:05, 40 min) and the **DB-ČD bus** to Nürnberg.

Straight down from the low-ceilinged area is the main hall, where you'll find four Metro entrances in the center (two for each direction). A Raiffeisen Bank **ATM** is along the right wall (with your back to the tracks, look for a black-and-yellow sign).

At **Wasteels travel office** (in the main hall—with your back to tracks, it's to the right under the stairs), Jaromír and Jaroslav offer reasonably friendly assistance. You can drop by here upon arrival to get a transit ticket without using the ATM (they take euro coins), and to confirm and buy your outbound train tickets. They can help you figure out international train connections, and they sell train tickets to anywhere in Europe—with domestic stopovers if you like—along with tickets for fast local trains and cheap international phone cards (no commission; Mon–Fri 9:00–17:00 or later, Sat 9:00–12:00 & 13:00–16:00, closed Sun, tel. 972-241-954, www.wasteels.cz). You can even leave your bags here for a short time.

The **Czech Railways ticket office** is in the middle of the main hall under the stairs. Its tiny ČD Travel center, on the left as you enter the main office, sells both domestic and international tickets, and is your best bet for information in English (Mon–Fri 9:00–17:00, closed Sat–Sun, tel. 972-241-861, www.cdtravel.cz). The regular ticket desks are faster if you already know your schedule and destination, but attendants are unlikely to speak English. You can also wait and get your tickets later at their more centrally located downtown branch (at Na Příkopě 31; see map on page 53).

Touristpoint (with your back to the tracks, it's on your right under the stairs) arranges last-minute rooms in hotels and pensions, as well as car rentals, sightseeing tours, and adrenaline experiences. They accept any currency and credit cards, and also sell maps and international phone cards. A phone is available for calling a cab—the driver will come to the desk to get you (daily 8:00–22:00, tel. 224-946-010, www.touristpoint.cz, info@touristpoint.cz).

Getting from the Main Station to Your Hotel: Even though

CONNECTIONS

the Main Station is basically downtown, it can be a little tricky to get to your hotel. The biggest challenge is that the **taxi** drivers at the train station's run-down "official" stand are a gang of no-neck mafia thugs who wait around to charge an arriving tourist five times the regular rate. (This is likely to change as station reconstruction progresses.) To get an honest cabbie, exit the station's main hall through the big glass doors, then cross 50 yards through a park to Opletalova street (a few taxis are usually waiting in front of the Hotel Chopin, on the corner of Jeruzalémská street). You can also call a taxi from the Touristpoint office, described earlier (AAA Taxi—tel. 14-014; City Taxi—tel. 257-257-257). Before getting into a taxi, always confirm the maximum price to your destination, and make sure the driver turns on the meter—it should cost no more than 300 Kč to get to your hotel. For more pointers on taking taxis, see page 42.

A better option may be to take the **Metro.** It's dirt cheap and easy, with frequent departures. Once you're on the Metro, you'll wonder why you would ever bother with a taxi (inside the station's main hall, look for the red *M* with two directions: Háje or Letňany). To purchase tickets from the automated machine by the Metro entrance, you'll need Czech coins (get change at a newsstand or grocery). Validate your ticket in the yellow machines *before* you go down the stairs to the tracks. To get to hotels in the Old Town, catch a Háje-bound train to the Muzeum stop, then transfer to the green line (direction: Dejvická) and get off at either Můstek or Staroměstská; these stops straddle the Old Town. For information on Prague's public transit, see page 40.

Most hotels I list in the Old Town are within a 20-minute **walk.** Exit the station into a small park. Walk across the park, and cross the street on the other side of it. Head down Jeruzalémská street to Jindřišská Tower and tram stop, walk under a small arch, then continue slightly to the right down Senovážná street. To the left at the end of the street, you'll see the Powder Gate, the grand entry into the Old Town. Alternatively, Wenceslas Square in the New Town is a 10-minute walk—exit the station, cross the park, and walk to the left along Opletalova street.

The nearest **tram** stop is to the right as you exit the station (about 200 yards). Tram #9 to takes you to the neighborhood near the National Theater and the Little Quarter, but is not useful for most hotels in the Old Town.

Holešovice Train Station (Nádraží Holešovice)

This station, slightly farther from the center, is suburban mellow. The main hall has all the services of the Main Station in a more compact area. On the left are international and local ticket windows (open 24 hours), an information office, and an AVE (AEX) office with last-minute accommodations (daily 12:00–20:00, tel. 972-224-660). On the right is an uncrowded café with Internet access (1 Kč/min, daily 8:00–19:30). Two ATMs are immediately outside the first glass doors, and the Metro is 50 yards to the right (follow signs toward *Vstup*, which means "entrance"; it's three stops to Hlavní Nádraží—the Main Station—or four stops to the city-center Muzeum stop). Taxis and trams are outside to the right (allow 300 Kč for a cab to the center).

Train Connections

Direct overnight trains connect Prague to Amsterdam, Frankfurt, and Zurich; several trains leave daily from Munich, Berlin, and Vienna. From the East, Prague is connected by convenient night trains with Budapest, Kraków, and Warsaw. Be sure you know which of Prague's two major stations your train uses—the Main Station (Hlavní Nádraží) or the Holešovice Station (Nádraží Holešovice). For more rail travel tips, see "Transportation" in the appendix.

Schedules: You'll find handy Czech train and bus schedules at www.idos.cz; for trains, you can also check out Germany's all-Europe timetable at http://bahn.hafas.de/bin/query.exe/en.

Tickets: You can make express or international reservations and buy tickets at the conveniently located **Czech Railways' travel center** in the Broadway Mall between Na Příkopě and Celetná streets, near the Powder Tower (see map on page 53). Ask whether discounts are available for your journey, as the rail company has a complex scheme of special offers (Mon–Fri 9:00–17:00, closed Sat–Sun; quick, helpful, English-speaking staff; inside the mall passageway by T.G.I. Friday's, look for blue neon *ČD* sign on your right, Na Příkopě 31; tel. 972-243-071, www.cdtravel.cz, prodej @cdtravel.cz). While Czech rail journeys are covered by various **railpasses**—including the Eurail Global pass, Eurail Selectpass, and various more focused regional passes—simply buying point-to-point tickets for domestic journeys is generally more affordable. For details on railpasses, see www.ricksteves.com/rail.

From Prague by Train to: Konopiště Castle (train to **Benešov,** hourly, 1 hr, then 30-min walk to castle), **Karlštejn** (2/hr, 40 min, then a 20-min walk to castle), **Křivoklát** (hourly, 1.5 hrs, transfer in Beroun), **Kutná Hora** (11/day, 1 hr, more with change in Kolín), **Terezín** (train to Bohušovice station, nearly hourly, 1–1.5 hrs; then 5-min taxi or bus ride), **Český Krumlov** (8/day, 1/day direct, 4 hrs—bus is faster, cheaper, and easier), **České Budějovice** (almost hourly, 2.5 hrs), **Třeboň** (7/day, 2.5 hrs, transfer at Veselí nad Lužnicí—get off at Třeboň–Lázně station, not Třeboň–Město), **Telč** (3/day, 4–5 hrs, requires 2 changes; bus is better), **Třebíč** (nearly hourly, 4–5 hrs, transfer in Brno; bus is better), **Slavonice** (5/day Mon–Fri, 3/day Sat–Sun, 2–3-hr bus to Telč, then 1-hr train to Slavonice), **Olomouc** (at least hourly, 2–3 hrs; use Olomouc for connections to **Wallachia**), **Valtice** (hourly, 4 hrs, 1 transfer), **Břeclav** (with connections on to **Mikulov Wine Region**—see page 262; 9/day direct, 3 hrs, most from Holešovice station), **Brno** (every 2 hrs direct, 2.5 hrs, more with changes), **Moravský Krumlov** (go to Brno, then take hourly 45-min train; bus from Prague to Brno is faster), **Berlin** (6/day, 4.5–5 hrs), **Munich** (2/day direct, 6.25 hrs; 6 more/day with express bus to Nürnberg then train to Munich, 5.25 hrs total; no night train), **Frankfurt** (almost hourly, 7–8.25 hrs), **Vienna** (5/day direct, 4–4.5 hrs, more with 1 change, 5–6 hrs), **Budapest** (3/day, 7 hrs; more with 2–3 changes, 8.5 hrs; 1 night train, 7.5 hrs), **Kraków** (1/day direct, 7.5 hrs; 4 more/day with 1–2 changes, 8.25 hrs; 1 night train, 9.5 hrs), **Warsaw** (1/day direct, 8.75 hrs; 3 more/day with 1–2 changes, 8.5–10 hrs; 1 night train, 10 hrs).

By Bus

Prague's main bus station is at Florenc, east of the Old Town (Metro: Florenc). But some connections use other stations, including Roztyly (Metro: Roztyly), Na Knížecí (Metro: Anděl), the Nádraží Holešovice train station (Metro: Nádraží Holešovice), or the main train station (Metro: Hlavní Nádraží). As with trains, be sure to confirm which station your bus uses.

From Prague by Bus to: Terezín (hourly, 50 min, departs from Nádraží Holešovice train station), **Český Krumlov** (7/day, 3.5 hrs, some leave from Florenc station, others leave from Na Knížecí station or Roztyly station), **Třeboň** (2/day, 2.5 hrs), **Telč** (5/day Mon–Fri, 3/day Sat–Sun, 2–3 hrs, some from Roztyly station; more with a transfer in Jihlava, 3 hrs total), **Třebíč** (7/day, 2.5 hrs, some from Roztyly station), **Lány** (6/day, fewer on weekends, 40 min), **Brno** (2/hr from Florenc station, 2.5 hrs), **Nürnberg,** Germany (every 2 hrs, 3.75 hrs, from main train station).

By Plane

Prague's modern, tidy, low-key **Ruzyně Airport,** located 12 miles (about 30 min) west of the city center, is as user-friendly as any airport in Western Europe or the US. The new Terminal 2 serves destinations within the EU except for Great Britain (no passport controls); Terminal 1 serves Great Britain and everywhere else. The airport has ATMs (avoid the change desks), desks promoting their transportation services (such as city transit and shuttle buses), kiosks selling city maps and phone cards, and a tourist service with few printed materials. Airport info: tel. 220-113-314, operator tel. 220-111-111.

Getting from the Airport to Downtown: It's easy. Leaving either airport terminal, you have five options, listed below from cheapest to priciest:

Dirt Cheap: Take bus #119 to the Dejvická Metro station, or #100 to the Zličín Metro station (20 min), then take the Metro into the center (26 Kč, info desk in airport arrival hall).

Budget: Take the airport express (AE) bus to the main train station (50 Kč, runs every half-hour daily 5:35–22:05, 40 min, look for the *AE* sign in front of the terminal and pay the driver, www .czech-transport.com). From the main train station, you can take the Metro, hire a taxi, or walk to your hotel, following the arrival instructions on page 34. However, note that Náměstí Republiky— served by the minibus shuttle described next—is a much handier place to arrive than the main train station, and well worth the negligible extra cost.

Moderate: Take the Čedaz minibus shuttle to Náměstí Republiky, at the entrance to the Old Town. The shuttle drops you off in front of the Czech Airlines office next to Hotel Marriott on V Celnici street (pay 120 Kč directly to driver, daily 7:30–19:00, 2/ hr, info desk in arrival hall).

Expensive: Take a Čedaz minibus directly to your hotel, likely with a couple of stops en route (480 Kč for a group of up to four, tel. 221-111-111). Look for a dispatcher on the curb in front of the arrival hall.

Splurge: Catch a taxi. Cabbies wait at the curb directly in front of the arrival hall. Airport taxi cabbies are honest but more expensive. Carefully confirm the total price before getting in. It should be a fixed rate of 600–700 Kč, with no meter.

By Car with a Driver

Mike's Chauffeur Service is a reliable, family-run company with fair and fixed rates around town and beyond. Friendly Mike's motto is, "We go the extra mile for you" (round-trip fares, with waiting time included, guaranteed through 2010 with this book: Český Krumlov-3,800 Kč, Terezín-1,900 Kč, Karlštejn-1,800 Kč, plus 5 percent gas surcharge, 4 percent surcharge for credit-card payment; these prices for up to 4 people, minivan for up to 6 and brand-new minibus for 7 also available; tel. 241-768-231, mobile 602-224-893, www.mike-chauffeur.cz, mike.chauffeur@cmail .cz). On the way to Krumlov, Mike will stop at no extra charge at Hluboká Castle or České Budějovice, where the original Bud beer is made.

Mike also offers "Panoramic Transfers" to **Vienna** (7,000 Kč, depart Prague at 8:00, arrive Český Krumlov at 10:00, stay up to 6 hrs, 1-hr scenic Czech riverside-and-village drive, then a

2-hr autobahn ride to your Vienna hotel, maximum 4 people), to **Budapest** (8,900 Kč, 2 hrs to Český Krumlov, then 1-hr scenic drive to Linz, followed by 5–6 hrs on expressway to Budapest), and to **Kraków** (8,900 Kč, with a stop at Auschwitz). Check Mike's website for special deals on last-minute transfers.

BEYOND
PRAGUE

DAY TRIPS

Prague has plenty to keep a traveler busy, but don't overlook the enjoyable day trips in the nearby Bohemian countryside. Within an hour of Prague (in different directions), you'll find a rich medieval town, a sobering concentration camp, and three grand castles. Descriptions and ratings follow:

▲▲**Kutná Hora**—Once home to the world's largest silver mine, this down-to-earth city is known for its opulent cathedral, built with riches from the mining bonanza, and a creepy church decorated with human bones.

▲▲**Terezín Concentration Camp**—This walled town served as an internment camp for Jews during World War II. Nearby, the town of Litoměřice offers charm and an opportunity to reflect on the camp.

▲**Konopiště** and ▲**Karlštejn**—Two of the country's most popular castles, both provide a good look at the Czech version of this European medieval architectural form. Konopiště has a better interior; Karlštejn has a better exterior.

Křivoklát—One of the purest Gothic castles in the country, it's a less touristy alternative to the other two castles. The nearby village of Lány, with the grave of Tomáš Masaryk, is a modern-day pilgrimage site for Czech patriots.

Kutná Hora

Kutná Hora (KOOT-nah HO-rah) is a refreshingly authentic town of 20,000, on top of what was once Europe's largest silver mine. In its heyday, the mine was so productive that Kutná Hora was Bohemia's "second city" after Prague. Much of Europe's standard coinage was minted here. By about 1700, the mining and minting petered out, and the city slumbered. Once rich, then ignored, Kutná Hora is now newly appreciated by tourists looking for a handy side-trip from Prague. Visitors are charmed by the wonderfully preserved town and its interesting sights: the fine St. Barbara's Cathedral, the fascinating silver mine, and the eerie Sedlec Bone Church.

Kutná Hora, unlike dolled-up Český Krumlov, is a typical

Czech town. The shops on the main square cater to locals, and the factory between the Sedlec Bone Church and the train station—since the 1930s, the biggest tobacco processor in the country—is now Philip Morris' headquarters for Central Europe. After touristy Prague, Kutná Hora is about as close to quintessential Czech life as you can get.

Getting to Kutná Hora

The town is 40 miles east of Prague. Direct trains from Prague's Main Station stop at Kutná Hora's Main Station, two miles from the town center (11/day, 1 hr; other trains are slower and require transfer in Kolín). From there, a local train shuttles visitors to Sedlec Station (near the Sedlec Bone Church), then to the central Město Station (near the rest of the sights).

In Prague, make sure to buy a ticket to the Kutná Hora Město Station rather than its Main Station—the price is nearly the same, and this gives you the flexibility to get off and on at any of the three Kutná Hora stations.

Planning Your Time

For the most efficient visit, visit the Sedlec Bone Church first. At Kutná Hora's Main Station, transfer to the local train or walk 10 minutes to the church. After your visit, ride the Bone Church's tourist minivan to St. Barbara's Cathedral in the town center. From the cathedral, walk to the silver museum and reserve your spot on the next English-language tour (or call the museum ahead to find out the schedule and reserve).

Orientation to Kutná Hora

Tourist Information

The main TI is on **Palackého Náměstí,** housed in the same building as the Alchemy Museum (April–Sept daily 9:00–18:00; Oct–March Mon–Fri 9:00–17:00, Sat–Sun 9:00–16:00; tel. 327-512-378, www.kutnahora.cz). It offers Internet access and also rents bicycles (220 Kč/day, mobile 605-802-874).

A small TI kiosk, with handy WCs, is in front of the **cathedral;** you can also hire a local guide here. Reserve ahead if you can (500 Kč/hr Tue–Sun, no tours Mon, tel. 327-516-710, mobile 736-485-408, infocentrum@kh.cz).

Sights in Kutná Hora

St. Barbara's Cathedral (Chrám Sv. Barbory)—The cathedral was founded in 1388 by miners, who dedicated it to their patron. The dazzling interior celebrates the town's sources of wealth, with

DAY TRIPS

frescoes featuring mining and minting. Even the Renaissance vault—a stunning feat of the two Gothic geniuses of Prague, Matyáš Rejsek and Benedict Ried—is decorated with miners' coats of arms. The artistic highlight is the Smíšek Chapel to the right of the altar. The late-Gothic frescoes—*The Arrival of the Queen of Sheba, The Trial of Trajan,* and especially the fresco under the chapel's window depicting two men with candles—are the only remaining works of a Dutch-trained master in Gothic Bohemia (50 Kč, daily 9:00–18:00 in summer, shorter hours off-season).

As you exit the cathedral, you'll see the Baroque Jesuit college on your left (currently being converted into an art gallery). Jesuits arrived here in 1626 with a mission: to make the Protestant population Catholic again. The statues of saints on the artificial terrace in front of the college were inspired by the statues on Charles Bridge in Prague.

Hrádek and the Czech Museum of Silver—At this museum, located in Kutná Hora's 15th-century castle, you'll see an exhibit on mining and an intriguing horse-powered winch that hoisted 2,000 pounds of rock at a time out of the mine. Then you'll don a miner's coat and helmet and climb deep into the mine for a wet, dark, and claustrophobic 45-minute tour of the medieval shafts that honeycomb the rock beneath the town (110 Kč, April–Oct Tue–Sun 10:00–18:00, closed Mon and Nov–March, tours generally every half-hour, tel. 327-512-159, www.cms-kh.cz). Try to time your visit to join an English-language tour (ask for Mr. Matuška, a charming retired miner). You can try calling ahead (the day before or the morning of your visit) to ask when English tours are scheduled—wait through the Czech recording, ask to speak with an English-speaker, and reserve a slot. Otherwise, drop by the museum soon after you arrive in Kutná Hora to find out the schedule and reserve.

Stone Fountain (Kamenná Kašna)—Because of intensive mining under the town, Kutná Hora has always struggled with the problem of obtaining clean drinking water. Water was brought to town by a sophisticated system of water pipes and stored in large tanks. At the end of the 15th century, the architect Rejsek built a 12-sided, richly decorated Gothic structure over one of these tanks. Although no longer functioning, the fountain survives unchanged—the only structure like it in Bohemia (on the square called Rejskovo Náměstí).

Stone House (Kamenný Dům)—Notice the meticulous detail in the grape leaves, branches, and animals on this house's facade and up in its gable. Talented Polish craftsmen delicately carved the brittle stone into what was considered a marvel of its time. Skip the boring museum of local arts and crafts inside (40 Kč, daily 10:00–17:00, Radnická 183).

Kutná Hora

DAY TRIPS

Alchemy Museum—The only one of its kind in the Czech Republic, this place is run by a gracious, eccentric Englishman who (upon request) will personally guide you into the surprisingly deep medieval cellars of this otherwise unassuming house. There you'll find a laboratory dedicated to the pursuit of *prima materia* (primal matter). The English descriptions do a good job explaining the goals and methods of alchemy and the fate of its failed practitioners. The rare Gothic tower in the rear of the house is set up as an alchemist's study (complete with ancient books), looking much as it did when a prince used this vaulted space in his quest to purify matter and spirit (50 Kč, daily April–Oct 10:00–17:00, Nov–March 10:00–16:00, on the main square in the same building as the TI, tel. 327-511-259, mobile 603-308-024, www.alchemy.cz).

Upstairs from the TI is another quirky museum, featuring a collection of baby strollers from the Victorian era to the present.

To Main Train Station & Bone Church (in Sedlec)

Aneské Náměstí

KUTNÁ HORA MĚSTO STATION

❶ Hotel u Vlašského Dvora, Hotel Garni & Restaurace Donna-U Žlutého Kola
❷ Pivnice Dačický Restaurant
❸ Dobrá Čajovna Teahouse
❹ Piazza Navona Restaurant

VOCELOVA
NA LÁVKÁCH
NA NÁMĚTÍ
ŠTEFÁNIKOVA
POTOČNÍ
LIBUŠINA
TYLOVA
UHELNÁ
RUDNÍ
K BĚLIDLU
SOKOLSKÁ
KONÁČOVA
❸
MĚSTSKÉ SADY
ŽIŽKOVA BRÁNA
ZA OCTÁRNOU
ČÁSLAVSKÁ
U LAZARA
ZAHRADNÍ
MACHÁČKOVO NÁBŘEŽÍ
POBŘEZNÍ
Creek
Vrchlice

200 Meters
200 Yards

DAY TRIPS

Italian Court (Vlašský Dvůr)—This palace, located on the site where Czech currency was once made, became Europe's most important mint and the main residence of Czech kings in the 1400s. Today, it hosts a museum on minting and local history. The entry fee gets you into the main Gothic hall (now a wedding chamber) and the Art Nouveau–decorated St. Wenceslas Chapel (70 Kč, April–Sept daily 9:00–18:00, shorter hours Oct–March, Havlíčkovo Náměstí). Neither the museum nor the building itself—largely a 19th-century imitation of the former palace—is particularly interesting. The flower-filled square in front, on the other hand, is worth a look...

Havlíček Square (Havlíčkovo Náměstí)—The monuments on this square are a Who's Who of important Czech patriots.

The statue in the middle of the square (and the square's namesake) is **Karel Havlíček** (1821–1856), the founder of Czech political journalism. From Kutná Hora, Havlíček ran an influential magazine highly critical of the Habsburg government. In 1851, he was forced into exile and detained for five years in the Tirolean Alps under police surveillance. His integrity is reflected by the quote inscribed on the statue: "You can try to bribe me with favors, you can threaten me, you can torture me, yet I will never turn a traitor." His motto became an inspiration for generations of Czech intellectuals, most of whom faced a similar combination of threats and temptations. Havlíček (whose name means "little Havel") was much revered in the 1970s and 1980s, when the *other* Havel (Václav) was similarly imprisoned for his dissent.

The bronze statue in front of the Italian Court honors the founder of Czechoslovakia, **Tomáš Garrigue Masaryk** (1850–1937; see page 106). The brief inscription on the back of the pedestal recounts the statue's history, which parallels the country's troubled 20th-century history: erected by Kutná Hora townspeople on October 27, 1938 (the eve of the 20th anniversary of Czech independence); torn down in 1942 (by occupying Nazis, who disliked Masaryk as a symbol of Czech independence); erected again on October 27, 1948 (by freedom-loving locals, a few months after the communist coup); torn down again in 1957 (by the communists, who considered Masaryk an enemy of the working class); and erected once again on October 27, 1991. Notice that the Czechs, ever practical, have left a blank space below the last entry....

On the wall to the left of the gate, you'll find a small bronze tablet covered with barbed wire. This is an unassuming little **memorial** to the victims of communist misrule and torture.

Walk down the steps into a little park, and then turn right to reach a great viewpoint. It overlooks the tent-shaped roof of the cathedral and the scenic valley below. You might want to take a rest on nearby benches under some linden trees—and think about those whom the memorial commemorates.

Market (Tržiště)—This double row of stalls selling fake Nike shoes and cheap jeans is as much a part of Czech urban life today as farmers markets were in the past. The stalls are often run by Vietnamese immigrants, the Czech Republic's third-largest minority (after Slovaks and Poles). Many came here in the 1970s as part of a communist solidarity program that sent Vietnamese workers to Czech textile factories. They learned the language, adapted to the environment, and, after 1989, set off on a road to entrepreneurial success that allowed them to bring over friends and relatives (Mon–Fri 7:30–16:45, shorter hours Sat, closed Sun, near Stone House).

Near Kutná Hora

Sedlec Bone Church (Kostnice u Sedlci)—Located a mile away from the center of town, in Sedlec, this little church looks normal on the outside. But inside, the bones of 40,000 people decorate the walls and ceilings. The 14th-century plagues and 15th-century wars provided all the raw material necessary for the creepily creative monks who made these designs. Those who first placed these bones 400 years ago wanted viewers to remember that the earthly church is a community of both the living and the dead, a countless multitude that will one day stand before God. Later bone-stackers were more interested in design than theology...as evidenced by the chandelier that includes every bone in the human body (50 Kč, daily April–Sept 8:00–18:00, March and Oct 9:00–17:00, Nov–Feb 9:00–16:00, tel. 327-561-143, www.kostnice.cz).

The Bone Church runs a **tourist minivan** that can shuttle you around town (35 Kč/person, requires three passengers or else pay the 105-Kč minimum fee, April–Sept 9:00–18:00, Oct–March 9:00–17:00, inquire at the desk, mobile 733-551-011).

Sleeping in Kutná Hora

Although one day is enough for Kutná Hora, staying overnight saves you money (hotels are much cheaper here than in Prague) and allows you to better savor the atmosphere of a small Czech town.

$$ Hotel u Vlašského Dvora and **Hotel Garni** are two newly renovated townhouses run by the same management. Furnished in a mix of 1930s and modern style, the hotels come with access to a fitness center and sauna. Hotel Garni is slightly nicer (Db-1,200

DAY TRIPS

Sleep Code

(18 Kč = about $1, country code: 420)
S = Single, **D** = Double/Twin, **T** = Triple, **Q** = Quad, **b** = bathroom, **s** = shower only. Unless otherwise noted, prices include breakfast.

To help you sort easily through these listings, I've divided the rooms into three categories based on the price for a standard double room with bath:

   $$$ Higher Priced—Most rooms 1,500 Kč or more.
   $$ Moderately Priced—Most rooms between
                      1,000–1,500 Kč.
   $ Lower Priced—Most rooms 1,000 Kč or less.

Kč, a few steps off main square at Havlíčkovo Náměstí 513, tel. 327-515-773, www.vlasskydvur.cz).

Eating in Kutná Hora

Pivnice Dačický has made a theme of its namesake, a popular 17th-century author who once lived in the house. Solid wooden tables rest under perky illustrations of medieval town life, and a once-local brew, also named after Dačický, flows from the tap. They serve standard Czech fare, as well as excellent game and fish. While its regulars still come here for the cheap lunch specials, during tourist season the crowd is mostly international. Service can be slow when a group arrives (daily 11:00–23:00, Rakova 8, tel. 327-512-248, mobile 603-434-367).

Dobrá Čajovna Teahouse also offers the chance to escape— not to medieval times, but to a Thai paradise. Filled with tea cases, water pipes, and character, this place is an ideal spot to dawdle away the time that this ageless town has reclaimed for you (daily 14:00–22:00, Jungmannovo Náměstí 16, mobile 777-028-481).

Restaurace Donna-U Žlutého Kola serves the fastest, tastiest Czech dishes in town, attracting a local crowd. There's a long menu in English, but the lunch specials are only listed on a separate sheet in Czech. When the weather's nice, sit in the shady courtyard behind the restaurant (open daily, lunch specials until 15:00, on Havlíčkovo Náměstí, right above Hotel Garni).

Piazza Navona features irritating English-language advertising ("the only true Italian restaurant in town"), but it still draws loyal customers thanks to its decent food and superb location on the main square (open daily).

Terezín Concentration Camp

Terezín (TEH-reh-zeen), an hour by bus from Prague, was originally a fortified town named after Habsburg Empress Maria Theresa (it's called "Theresienstadt" in German). It was built in the 1780s with state-of-the-art, star-shaped walls designed to keep out the Prussians. In 1941, the Nazis removed its 7,000 inhabitants and brought in 60,000 Jews, creating Terezín Concentration Camp. Ironically, the town's medieval walls, originally meant to keep

Petr Ginz, Young Artist and Writer

Born in 1928 to a Jewish father and non-Jewish mother, Prague teenager Petr Ginz excelled at art and was a talented writer who penned numerous articles, short stories, and even a science-fiction novel. Petr was sent to the concentration camp at Terezín in 1942, where he edited the secret boys' publication *Vedem (We Are Ahead),* writing poetry and drawing illustrations, and paying contributors with food rations he received from home.

Some of Petr's artwork and writings were preserved by Terezín survivors and archived by the Jewish Museum in Prague. In 2003, Ilan Ramon, the first Israeli astronaut and the son of a Holocaust survivor, took one of Petr's drawings—titled *Moon Country*—into space aboard the final, doomed mission of the space shuttle Columbia.

The publicity over the Columbia's explosion and Petr's drawing spurred a Prague resident to come forward with a diary he'd found in his attic. It was Petr's diary from 1941 to 1942, hidden decades earlier by Petr's parents and chronicling the year before the teen's deportation to Terezín. *The Diary of Petr Ginz* has since been published in more than 10 languages.

In the diary, Petr matter-of-factly documented the increasing restrictions on Jewish life in occupied Prague, interspersing the terse account with dry humor. In the entry for September 19, 1941, Petr wrote, "They just introduced a special sign for Jews" and drew the Star of David. He continued, "On the way to school I counted 69 'sheriffs,'" referring to people wearing the star.

Petr spent two years at Terezín before being sent to Auschwitz, where he died in a gas chamber. He was 16.

Germans out, were later used by Germans to keep the Jews in.

This was the Nazis' model "Jewish town," a concentration camp dolled up for propaganda purposes. Here, in this "self-governed Jewish resettlement area," Jewish culture seemed to thrive, as "citizens" put on plays and concerts, published a magazine, and raised their families. But it was all a carefully planned deception, intended to convince Red Cross inspectors that the Jews were being treated well. Virtually all of Terezín's Jews (155,000 over the course of the war) ultimately ended up dying either here (35,000) or in extermination camps farther east.

One of the notable individuals held at Terezín was Viennese artist Friedl Dicker-Brandeis. This daring woman, a leader in the Bauhaus art movement, found her life's calling in teaching children freedom of expression. She taught the kids in the camp to distinguish between the central things—trees, flowers, lines—and

To Litoměřice

FORMER PROTECTORATE
BOHEMIA AND MORAVIA

FORMER
DEUTSCHES
REICH

To Ústí
nad Labem

TEREZÍN
TOWN

PRAŽSKÁ

MÁCHOVA

HUSOVA

FUČÍKOVA

5 KVĚTNA

FORMER BORDER
SUDETENLAND

Nám.
Česko.
Armády

WATER
GATE

28 ŘÍJNA

PALACKÉHO

VODARENSKÁ

DLOUHÁ

TYRŠOVA

FORTRESS WALLS

N

400 Meters

400 Yards

Vegetable
Plots

To Bohušovice

peripheral things, such as the conditions of the camp. In 1944, Dicker-Brandeis volunteered to be sent to Auschwitz after her husband was transported there; she was killed a month later.

Of the 15,000 children who passed through Terezín from 1942 to 1944, fewer than 100 survived. The artwork they created at Terezín is a striking testimony to the cruel horror of the Holocaust. In 1994, Hana Volavková, a Terezín survivor and the director of the Jewish Museum in Prague, collected the children's artwork and poems in the book *I Never Saw Another Butterfly*. Selections of the Terezín drawings are also displayed and well-described in English in Prague's Pinkas Synagogue (see page 70).

The most well-known of the cultural activities that took place at Terezín was the children's opera *Brundibár*. Written just before the war, the anti-Fascist opera premiered secretly in Prague at a

Terezín

FORTRESS WALLS

SMALL FORTRESS

National Cemetery

To Prague

New Ohře River

Sights
❶ Main Square
❷ Museum of the Ghetto
❸ Magdeburg Barracks
❹ Dry Moat
❺ Small Fortress Entry Gate
❻ Model Cells, Washroom &
   Gavrilo Princip's Cell
❼ Art Museum
❽ Execution Ground & Mass Grave
❾ Hidden Synagogue
❿ Railway Tracks & Columbarium
⓫ Crematorium, Jewish Cemetery
   & Soviet Memorial

Other
⓬ Bus To/From Prague
⓭ Cafeteria
⓮ Parkhotel Restaurant

DAY TRIPS

time when Jewish activities were no longer permitted. From 1943 to 1944, the play, performed in Czech, ran 55 times in the camp. After the war it was staged internationally (including a successful run on Broadway) and was recently rewritten in the US as a successful children's book.

Today, Terezín is an unforgettable day trip from Prague for those interested in touring a concentration camp memorial and museum. Allow three to six hours to see the entire camp. With more time, stop in the nearby attractive town of Litoměřice (described later) for lunch before returning to Prague.

Getting to Terezín

The camp is about 40 miles northwest of Prague. It's most convenient to visit Terezín by bus (described next) or tour bus (see page 46).

Buses to Terezín leave hourly from Prague's Holešovice train station (Nádraží Holešovice, on Metro line C). When you get off the Metro (coming from the city center), head toward the front of the train, go upstairs, turn right, and walk to the end of the corridor. You'll see bus stands directly ahead, outside the station. The Terezín bus departs from platform 7 (direction: Litoměřice, buy ticket from driver).

You'll arrive in Terezín 50 minutes later at the public bus stop on the main square, around the corner from the Museum of the Ghetto. Some buses also stop earlier, by the Small Fortress. The driver and fellow passengers may tell you to get off there, but my self-guided tour works best if you begin at the stop in town (after the bus passes a field of crosses on your right and travels across the river).

For schedules, see www.idos.cz—you want "Terezín LT" (be sure to check the return schedule, too; for details on getting back to Prague, see "Terezín Connections," later).

Orientation to Terezín

Cost, Hours, Information: The 200-Kč combo-ticket includes all parts of the camp. Most sights, including the Museum of the Ghetto, Magdeburg Barracks, and Hidden Synagogue, are open daily April–Oct 9:00–18:00, Nov–March 9:00–17:30. The Columbarium and Crematorium are closed Sat. The Crematorium opens at 10:00 year-round and closes at 16:00 Nov–March, and the Small Fortress opens at 8:00 year-round and closes at 16:30 Nov–March. Tel. 416-782-225, mobile 606-632-914, www .pamatnik-terezin.cz.

Self-Guided Tour

Terezín Concentration Camp

On this visit, you'll see Terezín town and the Small Fortress, which is a long half-mile to the east across the river.

The bus from Prague drops you off at Terezín town's spacious ❶ **main square** (Náměstí Československé Armády). Picture the giant circus tent and barbed-wire fence that stood on this square for two years during the war. Inside, Jewish workers boxed special motors for German vehicles being used on the frigid Soviet front. As part of year-long preparations for the famous Red Cross visit (which lasted all of six hours on June 23, 1944), the tent and fence were replaced by flower beds (which you still see on the square today) and a pavilion for outdoor music performances.

Walk around the corner to the ❷ **Museum of the Ghetto,** where you can buy the Terezín combo-ticket (note movie show-times). You'll find two floors of exhibits about the development of the Nazi's "Final Solution" and a theater showing four excellent films. One film documents the history of the ghetto, and two focus on children's art in the camp. The fourth is made up of clips from *Der Führer schenkt den Juden eine Stadt (The Führer Gives a City to the Jews)* by Kurt Gerron. Gerron, a Berlin Jew, was a 1920s movie star who appeared with Marlene Dietrich in *Blue Angel*. Deported to Terezín, Gerron in 1944 was asked by the Nazis to produce a propaganda film. The resulting film depicts healthy (i.e., recently arrived) "Jewish settlers" in Terezín happily viewing concerts, playing soccer, and sewing in their rooms—yet an unmistakable, deadly desperation radiates from their pallid faces. The only moment of genuine emotion comes toward the end, when a packed room of children applauds the final lines of the popular anti-Nazi opera *Brundibár:* "We did not let ourselves down, we chased the nasty Brundibár away. With a happy song, we won it all." Even the Nazis were not fooled: Gerron and his wife were shipped to Auschwitz and the film was never shown in public.

To learn more about living conditions in the camp, walk over to the ❸ **Magdeburg Barracks.** Peek inside the large courtyard (you'll recognize it as the "soccer stadium" in Gerron's film), then continue upstairs. On the right are rooms reproducing the camp cabaret stage and exhibits documenting the prisoners' literary, musical, and theatrical activities. On the left is a meticulously restored camp dormitory, complete with three-tiered beds, eyeglasses, dolls, chess boards, and sewing kits.

As you exit from the barracks (notice the high-water marks from the 2002 flood on the house opposite), turn right around the corner and walk 100 yards to a brick gate. As you cross a bridge over a ❹ **dry moat,** imagine the moat filled with plots of vegetables grown by starving Jews for well-fed SS officers.

Turn left and walk along the moat. The top of the fortification walls on the other side were once equipped with benches and pathways. When you reach the main road, turn right across the New Ohře River (the original course of the river was diverted here when Terezín was built) and walk past the vast cemetery to the ❺ **Small**

Fortress—you'll see its black-and-white-striped gate. From 1940 to 1945, this fortress functioned as a Gestapo prison, through which 32,000 inmates passed (of whom nearly 10 percent died here)—chiefly members of the Czech resistance and communists. The 1,500 Jews interned here were treated with particular severity.

Inside the gate, turn left toward the notorious *Arbeit Macht Frei* sign (a postwar replica), painted above an arched gate. In the courtyard behind, you will first find ❻ **model prison cells.**

The **washroom** in the left corner was built solely for the purpose of fooling Red Cross inspectors. Turn the faucets: No pipes were ever installed to bring in water. The **shower room** farther to the left, on the other hand, was used to fool the Jews. Here they got used to the idea of communal bathing, so they wouldn't be suspicious when they were later taken to similar-looking installations at Auschwitz. (There were no gas chambers at Terezín—most of the deaths here were caused by malnutrition and disease and, to a lesser extent, executions.)

Before the Nazis, the Small Fortress was used as a prison by the Austrian monarchy. The little courtyard preserves the cell of the most famous prisoner from that time, Bosnian Serb **Gavrilo Princip,** whose assassination of Archduke Franz Ferdinand and his wife Žofie in 1914 sparked World War I (see page 182). Princip died here in 1918 of tuberculosis.

Return through the *Arbeit Macht Frei* gate, then turn left into a large courtyard. On your right is an ❼ **art museum** featuring two floors of paintings by prominent Czech artists, with themes of camp life and the Spanish Civil War. Farther to the left is a path leading to the ❽ **execution ground** and a **mass grave** of the victims.

At this point you could head to the handy cafeteria by the entry gate to the Small Fortress and take a break. The wood-and-metal chandeliers inside were produced by Jewish workers for the SS officers who once dined in these two rooms.

With more time, consider continuing your tour in Terezín town with the less-frequented sights that lie along or just off a main road called Dlouhá. At Dlouhá 17, look for the unique ❾ **hidden synagogue,** the only one of the camp's eight synagogues that survived. Although entry is included with your combo-ticket, you may need to ring the bell for the guard to open the door. Inside you'll find a courtyard; the bakery that used to be here hid the synagogue behind it. The atmospheric space is still inscribed with two Hebrew captions, which are translated as "May my eyes behold, how You in compassion return to Sinai," and "If I forget Jerusalem, may my tongue rot and my right arm fall off." These words indicate that the prayer room belonged to a congregation of

Zionists (advocates of a Jewish state), who, one would expect, were specifically targeted by the Nazis.

Continue down Dlouhá to the Bohušovice gate. On the ground, look for the remnants of ❿ **railway tracks.** In the early

years of the camp, Jews arrived at the train station in the nearby town of Bohušovice and then had to walk the remaining two miles to Terezín. This was too public a display for the Nazis, who didn't want locals to observe the transports and become suspicious, so the Jewish prisoners at Terezín were forced to construct a railway line that led right to Terezín...and back out again to Auschwitz.

As you exit the walled-in area, on the right you will find Jewish and Christian ceremonial halls and the main morgue; on the left is a **Columbarium,** or storage space for funerary urns. The Germans originally promised that the urns would be properly reburied after the war, but in 1945, to erase evidence, the ashes of Terezín victims (stored mainly in cardboard boxes) were dumped into the New Ohře River.

Continue along the road, then turn left past bucolic vegetable plots and fruit gardens to reach the ⓫ **Crematorium, Jewish Cemetery,** and a **Memorial to Soviet Soldiers.** Days before Terezín was liberated (on May 8, 1945), an epidemic of typhus spread through the camp. In the weeks after the war ended, scores of Soviet soldiers and medical workers who tried to contain the epidemic died, along with hundreds of former prisoners.

Our tour ends here. As you ponder Terezín, remember the message of all such memorials: Never again.

Eating in Terezín

In Terezín town, the **Parkhotel Restaurant** is the most elegant place for lunch (daily 10:00–22:00, around the block from the Museum of the Ghetto at Máchova 163, tel. 416-782-260).

The Small Fortress has a **cafeteria.** But avoid the stale sandwiches in the Museum of the Ghetto's dingy basement cafeteria, where most tour guides inexplicably shove their clients.

Terezín Connections

The bus for **Prague** leaves from Terezín's main square. If the return bus doesn't fit your schedule, consider taking a taxi from Terezín to the Bohušovice station (5 min from Terezín, trains to Prague depart nearly hourly, 1–1.5 hrs). There is no taxi service from Bohušovice to Terezín, making the train a good option only for the return journey. If you're continuing from Terezín to **Dresden,** Germany, take the train from Bohušovice to Ústí, then switch to the international express train.

Near Terezín: Litoměřice

With a bustling, beautifully restored Renaissance square, Litoměřice (lee-TOH-myer-zheet-seh, pop. 26,000), located three

miles north of Terezín, is a perfect lunch spot to lift your spirits after the bleakness of the camp. During the communist era, Litoměřice had the only seminary in the country. Today, there are still two huge Baroque churches here. Linger on the main square, Mírové Náměstí, and experience the life of this friendly, untouristy Czech town.

If arriving by bus from Terezín, get off at the first stop after the bridge; from here it's a two-minute, slightly uphill walk to the main square. From the square, several small streets filled with bakeries and convenience shops radiate outward. The onion-shaped tower is south, and the higher part of the square is due west. Stroll around and get lunch on the square (see "Eating in Litoměřice," later). After lunch, climb up the onion-shaped tower of the **Town Hall** (the guide in the tower loves to talk), but skip the uninteresting museum on the square.

The short street next to the Town Hall leads onto the city walls, with good views. The statue at the viewpoint depicts the Romantic poet **Karel Hynek Mácha** (1810–1836), who wrote the

most famous Czech poem, "Máj." He died in Litoměřice. In 1939, his body was ceremonially exhumed and transferred to the Slavín cemetery atop Prague's Vyšehrad hill. Mácha became a symbol of the irrepressible Czech spirit, stirring Czech nationalism during the occupations of the Nazis first, then the communists after. In November 1989, demonstrating students were headed for the grave of Mácha when they suddenly decided that they were tired of the communists...and thus started the Velvet Revolution.

KAREL HYNEK
MÁCHA

Getting to Litoměřice: Buses from Prague to Terezín continue on to Litoměřice (buses returning to Prague stop first in Litoměřice, then Terezín). Easier yet, it's a five-minute **taxi** trip between the camp and Litoměřice (about 150 Kč). The museum's ticket office will be happy to call a cabbie for you (such as Mr. Poláček, based in Terezín, tel. 606-833-480).

Eating in Litoměřice

The most convenient spot is the Czech fast-food joint **Joka,** which serves standard, ready-to-eat meals and good soups daily (at the top/northwest corner of the square). You can get a sandwich, sit on the benches under trees by the fountain, and enjoy the view of the Renaissance-era townhouses. **Salva Guarda** is a bit stuffy and service is slow, but it's a decent sit-down option (daily 11:00–23:00, under the arches at the bottom/southeast corner of the square).

Litoměřice Connections

To reach Litoměřice's bus station for the trip back to Prague (hourly, 1 hr), walk east on the main street (Dlouhá) down from the square to an intersection, cross it, and continue in the same direction along Na Kocandě street (an easy 10-min walk). The train station is nearby (though buses to Prague are preferable, as the train requires a transfer).

DAY TRIPS

Konopiště Castle

Konopiště (KOH-noh-peesh-tyeh), the huge, Neo-Gothic residence of the Archduke Franz Ferdinand d'Este, is 30 miles south of Prague.

Construction of the castle began in the 14th century, but today's exterior and furnishings date from about 1900, when the heir to the Habsburg throne, Archduke Franz Ferdinand, renovated his new home. As one of the first castles in Europe to have an elevator, a WC, and running water, Konopiště shows "modern" living at the turn of the 20th century. Touring the castle gives you a good sense of who this powerful Habsburg was, as well as a glimpse at one of the best medieval arms collections in the world (and lots of hunting trophies).

Archduke Franz Ferdinand
(1863–1914)

Archduke Franz Ferdinand was the nephew of the Habsburg Emperor Franz Josef, who ruled from 1848 to 1916 (longer than Queen Victoria). Ferdinand was the impatient successor to the Austro-Hungarian throne. Local legends (whose veracity historians categorically deny) say that Franz Ferdinand even built a chapel at Konopiště for the sole purpose of praying that his old, hated uncle might soon die...but the emperor went on to outlive the young archduke.

Franz Ferdinand fell out of his uncle's favor when he married a beautiful but low-ranking Czech countess, Žofie Chotková (often known by her German name, Sophie). Žofie was "only" aristocratic, not royal. To get out of his relatives' sight, Franz Ferdinand bought Konopiště and moved here.

Obsessed with hunting, Franz Ferdinand traveled around the world twice, shooting at anything in sight: deer, bears, tigers, elephants, and crocodiles. He eventually killed 300,000 animals, many of whom stare morbidly at you as hunting trophies covering the walls at Konopiště.

In the Kaiser's Pavilion on the grounds of Konopiště, Franz Ferdinand met with German Kaiser Wilhelm and tried to talk him out of plotting a war against Russia. Wilhelm argued that a war would work to the mutual benefit of Germany and Austria: Germans wanted colonies, and Austria—crippled by the aspirations of its many nationalities—could use a war to divert attention from its domestic problems. But Franz Ferdinand foresaw that war would be suicidal for Austria's overstretched monarchy.

Soon after, Franz Ferdinand and his wife went to Sarajevo, in the Habsburg-annexed territories of Bosnia and Herzegovina. On that trip, young Gavrilo Princip, a Bosnian Serb, shot the Habsburg archduke who so loved shooting. (Princip also shot and killed Žofie.) Franz Ferdinand's assassination ironically gave the Germans (and their pro-war allies in the Austro-Hungarian administration) the pretext for starting the war against Serbia and its ally, Russia. World War I soon broke out. The event Franz Ferdinand had tried to prevent was, in fact, sparked by his death.

While the stretch between the parking lot and the castle entrance is overrun by tour groups, the **gardens** and the **park** are surprisingly empty. In the summer, the flowers and goldfish in the rose garden are a big hit with visitors. The peaceful 30-minute walk through the woods around the lake (wooden bridge at the far end) offers gorgeous castle views.

Tucked away in the bushes behind the pond is a pavilion coated with tree bark, a perfect picnic spot. This simple structure, nicknamed the **Kaiser's Pavilion,** was the site of a fateful meeting between the German Kaiser Wilhelm and the Archduke Franz Ferdinand (explained in the sidebar).

Cost and Tours: Entrance to the castle is by one-hour guided tour only. Choose from three different routes: Route I (190 Kč, includes public and guest rooms, hunting hall, and shooting range), Route II (190 Kč, includes the oldest part of the castle, armory, elevator, and chapel), and Route III (300 Kč, includes private top-floor rooms of Franz Ferdinand and his family). All tickets are 30 percent cheaper if you join a Czech-speaking tour. While Route II gives you the most comprehensive look into the castle, its history, and celebrated collections, Route III—reopened after the rooms were meticulously restored to match 1907 photographs—launches you right into a turn-of-the-20th-century time capsule.

Hours and Information: Castle open May–Aug Tue–Sun 9:00–12:30 & 13:00–17:00; April and Oct Tue–Fri 9:00–15:00, Sat–Sun 9:00–16:00; Sept Tue–Fri 9:00–16:00, Sat–Sun 9:00–17:00; closed Nov–March and Mon year-round. Tel. 317-721-366, www.zamek-konopiste.cz.

Getting to Konopiště Castle: Trains from Prague's Main Station drop you in Benešov (hourly, 1 hr); a well-marked trail goes from the station to the castle (1.5 miles). As you exit the Benešov train station, turn left and walk along the street parallel to the railroad tracks. Turn left at the first bridge you see crossing over the tracks. Along the way you'll see trail markers on trees, walls, and lampposts—one yellow stripe between two white stripes. Follow these markers. As you leave town, watch for a marker with an arrow pointing to a path in the woods. Take this path to bypass the castle's enormous parking lot, which is clogged with souvenir shops and bus fumes.

Eating at Konopiště Castle

Three touristy restaurants sit under the castle, but I'd bring picnic supplies from Prague (or buy them at the grocery store by the Benešov train station). While the crowds wait to pay too much for lousy food in the restaurants, you'll enjoy the peace and thought-provoking ambience of a **picnic** in the shaded Kaiser's Pavilion. Or eat cheaply with locals on Benešov's main square (try **U Zlaté Hvězdy**—"The Golden Star").

Karlštejn Castle

One of the Czech Republic's top attractions, Karlštejn Castle (KARL-shtayn) was built by Charles IV in about 1350 to house the crown jewels of the Holy Roman Empire. While a striking, fairy-tale castle from a distance, it's not much inside. The highlight of the castle's interior—the much venerated and sumptuous Chapel of the Holy Cross (built to house the crown jewels)—can be seen only with an advance reservation.

Cost and Tours: The Chapel of the Holy Cross—basically the only thing inside Karlštejn worth seeing—is part of tour Route II (300 Kč). You can only visit this route with a group (15 people maximum per group, 1 group per hour), and reservations are required (30-Kč reservation fee per person, tel. 274-008-154 or 274-008-155, rezervace@stc.npu .cz). Route I is nowhere near as interesting (220 Kč, no reservation required, bigger groups, shorter tour).

Hours and Information: May–Sept Tue–Sun 9:00–12:00 & 13:00–18:00; April and Oct Tue–Sun 9:00–12:00 & 13:00–15:00; closed Nov–March and Mon year-round; tel. 274-008-154, www .hradkarlstejn.cz.

Getting to Karlštejn Castle: The castle, 20 miles southwest of Prague, is accessible by train (2/hr, 40 min, then a 20-min walk; depart from Prague's Main Station in the direction of Beroun). When you leave the Karlštejn station, turn right, walk to the next road, turn left, and cross the bridge over the river. From here, follow the pedestrian-only street up to the castle. Warning: This half-mile stretch has a concentration of crystal and souvenir shops as intense as Karlova street in Prague.

Hike to Srbsko: From Karlštejn Castle, an easy one-hour hike along a well-marked trail (look for markers with one red stripe between two white stripes) leads you away from the tourists through a quiet forest to Srbsko. There you'll find two good Czech restaurants and a train station (the Karlštejn–Prague train stops in Srbsko).

Křivoklát Castle

Křivoklát (KREE-vohk-laht), an original 14th-century castle, is beautiful for its simplicity and setting, amid hills and deep woods near the lovely Berounka River valley. Originally a hunting residence of Czech kings, it was later transformed into a royal prison that "entertained" a number of distinguished guests, among them the most notorious alchemist of the 1500s, Englishman Edward Kelly.

In summer, Křivoklát comes alive with craftspeople—woodcarvers, blacksmiths, and basket-weavers—who work as if it were the 15th century. The absence of tacky souvenir shops, the plain Gothic appearance, and the background noise of hammers and wood chisels give Křivoklát an engaging character.

The tour of the interior lasts a sensible half-hour. The highlight is the king's audience hall, with its delicately arched ceiling.

Cost, Hours, Information: 150 Kč with an English-speaking guide; 100 Kč if you go with a Czech group (pick up an explanation sheet in English, and you'll be fine with the Czechs). Open June–Aug Tue–Sun 9:00–12:00 & 13:00–17:00, closed Mon; May and Sept Tue–Sun 9:00–16:00, closed Mon; April and Oct Tue–Sun 9:00–15:00, closed Mon; Nov–Dec Sat–Sun 9:00–15:00, closed Mon–Fri; closed Jan–March, tel. 313-558-440, www.krivoklat.cz.

Getting to Křivoklát Castle: Trains leave Prague's Main Station for Beroun (hourly, 40 min), running through the delightful valley of the dreamy Berounka River. In Beroun, transfer to the cute little motor train to Křivoklát (dubbed by Czech hikers the "Berounka Pacific"; allow 1.5 hrs total for trip from Prague). From Křivoklát's train station, it's a 10-minute walk uphill to the castle. At the train station, confirm the schedule back—one train leaves just before noon, and three others depart in the afternoon.

Sleeping and Eating near Křivoklát

$ Hotel and Restaurant Sýkora, below the castle near the train station, has been a favorite among Czech hikers since the 1930s. If you want to stay for an evening concert in the castle courtyard or for a hike in the nearby woods, sleep in one of the hotel's 11 renovated rooms (Db-600 Kč, tel. 313-558-114, www.hotel-sykora .krivoklatsko.com, hotel.sykora@krivoklatsko.com, only Czech and German spoken). Insist on this promised price or cross the street to the nearby, much classier **$$ Hotel and Restaurant U Jelena** (Db-1,200 Kč, tel. 313-558-529, www.ujelena.eu, krivoklat @ujelena.eu).

Near Křivoklát: Lány

The village of Lány, about 15 miles from Křivoklát Castle, is close to patriotic Czech hearts. The castle in Lány served as the Czech "Camp David" for both Tomáš Garrigue Masaryk (the first president of Czechoslovakia, between the World Wars) and Václav Havel (the contemporary "father of the Czech Republic" and first post-communist president of the nation).

Masaryk and his family are buried in Lány's simple village cemetery. Masaryk's humble grave on a hill in the middle of the fields is a pilgrimage place for freedom-loving Czechs. The communists, wanting to erase Masaryk from the nation's memory, destroyed all statues of him (such as the one in Kutná Hora—see page 170) and barely mentioned his name in history textbooks. During the communist era, Czechs risked their careers by coming here on the Czech Independence Day to put candles on Masaryk's grave. Imagine: Every year, on October 28, the police sealed off all roads to the village of Lány, and anyone who wanted access had to show an ID card. When you arrived at work the next morning, the boss would be waiting at the door, asking, "Where were you yesterday—and why?"

After 1989, Václav Havel—the symbol of the new Czech freedom—strove to restore dignity to the presidency. He went back to the tradition of the first Czech president, making Lány his home away from home. Havel's weekend sojourns here symbolized a return to Czech self-governance.

Getting to Lány: The bus leaves Prague's Hradčanská Metro station for Lány KD (6/day, fewer on weekends, 40 min, direction: Rakovník). Check the schedule at www.idos.cz. The bus first stops on the main square of the town, then at the cemetery. There is no public transportation from Lány to Křivoklát Castle, but you can hike between the two (see next).

Hike to Křivoklát Castle: Consider making the 15-mile hike to Křivoklát Castle from Lány. From the cemetery, it's a five-minute walk to the trailhead on the main square, where you will also find two grocery stores for stocking up on supplies—there are no restaurants or stores until Křivoklát. With the help of a good map, follow the well-marked trail through woods and meadows (look for markers with one red stripe between two white stripes on trees, walls, and fences). This is one of the most beautiful hikes in the whole country, as it takes you through all the varieties of forests in Eastern Europe (beech, birch, poplar, oak, pine, spruce, fir), a hidden 1950s dam, and some stunning vistas. The *Praha-Západ* and *Křivoklátsko* hiking maps are excellent (sold in most Prague bookstores).

ČESKÝ KRUMLOV

Lassoed by its river and dominated by its castle, this enchanting town feels lost in a time warp. While Český Krumlov is the Czech Republic's answer to Germany's Rothenburg, it has yet to be turned into a medieval theme park. When you see its awe-inspiring castle, delightful Old Town of shops and cobbled lanes, characteristic little restaurants, and easy canoeing options, you'll understand why having fun is a slam-dunk here.

Český Krumlov (CHESS-key KROOM-loff) means, roughly, "Czech Bend in the River." Calling it "Český" for short sounds silly to Czech-speakers (since dozens of Czech town names begin with "Český"). However, "Krumlov" for short is OK.

Since Krumlov is the Czech Republic's second-most-visited town (1.5 million visits annually), there's enough tourism to make things colorful and easy—but not so much that it tramples the place's charm. This town of 15,000 attracts a young, bohemian crowd, drawn here for its simple beauty, cheap living, and fanciful bars.

Planning Your Time

Because you can visit the castle and theater only with a guide (and English-language tours are offered just a few times a day), serious sightseers should reserve both tours first thing in the morning in person at the castle and theater (or call the castle), and then build their day around the tour times. Those who hate planning ahead on vacation can join a Czech tour anytime with an English information sheet.

A paddle down the river to Zlatá Koruna Abbey is a highlight (three hours), and a 20-minute walk up to the Křížový Vrch (Hill of the Cross) rewards you with a fine view of the town and its unforgettable riverside setting. Other sights are quick visits and

Český Krumlov's History

With the sharp bend in the Vltava providing a natural moat, it's no wonder Český Krumlov has been a choice spot for eons. Celtic tribes first settled here a century before Christ. Then came German tribes. The Slavic tribes arrived in the ninth century. The Rožmberks—Bohemia's top noble family—ran the city from 1302 to 1602. You'll see their rose symbol all over town. In many ways, the 16th century was the town's Golden Age, when Český Krumlov hosted artists, scientists, and alchemists from all over Europe. In 1588, the town became home to an important Jesuit college. The Habsburgs bought the region in 1602, ushering in a more Germanic period. (After that, as many as 75 percent of the town's people were German—until 1945, when most Germans were expelled.)

The rich mix of Gothic, Renaissance, and Baroque buildings is easy to underappreciate. As you wander, look up...notice the surviving details in the stonework. Step into shops. Snoop into back lanes and tiny squares. Gothic buildings curve with the winding streets. Many precious Gothic and Renaissance frescoes were whitewashed in Baroque times (when the colorful trimmings of earlier periods were way out of style). Today, these precious frescoes are being rediscovered and restored.

With the town's rich German heritage, it was easy for Hitler to claim that this region—the Sudetenland—was rightfully part of Germany, and in 1938, the infamous Munich Agreement made it his. Americans liberated the town in 1945. Due to Potsdam Treaty-approved ethnic cleansing, three million Germans in

worthwhile only if you have a particular interest (Viennese artist Egon Schiele, puppets, torture, and so on).

The town itself is the major attraction. Evenings are for atmospheric dining and drinking. Sights are generally open 10:00–17:00 and closed on Monday.

Orientation to Český Krumlov

Český Krumlov is extremely easy to navigate. The twisty Vltava River, which makes a perfect S through the town, ropes the Old Town into a tight peninsula. Above the Old Town is the Castle Town. Český Krumlov's one main street starts at the isthmus and heads through the peninsula. It winds through town and continues across a bridge before snaking through the Castle Town, the castle complex (a long series of courtyards), and the castle gardens high above. The main square, Náměstí Svornosti—with the TI, ATMs, and taxis—dominates the Old Town and marks the center of the peninsula. All recommended restaurants and hotels are within a

Czech lands were sent west to Germany. Emptied of its German citizenry, Český Krumlov turned into a ghost town, partially inhabited by Roma (Gypsies—see sidebar on page 198).

In the post-WWII world drawn up by Stalin, Churchill, and FDR at Yalta, the border of the Soviet and American spheres of influence fell about here. While the communist government established order, the period from 1945 to 1989 was a smelly interlude, as the town was infamously polluted. Its now-pristine river was foamy with effluent from the paper mill just upstream, while the hills around the town were marred with apartment blocks of prefabricated concrete. The people who moved in never fully identified with the town—in Europe, a place without ancestors is a place without life. But the bleak years of communism paradoxically provided a cocoon to preserve the town. There was no money, so little changed, apart from a build-up of grime.

In the early 1990s, tourists discovered Český Krumlov, and the influx of money saved the buildings from ruin. Color returned to the facades, waiters again dressed in coarse linen shirts, and the main drag was flooded with souvenir shops.

With its new prosperity, the center of today's Český Krumlov looks like a fairy-tale town. In fact, movie producers consider it ideal for films. *The Adventures of Pinocchio* was filmed here in 1995, as was the opening sequence for the 2006 film *The Illusionist*.

few minutes' walk of this square. No sight in town is more than a five-minute stroll away.

Tourist Information

The helpful TI is on the **main square** (daily 9:00–19:00, July–Aug until 20:00, shorter hours in winter, tel. 380-704-622, www .ckrumlov.cz). Pick up the free city map. The 129-Kč *City Guide* book explains everything in town and includes a fine town and castle map in the back. The TI can check train, bus, and flight schedules. Ask about concerts, city walking tours in English, and canoe trips on the river. A second, less-crowded TI—actually a private business—is just below the **castle** (daily 9:00–19:00, tel. 380-725-110).

Arrival in Český Krumlov

By Train: The train station is a 20-minute walk from town (turn right out of the station, then walk downhill onto a steep cobbled path leading to an overpass into the town center). Taxis are standing by to zip you to your hotel (about 100 Kč), or call 602-113-113 to summon one.

By Bus: The bus station is just three blocks away from the Old Town (from the bus station lot, drop down to main road and turn left, then turn right at Potraviny grocery store to reach the center). Figure on 60 Kč for a taxi from the station to your hotel.

Helpful Hints

Internet Access: Fine Internet cafés are all over town, and many of my recommended accommodations offer Wi-Fi or Internet access. The TI on the main square has several fast, cheap, stand-up stations. Perhaps the best cybercafé is behind the TI by the castle (tel. 380-725-117).

Bookstore: Shakespeare and Sons is a good little English-language bookstore (daily 11:00–20:00, a block below the main square at Soukenická 44, tel. 380-711-203).

Laundry: The recommended **Pension Lobo** runs a self-service launderette near the castle. Since there are only a few machines, you may have to wait (200 Kč to wash and dry, includes soap, daily 9:00–20:00, Latrán 73).

Festivals: Locals drink oceans of beer and celebrate their medieval roots at big events such as the Celebration of the Rose (Slavnosti Růže), where blacksmiths mint ancient coins, jugglers swallow fire, mead flows generously, and pigs are roasted on open fires (June 18–20 in 2010). The summer also brings a top-notch international jazz and alternative music festival to town, performed in pubs, cafés, and the castle gardens (July 18–Aug 23 in 2010). During the St. Wenceslas celebrations, the square becomes a medieval market and the streets come alive with theater and music (Sept 24–28 in 2010). Reserve a hotel well in advance if you'll be in town for these events (for more details, see www.ckrumlov.cz).

ČESKÝ KRUMLOV

Tours in Český Krumlov

Walking Tours—Since the town itself, rather than its sights, is what it's all about here, taking a guided walk is the key to a meaningful visit. The TI sells tickets for two different guided walks. They are affordable, in English, and are time well-spent. Both meet in front of the TI on the main square. No reservations are necessary—just drop in and pay the guide. The **Old Town Tour** offers the best general town introduction and is most likely to run (250 Kč, daily May–Oct at 10:30 and 15:00, Nov–April at 11:00, weekends only in Feb, 1.5 hours). The **Brewing History Tour,** which is the most intimate of the many brewery tours in this land that so loves its beer, takes you through the Eggenberg Brewery (200 Kč, daily May–Oct

---

Parting of the Roses

A five-petal rose is not just the distinctive mark of Český Krumlov and the Rožmberk rulers (literally, "Lords from the Rose Mountain"). You'll find it, in five-color combinations, all over South Bohemia.

A medieval legend, depicted inside Český Krumlov's castle, explains the division of the roses in the following way: A respected nobleman named Vítek split the property he had accumulated during his lifetime among five sons. Each son was also assigned his own coat of arms, all of which shared the motif of a five-petal rose. The oldest son, Jindřich, received a golden rose in a blue field, along with the lands of Hradec and Telč. Vilém received a silver rose in a red field, with the lands of Landštejn and Třeboň. Smil was given a blue rose in a golden field and the lands of Stráž and Bystřice. Vok kept his father's coat of arms, a red rose in a white field, and became the lord in Rožmberk and Český Krumlov. Finally, the out-of-wedlock Sezima had to make do with a black rose and the tiny land of Ústí.

Over generations, the legend—which is corroborated by historical sources—served as a constant warning to the ambitious Rožmberks not to further split up their land. The Lords from the Rose Mountain were the rare Czech noble family that, for 300 years, strictly adhered to the principle of primogeniture (the oldest son gets all, and younger sons are subservient to him). Unlike Vítek, the patriarch, each successive ruler of the Rožmberk estates made sure to consolidate his possessions, handing more to his eldest son than he had received. As a result, the enterprising Rožmberks grew into the most powerful family in Bohemia. In 1501, their position as "first in the country after the king" became law.

at 12:30, Nov–April at 13:00, weekends only in Feb, 1 hr). For a self-guided town walk, consider renting an **audioguide** from the TI (60 Kč/hr).

Local Guides—Oldřiška Baloušková is a hardworking young guide who offers a wonderful tour around her hometown (400 Kč/hr, mobile 737-920-901, oldriskab@gmail.com). **Jiří (George) Václavíček,** a gentle and caring man who perfectly fits mellow Český Krumlov, is a joy to share this town with (450 Kč/hr, mobile 603-927-995, www.krumlovguide.cz, jiri.vaclavicek@gmail.com). **Karolína Kortušová** is an enthusiastic woman with great organizational skills. Her company, Krumlov Tours, can set you up with a good local tour guide, palace and theater admissions, river trips, and more (guides-400 Kč/hr, mobile 723-069-561, www.krumlov tours.com, info@krumlovtours.com).

Self-Guided Walk

▲▲▲Welcome to Český Krumlov

The town's best sight is its cobbled cityscape, surrounded by a bab-
bling river and capped by a dramatic castle. All of Český Krumlov's
modest sights are laced
together in this charming
walk from the top of the
Old Town, down its spine,
across the river, and up to
the castle.

• *Start at the bridge over the
isthmus, which was once the
fortified grand entry gate to
the town.*

Horní Bridge: From this "Upper Bridge," note the natural
fortification provided by the tight bend in the river. The last building in town (just over the river) is the Eggenberg Brewery (with
daily tours—see "Tours in Český Krumlov," earlier). Behind that,
on the horizon, is a pile of white apartment high-rises—built in
the last decade of the communist era and considered the worst
places in town to call home. Left of the brewery stands a huge
monastery (not generally open to the public). Behind that, on Kleť
Mountain, the highest hilltop, stands a TV tower that locals say
was built to jam Voice of America broadcasts. Facing the town, on
your left, rafters take you to the river for the sloppy half-hour float
around town to the take-out spot just on your right.

• *A block downhill on Horní (Upper) street is the...*

Museum of Regional History: This small museum gives you
a quick look at regional costumes, tools, and traditions. When you
pay, pick up the English translation of the displays (it also includes
a lengthy history of Krumlov). Start on the top floor, where you'll
see a Bronze Age exhibit, old paintings, a glimpse of noble life,
and a look at how the locals rafted lumber from Krumlov all the
way to Vienna (partly by canal). Don't miss the fun-to-study
ceramic model of Český Krumlov in 1800 (note the extravagant
gardens high above the town). The lower floor comes with fine folk
costumes and domestic art (50 Kč, daily 10:00–17:00, July–Aug
until 18:00, Horní 152, tel. 380-711-674).

• *Below the museum, a little garden overlook affords a fine castle view.
Immediately across the street, notice the Renaissance facade of...*

Hotel Růže: This former Jesuit college hides a beautiful
courtyard. Pop inside to see a couple of bronze busts that stand
like a shrine to the founders of Czechoslovakia. The one on the
right, dedicated by the Czech freedom fighters, commemorates the
first Czechoslovak president, Tomáš Garrigue Masaryk (in office

Český Krumlov

1. Castle View Apts.
2. Hotel Mlýn
3. Pension Olšakovský
4. Pension Lobo & Pension Danny
5. Pension Teddy
6. Pension Myší Díra & Maleček Boat Rental
7. Pension Anna
8. Hostel 99 & Hospoda 99 Rest.
9. Krumlov House Hostel
10. Na Louži Restaurant
11. Krčma u Dwau Maryí
12. Cikánská Jizba
13. Rest. u Dobráka
14. Laibon Restaurant
15. Rybářská Restaurace
16. Krčma v Šatlavské
17. Restaurace Barbakán
18. Dobrá Čajovna Teahouse
19. Start Short River Float
20. End Short River Float & Start Zlatá Koruna Float

Edvard Beneš and the German Question

Czechoslovakia was created in 1918, when the vast, multiethnic Habsburg Empire broke into smaller nations after losing World War I. The principle that gave countries such as Poland, Czechoslovakia, and Romania independence was called "self-determination": Each nation had the right to its own state within the area in which its people were in the majority. But the peoples of Eastern Europe had mixed over the centuries, making it impossible to create functioning states based purely on ethnicity. In the case of Czechoslovakia, the borders were drawn along historical rather than ethnic boundaries. While the country was predominantly Slavic, there were also areas with overwhelmingly German and Hungarian majorities. One of these areas—a fringe around the western part of the country, mostly populated by Germans—was known as the Sudetenland.

At first, the coexistence of Slavs and Germans in the new republic worked fine. German parties were important power brokers and participated in almost every coalition government. Hitler's rise to power, however, led to the growth of German nationalism, even outside Germany. Soon 70 percent of Germans in Czechoslovakia voted for the Nazis. In September 1938, the Munich Agreement ceded the Sudetenland to Germany, and the Czech minority had to leave (for more on the Munich Agreement, see "The Never-Used Fortifications" on page 229).

Edvard Beneš was the first Czechoslovak secretary of state (1918-1934) and later became the country's second president (1934-1948). Beneš led the Czechoslovak exile government in London during World War II. Like most Czechs and Slovaks, Beneš believed that after the hard feelings produced by the Munich Agreement, peaceful coexistence of Slavs and Germans in a single state was impossible. His postwar solution: move the Sudeten Germans to Germany, much as the Czechs had been forced out of the Sudetenland before. Through skillful diplomacy,

1918–1934; see sidebar on page 106). The bust on the left recalls Masaryk's successor, Edvard Beneš (in office 1934–1948).

• *Walk another block down the main drag, until you reach steps on the left leading to the...*

Church of St. Vitus: Český Krumlov's main church was built as a bastion of Catholicism in the 15th century, when the Roman Catholic Church was fighting the Hussites. The 17th-century Baroque high altar shows a totem of religious figures: the Virgin Mary (crowned in heaven); St. Vitus (above Mary); and, way up on top, St. Wenceslas, the patron saint of the Czech people—long considered their ambassador in heaven. The canopy in the back, though empty today, once supported a grand statue of a Rožmberk atop a horse. The statue originally stood at the high altar. Too

Beneš got the Allies to sign on to this idea.

Shortly after the end of World War II, three million people of German ancestry were forced to leave their homes in Czechoslovakia. Millions of Germanic people in Poland, Romania, Ukraine, and elsewhere met with a similar fate. Many of these families had been living in these areas for centuries. The methods employed to expel them included murder, rape, and plunder. (Today, we'd call it "ethnic cleansing.")

In 1945, Český Krumlov lost 75 percent of its population, and Czechs moved into vacated German homes. Having easily acquired the property, the new residents didn't take much care of the houses. Within a few years, the once-prosperous Sudetenland was reduced to shabby towns and uncultivated fields—a decaying, godforsaken region. After 1989, displaced Sudeten Germans—the majority of whom now live in Bavaria—demanded that the Czechoslovak government apologize for the violent way in which the expulsion was carried out. Some challenged the legality of the decrees, and for a time the issue threatened otherwise good Czech-German relations.

Although no longer such a hot-button diplomatic issue, the so-called Beneš Decrees remain divisive in Czech politics. While liberals consider the laws unjust, many others—especially the older generations—see them as fair revenge for the behavior of the Sudeten Germans prior to and during the war. In the former Sudetenland, where Czech landowners worry that the Germans will try to reclaim their property, Beneš is a hugely popular figure. His bust in Český Krumlov's Hotel Růže is one of the first memorials to Beneš in the country. The bridge behind the Old Town has been named for Beneš since the 1990s. The main square—the center of a thriving German community 70 years ago—is now, ironically, called "Square of Concord."

egotistical for Jesuits, it was later moved to the rear of the nave, and then lost for good. As you listen to the river, notice the empty organ case. While the main organ is out for restoration, the cute little circa-1716 Baroque beauty is getting plenty of use (see photos of the restoration work on the far wall, church open daily 10:00–19:00, Sunday Mass at 9:30, tel. 380-711-336).

• *Continuing on Horní street, you'll come to the...*

Main Square (Náměstí Svornosti): Lined with a mix of Renaissance and Baroque homes of burghers (all built on 12th-century Gothic foundations), the main square has a grand charm. There's continuity here. Lékárna, with the fine red Baroque facade on the lower corner of the square, is still a pharmacy, as it has been since 1620. McDonald's tried three times to get a spot here but was turned away each time. The Town Hall flies both the Czech flag and the town flag, which shows the rose symbol of the Rožmberk family, who ruled the town for 300 years.

Imagine the history that this square has seen: In the 1620s, the rising tide of Lutheran Protestantism threatened Catholic Europe. Krumlov was a seat of Jesuit power and learning, and the intellectuals of the Roman church allegedly burned books on this square. Later, when there was a bad harvest, locals blamed witches—and burned them, too. Every so often, terrible plagues rolled through the countryside. In a nearby village, all but two residents were killed by a plague.

But the plague stopped before devastating the people of Český Krumlov, and in 1715—as thanks to God—they built the plague

monument that stands on the square today. Much later, in 1938, Hitler stood right here before a backdrop of long Nazi banners to celebrate the annexation of the Sudetenland. And in 1968, Russian tanks spun their angry treads on these same cobblestones to intimidate locals who were demanding freedom. Today, thankfully, this square is part of an unprecedented time of peace and prosperity for the Czech people.

• *The following three museums are grouped around the main square.*

Puppet Museum: In three small rooms, you'll see fascinating displays of more than 300 movable creations (overwhelmingly of Czech origin, but also some from Burma and Rajasthan). At the model stage, children of any age can try their hand at pulling the strings on their favorite fairy tale (80 Kč, daily 10:00–18:00, longer hours in July–Aug, Radniční 29, tel. 380-713-422, www.inspirace .krumlov.cz). For more on Czech puppets, see page 144.

Torture Museum: This is just a lame haunted house: dark, with sound effects, cheap modern models, and prints showing off the cruel and unusual punishments of medieval times (80 Kč, daily 9:00–20:00, English descriptions, Náměstí Svornosti 1, tel. 380-766-343).

Egon Schiele Art Center: This classy contemporary art gallery has temporary exhibits, generally featuring 20th-century Czech artists. The top-floor permanent collection celebrates the Viennese artist Egon Schiele (pronounced "Sheila"), who once spent a few weeks here during a secret love affair. A friend of Gustav Klimt and an important figure in the Secession movement in Vienna, Schiele lived a short life, from 1890 to 1918. His cutting-edge lifestyle and harsh art of graphic nudes didn't always fit the conservative, small-town style of Český Krumlov, but townsfolk are happy today to charge you to see this relatively paltry collection (180 Kč, daily 10:00–18:00, Široká 70, tel. 380-704-011, www .schieleartcentrum.cz). The Schiele collection in Vienna's Belvedere Palace is far better.

• *From the main square, walk up Radniční street and cross the...*

Barber's Bridge (Lazebnicky Most): This wooden bridge, decorated with two 19th-century statues, connects the Old Town and the Castle Town. In the center stands a statue of St. John of Nepomuk, who's also depicted by a prominent statue on Prague's Charles Bridge (see page 68). Among other responsibilities, he's the protector against floods. In the great floods of August 2002, the angry river submerged the bridge (but removable banisters minimized the damage). Stains just above the windows of the adjacent building show you how high the water rose.

• *After crossing the bridge, hike up the hill. Your next stop is Krumlov Castle.*

Sights in Český Krumlov

▲▲Krumlov Castle (Krumlovský Zámek)

No Czech town is complete without a castle—and now that the nobles are gone, their mansions are open to us common folk. The Krumlov Castle complex includes bear pits, a rare Baroque theater, groomed gardens—and the castle itself (www.castle.ckrumlov.cz).

Round Tower (Zâmecká Věž)— The strikingly colorful round tower marks the location of the first castle, built here to guard the medieval river crossing. With its 16th-century Renaissance paint job colorfully restored, it looks exotic, featuring fancy astrological decor, terra-cotta symbols of the zodiac, and a fine arcade. Climb its 162 steps for a great view (30 Kč, daily 9:00–18:00, last entry 17:30).

Bear Pits—At the site of the castle drawbridge, the bear pits hold a family of European brown bears, as they have since the Rožmberks added bears to their coat of arms in the 16th century to demonstrate their (fake) blood relation to the distinguished Italian family of Orsini (the name means "bear-like"). Featured on countless coats of arms, bears have long been totemic animals for Europeans. Pronouncing the animal's real name was taboo in

Roma in Eastern Europe

Numbering 12 million, the Roma people constitute a bigger European nation than the Czechs, Hungarians, or the Dutch. The term "Gypsies," which used to be the common name for this group, is now considered both derogatory and inaccurate. It was derived from "Egypt"—the place that medieval Roma were mistakenly thought to have originated. In the absence of written records, the solution to the puzzle of Roma ancestry had to wait for 19th-century advances in the science of linguistics.

The Roma are descended from several low north-Indian castes (one of which may have given the Roma their name). A thousand years ago, the Roma began to migrate through Persia and Armenia into the Ottoman Empire, which later stretched across much of southeastern Europe. Known for their itinerant lifestyle, expertise in horse trading, skilled artisanship, and flexibility regarding private property, the Roma were both sought out and suspected in medieval Europe. In a similar way, *gadjos* (non-Roma) and their customs came to be distrusted by the Roma.

The Industrial Revolution removed the Roma's few traditional means of earning a livelihood, making their wandering lifestyle difficult to sustain. In the 1940s, Hitler sent hundreds of thousands of Roma to the gas chambers. After the war, communist governments in Eastern Europe implemented a policy of forced assimilation: Roma were required to speak the country's major language, settle in *gadjo* towns, and work in new industrial jobs. Today, few Roma can speak their own language well. Rather than producing well-adjusted citizens, the policy eroded time-honored Roma values and shattered the cohesiveness of their

ČESKÝ KRUMLOV

many cultures, and Czechs still refer to bears only indirectly. For example, in most Germanic languages the word "bear" is derived from "brown," while the Slavic *medvěd* literally means "honey-eater."

Castle—The immense castle is a series of courtyards with shops, contemporary art galleries, and tourist services. The interior is accessible only by tour, which gives you a glimpse of the places where the Rožmberks, Eggenbergs, and Schwarzenbergs dined, studied, worked, prayed, entertained, and slept. (By European standards, the castle's not much, and the tours move slowly.) Imagine traditional communities. It left the new Roma generation prone to sexual, alcohol, and drug abuse, and filled state-run orphanages with deprived Roma toddlers. When the obligation and right to work disappeared with the communist regimes in 1989, rampant unemployment and dependence on welfare joined the list of Roma afflictions.

As people all over Eastern Europe found it difficult to adjust to the new economic realities, they again turned on the Roma as scapegoats, fueling the latent racism that is so characteristic of European history. Many Roma now live in segregated ghettos, where even the most talented Roma children are forced to attend schools for the mentally disabled. Those who make it against the odds and succeed in mainstream society typically do so by turning their backs on their Roma heritage.

In this context, the Roma in Český Krumlov are a surprising success story. The well-integrated, proud Roma community (numbering 1,000 strong, or 5 percent of the town's population) is considered a curious anomaly even by experts. Their success could be due to a number of factors: It could be the legacy of the multicultural Rožmberks, or the fact that almost everyone in Český Krumlov is a relative newcomer. Or maybe it's that local youngsters, regardless of skin color, tend to resolve their differences over a beer in the local "Gypsy Pub" (Cikánská Jizba), with a trendy Roma band setting the tune.

While provincial politicians throughout the rest of Eastern Europe become national leaders by moving Roma into ghettos, Český Krumlov is living proof that Roma and *gadjos* can coexist happily.

being an aristocratic guest here, riding the dukes' assembly line of fine living: You'd promenade through a long series of elegant spaces and dine in the sumptuous dining hall before enjoying a concert in the Hall of Mirrors, which leads directly to the Baroque Theater (described next). After the play, you'd go out into the château garden for a fireworks finale.

Cost, Hours, Tours: To see the interior, you must take a one-hour escorted tour: Tour I (Gothic and Renaissance rooms, of the most general interest) or Tour II (19th-century castle life). Tours run June–Aug Tue–Sun 9:00–12:00 & 13:00–18:00, spring and fall until 17:00, closed Mon and Nov–March. Tours in Czech cost 130 Kč plus a 10-Kč reservation fee, leave regularly, and include an adequate flier in English that contains about half the information imparted by the guide (generally a student who's simply memorized the basic script). English tours are preferable, but cost more (240 Kč plus a 10-Kč reservation fee), run less frequently, and are often booked solid. Make your reservation when you arrive in town—just walk up to the castle office—or you can call 380-704-721, though the number is often busy. You'll be issued a ticket with your tour time printed on it. Be in the correct courtyard at that time, or you'll be locked out.

▲▲**Baroque Theater (Zámecké Divadlo)**—Europe once had several hundred Baroque theaters. Using candles for light and fireworks for special effects, most burned down. Today, only two survive in good shape and are open to tourists: one at Stockholm's Drottningholm Palace; and one here, at Krumlov Castle. During the 45-minute tour, you'll sit on benches in the theater and then go under the stage to see the wood-and-rope contraptions that enabled scenes to be scooted in and out within seconds (while fireworks and smoke blinded the audience). Due to the theater's fragility, the number of visitors is strictly regulated. There are only five English tours a day, limited to 25 people per group and generally sold out in advance. While it's a lovely little theater with an impressive 3-D effect that makes the stage look deeper than it really is, I wouldn't bother with the tour unless you can snare a spot on an English one. The theater is used only once a year for an actual performance, with attendance limited to Baroque theater enthusiasts. You can call 380-704-721 to get English-language tour times and reserve a space; but as with the castle tour, you will likely do best visiting the ticket office in person (380 Kč plus a 10-Kč reservation fee for English tour, 250 Kč plus a 10-Kč reservation fee for Czech tour, tours daily May–Oct only; English departures at 10:00, 11:00, 13:00, 14:00, and 15:00; buy theater tour tickets at castle ticket office).

Castle Gardens—This 2,300-foot-long garden crowns the castle complex. It was laid out in the 17th century, when the noble family would light it with 22,000 oil lamps, torches, and candles for special occasions. The lower part is geometrical and symmetrical—French-style. The upper is rougher—English-style (free, May–Sept daily 8:00–19:00, April and Oct daily 8:00–17:00, closed Nov–March).

Near Český Krumlov

Zlatá Koruna Abbey—Directly above the river at the end of a three-hour float by raft or canoe (see "Activities in Český Krumlov," later), this abbey was founded in the 13th century by the king to counter the growing influence of the Vítek family, the ancestors of the mighty Rožmberks. As you enter the grounds, notice the central linden tree, with its strange, cape-like leaves; it's said to have been used by the anti-Catholic Hussites when they hanged the monks. The short guided abbey tour takes you through the rare two-storied Gothic Chapel of the Guardian Angel, the main church, and the cloister. After the order was dissolved in 1785, the abbey functioned shortly as a village school, before being turned into a factory during the Industrial Revolution. Damage from this period is visible on the cloister's crumbling arches. The abbey was restored in the 1990s and opened to the public only a few years ago (95 Kč for a tour in Czech—generally runs hourly, 180 Kč for an English tour, Tue–Sun 9:00–15:30, until 16:30 June–Aug, closed Mon and Oct–March, call 380-743-126 to pre-arrange an English tour, access via river float, www.klaster-zlatakoruna.eu).

Šumava Mountains—The Šumava Mountains (SHOO-mah-vah) are, geologically, one of Europe's oldest ranges. Separating Bohemia from Bavaria, this long ridge, known in German as the Böhmerwald ("Czech Forest"), was the physical embodiment of the Iron Curtain for 40 years: The first 10 miles or so within the Czech border were a forbidden no-man's-land, where hundreds of Czechs were shot as they tried to run across to Germany. In 1989, the barbed wire was taken down, and the entire area—more than 60 miles long—was declared the Šumava-Bayerische Wald National Park. No development is permitted within the park, and visitors can't camp outside of designated areas. Since there's little industry nearby, these mountains preserve some of the most pristine woods, creeks, and meadows in Eastern Europe.

The gateway most easily accessible from Český Krumlov is the trailhead village of **Nová Pec,** a scenic 1.5-hour train ride away (5 direct trains/day). Nová Pec is located just beneath the slopes of the tallest mountain on the Czech side of the border, Plechý, a popular destination for hiking, biking, and cross-country skiing. Nová Pec's TI, which is 100 yards to the right of the train station, sells hiking and biking maps. You can rent bikes at the train station (150 Kč/day with train ticket, slightly more without one, reserve a few days ahead by calling 972-543-891 or emailing zstvlrdop@mail.cd.cz) or three miles away toward Plechý next to the Plešný parking lot (mobile 723-380-138).

Sleeping near Nová Pec: Both of these recommended B&Bs are about one mile outside of Nová Pec. Like almost everywhere else in this border region, German and Czech are the only ways to communicate.

$$ Pension Za Pecí has five new, tastefully decorated rooms (500 Kč/person, optional dinner-100 Kč, tel. 388-336-103, mobile 775-977-469, www.zapeci.com, mifudy@seznam.cz).

$$ Pension Hubertus sits on a sloping meadow and operates its three rooms on solar power. Owner Eva will pick you up from the train station if you ask (420–480 Kč/person, mobile 602-253-572, www.ubytovani.net—search for Hubertus).

ČESKÝ KRUMLOV

Activities in Český Krumlov

Český Krumlov lies in the middle of a valley popular for canoeing, rafting, hiking, and horseback riding. Boat-rental places are convenient to the Old Town, and several hiking paths start right in town.

▲▲▲Canoeing and Rafting the Vltava

Splash a little river fun into your visit by renting a rubber raft or fiberglass canoe for a quick 30-minute spin around Český Krumlov.

Or go for a three-hour float and paddle through the Bohemian forests and villages of the nearby countryside. You'll end up at Zlatá Koruna Abbey (described earlier), where the rafting company will shuttle you back to town—or provide you with a bicycle to pedal back on your own along a bike path. This is a great hot-weather activity. Though the river is far from treacherous, be prepared to get wet.

You'll encounter plenty of inviting pubs and cafés for breaks along the way. There's a little whitewater, but the river is so shallow that if you tip, you simply stand up and climb back in. (When that happens, pull the canoe up onto the bank to empty it, since you'll never manage to pour the water out while still in the river.)

Choose from a kayak, a canoe (fastest, less work, more likely to tip), or an inflatable raft (harder rowing, slower, but very stable). Prices are per boat (2–6 people) and include a map, a waterproof container, and transportation to or from the start and end points. Here are your options:

Quickie Circle-the-Town Float: The easiest half-hour experience is to float around the city's peninsula, starting and ending at opposite sides of the tiny isthmus. Heck, you can do it twice (350 Kč for 1–2 people in a canoe or raft).

Three-Hour Float to Zlatá Koruna Abbey: This is your best basic trip, with pastoral scenery, a riverside pub about two hours down on the left, and a beautiful abbey as your destination (about 9 miles, 700 Kč for 1–2 people). From there you can bike back or catch a shuttle bus home—simply arrange a return plan with the rental company.

Longer and Faster Trips: If you start upriver from Krumlov (direction: Rožmberk), you'll go faster with more whitewater, but the river parallels a road, so it's a little less idyllic. Longer trips in either direction involve lots of paddling, even though you're going downstream. Rafting companies can review the many day-trip options with you.

Rental Companies: Several companies offer this lively activity. Perhaps the handiest are **Půjčovna Lodí Maleček Boat Rental** (open long hours daily April–Oct, closed Nov–March, at recommended Pension Myší Díra, Rooseveltova 28, tel. 380-712-508, www.malecek.cz, lode@malecek.cz) and **Cestovní Agentura Vltava** (April–Oct daily 9:00–18:00, closed Nov–March, in Pension Vltava at Kájovská 62, tel. 380-711-988, www.ckvltava.cz). Vltava also rents mountain bikes (320 Kč/day) and can bring a bike to the abbey for you to ride back.

Hiking

For an easy 20-minute hike to Křížový Vrch (Hill of the Cross), walk to the end of Rooseveltova street, cross at the traffic light, then head straight for the first (empty) chapel-like Station of the Cross. Turning right, it's easy to navigate along successive Stations of the Cross until you reach the white church on the hill (closed), set in the middle of wild meadows. Looking down into the valley at the medieval city nestled within the S-shaped river, framed by the rising hills, it's hard to imagine any town with a more powerful *genius loci* (spirit of the place). The view is best at sunset.

For longer hikes, start at the trailhead by the bear pits below the castle. Red-and-white trail markers will take you on an easy six-mile hike around the neighboring slopes and villages. The green-and-yellow stripes mark a five-mile hiking trail up Kleť Mountain—with an altitude gain of 1,800 feet. At the top, you'll find the Kleť Observatory, the oldest observatory in the country (now a leading center for discovering new planets). On clear days, you can see the Alps (observatory tours-30 Kč, hourly July–Aug Tue–Sun 10:30–15:30, closed Mon, www.hvezdarna.klet.cz).

Horseback Riding

Head about a mile and a half out of town, beyond Křížový Vrch, for horseback rides and lessons at **Slupenec Horseback Riding Club** (300 Kč-1 hour outdoors or in the ring, 2,200 Kč-all-day ride, helmets provided, Tue–Sun 10:00–18:00, closed Mon, Slupenec 1, worth a taxi trip, tel. 380-711-052, www.jk-slupenec .cz, René Srncová).

Sleeping in Český Krumlov

Krumlov is filled with small, good, family-run pensions offering doubles with baths from 1,000 to 1,500 Kč and hostel beds for 300 Kč. Summer weekends and festivals (see page 190) are busiest and most expensive; reserve ahead when possible. Hotels (not

Sleep Code

(18 Kč = about $1, country code: 420)
S = Single, **D** = Double/Twin, **T** = Triple, **Q** = Quad, **b** = bathroom, **s** = shower only. Unless otherwise noted, prices include breakfast.

To help you sort easily through these listings, I've divided the rooms into three categories based on the price for a standard double room with bath:

$$$ Higher Priced—Most rooms 1,500 Kč or more.
$$ Moderately Priced—Most rooms between 1,000–1,500 Kč.
$ Lower Priced—Most rooms 1,000 Kč or less.

a Krumlov forte) have staff that speak some English and accept credit cards; pensions rarely have or do either. While you can find a room upon arrival here, it's better to book at least a few days ahead if you want to stay in the heart of town. Cars are not very safe overnight—locals advise paying for a garage.

In the Old Town
$$$ Castle View Apartments, run by local guide Jiří Václavíček, rents seven apartments. These are the plushest and best-equipped rooms I found in town—the bathroom floors are heated, all come with kitchenettes, and everything's done just right. Their website describes each stylish apartment (1,800–4,500 Kč depending on size, view, and season; the big 4,500-Kč apartment sleeps up to six, complex pricing scheme, reserve direct with this book to claim a 10 percent discount off their online prices, fourth night free, non-smoking, breakfast in a nearby hotel, Šatlavská 140, tel. 380-727-015, mobile 731-108-677, www.castleview.cz, info@castleview.cz).

On Parkán Street, Below the Square
Secluded Parkán street, which runs along the river below the square, has a row of pensions with three to five rooms each. These places have a family feel and views of the looming castle above.

$$$ Hotel Mlýn, at the end of Parkán, is a newly opened and tastefully furnished hotel with more than 30 rooms and all the amenities (Sb-2,400 Kč, Db-3,000 Kč, elevator, parking extra, Parkán 120, tel. 380-731-133, fax 380-747-054, www.hotelmlyn.eu, info@hotelmlyn.eu).

$$ Pension Olšakovský, which has a delightful breakfast area on a terrace next to the river, treats visitors as family guests (Db-1,000–1,250 Kč, includes parking, Parkán 114, tel. & fax 380-

ČESKÝ KRUMLOV

714-333, mobile 604-430-181, www.olsakovsky.cz, J.Olsakovsky @post.cz).

On Latrán Street, at the Base of the Castle

A quiet, cobbled pedestrian street (Latrán) runs below the castle just over the bridge from the Old Town. It's a 10-minute walk downhill from the train station. Lined with cute shops, the street has a couple of fine little family-run, eight-room pensions.

$$ Pension Lobo fills a modern and efficient concrete building with eight rooms. The pension operates a shuttle bus to Linz, Salzburg, and Vienna—see details under "Český Krumlov Connections" (Db-1,200 Kč, Tb-1,600 Kč, includes parking, Latrán 73, tel. & fax 380-713-153, www.pensionlobo.cz, lobo @ckrumlov.cz).

$ Pension Danny is a little funkier, with homier rooms and a tangled floor plan above a restaurant (Db-990 Kč, apartment Db-1,190 Kč, breakfast in room, Latrán 72, tel. 380-712-710, www .pensiondanny.cz, recepce@pensiondanny.cz).

On Rooseveltova Street, Between the Bus Station and the Old Town

Rooseveltova street, midway between the bus station and the Old Town (a four-minute walk from either), is lined with several fine little places, each with easy free parking. The key here is tranquility—the noisy bars of the town center are out of earshot.

$$ Little Pension Teddy offers three deluxe rooms that share a balcony overlooking the river and have original 18th-century furniture. Or stay in one of four modern-style rooms, some of which also face the river (Db-1,250 Kč, deluxe Db-1,400 Kč, cash only, staff may be unhelpful, free Wi-Fi and Internet access, parking-200 Kč, Rooseveltova 38, tel. 380-711-595, mobile 724-003-981, www.pensionteddy.cz, info@pensionteddy.cz).

$$ Pension Myší Díra ("Mouse Hole") hides eight sleek, spacious, bright, and woody Bohemian contemporary rooms overlooking the Vltava River just outside the Old Town (Db-900–1,400 Kč, bigger deluxe riverview Db-1,900 Kč, prices include transfer to/from bus or train station, Rooseveltova 28, tel. 380-712-853, fax 380-711-900, www.malecek.cz). The no-nonsense reception, which closes at 20:00, runs the recommended boat rental company (Půjčovna Lodí Maleček, at the same address), along with three similar pensions with comparable prices: **Pension Wok** down by the river, **Pension Margarita** farther along Rooseveltova, and **Pension u Hada.**

$$ Pension Anna is well-run, with two doubles, five apartments, and a restful little garden. Its apartments are spacious suites, with a living room and stairs leading to the double-bedded loft. The upstairs rooms can get stuffy during the summer (Db-1,250 Kč, Db apartment-1,550 Kč, extra bed-350 Kč, Rooseveltova 41, tel. & fax 380-711-692, www.pensionanna.euweb.cz, pension .anna@quick.cz). If you book a standard Db and they bump you up to an apartment, don't pay more than the Db rate.

Hostels

There are several hostels in town. Hostel 99 (closest to the train station) is clearly the high-energy, youthful party hostel. Krumlov House (closer to the bus station) is more mellow. Both are well-managed, and each is a five-minute walk from the main square.

$ Hostel 99's picnic-table terrace looks out on the Old Town. While the gentle sound of the river gurgles outside your window late at night, you're more likely to hear a youthful international crowd having a great time. The hostel caters to its fun-loving young guests, offering free inner tubes for river floats, rental bikes, and a free keg of beer each Wednesday. The adjacent and recommended Hospoda 99 restaurant serves good, cheap soups, salads, and meals (65 beds in 4- to 10-bed coed rooms-300 Kč, D-700 Kč, T-990 Kč, Internet access-1 Kč/min, laundry-200 Kč/load, use the lockers, no curfew or lockout, 10-min downhill walk from train station or two bus stops to Spicak, Vezni 99, tel. & fax 380-712-812, www .hostel99.com, hostel99@hotmail.com).

$ Krumlov House Hostel is take-your-shoes-off-at-the-door, shiny, hardwood-with-throw-rugs mellow. Efficiently run by a Canadian, it has a hip and trusting vibe and feels welcoming to travelers of any age (24 beds, 6 beds in two dorms-300 Kč per bed, Db-800 Kč, 2-person apartment-900 Kč, family room, no breakfast but there is a guests' kitchen, DVD library, laundry facilities, Rooseveltova 68, tel. 380-711-935, www.krumlovhostel.com, info @krumlovhostel.com).

Eating in Český Krumlov

Krumlov, with a huge variety of creative little restaurants, is a fun place to eat. In peak times, the good places fill fast, so make reservations or eat early.

Na Louži seems to be everyone's favorite little Czech bistro, with 40 seats in one 1930s-style room decorated with funky old advertisements. They serve inexpensive, tasty local cuisine and hometown Eggenberg beer on tap. If you've always wanted to play the piano for an appreciative Czech crowd in a colorful little tavern...do it here (daily 10:00–23:00, Kájovská 66, tel. 380-711-280).

Krčma u Dwau Maryí ("Tavern of the Two Marys") is a characteristic old place with idyllic riverside picnic tables, serving ye olde Czech cuisine and drinks. The fascinating menu explains the history of the house and makes a good case that the food of the poor medieval Bohemians was tasty and varied. Buck up for buckwheat, millet, greasy meat, or the poor-man's porridge (daily 11:00–23:00, Parkán 104, tel. 380-717-228).

Cikánská Jizba ("Gypsy Pub") is a Roma tavern filling one den-like, barrel-vaulted room. The Roma staff serves Slovak-style food (Slovakia is where most of the Czech Republic's Roma population came from). Krumlov has a long Roma history, and even today 1,000 Roma people live in the town (see sidebar on page 198). While this rustic little restaurant—which packs its 10 tables under a mystic-feeling Gothic vault—won't win any cuisine awards, you never know what festive and musical activities will erupt, particularly on Friday nights, when the owner's son's band, Cindži Renta (Wet Rag), performs here (Mon–Sat 15:00–24:00, closed Sun, 2 blocks toward castle from main square at Dlouhá 31, tel. 380-717-585).

Restaurace u Dobráka ("Good Man") is like eating in a medieval garage, with a giant poster of Karl Marx overseeing the action. Lojza, who's been tossing steaks on his open fire for years, makes sure you'll eat well. Locals know it as the best place for grilled steak and fish—expect to pay 350 Kč for a full meal. He charges too much for his beer in order to keep the noisy beer-drinkers away (open daily 17:30–24:00 from Easter until Lojza "has a shoebox full of money," Široká 74, tel. 380-717-776).

Laibon is the modern vegetarian answer to the carnivorous Middle Ages. Settle down inside or head out onto the idyllic river terrace, and lighten up your pork-loaded diet with soy goulash or Mútábúr soup (daily 11:00–23:00, Parkán 105).

Rybářská Restaurace ("Fisherman's Restaurant") doesn't look particularly inviting from the outside, but don't get discouraged. This is *the* place in town to taste freshwater fish you've never heard of (and never will again). Try eel, perch, shad, carp, trout, and more. Choose between indoor tables under fishnets or river-side picnic benches outside (daily 11:00–22:00, on the island by the millwheel).

Krčma v Šatlavské is an old prison gone cozy, with an open fire, big wooden tables under a rustic old medieval vault, and tables outdoors on the pedestrian lane. It's great for a late drink or game cooked on an open spit. *Medovina* is the hot honey wine (daily 12:00–24:00, on Šatlavská, follow lane leading to the side from TI on main square, mobile 608-973-797).

Restaurace Barbakán is built into the town fortifications, with a terrace hanging high over the river. It's a good spot for old-fashioned Czech cooking and beer, at the top of town and near the recommended Rooseveltova street accommodations (open long hours daily, reasonable prices, Horní 26, tel. 380-712-679).

Hospoda 99 Restaurace serves good, cheap soups, salads, and meals. It's the choice of hostelers and locals alike for its hamburgers, vegetarian food, Czech dishes, and cheap booze (meals served 10:00–22:00, bar open until 24:00, at Hostel 99, Vezni 99, tel. 380-712-812). This place is booming until late, when everything else is hibernating.

Dobrá Čajovna is a typical example of the quiet, exotic-feeling teahouses that flooded Czech towns in the 1990s as alternatives to smoky, raucous pubs. Though directly across from the castle entrance, it's a world away from the touristic hubbub. As is so often the case, if you want to surround yourself with locals, don't go to a traditional place...go ethnic. With its meditative karma inside and a peaceful terrace facing the monastery out back, it provides a relaxing break (daily 13:00–22:00, Latrán 54, mobile 777-654-744).

Český Krumlov Connections

Almost all trains to and from Český Krumlov require a transfer in the city of České Budějovice, a transit hub just to the north. České Budějovice's bus and train stations are next to each other. All bus and train timetables are online at www.idos.cz.

From Český Krumlov by Train to: České Budějovice (6/day, 1 hr), **Prague** (8/day, 1/day direct, 4 hrs; bus is faster, cheaper, and easier—see below), **Vienna** (6/day with at least one change, 5–6 hrs), **Budapest** (6/day with at least one change, 10–15 hrs).

From Český Krumlov by Bus to: Prague (7/day, 3.5 hrs, 180 Kč; 2 of the daily departures—12:00 and 16:45—can be reserved and paid for at TI, tickets can be bought from driver if seats are available), **České Budějovice** (transit hub for other destinations; about 2/hr, 30–50 min, 30 Kč). The Český Krumlov bus station, a five-minute walk out of town, is just a big parking lot with numbered stalls for various buses (bus info tel. 380-711-190). A good place to buy bus tickets online is www.studentagency.cz.

From České Budějovice to Třeboň, Telč, and Třebíč: An express bus goes from České Budějovice to the Moravian city of **Brno** (5/day Mon–Fri, 2/day Sat–Sun, 4.5 hrs). Along the way, it stops at **Třeboň** (30 min from České Budějovice), **Telč** (2 hrs from České Budějovice), and **Třebíč** (3.25 hrs from České Budějovice).

By Shuttle Bus or Private Car to Linz and Beyond: If you get to Linz, Austria, by shuttle bus or car, you'll have your choice of fast trains that run hourly from Linz to Munich, Salzburg, and Vienna. **Pension Lobo** in Český Krumlov runs a shuttle bus service to and from **Linz** (3/day, 75 min, 380 Kč), **Vienna** (1/day, 3 hrs, 950 Kč), and **Salzburg** (1/day, 3 hrs, 950 Kč). Reservations are required—call 380-713-153 or 777-637-374, send an email to lobo @ckrumlov.cz, or reserve in person at Pension Lobo or at the shuttle office on the main square (www.shuttlelobo.cz).

TŘEBOŇ, TELČ, AND TŘEBÍČ

Many travelers to South Bohemia visit only Český Krumlov. While it's delightful, three nearby towns are less packaged, more authentic, and, for many, equally worthwhile.

If you draw a line between České Budějovice (the capital of South Bohemia) and Brno (the capital of Moravia), you'll go right through the "Three Ts": Třeboň is an inviting medieval town famous for its peat spas, network of manmade lakes, and fish specialties. Tiny Telč has the Czech Republic's most impressive main square. And busy Třebíč is home to the country's most intact historic Jewish quarter.

Getting Around the "Three Ts"

An express bus line between the big cities of České Budějovice and Brno stops in Třeboň, Telč, and Třebíč (5/day Mon–Fri, 2/day Sat–Sun; České Budějovice to Třeboň—30 min, to Telč—2 hrs, to Třebíč—3.25 hrs, to Brno—4.5 hrs). You can reach České Budějovice easily by direct train from Prague (almost hourly, 2.5 hrs) or from Český Krumlov (6/day, 1 hr). In České Budějovice, the bus and train stations are next to each other. Direct buses also connect these towns to Prague and other destinations; see "Connections" for each destination.

Planning Your Time

With good planning—letting bus departures dictate the amount of time you spend in each town—you could reasonably leave Český Krumlov early in the morning, visit Třeboň and Telč, and arrive in Třebíč by evening. With more time, consider an evening in Telč for village relaxation and hiking, or move on to Třebíč for a bigger, more city-like feel.

Třeboň

Třeboň (TREH-bohn, pop. 18,000), a well-preserved medieval town centered around an inviting Renaissance square, is a charming place to explore a unique biosphere of artificial lakes that date back to the 14th century.

Over the centuries, people have transformed what was a flooding marshland into a clever and delightful combination of lakes, oak-lined dikes, wild meadows, Baroque villages, peat bogs, and pine woods. Rather than unprofitable wet fields, the nobles wanted ponds that swarmed with fish—and today Třeboň remains the fish-raising capital of the Czech Republic. Landscape architects in the 16th century managed to strike an amazing balance between civilization and nature, which today is a protected ecosystem (about 15 percent covered by water) with the biggest diversity of bird species in Eastern Europe. Nature enthu-

siasts come here to bird-watch, bike along dikes held together by the roots of centuries-old oaks, and devour the best fish specialties in the country.

While Třeboň enjoys plenty of tourism, its fish industry makes its relative affluence feel a little less touristy than other popular towns. Its peat spas have attracted patients from all over the world for decades—but since the facilities are small, Třeboň is never as overrun as some other, more famous spa towns.

Planning Your Time

With a full day in Třeboň, spend the morning enjoying the square, climbing up the Town Hall Tower, touring the Dean Church, and visiting the "Man and the Landscape" exhibition in the castle. (The castle itself and the brewery are less interesting.) After trying fish soup and trout for lunch, rent a bike and follow the educational trail along the ancient dikes. If it's hot, bring a bathing suit.

Soaking yourself in the peat of the spas is unforgettable; unfortunately, since the spa treatments are overbooked, it's difficult to get a spot (for details, see page 215). If you get in, build your day around it.

If you're here in October and November, lend a hand in the fascinating ritual of clearing the fish ponds, warming yourself with shots of potato rum as you wade through the mud.

Orientation to Třeboň

The old town—separated from newer construction by city walls, Renaissance gates, a water channel, and a castle garden—encircles the main square, Masaryk Square (Masarykovo Náměstí). Sights, hotels, restaurants, and ATMs are all within a couple blocks of Masaryk Square. From the train station, enter the square through the east gate. Standing in the middle of the square and facing west (with the station and gate at your back), the street to the left leads to the brewery and to Svět lake. The castle, which houses the "Man and the Landscape" exhibit, is at the far (west) end of the square.

Tourist Information

The TI, next to the Town Hall on Masaryk Square, hands out an exhaustive, glittering brochure called *The Region of Třeboň*, which includes a town map. They can reserve an English-speaking local guide with several days' advance notice (Mon–Fri 9:00–12:00 & 13:00–18:00, Sat–Sun 9:00–12:00 & 13:00–19:00, tel. 384-721-169, www.trebon-mesto.cz).

Arrival in Třeboň

The train station and the local bus stop are within easy walking distance from Masaryk Square.

By Train: Get off at the Třeboň–Lázně station—*not* the Třeboň–Město station. From Třeboň–Lázně, walk along the road directly in front of the station and you'll reach Masaryk Square in five minutes.

By Bus: The bus from Prague leaves you at the main bus station, a 20-minute walk (or 100-Kč taxi ride, tel. 384-722-200) west of the old town. Most buses arriving from České Budějovice continue from the main station to the Sokolská stop, which is a short walk through the castle park to Masaryk Square.

Helpful Hints

Internet Access: The user-friendly **Town Library** (Mon–Fri 8:00–17:00, closed Sat–Sun) and **Café Bar–Computer Center Roháč** (daily 18:00–2:00 in the morning) are in the same building by the castle park, at Na Sadech 349. **Lázně Berta** is just outside the east gate (daily 6:00–22:00).

Bike Rental: Hotel Zlatá Hvězda (on Masaryk Square, tel. 384-757-111) and the **newsstand** directly across the square at #85 (tel. 384-722-867) both rent decent mountain and trekking bikes (40 Kč/hr, 100 Kč/half-day, 200 Kč/day, hotel requires driver's license as a deposit).

Sights in Třeboň

Masaryk Square (Masarykovo Náměstí)—Třeboň's fine main square is typical of squares in the region, lined with col-

orful facades artfully blending both Renaissance and Baroque building styles. It was built by the town's 17th-century burghers, whose wealth came from the booming fish industry. The rectangular market plaza—with a humble plague column and fountain in the middle—feels just right. Grab a seat at one of the outdoor cafés, and watch local life circulate with the serenity of ducks on a lake.

While the tranquility comes naturally today, until 1989 it was a government requirement. At the square's lower end, above the bank door, a **propaganda relief** in the Social Realist style extols the virtue of working hard and stowing your money here for the common good. Higher up, a happy fisherman cradles a big fish, the reason for his wealth—and, since the 16th century, the wealth of Třeboň.

The **Town Hall Tower,** whose moderate height of 100 feet just fits with the size of the square, is worth the climb. Surveying the view from its top, you feel as if you can reach out and touch the circular old town. Beyond that, the lakes glimmer against the green backdrop of stately oaks (15 Kč, June–Sept daily

10:00–18:00, unpredictable hours Oct–May).

Across from the Town Hall, the impossible-to-miss, rampart-like white gable marks the famous 16th-century **Inn at the White Horse** (U Bílého Koníčka—look for the small horse on the facade).

At the other end of the square, notice the only modern building here, a **Spar supermarket.** Some 30 years ago, when the square was veiled in the shabby gray of communism, the regime decided to give it a facelift with a modern building that fit the medieval space like a UFO. After 1989, locals carefully added a facade and a new roof to the concrete box, effectively blending the former eyesore into the Old World townscape.

Castle (Zámek)—The castle is covered with rectangular sgraffiti, a characteristic decoration of the late 1500s (made by etching a design in plaster, revealing a different color underneath). As with other South Bohemian towns, all this sgraffiti is a reminder that the 16th century was Třeboň's heyday. Třeboň belonged to the Český Krumlov–based Rožmberk family. In 1600, Petr Vok—the last of the Rožmberks—moved here permanently after selling Český Krumlov to the emperor. He brought along his archive, still considered the most valuable collection of medieval documents in this part of Europe. The castle can only be visited with an escorted tour (in Czech, with an English flier). Your best basic castle visit is Route A, which includes Petr Vok's Renaissance rooms. Route B covers the 19th-century apartments, kitchens, and stables of the later, equally distinguished Schwarzenbergs (70–80 Kč for tours in Czech, English tours cost more and must be reserved a week ahead, buy at "cash box" ticket desk, tours go hourly or more, April–Oct Tue–Sun 9:00–11:45 & 12:45–17:00, closed Mon and Nov–March, tel. 384-721-193).

▲**"Man and the Landscape" Exhibit**—Located inside the castle, this is the best sight in town. Surprisingly modern, thoughtfully described in English, and further illuminated by excellent little video-on-command terminals, the exhibit covers the things that make this town distinct: lake-making, the fish industry, the peat spa treatment, and the natural environment. A highlight is the theater (just after the stuffed animals), where you can watch a 13-minute video that takes you fishing early in the morning, and a 20-minute video racing you through a year with nature in Třeboň. An hour here is time well-invested (50 Kč, Tue–Sun 9:00–17:00, closed Mon, enter from garden just outside castle and city wall, tel. 384-724-912).

City Wall and Park—The greenbelt that circles the town just outside its 16th-century wall makes for a delightful 15-minute walk. Along the way, you'll pass the town's famous but underwhelming spas.

TŘEBOŇ

Dean Church and Augustine Monastery (Děkanský Kostel a Augustiánský Klášter)—This Gothic church, with its unusual double nave (and obtrusive columns down the middle), is worth

a look if open during your visit. A highlight is its delicately curved statue of the *Madonna and Child* (c. 1390, painted limestone). Its Ivory Soap sweetness and a slinky S-shaped body are typical of late "beautiful style" Gothic. The artist, though anonymous, is known as the "Master of the Třeboň Madonna." The church once showcased more marvelous Gothic sculptures and altars, but these were deemed too

valuable, so they were zipped off to the Museum of Medieval Art in Prague's St. Agnes Convent (see page 60). Frescoes in the adjoining cloister, badly neglected until after 1989, show scenes from the life of St. Augustine. While the monastery library is long gone, Augustinians were some of the most ardent medieval copyists in the time before Gutenberg's moveable type revolutionized printing. Through the efforts of monks in this monastery, Třeboň became a center of medieval learning for Czechs and Austrians alike (30 Kč, July–Aug daily 9:00–11:30 & 13:30–17:00, or pop in just before the nearly nightly 18:30 Mass, if closed ring the parish home next door, Husova 142, rectory tel. 384-722-390).

Boating and Swimming—A motorboat sets out from the small wharf behind the brewery once an hour for a 30-minute (60 Kč) or 45-minute (90 Kč) cruise over the second-largest of Třeboň's lakes, Svět (daily 10:00–19:00). The nearest sandy beach is a 10-minute walk, to the right from the wharf along the dike.

Biking—The area is flat, so biking is a fun and convenient way to get around. A bike trip along the dirt trails on the ancient dikes is a great way to experience the land and water. Buy a cycling map from the TI, then follow the marked trails that snake along channels and through traditional villages.

Hiking—The best hiking is in the area of Nová Řeka (New River), directly east of town. Or catch a bus (or drive) to Chlum u Třeboně, and hike in the blueberry-filled pine woods along the Austrian border.

Peat Spa (Bertiny Lázně)—Třeboň is an important peat spa. Patients from all over the world come here for weeklong stays to get buried in the black, smelly sludge that's thought to cure aching joints and spines. Well…I guess it doesn't hurt to try. The complete peat bath *(slatinná koupel celková)* is combined with a full-body massage (don't try to sneak away before the nurse is finished with

The Lakes of Třeboň

The medieval lake-builders of Třeboň created an ingenious landscape of regulated channels, marshes turned into lakes, and fields changed into marshes. Birds and animals new to the region began to dwell here. Peat provided a rich soil for pines and blueberry bushes.

The good lake-builders knew that small is beautiful... but, of course, not all of them were good. The most famous of Třeboň lake-builders was Jakub Krčín, the architect of the largest lakes, Svět and Rožmberk. Krčín was a man driven more by his ego than by practical considerations. Much of the water in his huge, deep lakes is a dead zone, lacking enough oxygen to support large fish colonies. Though less celebrated, his predecessor, Štěpánek Netolický, was more of a fishing expert. He built small, and his lakes were successful. His Golden Channel, which connects dozens of lakes, is the region's biggest marvel.

The Třeboň lakes were built for flood control as well as fishing. The marshy area around the town used to be regularly flooded by the Lužnice River, and the artificial lakes were designed to absorb the floods. In 2002, the largest floods in Czech history tested the work of those medieval lake-builders. While the 20th-century dams built on the Vltava River to protect Prague failed, Třeboň's 16th-century dams held, vindicating Krčín and keeping Třeboň's feet dry.

you). It's worth it to have the opportunity to fully judge the power of peat and experience the surreal *One Flew Over the Cuckoo's Nest* atmosphere of Czech medical institutions.

While it's smart to book a spa treatment several months ahead (you'll receive a prompt confirmation and a reminder one month before your appointment), you can often snare a last-minute spot if there's a cancellation. Call the spa or ask your hotelier to inquire for you (tel. 384-754-457, www.berta.cz, sestra@berta.cz). To get to the spa, go through the east gate of the city walls; the spa is just off to your left.

Sleeping in Třeboň

Although there are many pensions in Třeboň, most only take spa guests who stay for a couple of weeks. These two hotels welcome guests even for one- or two-night stays on short notice.

$$$ Hotel Galerie has 12 renovated rooms and an artistically decorated breakfast room. Notice the slightly buried storage room by the reception hall that now serves as a semi-open wine cellar—since Třeboň stands on floating sands, no house in town

Sleep Code

(18 Kč = about $1, country code: 420)
S = Single, **D** = Double/Twin, **T** = Triple, **Q** = Quad, **b** = bathroom,
s = shower only. Unless otherwise noted, credit cards are
accepted and prices include breakfast.

To help you sort easily through these listings, I've divided
the rooms into three categories based on the price for a
standard double room with bath:

$$$ Higher Priced—Most rooms 1,500 Kč or more.
$$ Moderately Priced—Most rooms between
1,000–1,500 Kč.
$ Lower Priced—Most rooms 1,000 Kč or less.

has a basement. The Galerie manager can usually set up a spa
appointment even at the last minute—ask when you reserve (Sb-
1,300 Kč, Db-1,850 Kč, Tb-2,400 Kč, Internet access and Wi-Fi,
Rožmberská 35, tel. 384-385-293, fax 384-385-294, mobile 724-
093-876, www.hotel-trebon.cz, galerie@hoteltrebon.cz). The hotel
also runs a decent restaurant on the ground floor with tasty, cheap
lunch specials.

$ Hotel Bílý Koníček, on Masaryk Square, has managed to
revamp all 23 of its rooms. Although still only a pale shadow of
what was once a Renaissance inn—founded in 1544 and famous
throughout the country—its rooms are a good value (standard
Db-1,000 Kč, tel. 384-721-213, Masarykovo Náměstí 27, www
.hotelbilykonicek.cz, hotel@hotelbilykonicek.cz). Breakfast is not
included—that's probably a good thing, since the sausage-oriented
ground-floor restaurant is best avoided. Instead, walk around the
corner by the Town Hall to a little Happy Café bakery that serves
a large selection of fine pastries and good coffee from 7:00.

Eating in Třeboň

Since the 1200s, Třeboň has lived on a steady diet of fish. The variety of fish raised here is amazing...as are the chefs. Austrians and
Czechs alike drive for hours just to dine here. While you can find
trout and carp throughout the country, the perch and pike from
the lakes are unique. The pine woods south of the lakes are filled
with blueberries—when it's the season, the blueberry dumplings
are another must.

Šupina & Šupinka Restaurant ("Scale and Little Scale") is
run by the local fishers' union, which makes sure the meals are
top-notch. While the modern interior may not seem very atmospheric to visitors, it doesn't bother locals, who have good reason

TŘEBOŇ

to consider this one of the best fish restaurants in the country. Dig into the rare and refined appetizers, which include fried carp sperm, cod liver, pickled herring, and local crab. If you have only one fish dinner in the Czech Republic, the native pike perch here would be your best choice (daily 10:30–24:00; from Masaryk Square, walk past the Spar supermarket, then turn right into Novohradská Brána; tel. 384-721-149).

Na Rožmberské Baště is a little eatery with warm wooden walls and nets and fishing rods hanging from the ceiling (you can borrow one and bring in your own catch to be cooked). They serve cheap, tasty meals made from everything that swims in the surrounding lakes (Mon–Sat 10:30–23:30, Sun 10:30–22:30, on Rožmberská, tel. 384-721-893).

Schwarzenberská Pivnice is a large, colorful brewery/pub serving every variety of local Regent beer, including the fresh yeast kind you won't find in regular pubs. The only snacks available are Czech munchies, such as pickled sausage *(utopenec)* and pickled brie *(nakládaný hermelín)*—this place is for drinking (Mon–Fri 11:00–22:00, Sat–Sun 12:00–23:00, in Regent Brewery).

Třeboň Connections

While buses between Třeboň and Prague are about as fast as the train (2.5 hrs), bus departures are less frequent, and the bus station is far from the center of Třeboň.

From Třeboň by Train to: Prague (7/day, 2.5 hrs, transfer at Veselí nad Lužnicí). If going from Prague to Třeboň, get off at Třeboň–Lázně, not Třeboň–Město.

By Bus to: Prague (2/day, 2.5 hrs), **Český Krumlov** (10/day to České Budějovice, 30 min; then transfer to Český Krumlov—see page 187), **Telč** (5/day Mon–Fri, 2/day Sat–Sun, 90 min), **Třebíč** (5/day Mon–Fri, 2/day Sat–Sun, 2.75 hrs), **Brno** (5/day Mon–Fri, 2/day Sat–Sun, 4 hrs).

Telč

Telč (pronounced "telch," pop. 6,000) is famous for its castle and its glorious square, considered by many to be the country's best. The old town—just a fat square with a thin layer of buildings— is surrounded by a sophisticated system of protective ponds and defense walls. The general lay of the land has changed little since the 1300s. After 1800, all new construction took place outside the core. Today, Telč remains an unspoiled, sleepy Czech town where neighbors chat in pastry shops, Vietnamese traders in medieval arcade stalls sell dirt-cheap textiles to country folks, and the smell of goat dung from a pasture across the lake permeates the town after nightfall.

There are basically no attractions aside from the square and the castle. Telč is made to order as a lunch stop on the way to or from Slavonice, Třeboň, and Třebíč, or on the longer haul between Prague, Brno, and Vienna. An overnight stay here can be a relaxing village experience.

Orientation to Telč

Everything you'll need—including ATMs, shops, hotels, and restaurants—is on the main square (Náměstí Zachariáše z Hradce), easily reachable on foot from the bus station. For a taxi, call 603-255-048 and expect basic English.

Tourist Information

The TI has information on activities in the area, train and bus schedules, and Internet access (Mon–Fri 8:00–18:00, Sat–Sun 10:00–18:00, shorter hours off-season, tel. 567-112-407, www.telc -etc.cz). They can also help you find a room in one of the pensions on the square (see "Sleeping in Telč," later).

Helpful Hints

Festivals: Every year during the first two weeks of July, young musicians pour into Telč from all over Europe for the French–Czech Music Academy, which hosts workshops on classical music interpretation. The young virtuosos show off their skills in a number of concerts and recitals. The Telč Vacations (Prázdniny v Telči) festival, held during the first two weeks of August, makes the squares, gardens, and castle chambers come alive with folk music, open-air theater, and exhibitions.

Internet Access: The TI has one computer available to the public. The shop next to the TI also offers Internet access.

Bike Rental: You can rent bikes at the shop next to the TI (40 Kč/hour, 200 Kč/day, daily 9:00–18:00, tel. 567-243-562). Locals enjoy the half-day bike trip to the castle ruin of Roštejn and back (10 miles round-trip).

Boat Rental: During the summer, you can rent a boat for a lazy lake cruise. To get to the rental boats, walk through the gate between the castle and the square, then turn right on the path along the lake (40 Kč/hr; July–Aug daily 10:00–18:00; June

TELČ

Fri 13:00–18:00, Sat–Sun 10:00–18:00, closed Mon–Thu; no rentals Sept–May).

Sights in Telč

▲**Main Square (Náměstí Zachariáše z Hradce)**—Telč's spacious square, lined by fairy-tale gables resting on the characteris-

tic vaulted arcades that still cover local shops and bakeries, is the most impressive in the Czech Republic. The uniqueness of the square lies in its enormous size, unexpected proportions in such a small town, and the purity of its style—of the 40 houses lining the square, there isn't a single one younger than 300 years. A fire devastated the town in 1553, and it was rebuilt of stone. A plague that ravaged the region in 1780 skipped Telč, so the plague column was built on the square to thank God.

Telč Castle—In its early years, this castle belonged to the clan of the Five Roses (symbolized by a golden rose on a blue field; see the "Parting of the Roses" sidebar on page 191). In the 1500s, the nobleman Zachariáš z Hradce (for whom the grand main square is named) imported a team of Italian artists, who turned the earlier Gothic palace into a lavish Renaissance residence. (Their work also influenced most of the burgher houses in the square.) The castle can be toured only with an escort. You have two options: Tour A, the best basic castle tour, takes you through some stately Renaissance chambers. Tour B goes through the 19th-century apartments of the Lichtenstein family, who lived here until 1945. You'll most likely have a Czech-speaking guide and be given an English description to read as you go (160 Kč per tour; May–Aug Tue–Sun 9:00–12:00 & 13:00–17:00, closed Mon; April and Sept–Oct Tue–Sun 9:00–12:00 & 13:00–16:00, closed Mon; closed Nov–March; last tour one hour before closing). The castle is located at the end of the main square—you can't miss it.

Regional Museum of Telč—While humble, this little five-room exhibit gives you an interesting insight into the town (check out the 1895 town model and the WWI and WWII photos). Everything is well-explained in the English pamphlet you can borrow as you enter (30 Kč, daily 9:00–16:30, in the castle complex).

TELČ

Gustav Mahler and Jihlava

Gustav Mahler (1860–1911) was the most important composer in Vienna at the turn of the 20th century. Mahler composed some of the last of the classical symphonies and was the first to venture into the musical never-never-land of atonality (while his contemporary Arnold Schönberg, also Jewish, took up residence there). The age of harmony ended—by 1910 there was nothing to hold the world together, and shifts in art preceded the shots of World War I.

Mahler, born in the Czech village of Kaliště, spent the first 15 years of his life in Jihlava, at a house at Znojemská 4 that now functions as a vibrant cultural center and the composer's museum (tel. 567-167-132, www.jihlava.cz/gustavmahler). This is a worthwhile stop for music buffs en route from Prague to Telč.

Gallery of Jan Zrzavý—Tucked away in the garden to the right of the castle entrance, this small gallery is worth a peek to learn about pointillism. Zrzavý, one of the most prolific Czech painters, had a style similar to earlier Impressionists, but used dots (or points) instead of lines to construct images. Paintings in the five-room gallery evolve from his teen years on through the troubled first half of the 20th century, but without the angst you might expect. Don't try to make much sense of it. Just enjoy looking at the artist's slices of local life, from steelworks to villages, represented in his unusual style (30 Kč; April–Oct Tue–Sun 9:00–12:00 & 13:00–17:00, closed Mon; Nov–March Tue–Sun 9:00–12:00 & 13:00–16:00, closed Mon).

Sleeping in Telč

(18 Kč = about $1, country code: 420)

Many families living on or near the main square have turned parts of their homes into pleasant pensions that meld perfectly with the mellow feel of this town. At a pension, you get nicer rooms and more personal service for about half the price of the hotels, which bank on being the only places in town able to accommodate groups.

$$$ Hotel Telč, under the church tower across the square from the castle, has 10 simply furnished rooms (Sb-1,265 Kč, Db-1,580–1,870 Kč, extra bed-200 Kč, tel. 567-243-109, www.hoteltelc.cz, hotel.telc@tiscali.cz).

$$$ Hotel Celerin, also on the main square, is slightly bigger than Hotel Telč. Some of its comfy rooms have traditional burgher

TELČ

furniture (Sb-980–1,200 Kč, Db-1,530–1,750 Kč, more expensive rooms face square, cheaper rooms face garden, Wi-Fi, tel. 567-243-477, fax 567-213-581, www.hotelcelerin.cz, office@hotelcelerin.cz).

$ Penzion Patricia is run by a former high-school teacher (and her four-legged friends, Bibi and Borka) who, after 14 years in the US, returned to Telč with a mission: to turn her family's house into a showcase of Telč's hospitality. The eight rooms vary in size and style, but all come with queen-size beds imported from California. Breakfast is served on a terrace under the Romanesque church tower, and bonfires are lit in the garden along the former town walls, where you can grill meat or munch seasonal fruits (Sb-550 Kč, Db-940 Kč, Internet access, next to Hotel Telč on the main square at #38, tel. 567-213-342, mobile 776-691-300, www.pensionpatricia-telc.eu, patricia_telc@volny.cz).

$ Penzion Steidler has the most tastefully furnished rooms in town and a narrow, blooming garden that stretches all the way to the lake (Sb-500 Kč, Db-800 Kč, suite-1,600 Kč, parking-50 Kč, look for house #52 on the main square, tel. 567-243-424, mobile 721-316-390, www.telc-accommodation.eu, steidler@volny.cz).

$ Penzion Danuše is a well-managed, quiet place with four solid rooms (Db-1,000 Kč, Db suite-1,200 Kč, 30 yards off the main square at the corner of Palackého and Hradební 25, tel. 567-213-945, mobile 603-449-188, danuse.telc@seznam.cz).

Eating in Telč

All of these eateries are on the main square.

Šenk pod Věží ("Under the Tower") is ideal for a fancy Czech meal with extra touches. It has two small, atmospheric rooms with 100-year-old photographs and tranquil, outside seating in the back on the former town wall (daily 11:00–22:00, tel. 567-243-889).

Osvěžovna u Marušky, also directly beneath the tower, is popular with young locals who congregate here for coffee and cigarettes as much as for the food and beer. The walls are decorated by local artists and vacationing out-of-towners; jazz and classical concerts take place here twice a month (daily 11:00–24:00, mobile 603-398-128).

Pizzerie, on the corner by the plague column, has the best outside seating on the square and two modern, high-ceilinged rooms in the basement. Locals of all generations converge here for a surprisingly good and cheap Czech interpretation of the Italian theme. Sweet Czech ketchup rules the day, drowning every item on the long menu—be it pizza or pasta—in the same distinct flavor. Sicilian purists would not be amused (daily 11:00–22:00).

Telč Connections

From Telč to: Třeboň (5 buses/day Mon–Fri, 2/day Sat–Sun, 90 min), **Třebíč** (5 buses/day Mon–Fri, 2/day Sat–Sun, 45 min), **Brno** (5 buses/day Mon–Fri, 2/day Sat–Sun, 2.5 hrs), **Slavonice** (2 trains in morning, 3 in afternoon, 1 hr), **Prague** (3 trains/day, 4–5 hrs, requires 2 changes—bus is better; 5 buses/day Mon–Fri, 3/day Sat–Sun, 2–3 hrs; more with a transfer in Jihlava—3 hrs total). Note that some buses to Prague may arrive at Prague's Roztyly station (on the red Metro line) rather than the main bus station, Florenc.

Třebíč

A few miles east of Telč is the big, busy town of Třebíč (TREH-beech, pop. 40,000), with another wonderful main square and, just over its river, the largest intact Jewish ghetto in the country. While Prague's Jewish Quarter is packed with tourists, in Třebíč you'll have an entire Jewish town to yourself. Třebíč's Jewish settlement was relatively small. Its remains, though lonely and neglected, are amazingly authentic.

Orientation to Třebíč

Three hours in Třebíč is sufficient—everything's close by. The main square affords a fun slice-of-local-life look at a humble yet vibrant community, while the near-ghost town across the river was once the Jewish ghetto. The two main streets that run parallel to the river (which separates the ghetto from the Christian town) are connected by a maze of narrow passages, courtyards, and tunnels.

Tourist Information

The TI has two helpful branches: one on the main square and one in the ghetto's Rear Synagogue (both open daily 10:00–12:00 & 13:00–17:00, rental bikes at main square location, tel. 568-823-005, www.mkstrebic.cz).

Arrival in Třebíč

From the train station (with safe 24-hour luggage storage), cross the street behind the large waiting hall, and walk to the main square. To continue on to the ghetto, cross the river, following *Židovské Město* signs, marked with Stars of David. The cemetery is uphill.

Sights in Třebíč

▲**Charles Square (Karlovo Náměstí)**—Třebíč's main square is the third-biggest in the Czech Republic. A market square since the 13th century, it's still busy with a farmers market every morning. Třebíč was historically a mix of Christians and Jews, all living on the easy-to-defend bit of land between the river and the hill. As you'll see, that area is pretty tiny—and eventually the Christian community packed up and moved across the river for more space, establishing this square as the town's nucleus.

The statue of two Macedonian brothers—the saints Cyril and Methodius, who brought Christianity to Moravia and the Slavs in their own language, rather than Greek or Latin—was erected a thousand years after Methodius' death in 885. But forget all that history. Just circle the square, surveying today's Moravian scene. There are several fine pubs and cafés from which to people-watch. The small gallery in the four delightful vaulted rooms of the Painted House on the upper corner of the square is worth checking out to feel the artistic pulse of Moravia (next to the TI, displays temporary exhibits).

Opposite the bell tower, at #11, a lane leads across the river into the Jewish quarter, taking you directly to the Rear Synagogue (with a TI and small museum). Notice the grand views of the ghetto from the bridge.

▲**Jewish Ghetto (Židovské Město)**—The population of Třebíč's ghetto peaked in the 19th century at about 1,500. Only 10 Třebíč Jews survived the Holocaust. In the 1970s, the ghetto was slated for destruction, to be replaced by another ugly communist high-rise housing complex. But because the land proved unable to support a huge building project, the neighborhood survived. Today, it's protected by the government as the largest preserved Jewish quarter in

Europe. It comes back to life for one weekend a year during the Jewish festival (July 29–31 in 2010).

Coming here, you enter a place where time has stopped: The houses are essentially as the Jews left them more than 60 years ago. Many of the houses were resettled by Roma (see sidebar, page 198), who have done little to change the look and feel of the place. In Třebíč today, only one woman has a Jewish father. (Because you must have a Jewish mother to be legally Jewish, the Jewish population is officially zero.) The government wants the ghetto to be a living neighborhood, not a museum. Lines of drying clothes and kids kicking around a soccer ball on the cobblestones make today's ghetto come alive. After dark, it's *the* place for edgy nightlife.

The **Rear Synagogue** (Zadní Synagoga) is the visitors center, with a branch of the TI, plus displays of artifacts and a model of the once-thriving local Jewish community (40 Kč, daily 10:00–12:00 & 13:00–17:00). You can also hire a guide here. At the TI, confirm the hours of the nearby cemetery (listed below).

The **Front Synagogue** (Přední Synagoga) has functioned since 1954 as a Hussite Christian church. Though the synagogue is generally locked, you can peek through its gate to see how it was retooled for the plain Hus-style worship.

Jewish Cemetery—A 20-minute walk above the ghetto, this evocative memorial park is covered with spreading ivy, bushes of wild strawberries, and a commotion of 9,000 gravestones (the oldest dating to 1631). Notice how the tombstones follow the assimilation of the Jews, from simple markers to fancy 19th-century headstones that look exactly like those of the rich burghers in Christian cemeteries (daily May–Sept 8:00–20:00, March–April and Oct 8:00–18:00, Nov–Feb 9:00–16:00, confirm hours at the Rear Synagogue TI before ascending the hill).

St. Procopius Basilica—This enormous church looms over the town on a hill a five-minute walk above the main square and the ghetto. In a region of Baroque churches, this rich fusion of late Romanesque and early Gothic styles is a striking contrast. Unfortunately, it's viewable only with a tour (40 Kč, 45-min tours start every 30 min, May–Sept Tue–Fri 9:00–12:00 & 13:00–17:00, Sat–Mon 13:00–17:00, shorter hours and less-frequent tours Oct–April, tel. 568-610-022).

Sleeping in Třebíč

(18 Kč = about $1, country code: 420)

$$ Hotel Winkler, near the bus station, is an attractive little place with 15 comfortable rooms and flowers in the windows (Sb-770 Kč, Db-1,420 Kč, V. Nezvala 8, tel. 568-841-506, www.hotel-winkler .cz, recepce@hotel-winkler.cz).

$ Penzion u Synagogy, next to the Rear Synagogue, is as close as you can get to living in a Jewish ghetto, and includes free entry into the visitors center at the synagogue (Sb-470 Kč, Db-720 Kč, extra bed-120 Kč, Subakova 43, check in at Rear Synagogue TI, mobile 775-707-506, www.mkstrebic.cz).

$ Travellers' Hostel, near the Front Synagogue, has 55 dorm beds fitted into the meticulously restored home of a 16th-century baker. The oven still turns out warm bread, and a beer tap was installed even before the new roof, ensuring no guest leaves this party place without the two key elements of life (250 Kč per bunk in 8- to 10-bed dorm, 330 Kč in 4-bed dorm, Sb-600 Kč, Db-800 Kč, includes sheets and breakfast, Žerotínovo 19, tel. & fax 568-422-594, mobile 777-637-417, www.travellers.cz, trebic @travellers.cz).

Eating and Drinking in Třebíč

Neptune Restaurant, facing the Front Synagogue, serves good soup, fish dishes, and cheap daily lunch specials. This is the best place in the Jewish quarter, with fine indoor or outdoor seating (daily 11:00–22:00, mobile 776-350-850).

Měsíční Čajovna ("Moon Teahouse"), on the upper street in the middle of the ghetto, is made for contemplating times gone by in the company of young English-speaking locals (Sun and Tue–Fri 15:00–21:00, Sat 16:00–23:00, closed Mon, Skalní 2).

Občerstvení Jordan, in the midst of the action at #23 on the main square, has outside seating perfect for a fast salad, sandwich, or ready-made daily special. Go inside and order by pointing at what you want (Mon–Fri 6:30–18:00, Sat 8:00–12:00, Sun 14:00–18:00).

Třebíč Connections

From Třebíč to: Telč (5 buses/day Mon–Fri, 2/day Sat–Sun, 45 min), **Třeboň** (5 buses/day Mon–Fri, 2/day Sat–Sun, 2.75 hrs), **Brno** (5 buses/day Mon–Fri, 2/day Sat–Sun, 1.25 hrs; also 10 trains/day, 1.25 hrs), **Prague** (nearly hourly trains, 4–5 hrs, transfer in Brno—bus is better; 7 buses/day, 2.5 hrs). Note that some buses to Prague may arrive at Prague's Roztyly station (on the red Metro line), not the main bus station, Florenc.

TŘEBÍČ

SLAVONICE

Slavonice (SLAH-voh-neet-seh)—a charming little town of 2,700 people less than three miles from the Austrian border—is a perfect base for venturing into the most romantic of Czech landscapes. The town features two once-elegant Renaissance squares separated by a Gothic church and the Town Hall. In the surrounding countryside, hulking castle ruins top forested hills, deep woods surround lonely meadows, and WWII bunkers covered with sprawling blueberry bushes evoke the harsh realities of being a border town.

Centuries ago, this thinly populated borderland between Bohemia, Moravia, and Austria was filled with thieves and thugs—and was, therefore, nearly impossible to tax. Founded in the 1200s, the town was originally named Zlabings by the German settlers invited to colonize and civilize the region.

During the 14th century, when the main trading route between Prague and Vienna passed through here, Zlabings boomed. Most of the town's finest buildings date from this period. After the Thirty Years' War (1618–1648) the town declined, and, thanks to its ill fate, few new buildings broke the medieval harmony.

Following World War II, Zlabings' German residents—90 percent of the population—were forced out by vengeful Czechs (see "Edvard Beneš and the German Question" sidebar on page 194). Czech people moved in and simply occupied the homes of the former residents—sitting on their sofas and even wearing their clothes.

The town became fully Czech (and was officially renamed Slavonice), and a curtain of barbed wire sealed it from the West on three sides. This region—always sparsely populated, even more so after its predominantly German population was removed—grew wilder and full of forests throughout the Cold War, when it earned the nickname "Czech Canada" (Česká Kanada).

After 1989, the deep woods of the military zone were opened up to hikers and cyclists, the border a mile south of Slavonice was reopened, and Austrians began flocking here for cheap lunches and shopping sprees, boosting business and bringing a new period of relative prosperity to Slavonice. The children you see playing in the streets today—the grandkids of those Czech settlers from 1945—are enjoying good times once again. But something about this town, at the end of the Czech world just 20 years ago, still feels like Česká Kanada.

Orientation to Slavonice

Everything of interest is on Slavonice's main square, Náměstí Míru. The train and bus stations are each within a few minutes' walking distance of the center (head for the church tower, which overlooks the square).

Tourist Information

The TI, on the main square, hands out useful tourist maps of the Slavonicko region and sells the detailed *Česká Kanada* hiking map. They also have good Internet access (daily 9:00–12:00 & 13:00–18:00, shorter hours off-season, free English audioguide, Náměstí Míru, tel. 384-493-320, www.slavonice-mesto.cz).

The roads in the area are rarely used and ideal for **biking;** you can borrow bikes from each of the listed hotels (see "Sleeping in Slavonice," later).

Sights in Slavonice

The city tower and the simple town museum are nothing special and probably not worth your time (both open daily June–Aug, weekends only May and Sept, closed Oct–April). Instead, consider the following attractions.

Underground Passages—The medieval cellars under the town, connected by an intricate network of underground passages, are a hit with children and thin, short people. Starting from the entrance (on the main square, next to the TI), you can slip on boots and an overcoat and follow the flashlight of your guide, squeezing through a 30-minute subterranean tour of the town. While you'll see little more than dirty bricks, it's certainly a unique experience. It costs 40 Kč to join an existing tour. If you're visiting when a tour isn't already scheduled, you'll pay 240 Kč, the total cost of a tour for six people (July–Aug daily 9:00–18:00, call 775-906-330 to arrange a visit).

Sudetenland Defenses—Just outside Slavonice, hidden in a thick forest, is a network of armadillo-like concrete pillboxes and

The Never-Used Fortifications

As soon as Adolf Hitler came to power in Germany in 1933, Czechoslovakia grew nervous about invasion. The area around Slavonice was part of the so-called Sudetenland: It belonged to Czechoslovakia, but was predominantly inhabited by ethnic Germans (see sidebar on page 194). Czechoslovakia began constructing a ring of fortifications along its borders. Iron-enforced concrete bunkers were connected by underground tunnels.

By September 1938, when Hitler met with the French and the British in Munich to claim the Sudetenland, these fortifications were filled with 1.5 million mobilized Czechs and Slovaks. Morale was high, and nobody doubted that the French and British would honor treaties with Czechoslovakia and help the young democracy. But instead, British Prime Minister Neville Chamberlain proclaimed to the British public, "Why should we care about the fate of a quarreling people about whom we know nothing?"—and signed off on the Munich Agreement, ceding the German areas of Czechoslovakia to Hitler without even inviting Czech representatives to the negotiations. (Chamberlain won a Nobel Prize for this appeasement policy.) Alone, the Czechoslovak army—outnumbered by the Germans three to one—stood no chance. The frustrated soldiers were ordered home, and Czechs were forced out of the Sudetenland. Within six months, Hitler occupied the rest of the territory.

Today, the never-used bunkers along the hiking trails around Landštejn stand witness to the futility of appeasement policies and to the Czechs' bitter sense of betrayal. At the close of the war, this feeling led to the Czechs' siding with the Soviet Union, rather than with the unreliable French and British Allies. Ironically, the Munich Agreement probably saved Czechoslovakia from the fate of Poland, which was reduced to rubble during the war. Nevertheless, it took until 1989 for the Czechs to get over the frustration of the Munich Agreement in 1938, the communist takeover in 1948, and the failed "Prague Spring" uprising in 1968—moments when instead of being able to win their freedom, the Czechs had to give up without firing a single shot.

gun emplacements built by the Czechs in the 1930s, in anticipation of the Nazi takeover. The camouflaged mini-forts, barbed wire, and toy-like tank barriers evoke the futility of standing up to the Nazi war machine—you'll ponder the fine line between heroism and folly. A local duo is working to turn this area into the Museum of Fortifications. To get there, hike from Slavonice (1.25 miles) along the red-marked trail in the direction of Landštejn (see "Suggested Day Hike," later); or drive on the Slavonice–Stálkov road out of town and look for the *Muzeum Opevnění* sign on the left (park where you can and walk along the tiny road, then go through the lonely woods as if you were a 20th-century invader). You'll reach two bunkers fully equipped with 1930s periscopes and machine guns (daily July–Aug and on weekends May–June and Sept).

Landštejn Castle (Hrad Landštejn)—This region of thick forests and softly rolling hills is overseen by the stark ruins of the Gothic castle that once guarded the border. Though the castle itself is barren and looks like it was made of recently poured concrete, the commanding view from the top is worth the climb (40 Kč; June–Aug Tue–Sun 9:00–16:30, closed Mon; May and Sept Tue–Sun 9:00–15:30, closed Mon; April and Oct Sat–Sun 9:00–15:30, closed Mon–Fri; closed Nov–March; simple café inside castle gate, fancy Landštejnský Dvůr restaurant, two pubs by parking lot under castle; tel. 384-498-580, www.hradlandstejn .cz). On summer weekends, the castle serves as a venue for open-air folk and rock concerts.

Landštejn Castle is seven miles west of Slavonice, on the road to Nová Bystřice. Hardy travelers can reach the castle on foot (follow red-marked trail, see "Suggested Day Hike," below) or by bike (follow the road or get map at TI to go through the countryside). You can also reach it by bus (Slavonice–Nová Bystřice line, 3/day, weekdays only, 15 min, ask to be let off at Landštejn) or car (drive toward Nová Bystřice).

Suggested Day Hike: For a 14-mile hike, follow the red-marked trail from Slavonice to Landštejn via the work-in-progress Museum of Fortifications (described earlier), visit the castle (have lunch here), then descend along the yellow-marked trail in the direction of Dačice to Velký Troubný lake, a perfect swimming spot. From there, return to Slavonice along the red-and-white-marked nature trail.

Sleeping in Slavonice

All three recommended hotels are on the main square.

$$ Dům u Růže has 12 rooms in a restored late-19th-century house. Each room has its own bath and kitchen; the sauna and pool are 100 Kč/person extra (Sb-1,190 Kč, Db-1,390 Kč, Tb-1,590 Kč, breakfast-120 Kč, free parking, swimming pool, sauna, Wi-Fi, Náměstí Míru 452, tel. 384-493-004, mobile 603-493-879, www .dumuruze.cz, hotel@dumuruze.cz). They also rent bikes (30 Kč/ hr, 200 Kč/day).

$$ Hotel Besídka, between the two parts of the square separated by the church, hides eight ultra-modern, bright rooms behind a magnificent Renaissance facade. The striking combination of ancient and postmodern styles was designed by (and named

SLAVONICE

Sleep Code

(18 Kč = about $1, country code: 420)
S = Single, **D** = Double/Twin, **T** = Triple, **Q** = Quad, **b** = bathroom,
s = shower only. Unless otherwise noted, credit cards are
accepted and prices include breakfast.

To help you sort easily through these listings, I've divided
the rooms into two categories based on the price for a
standard double room with bath:

$$ Higher Priced—Most rooms 1,100 Kč or more.
$ Lower Priced—Most rooms less than 1,100 Kč.

after) the architects-cum-actors of Prague's popular avant-garde
theater, Sklep, who still converge here every New Year (Db-1,490
Kč, extra bed-490 Kč, free Wi-Fi, Horní Náměstí 522, tel. & fax
384-493-293, www.besidka.cz). The hotel also runs a restaurant
(described below).

$ Hotel Arkáda is more spartan (although all of the rooms
were recently renovated) and seems designed for hikers (Sb-690
Kč, Db-1,080 Kč, Náměstí Míru 466, tel. 384-408-408, fax 384-
408-401, www.hotelarkada.cz, info@hotelarkada.cz).

Eating in Slavonice

Restaurant Besídka is a welcoming place, with modern, artsy
decor, a solid Czech menu, excellent pizzas, and divine blueberry
dumplings. Their entertaining menu has choices ranging from
"Castro Breakfast" to "Cold and Chilly Tidbits" (daily 11:00–22:00,
tel. 384-493-293, see Hotel Besídka listing, above).

Slavonice Connections

The only way in and out of Slavonice is by train via **Telč** (2 trains
in morning, 3 in afternoon, 1 hr; see "Telč Connections" on page
223).

MORAVSKÝ KRUMLOV

Don't mistake the shabby industrial town of Moravský Krumlov (MOH-rahv-skee KROOM-loff) for its enchanting Bohemian counterpart, Český Krumlov. A "bend in the river" (the literal meaning of "Krumlov") is the only thing these two towns have in common.

Moravský Krumlov has two restaurants, and every store is closed by 17:00. In the evening, steam from the nearby nuclear power plant envelops the setting sun. The clumsy ugliness of the circa-1950s main square (rebuilt after the town was bombed by Russians in 1945) can feel strangely exotic after you've visited picture-perfect villages elsewhere in the country.

But despite its flaws, there's one big reason to visit Moravský Krumlov: discovering the masterpiece of the Czech Republic's greatest painter, Alfons Mucha, tucked away in the town's decaying castle. Laying eyes on Mucha's grand work in this improbable setting gives you the feeling of having discovered a true "back door."

While Mucha's masterpiece, *Slav Epic,* will almost certainly be in Moravský Krumlov until the summer of 2010, its location beyond this date is less certain. Mucha dedicated this series of paintings to the capital city Prague, but before it can claim the work, the city must provide a suitable structure for displaying it. Recent threats by Mucha's heirs to take the city to court for its incapacity (or unwillingness) to meet these terms has "inspired" the otherwise apathetic city officials to pick up their search. Until *Slav Epic*'s fate is decided, Moravský Krumlov will renew its lease on the painting every three months. Before venturing to the town to see it, call 515-300-720 or 515-322-789 to ask if it's still being displayed there.

History of Mucha's *Slav Epic*

Alfons Mucha (1860–1939), born in the nearby town of Ivančice, made a hugely successful commercial career for himself in Paris and in the US as *the* Art Nouveau poster artist and illustrator. In Paris, Mucha conceived the idea of dedicating the second half of his life to a work that would edify his nation. Throughout history, bards in every culture have composed poems eulogizing the best moments of their tradition. Mucha would do the same for the Czechs and the Slavs, on a grand, epic scale...and on canvas.

Mucha convinced the Chicago industrialist Charles Crane

to sponsor his project. Both men believed that the purpose of a truly patriotic work was to inspire human beings to understand one another better, thereby bring humanity closer together. Mucha returned home, and by 1912 finished the first three paintings (each 25 by 20 feet). It was another 16 years before Mucha could dedicate the cycle of 20 enormous canvases to the Czech nation and the city of Prague. The response of his fellow artists was lukewarm—in the experimental age of Picasso, Mucha's slinky style and overt nationalism were out of fashion.

During the war, the patriotic work was hidden from the Nazis and became damaged in the process. After years of restoration, the paintings were unveiled in 1963 in Moravský Krumlov's castle, near Mucha's birthplace.

Sights in Moravský Krumlov

▲▲▲ Mucha's *Slav Epic*

Every year, 20,000 people come to Moravský Krumlov solely to see Alfons Mucha's epic 20-canvas masterpiece. Mucha's huge paintings depict momentous events in Slav history.

His work is more than a timeline chronicle. *Slav Epic* rises above the typically shallow, overly nationalistic products of the politicized 19th century. A brilliant craftsman and designer, Mucha captures the viewer's attention with his strong composition and sense of color. Like any true artistic masterpiece, Mucha's work goes beyond the style of the time, beyond Art Nouveau, beyond Slavic.

Consider contemplating Mucha's canvases on three levels. First, with the help of the handout that you'll get at the ticket office, decipher the history. The great feast is the celebration of the Slavic pagan god; the zealous preacher is Jan Hus (the revolutionary Czech priest); and the subdued old man contemplating the dark horizon is the first Czech exile and great educator, John Amos Comenius (for more about Comenius, see page 246). Red is the color of war, white is the color of peace, blue is the past, and orange is the future.

When you get tired of being told what's what, step back and figure out Mucha's intention. His technique will help you. The grand-scale background, which shows the historic events, is executed in egg-based tempera. Against that low-resolution, foggy base, clear details come into focus: the terrified couple, the mother with the child, the bearded sage with the young man, the face of the lady-in-waiting. These figures are painted in oil, and the lucid detail tells the experience of a single, often-anonymous individual. The people within *Slav Epic* suggest that Mucha's artwork is not about monumental depiction of a particular event, but about the fate of the individual against the backdrop of history. The entire weight of events is condensed into the expressions on their faces. In the scene of a print shop, the young man in the foreground is Mucha's self-portrait.

Finally, step even farther back and contemplate the painting as a work of an Impressionist or an abstract artist. The fusion of colors stands far beyond any particular meaning. Like the tones of a 19th-century symphony, Mucha's visual concert has the power to stir the deepest emotions.

Cost, Hours, Location: 80 Kč, April–Oct Tue–Sun 9:00–12:00 & 13:00–16:00, July–Aug until 17:00, closed Mon and Nov–March, tel. 515-322-789. The ticket office sells a few brochures and pictures. Notice how out of place Mucha's characteristic posters feel here. Allow two hours to see *Slav Epic*—it's hard to appreciate the work in less time.

Sleeping in Moravský Krumlov

(18 Kč = about $1, country code: 420)
With easy connections in and out, only one hotel worth recommending, and no excuse to spend more time in Moravský Krumlov than it takes to see Mucha's masterpiece, I'd sleep elsewhere. But if you're looking to spend more time in the company of lanky Slavic heroes—or if you're simply stranded in Moravský Krumlov overnight—you won't regret your stay here:

$ Hotel Epopej ("Epic") was built in the early 1960s on the town's main square (Náměstí T.G. Masaryka) to accommodate far more visitors than actually ended up coming. The hotel and the restaurant deteriorated until both were closed down. Fortunately, the post-communism economic boom brought the need for a new, modern, business-class facility. The hotel's 20 rooms were renovated and equipped with modern amenities (Sb-600 Kč, Db-1,000 Kč, Tb-1,450 Kč, free Wi-Fi, tel. 515-321-317, fax 515-322-373, www.hotel-epopej.cz, recepce@hotelepopej.cz).

Eating in Moravský Krumlov

Restaurant Epopej, on the ground floor of the Hotel Epopej, is popular with locals attracted by both the varied menu (available in English) and cheap lunch specials (advertised only in Czech). Ask the waiter for today's special, and avoid the greasy Chinese dishes made by the restaurant's Vietnamese chef (daily 10:00–22:00). If you have time and money to waste, a slot-machine room *(Herna)*, located behind the restaurant bar, is more than willing to oblige (daily until 2:00 in the morning).

Moravský Krumlov Connections

From Moravský Krumlov to: Mikulov (2 trains/afternoon, 1.5 hrs, transfer in Hrušovany), **Brno** (hourly, 45 min; bus connections mainly on weekdays). Since Brno is right on the Prague–Vienna and Prague–Bratislava–Budapest train lines, Moravský Krumlov is a handy stop in the middle of a long travel day. (Consider taking the SC Pendolino train from **Prague's Main Station** to **Brno,** which is a bit faster than other trains; 2.5-hr trip.)

By Car: If you're driving to Moravský Krumlov, figure about 30 minutes from Třebíč or Mikulov, and one hour from Telč or Slavonice.

OLOMOUC

Olomouc (OH-loh-moats), the historical capital of Moravia, is a showcase of Baroque city planning. Today, it's the Czech Republic's fifth-largest city (pop. 100,700) and harbors Moravia's most prestigious university. Students rule the town. With its wealth of cafés, clubs, and restaurants, Olomouc is the place to taste vibrant local culture—without the hassles and scams of Prague.

Olomouc has pride. It's at a crossroads about 150 miles from each of the other great cities of the region (Prague, Wrocław, Kraków, Bratislava, and Vienna) and wants to play with the big boys. While it ruled Moravia from the 11th century until 1642, today it's clearly playing second fiddle to Prague in the modern Czech Republic. Locals brag that Olomouc has the country's second-most-important bishopric and its second-oldest university. Like Prague, it has its own fancy astronomical clock. Olomouc actually built its bell tower in the 19th century to be six feet taller than Prague's. Olomouc is unrivaled in one category: Its plague monument is the tallest and most grandiose anywhere.

Although Olomouc's suburbs sprawl with 1960s apartment complexes and factories, its historic core was spared Stalin's experiments in urban design. It's not lost in a time warp like the old-town areas of Český Krumlov, Telč, and Slavonice. It's simply workaday Moravia. Trams clatter through the streets, fancy boutiques sell stylish Versace fashions, and locals pack the busy pubs. Few tourists come here, so the town lives on its own booming economy.

In the mornings, proud farmers dig out their leeks and carrots and descend upon the colorful open-air market. Haná, the region that immediately surrounds Olomouc, is the most fertile in the Czech Republic. The big landowners here have never had trouble converting their meat, milk, and bread into gold and power. The most distinguished landowner of all has always been the Church.

Olomouc's History

The fortune and misfortune of Olomouc has always come from its strategic location at the intersection of Eastern Europe's main east-west and south-north routes: Merchants, pilgrims, kings, and armies had to pass through the city.

Until the 1640s, Olomouc was the second-largest city in the Czech lands. The king's younger brother governed Moravian politics from here, while the archbishop kept the spirits (and the lands) of Moravians in God's hands—that is, his own.

Olomouc was trashed by passing armies during the Thirty Years' War (1618-1648) and occupied by Sweden for the last eight of those years. More than 70 percent of the town's population died in battles or from plagues, and the Moravian capital was moved to Brno. In 1709, Olomouc burned to the ground...only to emerge from the ashes with a Baroque flair during the Habsburg years. The new Olomouc—filled with churches, colleges, statues, and fountains—became the largest Baroque town in the country. But its prosperity again ended abruptly, as Prussia (occupying what is now western Poland and eastern Germany) threatened to invade Vienna—and Olomouc was right in the way. The Habsburgs had Olomouc's students and monks leave, and replaced them with soldiers who would defend the city. They surrounded Olomouc with tall, thick walls, and what once was a cultural center became an immense fortress. The Prussians laid siege to the city, but never managed to take it. The ring of walls and moats that protected the town also ended up preventing the encroachment of modern-day architecture into the historic center.

Olomouc eventually began to thrive again, but it remains overshadowed by Brno. Today, it still comes in second as the economic powerhouse of Moravia. But ever since Palacký University was founded here in 1946—on the grounds of the centuries-old theological university—Olomouc has been Moravia's intellectual center.

Archbishops have ruled from here for a thousand years, filling the town with churches and monasteries. In 1946, these buildings were turned into departments of Palacký University.

Being a student town, Olomouc feels young and alive (though quiet during summer weekends and school vacations, when the students clear out). Olomouc has managed to blend the old and the new better than any other town in the country. The McDonald's on the Baroque main square is not an intruder, but simply a contented acknowledgment of modern times.

To generalize, the Moravians are seen as friendlier and more community-oriented than the more individualistic Bohemians.

This shows in voting patterns. In Moravia, left-leaning parties tend to do better than the pro-business candidates who dominate the electorates in Prague and Plzeň (a city in western Bohemia). Traditions are also more prized in Moravia: Diverse regional dialects and folk customs have flourished here but have long since disappeared in Bohemia.

Anything labeled "Haná" is from this particular part of Moravia—you'll notice plenty of Haná pride among locals. Olomouc is a fine place to just kick back for a day or two in a beautiful Baroque town with its Haná-centric gaze fixed on the future.

Planning Your Time

Olomouc is a delightful mix of Baroque space and 21st-century life. Don't approach the city as a sightseer; Olomouc is to be experienced and enjoyed. The only must-see "sights"—the two squares and the plague column—can be covered in an hour, but you can enjoy additional time in the city's restaurants, bars, and clubs.

If you're passing through, hop off the train for a three-hour lunch stop on the main square. Better yet, stay the night to relax and sample the rich nightlife. I enjoy the city enough to visit it as a long day trip from Prague. On a more leisurely visit, consider the worthwhile day trips to Kroměříž (with a sumptuous château, described later in this chapter) and the Wallachia region (see next chapter).

Orientation to Olomouc

Olomouc's historic core is small, compact, and just five tram stops from the train station. The core has two parts: the original settlement around the former royal palace and cathedral, and the royal town (west of the cathedral). The royal town is concentrated around two connected squares: Upper Square (Horní Náměstí), with the Town Hall and plague column; and Lower Square (Dolní Náměstí), with many restaurants.

Part of Olomouc's charm is that it's a Baroque town on a medieval street plan. Everything of sightseeing interest is contained within its historic core, defined by the circular greenbelt that follows the town's old wall (much like the famous Planty in Kraków).

Tourist Information

Olomouc's main TI, in the Town Hall on the Upper Square, has plenty of well-written fliers describing the town's main sights (daily 9:00–19:00, tel. 585-513-385, www.olomouc-tourism.cz; there's also a TI at the train station). They sell tickets to concerts and can set you up with a local guide (500 Kč/hr, reserve ahead).

Arrival in Olomouc

By Train: Olomouc's circa-1950s train station (Hlavní Nádraží) is downright cute: Bright, happy peasants still greet you with their banners, rakes, and trays of *koláče* (pastries). As you exit through the main station hall, you'll see three information offices on the left. First is the railway center, with 24-hour help on train connections (tel. 972-741-620). Next is a simple TI that offers basic help—such as directions to hotels—and can sell you a good town map (daily 6:45–12:00 & 12:30–17:45, Internet access for 1 Kč/min). And third is a city transit office, with information about trams and tickets (Mon–Fri 5:00–17:00, closed Sat–Sun).

Take the **tram** into the center. Trams #2, #4, and #6 stop in front of the train station and go past the cathedral (U Dómu, third stop), then continue to Koruna (fifth stop), right by the main square. Even if you're not arriving by train, consider riding this tram for an easy orientation to the city (see "Getting Around Olomouc," later).

Taxis are inexpensive (figure on 100 Kč to the center). Call Atlant-taxi (toll-free tel. 800-113-030) or Citytaxi (toll-free tel. 800-223-030).

Helpful Hints

Festivals: During the summer (July–Sept), the town organizes a cultural festival. Top Czech artists perform weekly under the open sky in the Town Hall courtyard or in one of the numerous churches and student clubs around town (www.okl .info). The Jesuit Konvikt (former monastery) simultaneously hosts a Baroque music festival. Outside of festival time, when school is in session (Sept–June), Olomouc is hopping, with good independent movie theaters (www.olomouckakina.cz) and live music in bars (see page 252). The town's main theater, Moravské Divadlo, regularly puts on opera performances (ticket office open Mon–Fri 9:00–18:00, closed Sat–Sun, located on the Upper Square next to Moravská Restaurace, tel. 585-223-533, pokladna@moravskedivadlo.cz).

Pharmacy: A 24-hour pharmacy is on Aksamitova street.

Internet Access: U Dominika has mellow decor and comfy chairs (Mon–Fri 9:00–21:00, Sat–Sun 10:00–21:00, across the street from Dominican monastery on the corner of Sokolská and Slovenská).

Walking Tours and Bike Rental: Poets' Corner Hostel organizes a daily walking tour and rents wheels by the day (for details, see hostel listing under "Sleeping in Olomouc").

Rickshaws: To cycle around on a rickshaw, look for the main stand in front of the TI on the square (50 Kč per ride, 100-Kč circuit goes around all fountains, 200 Kč also includes parks).

Local Guide: Štefan Blaho, who speaks English well, is a rare Olomouc guide ready to connect with curious visitors who figure out how much fun Olomouc is to visit—especially with a local (500 Kč/hr, tel. 581-208-242, mobile 602-729-613, www.olomouc-guide.cz, stefan@olomouc-guide.cz).

Getting Around Olomouc

Although Olomouc is walkable, I recommend taking the following tram ride for a good orientation.

Overview Tram Ride: The 10-minute tram ride from the train station (Hlavní Nádraží) to the Upper Square (stop: Koruna) is a handy way to get an overview of the city. It's easy. Trams #2, #4, and #6 make the route, going every few minutes. Tickets are good for 40 minutes, so you can hop on and off (8 Kč, buy at *tabák*

1. Hotel Arigone
2. Hotel u Dómu
3. Pension Antica
4. Pension u Jakuba
5. Pension na Hradbách
6. Pension u Anděla
7. Poets' Corner Hostel
8. Hanácká Hospoda Pub
9. Moravská Restaurace
10. Restaurant Vila Primavesi
11. Minipivovar Moritz
12. Mekáč (McDonald's)
13. Centrum Česká Jídelna
14. Café Caesar
15. Café Restaurant Konvikt
16. Café Mahler
17. Cukrárna Madlen
18. Café 87
19. Kratochvíle Teahouse
20. Pizza, Irish Bar, Etc.
21. Jazz Club Tibet
22. U-Klub
23. Internet Café

OLOMOUC

shops or yellow machines, or pay a little extra to buy on board from the driver).

In front of the train station stretches a modern town center with planned communist-era apartment blocks. While there are plenty of drawbacks to the city's communist heritage, one good leftover from that era is Olomouc's fine, still-subsidized public transit. As you ride, notice that people often forgo owning a car because of dirt-cheap monthly passes. It's second nature here.

Going downtown from the station, you peel through the city's architectural layers of history. Crossing the three branches of the river, you pass through the university district before reaching the center. A red light at the front of the car indicates your next stop. Hop out at "Koruna," and head toward the big square (Upper Square) a block to your left.

Sights in Olomouc

Olomouc is divided between its royal town (surrounding the magnificent Upper Square, with its famous plague column) and its bishop's town, or cathedral district (the other end of town, with the bishop's palace and Archdiocesan Museum). The huge university sprawls between these two former centers of power. Visitors connect the two zones with an easy 10-minute walk. The sights here are listed in that order: Upper Square and its surroundings (market and churches), cross-town walk, and cathedral.

The Royal Town

Upper Square (Horní Náměstí)—Standing in front of the Town Hall, surrounded by the vast square and the town's beautiful noble and bourgeois residences, you can imagine Olomouc's importance over the centuries. The fountain with an equestrian statue of Julius Caesar is dedicated to the legendary founder of the town (excavations reveal that it actually originated as a third-century Roman military camp—centuries after Caesar).

The Mahler Café is a reminder of the great composer Gustav Mahler (1860–1911). He lived and worked here until he moved to Vienna, claiming he needed better food.

Examine the town model. While designed for blind people, it gives anyone interested a feel—literally—for the medieval street plan, otherwise easily overlooked among all the Baroque grandeur.

On the square, take a look at the Town Hall, the fancy clock, the towering plague monument, and the seven mostly venerable fountains.

▲Town Hall—Olomouc's grand Town Hall is a testament to the city's 600 years of prominence in Moravia. The three wings around a rectangular courtyard once served as both council chambers and market halls. In the late 1400s, part of the building was converted into an armory, guards' house, and jail. On the outside, notice the beautiful Mannerist loggia, used for the entry into the council chambers and for ceremonial purposes (such as the mayor's declarations to the public). The coats of arms of many nations show that Moravia was part of the vast and multiethnic Habsburg Empire.

The Town Hall is busy with local weddings—if you see a festively decorated car parked on the square, it's probably waiting to zip a bride and groom away. You can visit the Town Hall's interior and climb the tower only with an escort (15 Kč, 30 min, daily at 11:00 and 15:00, book tickets and depart from the TI located within the Town Hall).

▲Astronomical Clock—The huge clock on the Town Hall was once far more complex than the one in Prague. Originally, it depicted the medieval universe divided into three spheres, but

The Baroque Fountains of Olomouc

Sprinkled around Olomouc's old town is a series of seven alle-gorical fountains with statues. Since pagan times, Olomouc—whose wealth has always been based on agriculture—has had a close relationship to water. Most of the fountains were inspired by classical mythology.

One features a statue of **Neptune,** the god of water. Another shows **Hercules** depicted as the guardian of Olomouc, holding the Moravian checkered eagle in his left hand and a mace in his right. **Jupiter,** the overlord of the gods, replaced an earlier sculpture of the only Christian saint who appeared on the fountains: St. Florian, protector from fires and floods.

The **Tritons** fountain—closely based on the one at Rome's Piazza Barberini—has the most developed composition: a pair of water spirits and a dolphin carrying a conch, with a fragile boy leading two dogs.

The culmination of the cycle is the eques-trian statue of **Caesar,** who looks proudly toward Michael Hill (where leg-end says he founded Olomouc). The water gods Morava and Danubius carry the coats of arms of Moravia and Lower Austria, and the dog rep-resents Olomouc's fidelity to the Austrian emperor.

The **Mercury** statue is artistically the most successful. Mercury fulfilled the same role in classical mythology as the archangel Michael in the Old Testament: He was the guide through the land of the dead and the messenger of gods.

The modern **turtle fountain,** at the end of the Town Hall, is the most entertaining. The turtle, who lives a long life, sym-bolizes ancient Olomouc's ability to hang in there. The city's history in maps and documents is inscribed on the turtle's pil-lar. Contribute to a new tradition—though the statue is only a few years old, the tail (on the dolphin statue) already shows signs of being rubbed by visitors to assure their return to Olomouc. This fountain is a meeting place for young mothers and a fun place to watch toddlers enjoy the art.

The placement of the fountains and statues at the inter-sections of roads and squares—reminiscent of stage props in Baroque theater—imitates the spectacular cycle of Bernini's fountains in Rome. Since the second half of the 18th century, every view down any main street in Olomouc has ended with a sculpture. Look for these as you sightsee, and you'll better appreciate the town as theater.

it was periodically rebuilt to correspond with new advances in knowledge. In 1898, purists worked to restore it to its original state. (A picture of this older version is in the window located a few steps to the left of the actual clock.)

Like Prague's clock, Olomouc's astronomical clock was intentionally destroyed by the Nazis in World War II. Today's version was rebuilt in 1953 by the communists, who had a kitschy flair for propaganda. In this one-of-a-kind clock made in the Socialist Realist style, you have earnest chemists and heroic mothers rather than saints and Virgin Marys. High noon is marked by a proletarian parade, when, for six minutes, a mechanical conga line of milkmaids, clerks, blacksmiths, medics, and teachers are celebrated as the champions of everyday society. Study the mosaic symbols of the 12 months (*leden* is January; circle down on the left—*červen* is June). The Haná region is agriculturally rich, so each month features a farm activity. As with any proper astronomical clock, there's a wheel with 365 saints, so you'll always know whose special day it is. But this clock comes with a Moscow-inspired bonus—red bands on the wheel splice in the birthdays of communist leaders (Lenin was born on the 112th day of the year in 1870; Stalin's saint was Toman—day 355). Note that the clock's designers were optimists—the year mechanism (on the bottom) is capable of spinning until A.D. 9999.

▲▲▲Column of the Holy Trinity (Sousoší Nejsvětější Trojice)—The artistic pride of Olomouc is the tallest plague col-

umn in Europe. Squares throughout Eastern Europe are dotted with similar structures, erected by locals to give thanks for surviving the plague. This one was started in 1716 by a local man named Render, who announced—with a confidence characteristic of the Haná region—that he would create a work that in "its height and ornamentation would not have a peer in terms of excellence." He donated his entire fortune, employing many great artists for decades to build the monument. Sadly, he died before its consecration, which occurred in the presence of the Habsburg ruler Maria Theresa, the Holy Roman Empress.

The Holy Trinity group on the highest point of the column features God the Father making a blessing, Christ with a cross sitting on a globe, and the dove in gold (representing the Holy Spirit) crowning everything. Tumbling with the Trinity, the archangel Michael—holding his fiery sword and shield—reminds us that the Church is in a constant struggle with evil. A third of the way down from the top of the column (past the golden cannonball—embedded there as a reminder of the 1758 Prussian siege), we see Mary—the mediator between heavenly and earthly spheres—carried off by angels during the Assumption.

The bottom third features three reliefs with allegories of the Christian virtues (Faith, Hope, and Charity), surrounded by six saints. Four of the saints are closely connected with the life of Jesus (saints Joachim and Anne—the parents of St. Mary—as well as St. Joseph and St. John the Baptist); the other two are the patron saints of Olomouc (saints Jerome and Lawrence). This particular arrangement of saints shows that universal faith is often combined with a distinctly local myth and belief.

It all sits atop a tiny (and rarely open) chapel where Maria Theresa knelt to pray—devout, yet green with envy. Olomouc had a plague column grander than Vienna's.

Lower Square (Dolní Náměstí)—Below the Upper Square stretches the more workaday Lower Square. Enjoy live music at the beer terrace or a bite at the fine Hanácká Hospoda pub (described later, under "Eating in Olomouc").

Find the communist-era **lamppost** with its twin 1970s speakers. Locals remember growing up with these mouthpieces of gov-

ernment boasting of successes ("This year, despite many efforts of sabotage on the part of certain individuals in service of imperialist goals, we have surpassed the planned output of steel by 195 percent"); calling people to action ("There will be no school tomorrow as all will join the farmers in the fields for an abundant harvest"); or quelling disturbances ("Some citizens may have heard about alien forces in our society taking advantage of this week's anniversary to spread unrest. This is to reassure you that the situation is firmly under control and nothing is happening in Olomouc or in Prague. Nevertheless, for their own safety, we suggest all citizens stay home").

Open-Air Market—As was the norm in medieval times, poor people traded tax- and duty-free items just outside the town walls. The city's market remains in the same spot, just outside the town wall a long block below the Lower Square. The town's circa-1900 brick market hall is of no interest today, but around it sprawls a

OLOMOUC

"From Armories Make Libraries": John Amos Comenius (1592–1670)

This motto, which inspired the transformation of Olomouc's military fortress into a lively university campus, came from Comenius, a.k.a. Jan Amos Komenský, one of the Czech Republic's most influential teachers and writers (pull out a 200-Kč banknote to have a look at him). You'll find his dictum embedded in the pavement at the entrance to Olomouc's former central armory, which is the main university library today.

Comenius was born into the Moravian Brethren faith, which was founded on the pacifist ideals of the Czech religious reformer Petr Chelčický (c. 1390–c. 1460). Having studied at universities in Germany, Comenius returned to Moravia as a young pastor to run the Protestant schools in Fulnek and Přerov. The beginning of the Thirty Years' War had a direct impact on him: His wife and two children died in a plague epidemic, and following the defeat of the Czech Protestants by the Catholic Habsburgs, Comenius had to choose exile over abandoning his faith. Personal misfortune went hand-in-hand with a professional one: During his escape through Poland, his entire library went up in flames, a fate that later befell many of his personal writings.

Surrounded by the chaos and destruction of war, Comenius believed that guns were no way to restore order—what the world really needed was a revolution in learning. He envisioned a liberal-arts education that would create citizens, rather than specialists, and proposed a new teaching system based on the novel principle of "school through play." To promote this idea, he wrote extensively. His works included a textbook aimed at making learning Latin fun for children, one of the first scholarly treatments of preschool education, and *Orbis Pictus* ("World

colorful open-air market. While Moravian farmers sell their vegetables and herbs, Vietnamese traders hawk knock-off jeans and cheap sunglasses (closed Sun, busiest on Wed and Sat, but fun any morning). The rough little snack bar sells *langoš* (a Hungarian cheese-and-grease doughnut, 13 Kč), cheap coffee, and good beer.

Churches—Since its origin, Olomouc has been the seat of bishops. The great number of churches—concentrated in such a small area—shows the strong presence of the Church here. Of the many churches in town, two are worth a peek (each one is a block off the Upper Square).

St. Michael's Church (Sv. Michal), located at the highest point in town, dominates Olomouc's skyline (free, open long hours daily). It's a fine, single-nave Baroque church full of illusory paintings, fake armor, and lovely Gothic frescoes hidden under Baroque whitewash. As it was rebuilt after looting by the in Pictures"), the first children's encyclopedia. His most famous and acclaimed work, *The Labyrinth of the World and the Paradise of the Heart* (written in Czech, not Latin), argued that all human knowledge and ambition is futile if unaccompanied by faith and charity. His fame spread across the Atlantic: In 1636, Comenius was asked to become the first president of Harvard University. Still hoping to return home (and afraid of sea journeys after he almost lost his life in a storm in the North Sea), Comenius declined the offer.

For the remainder of his wandering life, Comenius taught and wrote in Poland, Hungary, the Netherlands, England, and Sweden, never able to return home. Alfons Mucha powerfully captured Comenius' tragic fate as a homeless exile—a fate to be

shared by thousands of free-spirited Czechs—in one of the canvases of his *Slav Epic* (see the Moravský Krumlov chapter). During the communist era, Comenius' grave (in Naarden, near Amsterdam) became a shrine for Czech exiles; immediately after the fall of the Iron Curtain, the site was swamped with Czechs who came to pay their respects. Today, Comenius is considered one of the founders of modern education, and his legacy is alive far beyond Olomouc. In the Czech Republic and Slovakia, Comenius' birthday is celebrated as Teachers' Day, and the Comenius Medal is the highest UNESCO award for achievement in education.

Protestant Swedes during the Counter-Reformation, the Catholic propaganda is really cranked up. The three-domed ceiling—a reminder of the Trinity—is an unusual feature. From the cloister, stairs lead down to the 11th-century "rock chapel" and its tiny lake. The chair in the dark hole on the left is an invitation to pray or meditate. This humble grotto was the site of the first hermitage here on Olomouc's high rock. As Michael is the Christian antidote to paganism, archaeologists assume that this church sits upon a pagan holy spot.

St. Moritz's Church (Sv. Mořic) is a must-see for its pair of asymmetrical towers, which look more like fortresses. The church has an original Gothic vault, but its Gothic treasures are in a Prague museum. The altar and windows, while lovely, are Neo-Gothic, dating only from the 19th century. Climb the 200 steps to the tower to enjoy a commanding city view (15 Kč).

Strolling Between the Royal Town and the Cathedral

Connect the two sightseeing zones with a short walk along the city's main drag. Leaving the Upper Square on Ostružnická street, you'll pass real-estate offices (a home in a village or apartment here goes for about 1.5 million Kč, or about $90,000) and lots of bookstores (supplying 17,000 local university students).

When you hit the main road, Denisova, notice the fine gas streetlamp that lit the street in 1899, when the tram first ran. Follow the tram line toward the lacy spire of the cathedral in the distance.

The mix of facades, from Gothic to Art Nouveau, masks narrow medieval buildings. At Univerzitní street, a quick detour to the right leads past the Vertigo Bar (where students believe a mind is a wonderful thing to waste) to the grand and renovated University building on the left (with its handy Café Restaurant Konvikt and a courtyard with a nice view over the town wall).

Continuing up the main drag, you pass the Museum of Art (interesting) and the Natural History Museum (boring). If you visit the art museum (50 Kč, Tue–Sun 10:00–18:00, closed Mon, Denisova 47), save your ticket—it'll also get you into the Archdiocesan Museum (described later).

The big square called Náměstí Republiky is marked by a fountain inspired by Bernini's Triton Fountain in Rome (see "The Baroque Fountains of Olomouc" sidebar). The Jesuits, whose gorgeous church faces the square, founded the original university in the 16th century. This square marks the division between the royal town and the bishop's town. Ahead (past the square, veering a bit to the right), Mariánská street leads to the archbishop's stately 17th-century palace (closed to the public). On the slopes below the palace are Jesuit colleges (now university classrooms) and a Clarist convent (now a museum).

In the Bishop's Town, near the Cathedral

St. Wenceslas' Cathedral (Dóm Sv. Václava)—Supposedly, this has been the resident church of Olomouc's bishops ever since the Christian missionaries Cyril and Methodius visited in the ninth century. The present church has been rebuilt many times. While it maintains its Gothic lines, what you see is 19th-century pseudo-Gothic, with Neo-Renaissance paintings. The crypt houses a collection of liturgical ornaments—the second-largest in the country, after Loreta Church in Prague. Just inside the door, you can trace the lineage of local archbishops back 68 men, from today's archbishop to St. Methodius in 869.

▲**Archdiocesan Museum**—Opened in 2006, this is Olomouc's pride and joy. After his 1995 visit, Pope John Paul II asked the city to build this museum. The mission of this state-of-the-art museum is "In Glory and Praise—To Share a Thousand Years of Spiritual Culture in Moravia"...and it does just that.

This former royal castle, once the king's principal Moravian residence, later became home to Olomouc's archbishop. The exterior is a mix of Romanesque and Gothic elements. Inside you'll wander among some of the finest medieval art in Eastern Europe (all well-described in English). The centerpiece of the treasury is a monstrance with 1,800 diamonds and seven pounds of pure gold (from 1750). The bishop's gilded coach understandably gave the Holy Roman Empress Maria Theresa more reason for envy.

Then, wearing slippers to protect the not-so-hardwood floor, you shuffle through the staterooms lined with well-lit paintings. Don't miss the painting depicting the ceremonial arrival of the new archbishop in Olomouc in the mid-1700s. Survey the town: Except for the McDonald's, it's all there. See how the artist, playing with perspective a bit, shows the gate on the left dividing the royal town from the bishop's town. This day was a good one for the bishop, as the secular royal town is filled with Christian pageantry (50 Kč, free on Wed and Sun, open Tue–Sun 10:00–18:00, closed Mon, Václavské Náměstí 3, same ticket also gets you into the Museum of Art at Denisova 47).

Sleeping in Olomouc

$$$ Hotel Arigone, filling three tastefully renovated townhouses, is on the hill by St. Michael's Church. While some of the 40 rooms have 17th-century wooden ceilings and 19th-century-style furniture, most are furnished in a modern style and are accessible by elevator (Sb-2,000 Kč, Db-2,300 Kč, Internet access, Univerzitní 20, tel. 585-232-351, fax 585-232-350, www.arigone.cz, hotel @arigone.cz).

$$$ Hotel u Dómu, a six-room place on a quiet street next to the cathedral, is run with a personal touch that makes it popular with quirky visiting professors (Sb-1,400 Kč, Db-2,000 Kč, Tb-2,400 Kč, pay Internet access, free parking, Dómská 4, tel. 585-220-502, fax 585-220-501, www.udomu.3dpano.eu, hotel udomu@email.cz).

$$$ Pension Antica, in a Baroque house filled with meticulously restored furniture and hand-woven rugs, is a lively mixture of friendliness and tasteful opulence, courtesy of caring owner Míra (Db-2,000 Kč, Tb-3,000 Kč, Wi-Fi, Wurmova 1, tel. 585-242-368, mobile 731-560-264, www.antica.cz, pension@antica.cz).

$$ Pension u Jakuba rents six self-contained, Ikea-furnished apartments in a renovated 400-year-old house on a busy street. The pension also has seven quiet, modern rooms in a newly built

OLOMOUC

Sleep Code

(18 Kč = about $1, country code: 420)
S = Single, **D** = Double/Twin, **T** = Triple, **Q** = Quad, **b** = bathroom,
s = shower only. Unless otherwise noted, credit cards are accepted and prices include breakfast.

To help you sort easily through these listings, I've divided the rooms into three categories based on the price for a standard double room with bath:

$$$ Higher Priced—Most rooms 1,700 Kč or more.
  $$ Moderately Priced—Most rooms between 1,000–1,700 Kč.
    $ Lower Priced—Most rooms 1,000 Kč or less.

annex in the courtyard (Sb-800 Kč, Db-1,500 Kč, Tb-1,700 Kč, Qb-2,000 Kč, Internet access, 8 Května #9, to reach the reception walk through the passage and into the courtyard, parking available, tel. 585-209-995, mobile 777-747-688, www.pensionujakuba .com, ujakuba@iol.cz).

$ Pension na Hradbách rents four modern rooms, each with a personal touch (Sb-700 Kč, Db-1,000 Kč, Tb-1,500 Kč, no breakfast, Hrnčířská 3, tel. 585-233-243, mobile 602-755-848, nahradbach@quick.cz).

$ Pension u Anděla, across the street, is well-suited to be on Hrnčířská ("Potter's street"), a quiet row of two-story village houses with brightly painted facades and window-boxes full of geraniums. Two of the four simply furnished rooms overlook the bastion and park (Sb-600 Kč, Db-700 Kč, no breakfast but in-room fridge, downstairs restaurant can make breakfast the night before on request, Hrnčířská 10, tel. 585-228-755, mobile 602-512-763, www.uandela.cz).

$ *Hostel:* Poets' Corner Hostel fills two 1930s apartments near the town center. Tastefully furnished, immaculately clean, and run by a friendly Australian couple, Greg and Francie, the hostel fits in perfectly with Olomouc's character as a student town and ultimate Back Door destination in the Czech Republic. The common room has sofas, armchairs, a decent library, Czech CDs (and no TV), and holds a wealth of information on Olomouc and the surrounding area (dorm beds-300–350 Kč, Db-900 Kč, Tb-1,200 Kč, free Wi-Fi, laundry service-100 Kč/load, ring the doorbell at the entryway to the right of the Umbro shop to get into Sokolská 1, mobile 777-570-730, www.hostelolomouc.com, reservation @hostelolomouc.com). The hostel also rents bicycles (100 Kč/ day) and organizes walking tours of Olomouc that depart every morning in summer at 10:00 from the Astronomical Clock (voluntary contribution, 200 Kč/person is fine, no tours off-season).

Eating in Olomouc

Try the sour, foul-smelling, yet beloved specialty of the Haná region, Olomouc cheese sticks *(olomoucké tvarůžky)*. The milk goes through a process of natural maturation under chunks of meat. Czechs figure there are two types of people in the world: *tvarůžky*-lovers and sane people. The *tvarůžky* are so much a part of the Haná and Czech identity that when the European Union tried to forbid the product, the Czech government negotiated for special permission to continue to rot their milk. Zip a few of these stinkers in a baggie, and you can count on getting a train compartment to yourself.

OLOMOUC

Restaurants

Hanácká Hospoda, on the Lower Square, is a simple, hearty village pub that serves regional specialties to visitors and locals alike. Choose between the woody, non-smoking Moravian beer-hall interior or the best square seating outside. Mozart came here to escape a smallpox epidemic in Vienna, and he lived above this restaurant. Enjoy the funky menu. Dish #007, Guttery Breath of the Knight of Loštice (a.k.a. *tvarůžky*—the stinky cheese sticks described above), comes with a lid, mints, and the offer of a toothbrush—they only have one, so please return it. Dishes #40 to #81 are good local favorites. Daily specials are available only in the basement room (Mon–Sat 10:00–24:00, Sun 10:00–20:00, kitchen closes two hours earlier, Dolní Náměstí, tel. 585-237-186).

Moravská Restaurace ("Moravian Restaurant"), on the Upper Square, is the one touristy place in town. If you're feeling homesick, step in here, and you'll see happy tourists attracted by ads all over town, "authentic" Moravian folk costumes on the waiters, walls decorated with Moravian painted ceramics...and prices that will make you feel like you're back at home (essentially the same menu as Hanácká Hospoda for triple the price, daily 11:30–23:00, reservations recommended, Horní Náměstí, tel. 585-222-868).

Restaurant Vila Primavesi, to the left of St. Michael's Church, is located in a newly renovated, classy Art Nouveau villa—arguably one of Moravia's finest. The creative menu is rich in fish and game, and they have daily specials and a good wine selection. Seating is either inside, with ironed tablecloths, or on the terrace overlooking the city park (200–400-Kč entrées, daily 11:00–23:00, Univerzitní 7, tel. 585-204-852, mobile 777-749-288).

Minipivovar Moritz, which brews fresh yeasty beer on-site, serves Bohemian cuisine and specialties from Galicia (the region of Poland just east of here). Dine in their atmospheric circa-1900 cellar or on the park-like square, in front of the dilapidated, picturesque Maria Theresa Gate. Taking its name from a German-Jewish industrialist (Moritz Fischer), it opened near a former synagogue in 2006 (precisely 100 years after the death of the man responsible for developing Olomouc into a modern manufacturing center). Today Moritz is one of the trendiest places in town. Head down to the basement to check out the kosher beer-making process, the unique *pivovod* (system of beer pipes that leads under the street to the outdoor bar on the square), and the portrait of Moritz's grandmother, who set the standard for hospitality that the owners hope to match (daily 11:00–23:00, on Palachovo Náměstí at Nešverova 2, tel. 585-205-560, reservations recommended in the evenings).

Mekáč (McDonald's), on the Upper Square, is filled with teenagers and moms with kids during the week. On a weekend, you can sit here and watch folks from the countryside, dressed in their Sunday best and coming to town for a "Bikmek" taste of the world.

Centrum Česká Jídelna ("Czech Eatery") is ideal if you're short on time and want some local-style fast food. They offer a world of traditional Czech dishes, ready and warmed, as well as an array of sandwiches and salads. Choose your meal by pointing at what you want (Mon–Fri 6:30–18:00, Sat 7:30–12:00, closed Sun, directly opposite the clock).

Café Caesar, filling the Gothic vaults in the Town Hall, is a popular pizza place with fine outside seating within a flea's hop of the plague monument (daily 9:00–1:00 in the morning, tel. 585-229-287). The little gallery next door, run by the café, promotes local artists.

Café Restaurant Konvikt is a modern-feeling place in the delightfully restored former Jesuit college. They cater primarily to businessmen, though some philosophy students also wander here from the classrooms upstairs. In summer, they offer seating in a peaceful courtyard above the city walls and greenbelt (daily 11:00–24:00, Univerzitní 3, tel. 585-631-190).

Cafés, Teahouses, Pubs, and Clubs

Olomouc is the Moravian university town, and every aspect of student life (except sleeping) happens right in the old center. Being a student town, Olomouc is lively and cheap during the school year but slower in July, August, and September (although foreign students coming here for summer programs in languages, music, and history are doing their best to make up for the annual vacation energy drain).

Café Mahler, on the Upper Square, is a stylish place for coffee and cake (Mon–Sat 8:00–22:00, Sun 10:00–21:00), while **Cukrárna Madlen,** between the Upper Square and the Lower Square, is the local ice-cream paradise (Mon–Sat 8:00–21:00, Sun 9:00–21:00).

Café 87 has the longest list of espresso drinks, iced coffees, frappés, pancakes, and desserts in town. The handful of Olomouc expats converge here daily just before lunch to have the chocolate cake, which is heavenly but highly addictive (daily 10:00–19:00, between the art and natural-history museums on Náměstí Republiky).

Kratochvíle Teahouse offers a wide array of freshly harvested tea leaves, as well as coffee, Moravian wines, and the increasingly popular hookahs (water pipes). This contemplative, bamboo-lined space also hosts exhibitions, concerts, and author readings (Mon–Fri 11:00–23:00, Sat–Sun 15:00–23:00, Sokolská 36, mobile 603-564-120).

Captain Morgan's Pizza, Bar Rasputin, The Crack Irish Bar, and **Club Belmondo** fill the massive red-brick 18th-century town wall with nightlife inspired by various corners of Europe. Fueled by the vibrant local crowd, these spots are open much of the day, but they don't really start to swing until around 21:00, when the disco and live music begin. All are free except Club Belmondo, which charges a 100-Kč cover. Head to the corner of Mlýnská and Pavelčákova, just across the Třída Svobody from Maria Theresa Gate.

Jazz Club Tibet has nothing to do with Tibet, but it does offer good food and live jazz twice a week in a modern, pub-like setting (Mon–Fri 11:00–24:00, Sat 12:00–24:00, closed Sun, Sokolská 48, tel. 585-230-399). Across the street, the **Metropol** movie theater screens a mixture of artsy and mainstream flicks.

Konvikt is a hip club right next to the restaurant of the same name (described earlier). In summer, it's a popular hangout for foreign students (Mon–Sat 14:00–24:00, closed Sun, tel. 585-631-191).

U-Klub, a 10-minute walk out of the center in the dorms, is the university's concert hall. Bands play folk, jazz, rock, punk...you name it (Šmeralova 12, tel. 585-638-117).

Olomouc Connections

Olomouc is on several major rail lines (including the one from Prague to Kraków).

From Olomouc by Train to: Kroměříž (hourly, 1–1.5 hrs,

transfer in Hulín; see "Kroměříž Connections," later), **Prague** (at least hourly, 2–3 hrs), **Brno** (buses and trains at least hourly, 1.5 hrs), **Rožnov pod Radhoštěm** (7/day, most connections require transfer in Valašské Meziříčí, allow 2 hrs total; also consider bus), **Břeclav** (10/day, 2 hrs, may transfer in Brno or Přerov), **Kraków** (5/day, 4.5–6 hrs, transfer in Katowice, Poland, and possibly Přerov, Czech Republic; one 5-hr overnight train), **Vienna** (8/day, 3–4 hrs, transfer in Brno, Břeclav, or Přerov), **Budapest** (6/day, 5–8 hrs, transfer in Brno or Přerov).

From Olomouc by Bus to: Třeboň, Telč, and **Třebíč**—take the bus or train to **Brno** (see above), then take the bus in the direction of **České Budějovice** (5/day Mon–Fri, 2/day Sat–Sun—see page 208), **Rožnov pod Radhoštěm** (hourly, 1.75–2.25 hrs, most with change in Valašské Meziříčí).

Near Olomouc: Kroměříž

Whereas Olomouc was the official seat of the Moravian archbishops, Kroměříž (KROH-myehr-eezh) was the site of their lavish summer château. In 1948, this castle and its enormous gardens were nationalized and opened to the public. Kroměříž—showing off the richness of this corner of the Czech Republic—is the most lavish and best-renovated Rococo castle in the country. The 19th-century English-style park, with lakes, woods, and Chinese pavilions, is good for a walk or picnic.

While there are no other worthwhile sights in town, the pleasant square, streets filled with little bakeries, and a chance to experience a small Moravian town offers a perfect complement to the grandeur of the archbishop's estate. The town and château of Kroměříž combine for a perfect half-day excursion from Olomouc to enjoy the genteel art and gentle life of Moravia.

Orientation to Kroměříž

Getting to Kroměříž

From Olomouc, take one of the frequent trains in the direction of Přerov and Břeclav (hourly, 7:20 or 9:20 train is convenient). Get off at Hulín (the stop after Přerov on fast trains, 45 min), walk through the train station to the other side of the building, and hop on the small motor train to Kroměříž (departure scheduled to coincide with the arrival of Břeclav-bound trains, 8 min). On the way back, most trains from Kroměříž to Hulín connect with an Olomouc-bound train.

Tourist Information

The humble TI on the main square hands out a useful map with brief descriptions of all major sights, as well as a list of events (Mon–Fri 8:30–17:00, Sat–Sun 9:00–13:00, open weekdays until 18:00 in July–Aug, closed Sun Nov–April, Velké Náměstí 45/50, tel. 573-331-473, www.mesto-kromeriz.cz).

Arrival in Kroměříž

Turn right out of the train station, then take the first left over the bridge. The main square (Velké Náměstí) and the entrance to the château are an easy 10-minute walk away.

Helpful Hints

Music: Throughout the summer, the city government joins forces with art schools and conservatories to enliven historical spaces with weekly concerts. The quality of the performers and the unique setting—in the château halls and gardens—make a visit worthwhile (ticket booking and purchase at the TI on Velké Náměstí, www.hudba-kromeriz.cz). The Kroměříž Music Summer Festival is held in September (tel. 573-341-400).

Internet Access: DC Internet Café, located on the main square, is right below the town museum (40 Kč/hr, Mon–Fri 10:00–19:00, Sat–Sun 13:00–19:00, Velké Náměstí 39).

Sights in Kroměříž

Archbishop's Château (Arcibiskupský Zámek)—Dominating the main square and the whole town, this château was rebuilt in Baroque style by archbishop Karel Lichtenstein (dubbed the "Moravian Richelieu") after an earlier castle was severely damaged in the Swedish siege during the Thirty Years' War. The furniture and decorations are in the Rococo style (from the second half of the 18th century). The breathtaking chandeliers are made of Czech crystal.

The château is famous for one historic event: The Austrian parliament moved here from unstable Vienna during the tumultuous year of 1848, when a wave of revolutions spread across the Habsburg lands. The parliament drafted the first Austrian constitution in the château's main hall.

Hours: May–Sept Tue–Sun 9:00–17:00, closed Mon; April and Oct Sat–Sun 9:00–17:00, closed Mon–Fri; closed Nov–March. Tel. 573-502-011, www.azz.cz.

Tours: You can see the art gallery (described next) and climb the tower (40 Kč) on your own, but you can tour the château interior only with a guide (90 Kč with a Czech-speaking group). Try asking for an English-language tour—you'll pay double, and you might be the only one on the tour. Tours run about every hour and last 70 minutes, with the time about evenly split between the first floor (eight rooms) and second floor (which has a beautifully painted ceiling depicting the history of the bishopric, and overlooks a stunning library interior with 80,000 books).

Art Gallery: Art-lovers should consider visiting the bishop's art gallery. Sure, it's not the Louvre, but it's the best Moravian collection of European paintings from 1400 to 1800, with works by Titian, Lucas Cranach, Albrecht Dürer, and Paolo Veronese (60 Kč, same hours as château).

Castle Garden (Podzámecká Zahrada)—This green space, filled with little ponds, exotic trees, and Chinese pavilions, offers a peaceful refuge. It's in the English style—wilder and more natural than the geometrically designed French gardens (July–Aug daily 5:30–20:30; May–June and Sept Tue–Sun 9:00–17:00, closed Mon; April and Oct Sat–Sun only, closed Mon–Fri; closed Nov–March).

Sleeping in Kroměříž

Kroměříž works best as a day trip from Olomouc, but if you want to see a concert and stay the night, try **$$ Hotel Bouček.** This well-renovated, traditional townhouse on the main square rents 11 decent rooms (Sb-1,000 Kč, Db-1,500 Kč, extra bed-500 Kč, Velké Náměstí 108, tel. 573-342-777, www.hotelboucek.cz, hotel.boucek@seznam.cz).

Eating in Kroměříž

All of these eateries are on or just off the main square (Velké Náměstí).

Bistro u Zámku is a popular place to sip a frappé or iced coffee (daily, on the corner of main square next to the château).

Zámecká Myslivna ("Château Hunting Lodge") specializes in game. Your venison might have been shot by the archbishop, who still comes here during the summer (Sun–Thu 11:00–22:00, Fri–Sat 11:00–24:00, just off main square, Sněmovní Náměstí 41).

Radniční Kavárna is perfect if you want to eat on cushioned chairs outside, because it's a bit stuffy inside (daily 9:00–22:00, at top of main square across street from Town Hall).

Bistro Avion, a blue-collar self-service cafeteria on the main square, is good for a basic, filling meal (Mon–Fri 6:00–18:00, Sat 8:00–15:00, Sun 7:00–14:00). The place has no menu—just point to what looks good, and wash it down with Slovakia's best beer, Zlatý Bažant ("Golden Pheasant").

WALLACHIA

The mountainous region of Wallachia (vah-LAH-chee-ah)—where Slovakia and Poland meet the eastern edge of the Czech Republic—is ideal for an escape into nature, where you can enjoy both the ruggedness of the mountains and the easy tourist facilities of an accessible recreational area.

Wallachia (Valašsko) comprises three east–west ridges separating three long valleys. The Beskydy Mountains—the westernmost part of the Carpathian mountain range—make an impressive backdrop.

Wallachia has a sparse but proud population, the Wallachians (Valaši). They were originally Romanian shepherds who, following their sheep, drifted west along the pristine meadows and rugged canyons of the hauntingly beautiful Carpathians. In exchange for guarding the border, these shepherds received many privileges—most importantly, exemption from taxes.

Today, the Wallachians have their own tongue-in-cheek, tax-free "kingdom." In local restaurants and hotels, you can buy Wallachian "passports," which come with a brochure explaining in English why you should emigrate. The 90 Kč is a small price to pay for a passport when you consider that it frees you from the far-reaching clutches of the IRS.

Getting Around Wallachia

This region is best with a car. It's difficult, though doable, by public transportation. **Olomouc** is the nearest big city. To reach **Rožnov** pod Radhoštěm by train or bus from Olomouc, you'll need to transfer in Valašské Meziříčí (7 trains/day, allow 2 hrs total; hourly bus, 1.75–2.5 hrs). From **Rožnov,** a direct bus goes to **Prostřední Bečva/Pustevny** (4/day, 45 min).

Rožnov pod Radhoštěm

Rožnov pod Radhoštěm (ROHZH-novh pohd rahd-hosh-tyem), the largest town in the region and once a popular spa resort, may

not be worth an overnight stay, but it certainly merits a visit for its **Wallachian Open-Air Folk Museum** (Valašské Muzeum v Přírodě), rated ▲. The museum, which re-creates a traditional Wallachian village, is divided into three parts. Touring the "Little Wooden Town" is sufficient to give you a good sense of Eastern European mountain architecture, which blends here with elements of Moravian house-building. The museum is also the resting place for the most distinguished Wallachians, among them the incredible runner Emil Zátopek, who won three gold medals at the Helsinki Olympics in 1952.

Cost, Hours, Location: 50 Kč; May–Sept daily 8:00–18:00; April Tue–Sun 9:00–17:00, closed Mon; Jan–March and Oct Tue–Sun 9:00–16:00, closed Mon; closed most of Nov and part of Dec (www.vmp.cz). On Rožnov's main square, you'll find direction markers for the museum (it's a 10-min walk).

Tours: Although you can visit the complex on your own, to fully appreciate the site, call a few days ahead to reserve an English-speaking guide (400 Kč for an hour-long tour, reserve at tel. 571-757-111 between 6:00 and 14:00, prohlidka@vmp.cz).

Pustevny

Pustevny (POO-stehv-nee, "Hermitage") is a small, pleasant resort atop the Beskydy (BEH-skih-dee) Mountains' most sacred ridge, in a spot where a legendary hermit once lived. The style of the mountain huts here is an imaginative combination of Art Nouveau and wooden village architecture. Peak season is June through August for hiking, and Christmas through Easter for skiing. During other months restaurants are open only on weekends .

The 30-minute **hike** from Pustevny along the red-marked trail on the ridge toward the west will take you to a statue of Radegast, the old Slavic god of sun, friendship, and harvest. If you hike farther along the ridge for two miles, you'll reach the top of the sacred Radhošť mountain and statues of the Slavic ninth-century missionaries St. Cyril and St. Methodius. They hold a page of the beginning of the Gospel according to John, which they translated for the Slavic people more than 1,100 years ago. A wooden church dedicated to these two patrons of all Slavs stands behind the statue.

Hiking along the ridge from Pustevny in the opposite direction takes you through less-visited woods and into a virgin forest preserve at Kněhyně.

Getting to Pustevny

To get to Pustevny by **public transportation,** take a direct bus from Rožnov pod Radhoštěm (4/day, 45 min, stop is marked *Prostřední Bečva/Pustevny*).

If you're **driving,** you can reach the summit either from the south via Rožnov pod Radhoštěm and Prostřední Bečva, or from the north via Frenštát pod Radhoštěm and Trojanovice (which is linked to Pustevny by a scenic chairlift). From Frenštát, follow signs for Trojanovice, drive to the end of the road at the Ráztoka Hotel, then walk 500 yards to find the chairlift (50 Kč one-way, 80 Kč round-trip, in summer runs daily once an hour 9:00–18:00, off-season until 16:00, 15-min ride). On arrival in Pustevny, be sure to check the schedule for the last chairlift back down to Trojanovice.

Sleeping and Eating at Pustevny

(18 Kč = about $1, country code: 420)

$$ Hotel Maměnka, a century-old, recently renovated historical landmark, fits sumptuously furnished rooms into a wooden structure that uniquely blends Art Nouveau with regional architecture (Db-1,300 Kč, suite Db-2,800 Kč, tel. 556-836-207, mobile 736-682-289, www.libusin-mamenka.cz, libusin@libusin-mamenka .cz). Its newly built **Koliba Valaška** annex, with similar rooms, is an opulent imitation of a shepherd's lodge. Hotel Maměnka is home to the classy-looking **Restaurant Libušín,** while the annex's **Restaurant Koliba** is geared more toward satisfying city Czechs' demand for rural fare in a traditional setting.

$ Hotel Tanečnica, large and modern, is a solid, standard, circa-1980 Czech mountain lodge (Db-1,250 Kč, swimming pool, tel. 556-835-341, www.hoteltanecnica.cz). The nearby **Koliba u Záryša** restaurant, with a more down-to-earth, scruffy shepherd's-hut setting than Restaurant Koliba, serves Wallachian food (such as cabbage soup and the pan-Carpathian specialty *halušky*—potato and flour gnocchi with sheep cheese and bacon) as well as the owner/cook's imaginative creations (such as oven-baked *živáňská pečeně*—a mixture of beef tenderloin, pork, or lamb in spices, wine, and vegetables).

MIKULOV WINE REGION

The Mikulov region produces the Czech Republic's most famous wine. The village of Pavlov, with its beautiful rural architecture and wine cellars filled with singing Moravians, is the ideal place to experience Moravia's wine culture. The surrounding Pálava Hills and water sports make days here as enjoyable as the nights. The historic town of Mikulov—the center of the region—is a pleasant lunch stop between Pavlov and Lednice. And the large Lednice–Valtice complex of castles and 19th-century English-style parks is a unique feat of environmentally friendly landscaping.

Getting Around the Mikulov Wine Region

The main railway junction of Břeclav is the gateway to the Mikulov wine region.

By Train and Bus from Břeclav to: Mikulov (10 trains/day, 30 min, goes through Valtice), **Valtice** (10 trains/day, 15 min), **Lednice** (8 buses/day Mon–Fri, 4/day Sat–Sun, 20 min; on summer weekends, a cute historical train runs between Břeclav and Lednice: 4/day, 20 min), **Prague** (9/day direct, 3 hrs, most arrive at Prague's Holešovice station), **Olomouc** (10/day, 2 hrs, may transfer in Brno or Přerov). To get to **Pavlov,** you'll first take the train to Mikulov (see above), then a bus to Pavlov (4/day Mon–Fri, 1/day Sat–Sun, 30 min).

By Car: Although it's possible to connect all these destinations by public transportation, renting a car in Břeclav or elsewhere can save lots of time (see Mikulov's "Helpful Hints" on page 267).

MIKULOV WINE REGION

Pavlov and the Pálava Hills

The traditional village of Pavlov, stretching from the banks of the Nové Mlýny dam up toward the dramatic hilltop ruin of Dívčí Hrady ("Girls' Castle"), has everything you need for a fun one- or two-day wine adventure. In deep brick cellars, you can taste local wines and spicy Hungarian salami while hearing the dreamy tunes of Moravian songs. You'll see Moravian village architecture; choose from a wealth of neat, family-run pensions; take nature walks along the wooded slopes of the white Pálava Hills; and tackle an expanse of water however you like, from swimming to windsurfing.

The only drawback is communication: While German works well, few locals speak more than broken English. But fear not— the genuine hospitality of the locals makes struggling with the language barrier both fun and rewarding. So be brave, and pull your hands and your phrase books out of those pockets.

Sights in Pavlov

Wandering the Town—Česká street, stretching from under the hill to the parking lot above the church, is lined with traditional vintners' houses. The owners live on the first floor, wine is pressed on the ground floor, and extensive cellars run deep into the mountain. The farmsteads along the park by the church are some of the finest examples of Moravian Baroque village architecture.

Wine Cellars—Ask your host whether a dulcimer band is playing in any of the wine cellars. Locals often bring their guitars along. September is a wild month here—the whole country converges on the region, and everyone drinks the hugely popular young wine *(burčák)*.

Floating on the River—During the day, the Yacht Club at the bottom of the village rents a variety of floatables, including paddleboats, canoes, and windsurfing boards. The shallow water is warm for most of the summer, and the beaches seem endless.

Three successive dams, planned for decades as part of an immense irrigation project intended to water most of southern Moravia, were completed in the early 1990s. By then, the collectivized fields and vineyards had been returned to individual owners. For these small producers, building channels or pumping water from the dams turned out to be too expensive. So in the end, the costly project boosted the local economy only indirectly—by drawing in thousands of fishing and sailing enthusiasts.

Hiking in the Pálava Hills—For a perfect half-day hike, follow the green-marked trail from the church past Pension a Restaurace Florián, then up through the beech woods to the ruined castle (1.5 miles, 45 min). Continue on the ridge, on the red-marked trail, to the highest point of the hills, called Děvín (1 hr). Descend on the other side of the mountain to Klentnice. From here you can return to Pavlov either along the blue-marked trail through the woods on the western slopes of the Pálava Hills, or along the educational winemaking route (marked by white signs with diagonal green stripes) through the vineyards east of the hills.

Sleeping and Eating in Pavlov

During hot summer months and in September, getting a room on short notice can be difficult—book ahead.

$$ Hotel Iris, part of a Czech chain, is the only real hotel in the village. Its 22 rooms are relatively expensive, but it's a suitable fallback if the pensions (listed next) are full. The standardized experience comes with TV, a sauna, and a fitness center. The ease of communication in English might make up for the lack of village ambience (Sb-850 Kč, Db-1,700 Kč, Internet access, rental bikes,

MIKULOV WINE REGION

Sleep Code

(18 Kč = about $1, country code: 420)
S = Single, **D** = Double/Twin, **T** = Triple, **Q** = Quad, **b** = bathroom,
s = shower only. Unless otherwise noted, credit cards are
accepted, English is spoken, and breakfast is included.

   To help you sort easily through these listings, I've divided
the rooms into two categories based on the price for a
standard double room with bath:

   $$ Higher Priced—Most rooms 1,200 Kč or more.
   $ Lower Priced—Most rooms less than 1,200 Kč.

---

tel. 519-515-310, www.hotel-iris.cz, hotel.iris@vasstav.cz).

   $ Pension a Restaurace Florián, with six homey rooms, is
run by an energetic woman who speaks no English. From June to
October, she has an English-speaking student on hand to help out.
They would like to see more Americans come to Pavlov, so even if
their place is booked up, ask for help arranging a room elsewhere.
They make you feel like part of the family—home-cooking is
available all day. In the evenings, they run a wine cellar–restaurant
behind the pension. They're also able to recommend other nearby
wine cellars where English is spoken (Db-1,000 Kč, 5 percent
discount for readers of this book for 2 or more nights, Podhradní
195, tel. 519-515-323, mobile 736-760-463, www.pensionflorian.cz,
info@pensionflorian.cz).

   $ Pension u Bednářů rents 23 rooms scattered through three
houses—two traditional, one hotelesque. The owners, who speak
only German, also run their own wine cellar–restaurant (Db-900
Kč, rooms #110–113 have no windows, tel. 519-515-110, fax 519-515-
341, mobile 607-108-450, www.penziony.breclavsko.com, penziony
@breclavsko.cz).

Mikulov

An important border town on the amber road from the Baltic Sea
to the Adriatic, Mikulov (MEE-kuh-lohv; think "Mikulov, not
war") was briefly the capital of Moravia. When the Austrian kings
expelled the Jews from Austria in the early 1400s, the Jews settled
here on the border, making up half the town's population and
forming the largest Czech Jewish community outside of Prague.
The railway line to Vienna bypassed Mikulov, condemning it
to a stagnation that mercifully protected it from Industrial Age

Mikulov Wines

Czech wine is more than just a drink—it's a way of life. Although the Moravians might not have captured the sweetness of the Portuguese varieties, they did manage to ferment the taste of grapes into their own authentic culture. Without experiencing the wine tradition of southern Moravia, you will have missed a good part of the country's spirit.

Wine has been made in the Mikulov region since Roman times. Because no Roman soldier would fight without his daily two-liter ration of wine, and because it was difficult to transport unpasteurized wine over long distances, the 10th legion of Marcus Aurelius planted its own vines on this region's limestone hills (which reminded them of their homes in Tuscany). The Slavs and the Germans found the vines long after the Romans were gone and continued the tradition. In the 16th century, Anabaptist refugees from Switzerland brought new energy to the winemaking process. Today, the warm climate and the soil rich in calcium (from the limestone) make the Mikulov region one of the best wine-producing areas in Eastern Europe.

The most commonly used grapes are Ryzlink, Veltlínské Zelené, Rulandské Bílé, Chardonnay, and Sauvignon for whites, and Svatovavřinecké, Frankovka, and Cabernet Sauvignon for reds. The locally bred grapes are Pálava and Aurelius.

The variety of grape is only one factor that contributes to each wine's distinct taste. Vintners discern wines by the type of soil in which they grow; the orientation of the slope (which determines the amount of sun); and—most importantly—the sugar

construction. Mikulov was the seat of the leading Moravian rabbi until World War II.

Today, all that remains of Mikulov's past glory are a synagogue, a cemetery, and a few traditional houses along Husova street below the castle. Still, it's an enjoyable and historic town that comes alive during vintage festivals. Mikulov makes a good lunch stop if you're driving to Lednice or Vienna.

Orientation to Mikulov

Tourist Information

The TI on the main square is a wealth of information about the entire region. They give out free maps and good biking informacontent. The best wines are from hand-picked late vintages, with sugar content reaching 27 percent.

The quirky local specialties are straw and ice wines. The grapes for straw wines mature in barns for months spread on dry straw. Ice wines—a Moravian and German specialty—are made by storing grapes for most of the winter, then pressing them at –6 degrees Celsius. As these two wines are very difficult to make—the process is practically alchemy, as even the best vintners cannot predict which grapes will turn into a good ice wine—they are also the most expensive. A tiny .3-liter bottle (about 10 oz.) costs more than 700 Kč.

The communists mismanaged wine production by using bad shoots prone to diseases. Over the last 20 years, vintners have replaced most of these old vines with young, quality ones. Moravian wines improve from year to year. Look for vintages from odd years—in the past decade these have been better than even years. Among older vintages, 1994 was outstanding.

One of the most prominent wine companies in the country is Reisten, the exclusive supplier to Prague's luxury restaurants and the president of the Czech Republic. Reisten produces its wines in Pavlov, in the cellars next door to Restaurace u Venuše. The owner will take you down for a tasting (open most of the day; coming from the church and Florián, turn left by Restaurace u Venuše and then look on your right for a small *Reisten* sign; tel. 519-515-222, mobile 777-151-299).

tion, and can help you arrange accommodations (Mon–Fri 8:00–18:00, Sat–Sun 9:00–18:00, tel. 519-510-855 or 519-512-200, www.mikulov.cz).

Helpful Hints

Bike Rental: A popular way to explore the surrounding wine region is on bicycle (the TI hands out a free map describing trails and can direct you to a rental place).

Car Rental: If you're arriving in the Czech Republic by train from Vienna or Budapest and will need to return there, consider getting off in nearby Břeclav to pick up a rental car. **Bors** in Břeclav is handy and rents Renaults (1 day starts at 700 Kč, Mon–Fri 8:00–17:00, Sat 8:00–11:00, closed Sun, tel. 519-444-242, mobile 731-606-242, www.bors.cz, safrankova@bors.cz). To get to Bors from Břeclav's train station, either take a cab (less than 50 Kč) or walk for 10 minutes (exit into park, turn left, walk along main street past the post office, then under railway bridge to gas station and Bors Renault dealership).

Sights in Mikulov

Of the scant sights in town, only the **synagogue museum,** which chronicles the history of local Jews, is worth a visit (daily July–Aug 10:00–17:00, May–June and Sept 13:00–17:00, closed Oct–April, on Husova street). You can skip the large castle complex in the middle of the town; the castles in nearby Lednice and Valtice are far more interesting (described later in this chapter).

Sleeping in Mikulov

$$ Hotel Tanzberg is a beguiling Baroque townhouse, formerly the home of one of Mikulov's richest Jewish families. When you step in the atmospheric interior, you're transported back to the 1930s (Sb-1,000 Kč, Db-1,200 Kč, apartment-2,200 Kč, across from synagogue at Husova 8, tel. 519-510-692, fax 519-511-695, www.hotel-tanzberg.cz, hotel@hotel-tanzberg.cz).

Eating in Mikulov

Restaurace Alfa, the best restaurant in town, is on the main square in the white Renaissance house with sgraffiti decorations. Their fresh daily specials, available from 11:00, land on your table before the foam settles on your beer (daily 10:00–22:00, Náměstí 27, tel. 519-510-877).

At **Le Patio Café,** in a graceful Renaissance courtyard complete with balconies and a gallery, you can peacefully sip a Turkish coffee and munch sweet Moravian crêpes under the blue sky (open daily, enter from left side of same house as Restaurace Alfa and walk through the passageway).

Mikulov Connections

From Mikulov to: Pavlov (4 buses/day Mon–Fri, 1/day Sat–Sun, 30 min), **Lednice** (2 buses Mon–Fri afternoons only, 20 min), **Valtice** (10 trains/day, 15 min), **Moravský Krumlov** (2 trains every afternoon, 1.5 hrs, transfer in Hrušovany), **Vienna** (8 trains/day, 2 hrs, transfer in Břeclav).

MIKULOV WINE REGION

Lednice and Valtice

The twin towns of Lednice and Valtice—connected by a lush, walkable greenbelt—each boast a proud castle. Located along

the Austrian border southeast of Mikulov, they make up one of the Czech Republic's most visit-worthy castle regions.

Since the 1200s, Lednice and Valtice have been part of the Mikulov-based Lichtenstein family. The Lichtensteins were to South Moravia what the Rožmberks were to South Bohemia: either caring benefactors who turned marshes and beech woods into the promised land, or despotic aristocrats who mercilessly impoverished their serfs...depending on whom you ask. While the Rožmberks died out in the early 1600s, the Lichtensteins thrived during the Thirty Years' War (they wisely stayed loyal to the victorious Habsburgs) and continued to enrich the region until the 1940s. While Valtice was their winter residence, they summered at Lednice (even though Lednice means "fridge," so named because this stretch of the Dyje River is known for frequent frosts). Of the two castles, Lednice is more interesting to tour.

An even more compelling reason to make the short side-trip from Mikulov or Břeclav is the spectacular 19th-century English-style park, which extends for miles between the Lednice and Valtice castles. Native oaks and exotic cedars span their gnarled branches over wild meadows and green lakes, Romantic castles and Taj Mahal–style minarets rise in the middle of woods like apparitions, and rare birds silently glide through the sky.

Orientation to Lednice and Valtice

The "Lednice–Valtice Area" (Lednicko–Valtický Areál) is composed of two small towns, about four miles apart: Lednice (LEHD-neet-seh, pop. 2,400) and Valtice (VAHLT-eet-seh, pop. 3,600).

Tourist Information

Lednice's TI, by the main parking lot in front of the entrance to the Lednice Castle, has free Internet access and sells an inexpensive info brochure and maps of the garden complex (June–Aug daily 8:00–17:00, shorter hours April–May and Sept–Oct, closed Nov–March; tel. 519-340-986, www.lednice.cz). For information on Valtice, see www.radnice-valtice.cz.

Sights in Lednice

Lednice Castle (Zámek Lednice)—This castle is the Moravian answer to England's Windsor Castle, an immense structure built in the English Neo-Gothic style. Today, the castle houses the university for winemakers; anyone is welcome to sign up for a short summer course.

To tour the palace, choose between two routes: Route A (80 Kč) goes through the halls, and Route B (100 Kč) goes through the apartments. With either one, you can pay 50 Kč extra for a tour in English (May–Aug Tue–Sun 9:00–12:00 & 13:00–17:15, closed Mon; Sept Tue–Sun 9:00–12:00 & 13:00–16:15, closed Mon; April and Oct Sat–Sun only 9:00–12:00 & 13:00–15:15, closed Mon–Fri; closed Nov–March; tel. 519-340-128, www.zamek-lednice.info).

Castle Parks—From Lednice Castle, parks extend both north and south. The 19th-century nobles loved everything Romantic, peppering these woods with a quirky architectural hodgepodge: a Neo-Roman aqueduct, a Neo-Gothic castle ruin, a Neo-Greek temple, a victory column, a rendezvous pavilion, and so on. Navigate between these perfect spots to bring a date with the help of the map from the TI.

Cost: Depending on how many of the recommended park attractions you visit, plan on spending about 190–230 Kč per person.

Getting There: To reach the minaret from Lednice Castle, you can walk (1 mile), hire a horse carriage (60 Kč/person, 30 min), or take a boat. Boats and carriages depart from the little dam just behind the castle; prices depend on the number of riders. Although most horse-carriage rides throughout Europe are tourist traps, here it feels appropriate to ride through the alleys like the nobles once did—even the school groups do it. A good plan is to ride to the minaret and walk back.

❷ Self-Guided Tour: Here are some highlights of the parks.

The **Palm Greenhouse,** located near the castle entrance, takes you from Moravia to the tropics (50 Kč, similar hours as castle but open even during winter). Notice the construction above you: one of the oldest examples of a cast-iron roof in Europe. Created in England in the 1830s, this innovation was one of the great technical marvels of the 19th century, gradually spreading to create spacious train stations and market halls throughout Europe.

From the greenhouse, it's a five-minute walk to the predator bird show; en route, you'll see a small **archery stand.** If you've ever dreamed of being William Tell, stop here and try your skill on the medieval and modern crossbows. No need to bring an apple or a son—they provide the target discs and instruction (60 Kč for five shots, daily in summer, weekends only in spring and fall).

The 45-minute show of live **predator birds** features more than 20 kinds of birds from all over the world. The falcons, merlins, marsh harriers, buzzards, and goshawks demonstrate their hunting skills on simulated rabbits and quails. Some are breathtakingly fast, others comically slow. You can leave whenever you want (35 Kč for short visit, 70 Kč for whole show, pick up English brochure in ticket tent that describes every bird; July–Aug

daily at 11:30, 14:15, and 16:30; May–June and Sept weekends at 12:00 and 15:00, plus occasional shows during the week; call 608-100-440 for details).

My favorite part of the park stretches north, from the castle to the minaret. The **minaret** is an impressive bit of Romantic-era garden planning that copies the kind of Muslim-style minarets that flank the Taj Mahal in India. Those climbing its 302 winding steps (60 Kč) are rewarded with a grand view. Locals say that Count Alois Josef I intended to build a new church for the village of Lednice, but no plan seemed quite right to the villagers. Their pickiness finally irritated the count so much that he decided to build a mosque with a minaret instead of a church. The mosque never materialized, but the minaret did (completed in 1804). Since the ground around the Dyje River is made up of moving sands, the 200-foot-tall tower had to be anchored almost as deep underground, on beech and oak pilings. The minaret's architect, Josef Hardtmuth, was a versatile genius. The most successful of his patents was the idea of mixing graphite and mud and coating it with wood. The pencil factory he founded (which bears his name) is still one of the largest in Europe.

One scholar believes the minaret is actually a few centuries older. For a short period, the area was part of the vast Mogul Empire, ruled by Persian-speaking Muslims and centered in northern India. The great Mogul emperor Aurangzeb (1618–1707) subdued even the mighty Turks and expanded his empire from Sri Lanka to southern Moravia. The minaret, which marks the northernmost point of his exploits, was purportedly built by the Delhi "World Conqueror" to give thanks to Allah.

The four Arabic inscriptions on the sides of the minaret roughly translate: "There is no God except God, and Muhammad is his prophet. The world betrayed its people. Do not forsake your worldly possessions. There is no difference between wealth and renunciation. True happiness can be reached only in the world beyond. Only through industry and hard work can you reach well-being in this world. When fate stands against you, all plans lose meaning; indeed, without the help of fate, man does not reach redemption."

Lednice and Valtice Connections

Consider taking the bus to Lednice, walking through the gardens to Valtice (a level four-mile stroll), and then taking the train from there.

From Lednice to: Mikulov (2 buses/afternoon Mon–Fri only, 20 min), **Vienna** (8 trains/day, 1.75 hrs, transfer in Břeclav).

From Valtice to: Mikulov (10 trains/day, 15 min), **Prague** (hourly trains, 4 hrs, 1 transfer), **Olomouc** (3 trains/day, 2.5–4 hrs, several transfers).

MIKULOV WINE REGION

CZECH HISTORY

The Czechs have always been at a crossroads of Europe—between the Slavic and Germanic worlds, between Catholicism and Protestantism, and between Cold War East and West. As if having foreseen all of this, the mythical founder of Prague—the beautiful princess Libuše—named her city "Praha" (meaning "threshold" in Czech). Despite these strong external influences, the Czechs have retained their distinct culture...and a dark, ironic sense of humor to keep them laughing through it all.

Charles IV and the Middle Ages

Prague's castle put Bohemia on the map in the ninth century. About a century later, the region was incorporated into the German Holy Roman Empire. Within two hundred years, Prague was one of Europe's largest and most highly cultured cities.

The 14th century was Prague's Golden Age, when Holy Roman Emperor Charles IV (1316–1378) ruled. Born to a Luxemburg

nobleman and a Czech princess, Charles IV was a dynamic man on the cusp of the Renaissance. He spoke five languages, counted Petrarch as a friend, imported French architects to make Prague a grand capital, founded the first university north of the Alps, and invigorated the Czech national spirit. (He popularized the legend of the good king Wenceslas to give his people a near-mythical, King Arthur–type cultural standard-bearer.) Much of Prague's history and architecture (including the famous Charles Bridge, Charles University, and St. Vitus Cathedral) can be traced to this man's rule. Under Charles IV, the Czech people gained esteem among Europeans.

Jan Hus and Religious Wars

Jan Hus (c. 1370–1415) was a local preacher and professor who got in trouble with the Vatican a hundred years before Martin Luther. Like Luther, Hus preached in the people's language rather than Latin. To add insult to injury, he complained about Church corruption. Tried for heresy and burned in 1415, Hus became both a religious and a national hero. While each age has defined Hus to its liking, the way he challenged authority while staying true to himself has long inspired and rallied the Czech people. (For more on Hus, see page 54.)

Inspired by the reformist ideas of Hus, the Czechs rebelled against both the Roman Catholic Church and German political control. This burst of independent thought led to a period of religious wars—and ultimately the loss of autonomy to Vienna. Ruled by the Habsburgs of Austria, Prague stagnated—except during the rule of King Rudolf II (1552–1612), a Holy Roman Emperor. With Rudolf living in Prague, the city again emerged as a cultural and intellectual center. Astronomers Johannes Kepler and Tycho Brahe flourished, as did other scientists, and much of the inspiration for Prague's great art can be attributed to the king's patronage.

Not long after this period, Prague entered one of its darker spells. The Thirty Years' War (1618–1648) began in Prague when Czech Protestant nobles, wanting religious and political autonomy, tossed two Catholic Habsburg officials out of the window of the castle. (This was one of Prague's many defenestrations—a uniquely Czech solution to political discord, in which offending politicians were thrown out the window.) The Czech Estates Uprising lasted for two years, ending in a crushing defeat of the Czech army in the Battle of White Mountain (1620), which marked the end of Czech freedom. Twenty-seven leaders of the uprising were executed (today commemorated by crosses on Prague's Old Town Square), most of the old Czech nobility was dispossessed, and Protestants had to convert to Catholicism or leave the country. Often called "the first world war" because it engulfed so many nations, the Thirty Years' War was particularly tough on Prague. During this period, its population dropped from 60,000 to 25,000. The result of this war was 300 years of Habsburg rule from afar, as Prague became a German-speaking backwater of Vienna.

Czech Nationalist Revival

The end of Prague as a "German" city came gradually. As the Industrial Revolution attracted Czech farmers and peasants to the cities, the demographics of the Czech population centers began

Notable Czechs

These prominent historical figures are listed in chronological order.

St. Wenceslas (907–935): Bohemian duke who allied the Czechs with the Holy Roman Empire. He went on to become the Czech Republic's patron saint, and it is he who is memorialized as a "good king" in the Christmas carol. For more on Wenceslas, see page 77.

Jan Hus (c. 1370–1415): Proto-Protestant Reformer who was burned at the stake (see page 54).

John Amos Comenius (Jan Amos Komenský in Czech, 1592–1670): "Teacher of Nations" and Protestant exile, whose ideas paved the way for modern education (see page 246).

Antonín Dvořák (1841–1904): Inspired by a trip to America, he composed his *New World Symphony*. For more on Czech composers, see page 148.

Tomáš Garrigue Masaryk (1850–1937): Sociology professor, writer, politician, and spiritual reformer. He was idolized during his lifetime as the "dearest father" of the Czechoslovak democracy (see page 106).

Jára Cimrman (c. 1853–1914): Illustrious but fictional inventor, explorer, philosopher, and all-around genius. Despite being overwhelmingly voted the "Greatest Czech of All Time" in a recent nationwide poll, he was not awarded the title. For details on the controversy, see page 94.

Alfons Mucha (1860–1939): You might recognize his turn-of-the-century Art Nouveau posters of pretty girls entwined in vines. Visit his museum in Prague, marvel at his stained-glass window in St. Vitus Cathedral, and make a pilgrimage to see his magnum opus, the *Slav Epic* (which will most likely stay in the town of Moravský Krumlov at least until the summer of 2010).

Franz Kafka (1883–1924): While working for a Prague insurance firm, he wrote (in German) *The Metamorphosis* (man awakes as a cockroach), *The Trial, The Castle,* and other psychologically haunting stories and novels.

Milan Kundera (1929–): Wrote the novel *The Unbearable Lightness of Being* (which became a film), among others. For more on Czech authors and filmmakers, see page 299.

Václav Havel (1936–): The country's first post-Soviet president, also known as a playwright and philosopher.

Madeleine Albright (1937–): Born in Prague as Marie Jana Korbelová, Albright was the first woman to serve as United States Secretary of State, from 1997-2001, under Bill Clinton.

Martina Navrátilová (1956–): Tennis star of the 1980s. For more on Czech sports, see page 153.

It's Not You, It's Me: The Velvet Divorce

In the autumn of 1989, hundreds of thousands of Czechs and Slovaks streamed into Prague to demonstrate on Wenceslas Square. Their "Velvet Revolution" succeeded, and Czechoslovakia's communist regime peacefully excused itself. But that was only the first step. In that age of new possibility, the two peoples of Czechoslovakia began to wonder if, in fact, they belonged together.

Ever since they joined with the Czechs in 1918, the Slovaks felt they were ruled from Prague (unmistakably the political, economic, and cultural center of the country), rather than from their own capital. And the Czechs, for their part, resented the financial burden of carrying their poorer neighbors to the east. In the post-communist world, the Czechs found themselves with a 10 percent unemployment rate...compared with 20 or 30 percent unemployment in the Slovak lands. In this new world of flux and freedom, long-standing tensions came to a head.

The dissolution of Czechoslovakia began over a hyphen, as the Slovaks wanted to rename the country Czecho-Slovakia. Ideally, this symbolic move would come with a redistribution of powers: two capitals and two UN reps, but one national bank and a single currency. The Slovaks were also less enthusiastic about abandoning the communist society altogether, since the Soviet regime had left them with a heavily industrialized economy that depended on a socialist element for survival.

Initially, many Czechs couldn't understand the Slovaks'

to shift. Between 1800 and 1900, though it remained part of the Habsburg Empire, Prague went from being an essentially German town to a predominantly Czech one. As in the rest of Europe, the 19th century was a time of great nationalism, when the age of divine kings and ruling families came to a fitful end. The Czech spirit was stirred by the completion of Prague's St. Vitus Cathedral, the symphonies of Antonín Dvořák, and the operas of Bedřich Smetana performed in the new National Theater.

After the Habsburgs' Austro-Hungarian Empire suffered defeat in World War I, their vast holdings broke apart and became independent countries. Among these was a union of Bohemia, Moravia, and Slovakia, the brainchild of a clever politician named Tomáš Garrigue Masaryk (see page 106). The new nation, Czechoslovakia, was proclaimed in 1918, with Prague as its capital.

Troubled 20th Century

Independence lasted only 20 years. In the notorious Munich Agreement of September 1938—much to the dismay of the demands. The first post-communist president of Czechoslovakia, Czech Václav Havel, made matters worse when he took a rare trip to the Slovak half of his country in 1990. In a fit of terrible judgment, Havel boldly promised he'd close the ugly, polluting Soviet factories in Slovakia, seemingly oblivious to the fact that many Slovaks still depended on these factories for survival. Havel left in disgrace and visited the Slovak lands only twice more in the next two and a half years.

In June 1992, the Slovak nationalist candidate Vladimír Mečiar fared surprisingly well in the elections—suggesting that the Slovaks were serious about secession. The politicians plowed ahead, getting serious about the split in September 1992. The transition took only three months from start to finish.

The people of Czechoslovakia never actually voted on the separation; in fact, public opinion polls in both regions were two-thirds *against* the split. This makes Slovakia quite possibly the only country in the history of the world to gain independence... even though its citizens didn't want it.

The Velvet Divorce became official on January 1, 1993, and each country ended up with its own capital, currency, and head of state. The Slovaks let loose a yelp of excitement, and the Czechs emitted a sigh of relief. For most the divorce dissolved tensions, and a decade and a half later, Czechs and Slovaks still feel closer to each other than to any other nationality.

Czechs and Slovaks—Great Britain and France peacefully ceded to Hitler the so-called "Sudetenland" (a fringe around the edge of Bohemia, populated mainly by people of German descent; see sidebar on page 229). It wasn't long before Hitler seized the rest of Czechoslovakia...and the Holocaust began.

For centuries, Prague's cultural makeup had consisted of a rich mix of Czech, German, and Jewish people—historically, they were almost evenly divided. But only 5 percent of the Jewish population survived the Holocaust. And after World War II ended, the three million people of Germanic descent who lived in Czechoslovakia were pushed into Germany. Their forced resettlement—which led to the deaths of untold numbers of Germans—was the idea, among others, of Czechoslovak President Edvard Beneš, who had been ruling from exile in London throughout the war (see page 194). As a result of both of these policies (the Holocaust and the expulsion of Germans), today's Czech Republic is largely homogenous—about 95 percent Czechs.

Although Prague escaped the bombs of World War II, it went directly from the Nazi frying pan into the communist fire. A local uprising freed the city from the Nazis on May 8, 1945, but the Soviets "liberated" them on May 9.

The early communist era (1948–1968) was a mixture of misguided zeal, Stalinist repressions, and attempts to wed socialism with democracy. The "Prague Spring" period—initiated by a young generation of reform-minded communists in 1968—came to an abrupt halt under the treads of Soviet tanks.

The uprising's charismatic leader, Alexander Dubček, was exiled (and made a backwoods forest ranger), and the years following the unsuccessful revolt were particularly disheartening. In the late 1980s, the communists began constructing Prague's huge Žižkov TV tower (now the city's tallest structure)—not only to broadcast Czech TV transmissions, but also to jam Western signals. The Metro, built at about the same time, was intended for mass transit, but was also designed to be a giant fallout shelter for protection against capitalist bombs.

But the Soviet empire crumbled. Czechoslovakia regained its freedom in the student- and artist-powered 1989 "Velvet Revolution" (so called because there were no casualties...or even broken windows). Václav Havel, a writer who had been imprisoned by the communist regime, became Czechoslovakia's first postcommunist president. In 1993, the Czech and Slovak Republics agreed on the "Velvet Divorce" and became two separate countries. Two other major turning points were May 1, 2004, when the Czech Republic joined the European Union (see sidebar on page 104); and January 1, 2008, when the country entered the Schengen Agreement, effectively erasing its borders for the purposes of travel.

Havel ended his second (and, constitutionally, last) five-year term in 2003. While he's still admired by Czechs as a great thinker, writer, and fearless leader of the opposition movement during the communist days, many consider him to have been less successful as a president. Some believe that the split of Czechoslovakia was partly caused by Havel's initial insensitivity to Slovak demands.

The current president, Václav Klaus, was the pragmatic author of the economic reforms in the 1990s. Klaus' surprising win in the 2003 election symbolized a change from revolutionary times, when philosophers became kings, to modern humdrum politics, when offices are gained by bargaining with the opposition (Communist votes in the Parliament were the decisive factor in Klaus' election).

In 2008, Klaus was narrowly re-elected by the Parliament for a second term, despite revelations that his economic reforms had resulted in widespread corruption in the privatizing business sector. The scandal became the defining issue of the election, with Klaus and his conservative party denying responsibility for (and even the existence of) the abuses. The Greens and the Social Democrats had

The Wisdom of Babička Míla ("Granny Míla")

Co-author Honza Vihan's grandmother, Bohumila Vihanová (February 17, 1907–August 18, 2008), was born in the Austro-Hungarian town of Prag (today's Praha), which was then ruled from Vienna. In the 101 years of her life, she lived under seven different governments: Habsburgs, interwar Czechoslovakia, Nazis, communists, post-communist Czechoslovakia, the Czech Republic, and the European Union. Wise beyond even her many years, she counseled family and visitors alike as follows:

- "I liked each change, because it always brought something new."
- "You must be able to take the best from whatever comes."
- "Nothing good that you do is ever lost; it always stays somewhere and surfaces when needed."
- "When the communists took over, that was bad—really bad. But then, my mother used to say, 'There's no point in crying over spilled milk. There's enough water in it already.' So I tried to get by, and somehow we managed to live through it all."
- "The main thing is to keep your inner balance."
- "You should never take yourself too seriously."
- "Let everyone believe whatever they want, as long as they behave accordingly."
- "Money will always be here. We won't."
- "Parents should never mix in their children's lives."
- "Good health and happy mind!"

chosen as their candidate University of Michigan economic professor Jan Švejnar, the most outspoken critic of Klaus' reforms in the 1990s. And though public support was evenly divided between the two candidates, behind-the-scenes deals in the Parliament allowed the ruling conservatives to maintain their majority and keep Klaus in power.

In the first half of 2009, the Czech Republic held the rotating presidency of the EU, during which time they focused on ending Europe's energy dependence on Russia and on more workforce mobility. Halfway through the presidency, Czech minority parties, along with two defectors from the conservatives, pushed a vote of nonconfidence through the Parliament, leaving the country and the EU without a prime minister—and thereby effectively confirming the widespread European suspicion that the Czechs were unreliable. Ironically, one of the defectors' objections was the government's willingness to allow the US to build a part of its anti-missile defense system on Czech territory, a plan that was shelved by the Obama administration in September 2009.

Klaus has polarized the country like no other figure in modern history, bringing into visible confrontation the old attitude of suppressing past trauma and the new attitude of learning from your history.

Today, while not without its problems, the Czech Republic is still enjoying a growing economy and a strong democracy, and Prague has emerged as one of the most popular tourist destinations in Europe.

APPENDIX

Contents

Tourist Information

Tourist Offices

The Czech national tourist office **in the US** is a wealth of information. Before your trip, get the free general information packet and request any specifics you may want (such as regional and city maps and festival schedules). Basic information and a map are free; additional materials are $4 (prepaid by check). Call 212/288-0830 or visit www.czechtourism.com (info-usa@czechtourism.com).

In the Czech Republic, your best first stop in every town is generally the tourist information office—abbreviated **TI** in this book. Try to arrive, or at least telephone, before it closes. Have a list of questions ready, and pick up maps, brochures, and walking-tour information. Most of these TIs are located on the main square of their town, and offer English-speaking staff, a free town map, and information on public transportation (including bus and train schedules), walking tours, special events, and nightlife recommendations. Many TIs have information on the entire country or at least the region, so try to pick up maps for destinations you'll be visiting later in your trip. Almost all of the TIs in the Czech Republic are run by the town governments, which means their information isn't colored by a drive for profit.

Communicating

Hurdling the Language Barrier

The language barrier in the Czech Republic is no bigger than in Western Europe. In fact, I find that it's even easier to communicate in Český Krumlov than it is in Madrid. Immediately after the Iron Curtain fell in 1989, English speakers were rare. But today, you'll find that most people in the tourist industry—and just about all young people—speak English well.

Of course, not everyone speaks English. You'll run into the most substantial language barriers in situations when you need to deal with a clerk or service person aged 40 or above (train station and post-office staff, maids, museum guards, bakers, and so on). Be reasonable in your expectations. Czech post-office clerks and museum ticket-sellers are every bit as friendly, cheery, and multilingual as ours are in the US. Luckily, it's relatively easy to get your point across in these places. I've often bought a train ticket simply by writing out the name of my destination; the time I want to travel (using the 24-hour clock); and, if necessary, the date I want to leave (day first, then month, then year). Here's an example of what I'd show a ticket-seller at a train station: "Olomouc – 17:30 – 15.7.2010."

If you speak German, it will likely come in handy—especially in the south of the country, where the economy depends in part on Austrian tourists from across the border.

Of course, the easiest way to hurdle the language barrier in any country is to learn some of the local words (see "Czech Survival Phrases" on page 307).

Pronunciation

Czech, a Slavic language closely related to its Polish and Slovak neighbors, bears little resemblance to Western European languages. Slavic pronunciation can be tricky. In fact, when the first Christian missionaries, Cyril and Methodius, came to Eastern Europe a millennium ago, they invented a whole new alphabet to represent these strange Slavic sounds. Their Cyrillic alphabet is still used today in the eastern Slavic countries (such as Serbia and Russia).

Fortunately, the Czechs long ago converted to the same Roman alphabet we use, but they've added lots of different diacritics—

little markings below and above letters—to represent a wide range of sounds. An acute accent *(á, é, í, ó, ú, ý)* means you linger on that vowel; it does not indicate stress, which invariably falls on the first syllable. The letter *c* always sounds like "ts" (as in "cats"). The little accent *(háček)* above the *č, š,* or *ž* makes it sound like "ch", "sh", or "zh" (as in "leisure"), respectively. A *háček* over *ě* makes it sound like "yeh."

Czech has one sound that occurs in no other language: *ř* (as in "Dvořák"), which sounds like a cross between a rolled "r" and "zh." Another unusual sound is *ň*, which is pronounced "ny" (as in "canyon"). These sounds are notoriously impossible for foreigners to duplicate; it's easiest just to replace them with simple "r" and "n" sounds.

Give it your best shot. Use the phrases listed later in this chapter. The locals will appreciate your efforts.

Telephones

Smart travelers get comfortable using the telephone to reserve or reconfirm rooms, get tourist information, reserve restaurants, confirm tour times, or phone home. Generally the easiest, cheapest way to call home is to use an international phone card purchased in the Czech Republic. This section covers dialing instructions, phone cards, and types of phones. (For more in-depth information, see www.ricksteves.com/phoning.)

How to Dial

Calling from the US to Europe, or vice versa, is simple—once you break the code. The European calling chart within this chapter will walk you through it.

Dialing Domestically in the Czech Republic

The Czech Republic has a direct-dial phone system (no area codes). To call anywhere within the Czech Republic, just dial the number. For example, one of my recommended Prague hotels is 224-812-041. To call it from a Prague train station, just dial 224-812-041. If you call it from Český Krumlov, it's the same: 224-812-041. All phone numbers in the Czech Republic are nine digits. If a number starting with 0800 doesn't work, replace the 0800 with 822.

Dialing Internationally to or from the Czech Republic

If you want to make an international call, follow these steps:

European Calling Chart

Just smile and dial, using this key:
AC = Area Code, LN = Local Number.

European Country	Calling long distance within ...	Calling from the US or Canada to ...	Calling from a European country to ...
Austria	AC + LN	011 + 43 + AC (without the initial zero) + LN	00 + 43 + AC (without the initial zero) + LN
Belgium	LN	011 + 32 + LN (without initial zero)	00 + 32 + LN (without initial zero)
Bosnia-Herzegovina	AC + LN	011 + 387 + AC (without initial zero) + LN	00 + 387 + AC (without initial zero) + LN
Britain	AC + LN	011 + 44 + AC (without initial zero) + LN	00 + 44 + AC (without initial zero) + LN
Croatia	AC + LN	011 + 385 + AC (without initial zero) + LN	00 + 385 + AC (without initial zero) + LN
Czech Republic	LN	011 + 420 + LN	00 + 420 + LN
Denmark	LN	011 + 45 + LN	00 + 45 + LN
Estonia	LN	011 + 372 + LN	00 + 372 + LN
Finland	AC + LN	011 + 358 + AC (without initial zero) + LN	999 (or other 900 number) + 358 + AC (without initial zero) + LN
France	LN	011 + 33 + LN (without initial zero)	00 + 33 + LN (without initial zero)
Germany	AC + LN	011 + 49 + AC (without initial zero) + LN	00 + 49 + AC (without initial zero) + LN
Gibraltar	LN	011 + 350 + LN	00 + 350 + LN
Greece	LN	011 + 30 + LN	00 + 30 + LN
Hungary	06 + AC + LN	011 + 36 + AC + LN	00 + 36 + AC + LN
Ireland	AC + LN	011 + 353 + AC (without initial zero) + LN	00 + 353 + AC (without initial zero) + LN

European Country	Calling long distance within ...	Calling from the US or Canada to ...	Calling from a European country to ...
Italy	LN	011 + 39 + LN	00 + 39 + LN
Montenegro	AC + LN	011 + 382 + AC (without initial zero) + LN	00 + 382 + AC (without initial zero) + LN
Morocco	LN	011 + 212 + LN (without initial zero)	00 + 212 + LN (without initial zero)
Netherlands	AC + LN	011 + 31 + AC (without initial zero) + LN	00 + 31 + AC (without initial zero) + LN
Norway	LN	011 + 47 + LN	00 + 47 + LN
Poland	LN	011 + 48 + LN (without initial zero)	00 + 48 + LN (without initial zero)
Portugal	LN	011 + 351 + LN	00 + 351 + LN
Slovakia	AC + LN	011 + 421 + AC (without initial zero) + LN	00 + 421 + AC (without initial zero) + LN
Slovenia	AC + LN	011 + 386 + AC (without initial zero) + LN	00 + 386 + AC (without initial zero) + LN
Spain	LN	011 + 34 + LN	00 + 34 + LN
Sweden	AC + LN	011 + 46 + AC (without initial zero) + LN	00 + 46 + AC (without initial zero) + LN
Switzerland	LN	011 + 41 + LN (without initial zero)	00 + 41 + LN (without initial zero)
Turkey	AC (if there's no initial zero, add one) + LN	011 + 90 + AC (without initial zero) + LN	00 + 90 + AC (without initial zero) + LN

APPENDIX

- The instructions above apply whether you're calling a land line or mobile phone.
- The international access codes (the first numbers you dial when making an international call) are 011 if you're calling from the US or Canada, or 00 if you're calling from virtually anywhere in Europe (except Finland, where it's 999 or another 900 number, depending on the phone service you're using).
- To call the US or Canada from Europe, dial 00, then 1 (the country code for the US and Canada), then the area code and number. In short, 00 + 1 + AC + LN = Hi, Mom!

Dial the international access code (00 if you're calling from Europe, 011 from the US or Canada).

Then dial the country code of the country you're calling (420 for the Czech Republic).

Then dial the local number. For example, to call the recommended Prague hotel from the US, dial 011 (the US international access code), 420 (the Czech Republic's country code), and 224-812-041.

To call my office in Edmonds, Washington, from the Czech Republic, I dial 00 (Europe's international access code), 1 (the US country code), 425 (Edmonds' area code), and 771-8303.

Note: You might see a + in front of a European number. When dialing the number, replace the + with the international access code of the country you're calling from (00 from Europe, 011 from the US or Canada).

Public Phones and Hotel-Room Phones

To make calls from public phones, you'll need a prepaid phone card. There are two different kinds of phone cards: international and insertable. Cards purchased in the Czech Republic will work only within the country, not elsewhere in Europe. If you have a live card at the end of your trip, give it to another traveler to use.

International Phone Cards: These are the cheapest way to make international calls from Europe—with the best cards, it costs literally pennies a minute. They also work for local calls. To use the card, you'll dial a toll-free access number, then enter your scratch-to-reveal PIN number. You can use international phone cards from any type of phone, even your hotel-room phone (but ask at the front desk if the hotel charges any fees for placing toll-free calls). Currently the only brand widely available in the Czech Republic is **Smartcall** (look for a black-and-orange advertisement), which you can buy at newsstands, exchange bureaus, Internet cafés, hostels, souvenir shops, and mini-marts in tourist towns such as Prague or Český Krumlov (they're not available in less touristy towns, like Olomouc). The cards come in denominations of 150 Kč, 300 Kč, 500 Kč, and 1,000 Kč. Because they're occasionally duds, avoid the high denominations.

Insertable Phone Cards: This type of card can be used only at pay phones and can be purchased at any post office. It's handy and affordable for domestic calls, but more expensive for international calls. Simply take the phone off the hook, insert the prepaid card, wait for a dial tone, and dial away. The price of the call (local or international) is automatically deducted while you talk. Dialing 970 before the international access code (970-00-1 for calls to the US) saves you about half the price on international calls (20 cents per minute to the US or other EU countries), but is still more expensive than an international phone card.

Hotel-Room Phones: Calling from your room can be cheap for local calls (ask for the rates at the front desk first), but is often a rip-off for long-distance calls (unless you use an international phone card, explained earlier). Incoming calls are free, making this a cheap way for friends and family to stay in touch (provided they have a good long-distance plan for calls to Europe—and a list of your hotels' phone numbers).

US Calling Cards: These cards, such as the ones offered by AT&T, Verizon, or Sprint, are the worst option. You'll nearly always save a lot of money by using instead an international phone card purchased in Europe.

Mobile Phones

Many travelers enjoy the convenience of traveling with a mobile phone.

Using Your Mobile Phone: Your US mobile phone works in Europe if it's GSM-enabled, tri-band or quad-band, and on a calling plan that allows international calls. For example, with a T-Mobile phone, you'll pay $1 per minute to make or receive a call, and about $0.35 apiece for text messages.

You can save money if your phone is electronically "unlocked"— then you can simply buy a **SIM card** (a fingernail-sized chip that stores the phone's information) in Europe. SIM cards, which give you a European phone number, are sold at mobile-phone stores and some newsstand kiosks for $5–15. When you buy the card, you'll also buy some prepaid calling time. Simply insert the SIM card in your phone (usually in a slot behind the battery), and it'll work like a European mobile phone. When buying a SIM card, always ask about fees for domestic and international calls, roaming charges, and how to check your credit balance and buy more time.

Many **smartphones,** such as the iPhone or BlackBerry, work in Europe—but beware of sky-high fees, especially for data downloading (checking email, browsing the Internet, watching videos, and so on). Ask your provider in advance how to avoid unwittingly "roaming" your way to a huge bill. Some applications allow for cheap or free smartphone calls over a Wi-Fi connection (see "Calling over the Internet," later).

Using a European Mobile Phone: Local mobile-phone shops all over Europe sell basic phones for $50–100. You'll also need to buy a SIM card (explained earlier) and prepaid credit for making calls. If you remain in the phone's home country, domestic calls are reasonable, and incoming calls are free. You'll pay more if you're "roaming" in another country. If your phone is "unlocked," you can swap out its SIM card for a new one in other countries.

APPENDIX

Calling over the Internet

Some things that seem too good to be true...actually are true. If you're traveling with a laptop, make calls using VoIP (Voice over Internet Protocol). With VoIP, two computers act as the phones, and the Internet-based calls are free (or you can pay a few cents per minute to call from your computer to a telephone). The major providers are Skype (www.skype.com) and Google Talk (www.google.com/talk).

Useful Phone Numbers

Emergencies

Dial 112 for medical or other emergencies. For police, dial 158.

Directory Assistance

Dial 1188 (12–27 Kč/min).

Embassies

United States: Call 257-022-000. It's in Prague's Little Quarter below the castle (passport services Mon–Fri 9:00–11:30, Tržiště 15, www.usembassy.cz, ACSPrg@state.gov).
Canada: Call 272-101-800. It's north of the Castle Quarter (consular services Mon-Fri 8:30–12:30, Muchova 6, www.canadainternational.gc.ca/czech-tcheque, canada@canada.cz).

Travel Advisories

US Department of State: tel. 202/647-5225, www.travel.state.gov
Canadian Department of Foreign Affairs: Canadian tel. 800-267-6788, www.dfait-maeci.gc.ca
US Centers for Disease Control and Prevention: tel. 800-CDC-INFO (800-232-4636), www.cdc.gov/travel

The Internet

The Internet can be an invaluable tool for planning your trip (researching and booking hotels, checking bus and train schedules, and so on). It's also useful to get online periodically as you travel to reconfirm your trip plans, check the weather, catch up on email, blog or post photos from your trip, or call folks back home (explained above, in "Calling over the Internet").

Some hotels offer a computer in the lobby with Internet access for guests.

Smaller places may sometimes let you sit at their desk for a few minutes just to check your email, if you ask politely. If you're traveling with a laptop, see if your hotel has Wi-Fi (wireless Internet access) or a port in your room where you can plug in a cable to get online. Most hotels offer Wi-Fi for free; others charge by the minute.

If your hotel doesn't have access, ask your hotelier to direct you to the nearest place to get online. Most of the towns where I've listed accommodations also have Internet cafés. Many libraries offer free access, but they also tend to have limited opening hours, restrict your online time to 30 minutes, and may require reservations.

Most computers are set to type using the Czech alphabet. To switch to English, click on the "CZ" at the bottom of the screen to toggle to "EN."

Mail

Get stamps at the neighborhood post office, newsstands within fancy hotels, and some mini-marts and card shops. While you can arrange for mail delivery to your hotel (allow 10 days for a letter to arrive), phoning and emailing are so easy that I've dispensed with mail stops altogether.

Transportation

By Car or Train?

Within Prague, a car is a worthless headache. If you're staying mostly in Prague and tackling a few convenient side-trips (such as Kutná Hora and Český Krumlov), public transportation works well. If you'll be venturing farther into the countryside, trains and buses will get you where you need to go—but renting a car gives you greater flexibility. For connecting Prague to international destinations (like Budapest or Kraków), stick with the train.

Trains

Trains are fairly punctual (generally running about 10 min late) and cover cities well, but frustrating schedules make a few out-of-the-way destinations I recommend not worth the time and trouble for the less determined (try buses instead—described later).

Schedules: For Czech train and bus timetables, visit www .idos.cz (train info tel. 221-111-122, little English spoken), or Germany's excellent all-Europe rail timetable: http://bahn.hafas .de/bin/query.exe/en. Consider buying the *Traťové Jízdní Řády*, a comprehensive, easy-to-use schedule of all trains in the country (includes English instructions, sold at major station ticket windows for 30 Kč). Although it's easy to look up a connection on the

Internet, having the printed schedule and a map of railway lines with you gives you freedom to easily change or make new plans as you travel.

Tickets and Tips: Tickets within the Czech Republic are valid for two days, and international tickets are good from three days to two months (the shorter-term ones are often cheaper). Your ticket is valid for travel along the entire stretch from Prague to your destination, not just for one trip on a specific train—so take advantage of the freedom it gives you and hop on and hop off along the way. You'll rarely need a reservation, except for international night trains.

If you have one or more companions traveling with you by train, ask for a group ticket. This gets you a 50 percent discount for every extra ticket (i.e., only the first person pays full price).

The Czech railway system has a rather complex system for discounts on international tickets. If you're heading to a city near the Czech border (such as Vienna, Bratislava, Dresden, or Nürnberg), it sometimes pays to buy two separate tickets: one to the Czech border, and another from the border to your destination. This also

Czech Public Transportation

(Map showing rail and bus routes)

POLAND

To Wrocław

Hradec
Králové

Jeseník

To Wrocław

Opava

Bohumín

To Katowice
& Kraków

Lichkov

Ostrava

Petrovice

Pardubice

Zábřeh

Český
Těšín

Olomouc

Hranice

Frenštát

Havlíčkův
Brod

Přerov

Rožnov Pod
Radhoštěm

REPUBLIC

Jihlava

Kroměříž

To
Žilina

Okříšty

Brno

Třebíč

Telč

Moravský
Krumlov

SLOVAKIA

Slavonice

Znojmo

Mikulov

Břeclav

To Vienna

To
Bratislava

AUSTRIA

----- Rail
---- Bus

allows you to take advantage of particular discounts in that country, such as the group discount.

In downtown Prague, you can buy tickets and make express or international reservations at the handy Czech Railways travel center located in the Broadway Mall between Na Příkopě and Celetná streets (see page 159).

Railpasses: The Czech Republic is covered by its own railpass, a Germany-Czech railpass, the five-country European East pass, the Eurail Global pass, and the Eurail Selectpass. If your train travel will be limited to a handful of rides and/or short distances (e.g., within the Czech Republic), you're probably better off without a pass—Czech tickets are cheap to buy as you go. If you're combining Prague with international destinations, a railpass could save you money. For all the details, check out my free Railpass Guide at www.ricksteves.com/rail.

Buses

To reach many of the destinations in this book, buses are faster and cheaper than trains. Buses are also generally more punctual.

No reservations are necessary, but they're highly recommended if you're traveling on a popular route (such as from Prague to Český Krumlov). To make online reservations, use www.studentagency .cz; if you're in Prague, visit the ticket office at the Florenc bus station (Metro: Florenc). For other routes, simply buy tickets directly from the driver (who appreciates exact change and might have difficulty breaking large bills). You'll be required to put big bags in the luggage compartment under the bus (12–24 Kč extra, depending on the distance), so have a small day bag ready to take on the bus with you. Most buses don't have bathrooms, nor do they stop for bathroom breaks.

Always let the bus driver know where you want to get off. Some stops may require a request (for example, the Small Fortress at Terezín Concentration Camp), and most bus drivers are happy to let you know when your stop is coming up.

Car Rental and Leasing

To rent a car in the Czech Republic, you must be at least 21 years old with a valid license and an International Driving Permit (see "Driving," later). Drivers under the age of 25 may incur a young-driver surcharge, and some companies might not rent to those

Driving in The Czech Republic: Distance & Time

To Wrocław
170m • 4h
330m • 6.5h
To Kraków

POLAND

Kutná Hora
CZECH REPUBLIC
Olomouc
50m • 1.5h
2.25m • 5.5h
To Kraków

60m • 1.25h
80m • 1.5h
Jihlava
95m • 2h
40m • .5h
55m • 1h
30m • 1h
Rožnov Pod Radhoštěm

Telč Třebíč
Brno
Kroměříž

40m • 1h
15m • .5h
35m • 1h
20m • .5h
40m • 1h
30m • 1h
25m • .75h
80m • 1.25h
30m • .75h

Moravský Krumlov
Mikulov
SLOVAKIA

35m • 1h
25m • .75h

Slavonice
45m • 1h

125m • 3h

Vienna
Bratislava

over age 70. If you're considered too young or old, look into leasing (explained later), which has less-stringent age restrictions.

Research car rentals before you go. Especially during peak season, the best deals at Czech car-rental companies need to be arranged two to three weeks ahead. Renting from a local Czech company (see page 39) is as convenient as using Budget or Avis; most will bring the car to your hotel. There are about a hundred car-rental companies in Prague. Alimex Thrifty is a good bet (see page 39). Or do a Google search from home, take your pick, and reserve by email.

Czechs are once again proud of their locally built Škoda cars (since the 1920s, the Ford of Eastern Europe). Now owned by Volkswagen, Škoda is the biggest post-communist success story in the country. By renting one, you'll learn why most Eastern Europeans stay loyal to the brand, even as cheap Japanese cars inundate the market. (In an ironic twist, the word "Škoda"—which is the family name of an early owner of the company—also means "damage" in Czech.)

When renting, I usually get a Škoda Fabia; for more luggage space and more oomph, step up to the Škoda Octavia. On average, you should be able to get a Škoda with full insurance and unlimited mileage for $50–70 per day. Škodas usually have manual transmission and come with alarms; you might want to supplement the alarm with a lock for the steering wheel or stick shift.

If you want an automatic, reserve the car at least a month in advance and specifically request an automatic. You'll pay about 40 percent more to rent a car with an automatic instead of a manual transmission.

When picking up the car, check it thoroughly and make sure any damage is noted on your rental agreement. Find out how your car's headlights, turn signals, wipers, and gas cap function.

If you drop your car off early or keep it longer, you'll be credited or charged at a fair, prorated price. But always keep your receipts in case any questions arise about your billing.

Returning a car at a big-city train station can be tricky; get precise details on the car drop-off location and hours. When you return the car, make sure the agent verifies its condition with you.

Car Insurance Options

Accidents can happen anywhere, but when you're on vacation, the last thing you need is stress over car insurance. Limit your financial risk by choosing one of these three options: Buy Collision Damage Waiver (CDW) coverage from the car-rental company, get coverage through your credit card (free, but more complicated), or buy coverage through Travel Guard.

While each rental company has its own variation, the basic **CDW** costs $15–25 a day (figure roughly 25 percent extra) and reduces your liability, but does not eliminate it. When you pick up the car, you'll be offered the chance to "buy down" the basic deductible to zero (for an additional $10–30/day; this is often called "super CDW").

If you opt for **credit-card coverage,** there's a catch. You'll technically have to decline all coverage offered by the car-rental company, which means they can place a hold on your card (which can be up to the full value of the car). In case of damage, it can be time-consuming to resolve the charges with your credit-card company. Before you decide on this option, quiz your credit-card company about how it works and ask them to explain the worst-case scenario.

Finally, you can buy CDW insurance from **Travel Guard** ($9/day plus a one-time $3 service fee covers you for up to $35,000, $250 deductible, tel. 800-826-4919, www.travelguard.com). It's valid everywhere in Europe except the Republic of Ireland, and some Italian car-rental companies refuse to honor it. Residents of Washington state aren't eligible for this coverage.

For more fine print about car-rental insurance, see www.rick steves.com/cdw.

APPENDIX

Leasing

For trips of two and a half weeks or more, leasing (which automatically includes zero-deductible collision and theft insurance) is the best way to go. By technically buying and then selling back the car, you save lots of money on tax and insurance. Leasing provides you a new car with unlimited mileage and a 24-hour emergency assistance program. You can lease for as little as 17 days to as long as six months. Car leases must be arranged from the US. One of many reliable companies offering affordable lease packages is Europe by Car (US tel. 800-223-1516, www.ebctravel.com). Because leasing companies serve fewer locations, you'll have to pick up and drop off your car outside the Czech Republic; Munich is the closest city to Prague that has leasing services.

Driving

To drive in the Czech Republic, you are required to have an International Driving Permit (get through your local AAA office before you go; $15 plus two passport photos; www.aaa.com). Also be sure to bring along your valid US driver's license.

STOP AND LEARN THESE ROAD SIGNS

Speed Limit (km/hr) — Yield — No Passing — End of No Passing Zone

One Way — Intersection — Main Road — Freeway

Danger — No Entry — No Entry for cars — All Vehicles Prohibited

Parking — No Parking — Customs — Peace

During the communist era, Eastern Europe's infrastructure lagged far behind the West's. Now that the Iron Curtain is long gone, superhighways are popping up like crazy all over the Czech Republic. You'll sometimes discover that a much faster freeway option has been built between major destinations since your three-year-old map was published (a good reason to travel with the most up-to-date maps available). As soon as a long-enough section is completed, the roads are opened to the public. Only rarely are backcountry roads the only option (as with part of the trip between Prague and Český Krumlov). These can be bumpy and slow, but they're almost always paved (or, at least, they once were).

Learn the universal road signs. Seat belts are required, and two beers under those belts are enough to land you in jail. Children under age 12 must ride in the back, and children under 80 pounds must have a child safety seat. You're required to have your headlights on anytime the engine is running, even in broad daylight. (The lights of many newer cars automatically turn on and off with the engine—ask when you pick up your car.)

Fuel: Be sure you know which type of fuel your rental car takes. At about $1.50 per liter ($6 per gallon) for unleaded ("Natural 95"), gas in the Czech Republic is still somewhat cheaper than in Western Europe. If driving a diesel car, you're in luck—it's called "diesel" at the pump.

Tolls: If you're driving on highways in the Czech Republic, you're required to buy a toll sticker *(dálniční známka)* at the border, a post office, or a gas station (200 Kč/15 days, 300 Kč/2 months). Your rental car may already come with the necessary sticker—ask.

Parking: You'll pay about $10–15 a day to park safely in Prague. Formerly notorious for its Russian car-theft gangs, Prague is safer now—but it's still wise to be careful. Ask at your hotel for advice. In small towns, such as Třeboň or Slavonice, it's better to stay on the safe side when parking overnight. Again, ask at your hotel for advice. I keep a pile of coins in my ashtray for parking meters, public phones, launderettes, and wishing wells.

Cheap Flights

While trains are usually the best way to connect places that are close together, a flight can save both time and money on longer journeys.

A visit to www.skyscanner.net sorts out the numerous options offered by the many discount airlines, enabling you to see the best schedules for your trip and come up with the best deal. Other good search engines include www.mobissimo.com and www.wegolo.com.

Well-known cheapo airlines in Europe include easyJet (www.easyjet.com) and RyanAir (www.ryanair.com). Smart Wings (www.smartwings.com) is based in the Czech Republic.

Be aware of the potential drawbacks of flying on the cheap: nonrefundable and nonchangeable tickets, minimal customer assistance, the typical use of airports far outside town, and pricey baggage fees. If you're traveling with lots of luggage, a cheap flight can quickly become a bad deal, due to per-piece baggage fees. To avoid unpleasant surprises, read the small print before you book.

Resources

Resources from Rick Steves

Rick Steves' Prague and the Czech Republic is one of more than 30 titles in a series of **books** on European travel, which includes country guidebooks, city and regional guidebooks, and my budget-travel skills handbook, *Rick Steves' Europe Through the Back Door.* My phrase books—for German, French, Italian, Spanish, and Portuguese—are practical and budget-oriented. My other books are *Europe 101* (a crash course on art and history, newly expanded and in full color), *Travel as a Political Act* (a travelogue sprinkled with advice for bringing home a global perspective), *European Christmas* (on traditional and modern-day celebrations), and *Postcards from Europe* (a fun memoir of my travels). For a complete list of my books, see the inside of the last page of this book.

My **TV series,** *Rick Steves' Europe,* covers European destinations in 100 shows, with two episodes focused on Prague and the Czech Republic. My weekly public radio show, *Travel with Rick Steves,* features interviews with travel experts from around the world, including the Czech Republic. All the TV scripts and radio shows (which are easy and free to download to an iPod or other MP3 player) are at www.ricksteves.com.

If your travels take you beyond the Czech Republic to France, Italy, or Great Britain, take advantage of my free self-guided **audio tours** of the major sights in Venice, Florence, Rome, Paris, and London. Simply download them from www.ricksteves.com or iTunes (search for "Rick Steves' tours" in the iTunes Store), then transfer them to your iPod or other MP3 player.

Maps

The black-and-white maps in this book are concise and simple. My staff, who are well-traveled in the Czech Republic, have created these maps to help you locate recommended places and get to local TIs, where you can pick up a more in-depth map of the city or region (usually free).

It's essential to buy a good city map for your time in Prague (for pointers, see page 33). Many of Prague's bookstores also have road, hiking, and cycling maps covering the entire country. One of the best is the Kiwi Map Store near Wenceslas Square (see page 145). Before you buy a map, look at it to be sure it has the level of detail you want.

For drivers, I'd recommend a 1:100,000 atlas of the Czech Republic. If you have hiking plans (near Křivoklát, around

Begin Your Trip at www.ricksteves.com

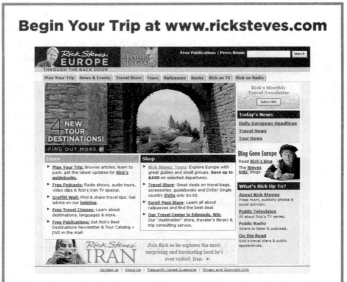

At our travel website, you'll find a wealth of free information on European destinations, including fresh monthly news and helpful tips from thousands of fellow travelers. You'll also find my latest guidebook updates (www.ricksteves.com/update) and my travel blog.

Our **online Travel Store** offers travel bags and accessories specially designed by Rick Steves to help you travel smarter and lighter. These include our popular carry-on bags (roll-aboard and rucksack versions), money belts, totes, toiletries kits, adapters, other accessories, and a wide selection of guidebooks, planning maps, and DVDs.

Choosing the right **railpass** for your trip—amidst hundreds of options—can drive you nutty. We'll help you pick the best pass for your needs, plus give you a bunch of free extras.

Rick Steves' Europe Through the Back Door travel company offers **tours** with more than two dozen itineraries and about 300 departures reaching the best destinations in this book...and beyond. We offer several tours that visit Prague and destinations in the Czech Republic, including our eight-day Prague and Budapest Tour; our 12-day Berlin, Prague, and Vienna tour (which also includes the charming village of Český Krumlov); and our 17-day Best of Eastern Europe tour. You'll enjoy great guides, a fun bunch of travel partners (with small groups of generally around 28), and plenty of room to spread out in a big, comfy bus. You'll find European adventures to fit every vacation length. For all the details, and to get our Tour Catalog and a free Rick Steves Tour Experience DVD (filmed on location during an actual tour), visit www.ricksteves.com or call the Tour Department at 425/608-4217.

Český Krumlov, in the Šumava or Beskydy Mountains, around Třeboň, or near Slavonice), get the excellent 1:50,000 *Edice Klub Českých Turistů* maps, or the less detailed but sufficient 1:100,000 *Kartografie Praha* maps. Train travelers usually manage fine with the freebies they get at the local tourist offices.

Other Guidebooks

If you're like most travelers, this book is all you need. But if you're heading beyond my recommended destinations, $40 for extra maps and books is money well-spent. One budget tip can save the price of an extra guidebook. Note that none of the following books is updated annually; check the publication date before you buy.

Lonely Planet's guides to the Czech and Slovak Republics and Prague are thorough, well-researched, and packed with good maps and hotel recommendations. The similar Rough Guides to these destinations are hip and insightful, written by British researchers.

Students and vagabonds will like the highly opinionated Let's Go series, which is updated by Harvard students. *Let's Go Eastern Europe* is best for backpackers who travel by train or bus, stay in hostels, and seek out the youth and nightlife scene.

Older travelers enjoy guides from Frommer's, even though, like the Fodor's guides, they ignore alternatives that enable travelers to save money by dirtying their fingers in the local culture.

The popular, skinny green Michelin Guides are excellent, especially if you're driving. Michelin Guides are known for their city and sightseeing maps, dry but concise and helpful information on all major sights, and good cultural and historical background. English editions are sold in Europe at gas stations and tourist shops. The encyclopedic Blue Guides are dry but just right for scholarly types.

The Eyewitness series is popular for great, easy-to-grasp graphics and photos, 3-D cutaways of buildings, aerial-view maps of historic neighborhoods, and cultural background. But written content in Eyewitness is relatively skimpy, and the books weigh a ton. I simply borrow them for a minute from other travelers at certain sights to make sure that I'm aware of that place's highlights.

The *Time Out* travel guide to Prague provides good, detailed coverage, particularly on arts and entertainment.

Recommended Books and Movies

The most famous Czech literary figure is the title character of Jaroslav Hašek's *Good Soldier Švejk,* who frustrates the World War I Austro-Hungarian army he serves by cleverly playing dumb.

Bohumil Hrabal, writing in a stream-of-consciousness style, mixed tales he had heard in pubs from sailors, self-made philosophers, and kind-hearted prostitutes into enchanting fictions that expressed the Czech spirit and sense of humor better than any other work. His best are *I Served the King of England, The Town Where Time Stood Still,* and *Too Loud a Solitude.* (Jiří Menzel turned some of Hrabal's writings into films, including the recently released *I Served the King of England* and the Oscar-winning *Closely Watched Trains;* for more on Czech cinema, keep reading.)

Other well-known Czech writers include Václav Havel (playwright who went on to become Czechoslovakia's first post-communist president—he authored many essays and plays, including *The Garden Party*); Milan Kundera (author of *The Unbearable Lightness of Being,* set during the "Prague Spring" uprising); and Karel Čapek (novelist and playwright who created the robot in the play *R.U.R.*).

But the most famous Czech writer of all is the existentialist great, Franz Kafka, a Prague Jew who wrote in German about a person turning into a giant cockroach *(The Metamorphosis)* and an urbanite being pursued and persecuted for crimes he knows nothing about *(The Trial).*

Some lesser-known Czech writers are also worth discovering. Arnošt Lustig's *Dita Saxová* covers the fate of Czech Jews during the war, while Ota Pavel's *Golden Eels* and Josef Škvorecký's *The Cowards (Zbabělci)* describe the world of a generation coming of age just after the war. Dominika Dery's *The Twelve Little Cakes* is a delightful memoir of her childhood (spent near Prague) at the end of communism in the late 1970s and early 1980s. So far, the definitive book of the 1989 generation is Jáchym Topol's *Sister.* Topol captures "the years after the Time exploded" in a rich mixture of colloquial Czech that's full of German and English loanwords and neologisms. Alex Zucker's English translation does an excellent job of capturing these nuances.

Nobel Prize–winning poet Jaroslav Seifert experienced during his long life all the diverse movements of the 20th century—Dadaism, Surrealism, communism, anti-communism—and created a medium of his own, in which everyone finds a poem to his or her own liking.

The Czech film tradition has always been strong, and the 1960s were its heyday, giving birth to Jiří Menzel's *Closely Watched Trains* and *Larks on the String,* Ivan Passer's *Intimate Lighting,* and Miloš Forman's *Firemen's Ball* and *Loves of a Blonde.* After his 1968 escape from communist Czechoslovakia, Forman made it big in the US with films such as *One Flew Over the Cuckoo's Nest* and *Amadeus.*

Two Czech filmmakers made a mark on the international stage after 1989: Jan Svěrák (*The Elementary School* and the Oscar-winning *Kolya*) and Jiří Hřebejk (*Divided We Fall,* nominated for an Oscar). More recently, Vít Klusák and Filip Remunda created a sensation with their hilarious, original, and disturbing documentary, *Czech Dream,* about the opening of a fake hypermarket invented and massively advertised by the directors themselves.

One of the most inspiring Czech artists is painter, animator, director, and surrealist Jan Švankmajer. His *Something from Alice, Lesson Faust,* and *Food* combine all of the author's artistic skills into a highly original style that is guaranteed to change the way you look at the world. His two most recent films—*Little Otík* and *Mad*—blend in more realism.

The Czechs have a wonderful animation tradition that successfully competes with Walt Disney in Eastern Europe and China. *Pat a Mat, Krteček (The Little Mole),* or *Maxipes Fík* are intelligent gifts to bring to your little ones at home.

Holidays and Festivals

This list includes many—but not all—major festivals, plus national holidays observed throughout the Czech Republic. Before planning a trip around a festival, make sure you verify the dates by checking the festival's website or contacting the Czech national tourist information office in the US (tel. 212/288-0830, www.czechtourism.com, info-usa@czechtourism.com). They can also provide specifics and a more comprehensive list of festivals.

Jan 1	New Year's Day
Jan 19	Anniversary of Jan Palach's death (flowers in Wenceslas Square)
Mid-March	One World International Human Rights Film Festival, Prague (www.oneworld.cz)
Easter Sunday and Monday	April 4–5 in 2010, April 24–25 in 2011
April 30	Witches' Night (bonfires)
May 1	Labor Day and Day of Love
May 8	Liberation Day
May (last 3 weeks)	"Prague Spring" Music Festival, Prague (www.festival.cz)
Mid-May	Prague International Marathon, Prague (May 9 in 2010, www.pim.cz)
Early June	Festival of Song, Olomouc
Mid-June	Celebration of the Rose, Český Krumlov (June 18–20 in 2010, medieval festival, music, theater, dance, knights' tournament)
July 5	Sts. Cyril and Methodius Day
July 6	Jan Hus Day

Mid-July–mid-Aug	International Music Festival in Český Krumlov (July 16–Aug 21 in 2010, www.festivalkrumlov.cz)
July–Aug	Summer of Culture, Olomouc (www.okl .info)
July–Aug	Prague Proms, Prague (music festival, www.pragueproms.cz)
Aug (first 2 weeks)	Telč Vacations Festival, Telč (folk music, open-air theater, exhibitions)
Aug–Sept	Dvořák's Prague Music Festival, Prague (Aug 20–Sept 4 in 2010, www.dvorak ovapraha.cz)
Sept	Radio Autumn, Prague (international music festival of radio orchestras)
Sept 28	St. Wenceslas Day (celebrates national patron saint and Czech statehood)
Oct	International Jazz Festival, Prague
Oct 28	Independence Day
Nov 17	Velvet Revolution Anniversary
Dec	Christmas markets, Prague
Dec 5	St. Nicholas Eve, Prague (St. Nicholas, devils, and angels walk the streets in search of nice—and naughty—children)
Dec 24–25	Christmas Eve and Christmas Day
Dec 26	Feast of St. Stephen
Dec 31	St. Sylvester's Day, Prague (fireworks)

Conversions and Climate

Numbers and Stumblers

- Europeans write a few of their numbers differently than we do. 1 = 1, 4 = 4, 7 = 7.
- In Europe, dates appear as day/month/year, so Christmas is 25/12/10.
- Commas are decimal points and decimals commas. A dollar and a half is 1,50, and there are 5.280 feet in a mile.
- When counting with fingers, start with your thumb. If you hold up your first finger to request one item, you'll probably get two.
- What Americans call the second floor of a building is the first floor in Europe.
- On escalators and moving sidewalks, Europeans keep the left "lane" open for passing. Keep to the right.

Metric Conversions (approximate)

A kilogram is 2.2 pounds and 1 liter is about a quart, or almost four to a gallon. A kilometer is six-tenths of a mile. I figure kilometers to miles by cutting them in half and adding back 10 percent of the original (120 km: 60 + 12 = 72 miles, 300 km: 150 + 30 = 180 miles).

1 foot = 0.3 meter	1 square yard = 0.8 square meter
1 yard = 0.9 meter	1 square mile = 2.6 square kilometers
1 mile = 1.6 kilometers	1 ounce = 28 grams
1 centimeter = 0.4 inch	1 quart = 0.95 liter
1 meter = 39.4 inches	1 kilogram = 2.2 pounds
1 kilometer = 0.62 mile	32°F = 0°C

Clothing Sizes

When shopping for clothing, use these US-to-European comparisons as general guidelines (but note that no conversion is perfect).

- Women's dresses and blouses: Add 30 (US size 10 = European size 40)
- Men's suits and jackets: Add 10 (US size 40 regular = European size 50)
- Men's shirts: Multiply by 2 and add about 8 (US size 15 collar = European size 38)
- Women's shoes: Add about 30 (US size 8 = European size 38½)
- Men's shoes: Add 32–34 (US size 9 = European size 41; US size 11 = European size 45)

Climate

The first line is the average daily high temperature; second line, the average daily low; third line, number of rainy days. For more detailed weather statistics for destinations throughout the Czech Republic (as well as the rest of the world), check www.world climate.com.

J	F	M	A	M	J	J	A	S	O	N	D
31°	34°	44°	54°	64°	70°	73°	72°	65°	53°	42°	34°
23°	24°	30°	38°	46°	52°	55°	55°	49°	41°	33°	27°
13	11	10	11	13	12	13	12	10	13	12	13

Temperature Conversion:
Fahrenheit and Celsius

Europe takes its temperature using the Celsius scale, while we opt for Fahrenheit. For a rough conversion from Celsius to Fahrenheit, double the number and add 30. For weather, remember that 28°C is 82°F—perfect. For health, 37°C is just right.

Essential Packing Checklist

Whether you're traveling for five days or five weeks, here's what you'll need to bring. Remember to pack light to enjoy the sweet freedom of true mobility. Happy travels!

- ❏ 5 shirts
- ❏ 1 sweater or lightweight fleece jacket
- ❏ 2 pairs pants
- ❏ 1 pair shorts
- ❏ 1 swimsuit (women only—men can use shorts)
- ❏ 5 pairs underwear and socks
- ❏ 1 pair shoes
- ❏ 1 rainproof jacket
- ❏ Tie or scarf
- ❏ Money belt
- ❏ Money—your mix of:
  - ❏ Debit card for ATM withdrawals
  - ❏ Credit card
  - ❏ Hard cash in US dollars ($20 bills)
- ❏ Documents (and back-up photocopies)
- ❏ Passport
- ❏ Printout of airline e-ticket
- ❏ Driver's license
- ❏ Student ID and hostel card
- ❏ Railpass/car rental voucher
- ❏ Insurance details
- ❏ Daypack
- ❏ Sealable plastic baggies
- ❏ Camera and related gear
- ❏ Empty water bottle
- ❏ Wristwatch and alarm clock
- ❏ Earplugs
- ❏ First-aid kit
- ❏ Medicine (labeled)
- ❏ Extra glasses/contacts and prescriptions
- ❏ Sunscreen and sunglasses
- ❏ Toiletries kit
- ❏ Soap
- ❏ Laundry soap
- ❏ Clothesline
- ❏ Small towel
- ❏ Sewing kit
- ❏ Travel information
- ❏ Necessary map(s)
- ❏ Address list (email and mailing addresses)
- ❏ Postcards and photos from home
- ❏ Notepad and pen
- ❏ Journal

If you plan to carry on your luggage, note that all liquids must be in three-ounce or smaller containers and fit within a single quart-size baggie. For details, see www.tsa.gov/travelers.

Hotel Reservation

To: _____   _____
            hotel   *email or fax*

From:_____   _____
            name   *email or fax*

Today's date: _____ /_____ /_____
                    day   *month*   *year*

Dear Hotel _____ ,
Please make this reservation for me:

Name: _____

Total # of people: _____   # of rooms: _____   # of nights: _____

Arriving: _____ /_____/ _____   My time of arrival (24-hr clock): _____
              day   *month* *year*   (I will telephone if I will be late)

Departing: _____/_____ /_____
                day   *month* *year*

Room(s): Single___   Double ___   Twin___   Triple ___   Quad___

With: Toilet ____   Shower____   Bath ___   Sink only___

Special needs: View___   Quiet___   Cheapest ___   Ground Floor___

Please email or fax confirmation of my reservation, along with the type of room reserved and the price. Please also inform me of your cancellation policy. After I hear from you, I will quickly send my credit-card information as a deposit to hold the room. Thank you.

_____
Name

_____
Address

_____
City   *State*   *Zip Code*   *Country*

Before hoteliers can make your reservation, they want to know the information listed above. You can use this form as the basis for your email, or you can photocopy this page, fill in the information, and send it as a fax (also available online at www.ricksteves.com/reservation).

Czech Survival Phrases

English	Czech	Pronounced
Hello. (formal)	*Dobrý den.*	DOH-bree dehn
Hi. / Bye. (informal)	*Ahoj.*	AH-hoy
Do you speak English?	*Mluvíte anglicky?*	MLOO-vee-teh ANG-lits-kee
Yes. / No.	*Ano. / Ne.*	AH-no / neh
Please. / You're welcome. / Can I help you?	*Prosím.*	PROH-zeem
Thank you.	*Děkuji.*	DYACK-khuyi
I'm sorry. / Excuse me.	*Promiňte.*	PROH-meen-teh
Good.	*Dobře.*	DOHB-zhay
Goodbye.	*Na shledanou.*	nah SKLEH-dah-now
one / two	*jeden / dva*	YAY-dehn / dvah
three / four	*tři / čtyři*	tree / chuh-TEE-ree
five / six	*pět / šest*	pyeht / shehst
seven / eight	*sedm / osm*	SEH-dum / OH-sum
nine / ten	*devět / deset*	DEHV-yeht / DEH-seht
hundred	*sto*	stoh
thousand	*tisíc*	TYEE-seets
How much?	*Kolik?*	KOH-leek
local currency	*koruna (Kč)*	koh-ROO-nah
Where is...?	*Kde je...?*	gday yeh
...the toilet	*...vécé*	vayt-SAY
men	*muži*	MOO-zhee
women	*ženy*	ZHAY-nee
water / coffee	*voda / káva*	VOH-dah / KAH-vah
beer / wine	*pivo / víno*	PEE-voh / VEE-noh
Cheers!	*Na zdraví!*	nah zdrah-VEE
The bill, please.	*Účet, prosím.*	OO-cheht PROH-zeem

Here are some English words that all Czechs know: super, OK, pardon, stop, menu, problem, and no problem.

Czech Place Names

Here's a rough pronunciation key for places mentioned in this book. For pronunciation help for specific sights and neighborhoods in Prague, see page 43.

Name	Pronounced
Beskydy (mountains)	BEH-skih-dee
Brno	BURR-noh
České Budějovice	CHESS-keh BOO-dyeh-yoh-vee-tseh
Český Krumlov	CHESS-key KROOM-loff
Karlštejn (castle)	KARL-shtayn
Konopiště (castle)	KOH-noh-peesh-tyeh
Křivoklát (castle)	KREE-vohk-laht
Kroměříž	KROH-myehr-eezh
Kutná Hora	KOOT-nah HO-rah
Lednice	LEHD-nee-tseh
Litoměřice	LEE-toh-myer-zhee-tseh
Mikulov	MEE-kuh-lohv
Moravský Krumlov	MOH-rahv-skee KROOM-loff
Mucha (artist)	MOO-kah
Olomouc	OH-loh-moats
Pálava (hills)	PAH-lah-vah
Pavlov	PAHV-lohv
Pustevny	POO-stehv-nee
Rožnov	ROHZH-nohv
Slavonice	SLAH-voh-neet-seh
Šumava (mountains)	SHOO-mah-vah
Telč	telch
Terezín	TEH-reh-zeen
Třebíč	TREH-beech
Třeboň	TREH-bohn
Trojanovice	TROH-yah-noh-vee-tseh
Valašsko	vah-LAH-she-skoh
Valtice	VAHL-tee-tseh

INDEX

INDEX

INDEX

MAP INDEX

Rick Steves
EUROPEAN TOURS

ADRIATIC • ATHENS & THE HEART OF
GREECE • BARCELONA & MADRID • BELGIUM
& HOLLAND • BERLIN, VIENNA & PRAGUE
BEST OF EUROPE • BEST OF ITALY
BEST OF TURKEY • BULGARIA • EASTERN
EUROPE • ENGLAND • FAMILY EUROPE
GERMANY, AUSTRIA & SWITZERLAND
HEART OF ITALY • IRELAND • ISTANBUL
LONDON • PARIS • PARIS & HEART OF
FRANCE • PARIS & SOUTH OF FRANCE
PORTUGAL • PRAGUE & BUDAPEST • ROME
SAN SEBASTIAN & BASQUE COUNTRY
SCANDINAVIA • SCOTLAND • SICILY
SOUTH ITALY • SPAIN & MOROCCO
ST. PETERSBURG, TALLINN & HELSINKI
VENICE, FLORENCE & ROME • VILLAGE
FRANCE • VILLAGE ITALY • VILLAGE TURKEY

VISIT **TOURS.RICKSTEVES.COM**

Great guides, small groups, no grumps

Free information and great gear to

▶ Plan Your Trip

Browse thousands of articles and a wealth of money-saving tips for planning your dream trip. You'll find up-to-date information on Europe's best destinations, packing smart, getting around, finding rooms, staying healthy, avoiding scams and more.

▶ Eurail Passes

Find out, step-by-step, if a rail pass makes sense for your trip—and how to avoid buying more than you need. Get a bunch of free extras!

▶ Graffiti Wall & Travelers' Helpline

Learn, ask, share—our online community of savvy travelers is a great resource for first-time travelers to Europe, as well as seasoned pros.

Rick Steves' Europe Through the Back Door, Inc.

NOW AVAILABLE

RICK STEVES APPS FOR THE iPHONE OR iPOD TOUCH

With these apps you can:

► Spin the compass icon to switch views between sights, hotels, and restaurant selections—and get details on cost, hours, address, and phone number.

► Tap any point on the screen to read Rick's detailed information, including history and suggested viewpoints.

► Get a deeper view into Rick's tours with audio and video segments.

Go to iTunes to download the following apps:

Rick Steves' Louvre Tour

Rick Steves' Historic Paris Walk

Rick Steves' Orsay Museum Tour

Rick Steves' Versailles

Rick Steves' Ancient Rome Tour

Rick Steves' St. Peter's Basilica Tour

Once downloaded, these apps are completely self-contained on your iPhone or iPod Touch, so you will not incur pricey roaming charges during use overseas.

Rick Steves books and DVDs are available at bookstores and through online booksellers.
Rick Steves guidebooks are published by Avalon Travel, a member of the Perseus Books Group.
Rick Steves apps are produced by Übermind, a boutique Seattle-based software consultancy firm.